MAGNIFICENT
BUT NOT WAR

MAGNIFICENT BUT NOT WAR

The Battle for Ypres, 1915

by

JOHN DIXON

LEO COOPER

First published in Great Britain 2003 by
LEO COOPER
an imprint of
Pen & Sword Books Limited
47 Church Street
Barnsley
South Yorkshire
S70 2AS

ISBN 1 84415 002 X

A catalogue record for this book
is available from the British Library.

Typeset in 10.5/12.5pt Plantin by
Phoenix Typesetting, Burley-in-Wharfedale, West Yorkshire

Printed in England by
CPI UK

No one who has not had actual personal experience of war can have the very slightest idea of what it means, the unutterable demands it makes, the unutterable sacrifices it entails. To try and represent war on paper or canvas is futile, on the stage merely grotesque. It cannot be copied; it exists only in the original.

The History of the Suffolk Regiment 1914–1927
by Lieutenant Colonel C.C.R. Murphy.

Contents

Appendices

Acknowledgements

A book of this size does not just happen in isolation. It has taken a number of years to prepare and in those years there have been many times when it has been necessary for me to ask the help and guidance of many people and organizations who for the most part have helped without hesitation.

I have no doubt that this work could not have been completed without the guidance and unreserved help of Ray Westlake, who has given of his time and resources to help in any way possible. I am also grateful to Barbara Westlake who has encouraged me with kind words and many cups of coffee over the years.

As an active member of the South Wales Branch of the Western Front Association I have many friends whom I have bounced ideas off over the years and I suppose I have been talking about the Second Battle of Ypres for a long time now. Among these I would like to mention are Gareth Scourfield who has accompanied me on many trips to Ypres; Peter Gorman who has found books on the Canadian involvement for me; Gwyn Prescott who has always listened and found my ideas of interest; Viv John who has straightened out many of the misconceptions I have held over the years; Paul Kemp who has helped with queries concerning medals and awards and our present Chairman, Vernon Davies, who has encouraged me in many, many ways to get this work together. It is possible that these friends will not have been aware of their help since sometimes it is indirect and less tangible than at others. Thanks also should go to the party of the Branch (Vic and Angela Evans, Terry Powell, Trevor Price, Peter Gorman, Gareth Scourfield, Barry Johnson, Gareth Harris, Hugh Edwards, Angus Evans, Martin Everett, Pat Evans, Margaret Gregory, Len Jones, Vernon Davies and David

Hughes) that visited the Second Ypres Battlefield in 2001 with me as a guide – their perseverance, patience and allowance for my enthusiasm is much appreciated.

There have been a number of organizations which have helped at various times throughout the work but none more so than the South Wales Borderers and Monmouthshire Regiment Museum in Brecon. Martin Everett and Celia Green are to be thanked for always finding useful material concerning the service of the Monmouthshire Regiment during the battle. Cardiff Central Library reference section has a good collection of material on the Great War and I am grateful to the staff there for all the efficient help they have offered over a long period of time. I have also gleaned information from the Imperial War Museum, the Welsh Regiment Museum, the Gloucester Regiment Museum and others and to all of these I am grateful.

In all my research I have been encouraged by my wife Francesca. She has taken an interest in all I do in relation to the Great War, accompanies me on battlefield tours and has walked the Ypres salient with me in all kinds of weather while I researched some odd little corner of the battle. Without her help, encouragement and understanding it is unlikely that this work could have come to completion.

Special thanks are due to Barry Johnson who read the manuscript with a knowledgeable and professional eye and suggested alterations to improve the text. I am particularly grateful since Barry volunteered his services when there were other calls on his time.

I am also very grateful to Patricia Gilbert-Chappell who read the final draft of the manuscript under some pressure and has provided further help and encouragement.

The following publishers are thanked for allowing me to quote material from published works; Thomas Harmsworth Publishing Company; The Crowood Press; Great Northern Publishing; The Imperial War Museum; Leo Cooper. The PPCLI Regimental Museum, Calgary, Alberta is thanked for permission to reproduce the painting by W.B. Wollen of the Regiment in action on Frezenberg Ridge.

John Dixon
January 2003

Preface

I have been asked many times why I have taken a special interest in the Second Battle of Ypres. To that question there is no simple answer since it has to do with many facets both historic and personal.

I suppose in the first instance both these things come together, since I remember stories of Ypres from when I was a child asking questions about the splendid war memorial in the Congregational Church in my home town of Cwm in the Monmouthshire valleys. So the story goes back many years and there was a gap of perhaps twenty years from the first time I heard of Ypres before I finally visited it. I was immediately taken with the town and its people. It is, quite simply, a beautiful town. Research into almost anything has been something I have always liked to do. I like to dig into things to find out the detail that few people care about. So although at the time of my first visit to Ypres over twenty years ago I was still studying for my doctorate at the University of Wales, I knew I would be back to discover more about the town and the part it played in one of the most horrific wars the world has known. That at least explains why I should be interested in Ypres.

The reasons for my interest in the Second Battle of Ypres are perhaps more involved. My home town is not too far from the market town of Abergavenny which had been the HQ of the 3rd Battalion the Monmouthshire Regiment. In the town, at the end of Frogmore Street, is a splendid war memorial to the Battalion and it was there that I first became aware of the date of 8th May 1915, and from there an interest that has developed into this book. It was on 8th May, the Battle of Frezenberg Ridge, that the 3rd Monmouths were almost wiped out and, as I was to discover, that was not special for this awful battle. I researched the service of this battalion and the other battalions of the regiment; in this battle all three battalions served within a few miles of one another. From those beginnings the interest simply spread to include the whole of the Second Battle of Ypres.

There are other reasons. I always see 1915 as the year in which the war developed into that with which the Great War is commonly associated. The Second Battle of Ypres was by later standards small, and at least in that context, is more readily understood than say the Battle of the Somme or the Third Battle of Ypres (Passchendaele) which are, in many ways, multiples of the Second Battle of Ypres simply repeated over and over. But even though it is easier to grasp as a whole it is often overshadowed by the later and bigger battles of the Great War. Perhaps this leads to the most significant reason for wanting to try and produce a book on the battle. There is not, to my knowledge, a book that deals with the battle comprehensively, though there are excellent works on various parts of the battle. I hope that this work helps to redress the balance and give some greater recognition for the men who fought and suffered within the salient of 1915. And, perhaps, there lies another facet of the reason for my interest in this battle. I want the men to be remembered for an effort which was no less great than those who fought and died in any other battle of the Great War; they too have a story to be told.

This all helps to explain the "why?" behind the book. The title I have chosen "Magnificent But Not War" is a paraphrase of the words of *Maréchal* Bosquet (1810–1861) from another occasion when the French and British were allies. When he witnessed the Charge of the Light Brigade (1854) during the Crimean War, he is said to have commented *"C'est magnifique, mais ce n'est pas la guerre"* (It is magnificent but it is not war). It seems appropriate that a French sentiment should be applied to a battle which saw magnificent defence and gallant, if futile and costly, counter-attacks. If I can explain the battle such that it is clear that there was tremendous gallantry, self sacrifice, terror and horror in equal quantities then I may just have succeeded in doing justice to the men of all nations who fought in it.

Most importantly I want to raise the profile of what is really a little known and understood battle of 1915. Let us not forget the men of 1915 who were forced to hold the line while Britain mobilized the great citizen army that was to grow in strength and confidence and which achieved the final victory of 1918.

Throughout the text there are numerous quotations from War Diaries, Regimental Histories and published works, and first hand accounts. As far as possible the punctuation and abbreviations have been left as in the original since this is considered the most appropriate approach. Minor changes have been made where the sense is not immediately clear. Also, where necessary the spelling of the place names adopted is that of the Official History – this is somewhat different in many cases from that used today but in all cases the places are readily recognizable. The contemporary accounts of the battle all use the Imperial units for measurement and these have been adopted here where necessary.

CHAPTER ONE

The Scene is Set
Winter 1914 – 1915

Nineteen-fifteen. The winter in Flanders was hard on everyone in the trenches. The euphoria of August, 1914 had long since disappeared and thoughts of "over by Christmas" had become long lost dreams. There had been those soldiers who had liked to think that it was a possibility until the end of the Christmas Truce had dispelled such naïve notions and the killing continued into the new year. As 1914 passed into 1915 there was no end in sight and it was becoming clear to the two huge armies facing each other from the frozen trenches, across the battle scarred landscape, that this was to be no easy conflict and that there could be no swift victory as envisaged in August of 1914.

The Germans had spent much of the late summer and autumn of 1914 consolidating their gains in France and Flanders to take the best advantage they could from their early momentum. They had, to some extent, chosen their ground for the continuation of the fighting as a direct result of their onslaught of August 1914. Whilst their original plan for a rapid victory in the west had been thwarted there was no reason why they should withdraw from all the ground they held. The Allies, for their part, had fought steadily and often very bravely against superior numbers, to achieve little, as they were forced to give ground to the advancing Germans. The French had suffered enormous losses in the early months of the war in futile gestures of gallantry, more appropriate to earlier wars. An example of this was in the Battle of the Frontiers where the French army sustained an estimated 300,000 casualties in a matter of weeks. The British for their part had lost much of its professional Regular Army in the fighting at Mons, on the Retreat

1

and the fighting on the Aisne and the Marne and in the fighting around Ypres in the autumn of 1914. These battles had been those which had stemmed the German tide across western Europe, but they had placed the Allies under severe pressure and as such they were no closer to victory than they had been at the outset of the war.

For the British the medieval town of Ypres was, by the end of 1914, a place of sad memories and gallant fighting. The British had stood in front of the town, with their French allies, throughout October and November 1914, to deny the Germans its capture. During this fighting the relatively small British force was fought almost to a complete stand-still against a numerically superior German force. Nevertheless, when the battle finished they had succeeded in holding the ground and, in so doing, had managed to hold on to a small piece of Belgium, a country which was by that time almost completely occupied by the Germans. It was during this fighting that such names as Gheluvelt and Nonne Boschen were to become battle honours for the severely pressed and weary regiments of the British Army – actions which were to set the standard for the fighting and defence of Ypres for the years to come. During this fighting the pressure had been so great that it had been inevitable that ground should be given up to the Germans. Some of this ground was along the higher ground to the east of Ypres and, in particular, portions of the Passchendaele Ridge fell into the Germans' hands. The British still retained possession of most of this ridge, around Broodseinde for instance, and of all the low ridges between there and the town of Ypres itself, but the loss of the high ground was to have an effect down the long bloody years of the war in front of Ypres. The line established after this battle, known as the First Battle of Ypres which took place between 19th October and 22nd November 1914 , left the Germans in sight of Ypres, and tantalizingly close, whilst the British and the French had been forced back into defending a curved, almost semi-circular, line that enclosed what was to become known as the Ypres salient. There was no option for the Germans as winter settled in over Flanders but to hold the ground they had won and to look to the future when they hoped they would be able to capture the town, and with it the rest of Belgium, and make up for their cavalry being forced out of the town as the Allied forces arrived in early October 1914. The story of the Germans' efforts and that of the Allies during the struggle in front of the town in spring 1915 is told in the coming pages.

After the battles for Ypres in 1914 there was a redistribution of the Allied force which saw the British effort moved to the right; that is, to the south of Ypres. The area to become known as the salient was, for the winter of 1914–15, manned mostly by the French as they took over the central portion in front of Ypres from the British I Corps. The

2

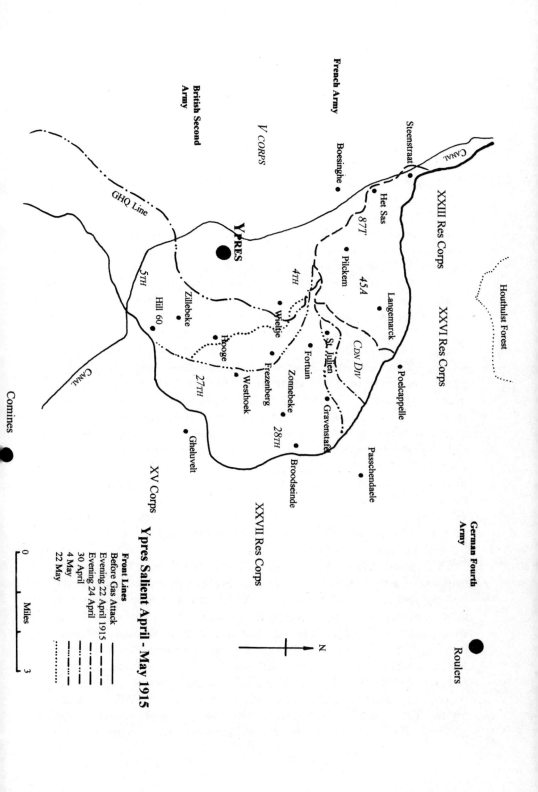

Ypres Salient April - May 1915

Front Lines
Before Gas Attack
Evening 22 April 1915
Evening 24 April
30 April
4 May
22 May

N

0   Miles   3

French Army

British Second Army

V CORPS

GHQ Line

YPRES

Steenstraat

CANAL

Het Sas

87T

Boesinghe

Pilckem

45A

4TH

Langemarck

Poelcappelle

CDN DIV

St. Julien

Wieltje

Zillebeke

Hill 60

5TH

Hooge

Fortuin

Frezenberg

Zonnebeke

Gravenstafel

Westhoek

27TH

28TH

Broodseinde

Passchendaele

CANAL

Gheluvelt

Comines

XV Corps

XXVII Res Corps

XXVI Res Corps

XXIII Res Corps

Houthulst Forest

German Fourth Army

Roulers

French then held the line from the Ypres – Comines Canal, south-east of Ypres, to the junction with the Belgian Army near Dixmude which, in turn, carried the front line to the coast near Nieuport. The British held the line from the Ypres – Comines Canal south to La Bassée. There were a number of reasons for this rearrangement. The British Army had suffered a large number of casualties since its arrival in Flanders and although the Government of the day was working hard to mobilize the large army required for a European war, there had not been sufficient time for it to take the field. Thus, when it became necessary to relieve the defenders of Ypres there were significant shortages of manpower so as to make this very difficult. Further, from the point of view of command it was going to be easier for the Allies to control their troops if they could be gathered together rather than be separated by each other's forces along the line. The French, on the other hand, had mobilized an army, based on conscription and long term reserve and territorial service, which they had been able to put into the field relatively quickly. It is true to say that many of the French units were not of the highest quality but it must be remembered that they had sufficient men under arms so that they could, if necessary, hold most, if not all, of the Western Front. Indeed for a spell shortly after the First Battle of Ypres this was almost the case, as the British were confined to a small section of the Front of no more than thirty miles long or a little over five per cent of the entire front line length, while the Belgians held an even smaller section with their very small standing army. It was a huge commitment for the French Army but the defence of its homeland was uppermost, especially since much of the military thinking in the country had been coloured by the defeat it had suffered in the Franco-Prussian war of 1870. Although it had suffered heavy casualties during the 1914 fighting, the military leaders were sufficiently optimistic as 1915 began to believe that the Germans could be defeated during the year. It is, to some extent, to this optimism that the British presence in front of Ypres in the spring of 1915 is due.

Throughout the winter of 1914–15 the British had been steadily bringing its army together, with the mobilization of the Territorial Force and the formation of Kitchener's New Armies. It was, of necessity, a process which could not be completed overnight. The Territorial Force was reasonably strong, prepared, and with a good standard of basic training. There was no commitment for any member of the Territorial Force to serve overseas. That particular obligation required a further commitment from each individual soldier of the Force. It is fair to say that in the years before the Great War the numbers of soldiers signing for this extra commitment were small. This changed rapidly on the declaration of war and in general the Territorials were as enthusiastic

4

to serve overseas as anyone else. However, the Territorial Force was seen by some, particularly Lord Kitchener, as not being the best way to enlarge an army on a scale suitable for European conflict since he considered it to be a very second rate resource. This thinking had been based on his experience of the French Territorial system, which although quite different to that operated in Britain, became the model for his argument. In France Territorials were time served reservists and mostly middle aged whilst in Britain Territorials were mostly young men who enjoyed basic military training and a two weeks summer camp. They were far better as the raw material for an army than their French namesakes. However, as a consequence of this thinking, the so called "New Armies" were raised, as Kitchener called for hundreds of thousands of men to volunteer for the colours. These armies, raised as they were from almost completely untrained men and recalled Boer War veteran NCO's and officers, further slowed down the process of putting a significant force in the field. For their part, the Territorials began to arrive in France in September 1914 and were attached to Regular divisions where they were used to fill gaps in the line that the fighting to that date had caused. It was, perhaps, not the best use of these men, but the shortages on the battlefields and the attitude of the War Office to their usefulness meant that their inclusion was inevitable and was to continue throughout the rest of the year. Lord Kitchener had decided that the British Territorials, or perhaps more appropriately the Territorial system, had no real part to play in the war.[1] It is with these matters in mind that he had sanctioned the formation of the New Armies. In these New Armies, Kitchener hoped to bring the ordinary citizens of Britain to war readiness in a short period of time. Kitchener had failed to accept that by not using the Territorial Force as a framework for a new army he was in fact delaying his own objectives. However, to his credit Kitchener had realized that the war would not be over quickly and saw the building of an army as something that could not be completed as quickly as the demands of the battlefields may require. His thinking was essentially long term and was really looking forward to the large set piece battles of the later years of the war. Whilst this may have been entirely appropriate thinking and planning, at the same time it was placing increasing difficulties on the British Expeditionary Force and its French allies. In the event Kitchener's New Army divisions began arriving in France in the spring of 1915 with the arrival of the 9th Scottish Division in early May of that year, but even then it was some time before they were entirely ready to take part in any large-scale battle. For all that, the enthusiasm of the New Armies should not be understated and as 1915 progressed their importance to the war effort steadily grew.

5

Whilst all of this was going on the British Empire was also mobilizing its colonies and Dominions as men from across perhaps the greatest empire ever known, were caught up in the war fever sweeping the world. This was at such a height in Canada that Andrew Hamilton Gault privately funded the formation of a new unit that was to become known as the Princess Patricia's Canadian Light Infantry. This unit was offered for service and on its acceptance became the first Canadian unit to enter the fighting on the Western Front. It was a unit composed largely of ex-patriot Britons who between them had served, so the story goes, in all but one of the regular regiments of the British Army. The raising of the Patricia's serves to show the attitude there was across the world as Canadians, Australians and New Zealanders, to name but a few, were drawn into the war. Further, the Indian Army was put on a war footing and an Indian Army Corps was sent to the Western Front during the first winter of the war, as some of their garrison duties in the sub-continent were taken over by Territorial units from Britain. Many of the Indian Army units were to see action on the Western Front throughout 1915. It was a large effort on the part of the British and their Empire and it could not be accomplished quickly. Throughout the first winter of the war some of these men from the outposts of Empire began to arrive in France and Flanders. It was early 1916, however, before the Anzacs were to arrive in Flanders for they were to experience the awful-ness of Gallipoli before they reached the Western Front. With these new men there arrived new hope that 1915 would be a decisive year and that, perhaps the war that had already lasted longer than many of the population could believe, would be brought to a close.

As the armies in France swelled in size it was decided that the British Army would take on a greater responsibility in terms of the length of line it held. This would then allow the French to relieve some of its troops and to strengthen other parts of the line that it would not have otherwise been able to do. Initially the plan had been for all the French troops in the vicinity of Ypres to be replaced by British units so that they could take over the line as far as the Belgian army near Dixmude. This plan meant that the British were to take control of the sweep of trenches in front of Ypres once again. In the early months of 1915 this had been largely accomplished and, but for the new plans committing British troops to fighting in Gallipoli, the line from La Bassée in France to Dixmude in Flanders would have been an entirely British commitment. However, the other commitments in Gallipoli left a small deficit in the requirement for the British to man this line completely and this resulted in two French divisions being required between the British and the Belgians from roughly Het Sas to Dixmude along the Yser Canal to the north of Ypres. At first these were the 11th Division, a regular unit, and the 87th Territorial Division. However, before the fighting for Ypres in the spring of 1915 had begun, it had been decided that the 11th Division would be replaced by the 45th Algerian Division, a colonial unit which was considered to be somewhat inferior to the unit it replaced. The 87th Territorial Division would remain on the northern flank of the salient where it had spent most of the winter. More will be said of these divisions later. Thus by the spring of 1915 the front line in front of Ypres was held mostly by the British with the French and the Belgians successively holding the left flank.

The line established by these redistributions of resources was seen essentially as a holding position by the Allied commanders. There were no plans, at this stage of the war, for offensive action in front of Ypres and, in view of the gradual build-up of British forces in Flanders, it was a holding position that at least some hoped would not be tested too soon. It was eventually decided that the first offensive actions of 1915 were to take place further south and would include battles at Neuve Chapelle, Aubers Ridge and Festubert. All available resources were to be directed towards these areas of northern France and if possible the status quo was to be maintained in front of Ypres. This commitment to an offensive, having been made, needed to be adhered to if there were to be any chance of success, so that all aspects could be put in readiness, and this was to place further constraints on those forces ranged in front of Ypres. For these it meant that there was little in the way of available reserves of both men and equipment as both were directed to the build-up for battle further south. This was made even worse when the shortage of artillery shells that dogged the British throughout 1915 is considered. For the artillery at Ypres there was an ammunition shortage without the thought of any action being fought, since the supply of shells, such as it was, was directed to areas considered to be of greater importance; in this case, Gallipoli and the offensive in France. With this evidence it must be assumed that the Allied command had assessed the situation in Flanders, seen it to be satisfactory for the time being and had considered that a German offensive was unlikely. Perhaps this was justified, bearing in mind the significant German advance that had been held in the First Battle of Ypres and also since there had been a significant withdrawal of German troops to the Eastern Front at the beginning of the year. But, as will become clear, evidence to the contrary was ignored when it became available in early April 1915.

For their part the Germans had their own problems, though these were somewhat different. During the initial rush of the German Army there had been significant successes as it had swept all before it. The Belgians had but a small army and it been more or less overwhelmed as Liege, Brussels and other Belgian cities were overrun. The French, too, had had their problems in dealing with the invader, as hundreds of thousands of men had been lost in the first few weeks of the war to stem the tide that had looked at one stage as if it would sweep over Paris. That it did not happen was reflected in the determined defence by both the French, in particular, and the British. Thus, by the time the Germans had been halted in their first rush, they too had suffered serious heavy casualties and, with the loss of momentum of their advance in 1914, they had probably lost their chance of finishing the war quickly. To add to their problems in the west the Germans were also fighting in the east against Russia who had entered the war as a French ally. It is fair to say that the Russian war machine was relatively slow to mobilize its great strength but had nevertheless done so far more quickly than the Germans had anticipated and had taken the field in August 1914, to pose an increasingly large threat to the Germans. For the Germans this meant fighting in East Prussia and, at the end of August, they had won a significant victory at Tannenberg, which had helped to lessen their immediate problems, as they had hoped to deal with the western Allies before Russia could fully mobilize. However, the war on two fronts meant a huge commitment for the German army in terms of men and material so that the German objectives of European domination could be realized. It had been foreseen that a swift victory in the west would be needed, but when this was not forthcoming the Germans realized that there was likely to be an increasing commitment to the war in the east. Thus, by early 1915 the German army, though large, was spread somewhat thinly to handle the war on two fronts, relying on its allies to deal with the threat in the Balkans, Italy[2] and Gallipoli. All of this meant that the Germans in front of Ypres, though numerically superior to the defenders, were not necessarily in a better position in terms of the reserves of men and material that were available to them. They had such far ranging commitments for both, and although in 1915 they were still better prepared for war than the British or the French, there were limitations to their resources also. It is a fact that the Germans in front of Ypres could not expect any reinforcement for either defence or attack; that is, the six army corps ranged around the salient were all that were available for every eventuality in the area. True, they were well equipped and supported by artillery, but there were no more troops immediately available. It is perhaps this situation that brought about the suggestion for the use of poison gas, as a way of making their resources more effective and of gaining ground cheaply and quickly by clearing it of the enemy. Certainly the Second Battle of Ypres was seen by the Germans as an experiment of that kind of thinking, but it was

8

an experiment that had not been thought through as thoroughly as it should have been, and was to lead to further problems for them as the war progressed.

Thus, by the spring of 1915, the combatant nations were all facing their own problems and were looking for ways of alleviating the situation. On the Western Front the scene was set for the British and French to begin operations against Aubers Ridge and in Artois, while the Germans were looking to consolidate along most of the line and experiment at Ypres. It is with this experiment that the following narrative is concerned.

The story of the Second Battle of Ypres is one which is influenced by the wider issues mentioned above and the detailed account of the four phases of the battle needs to bear this in mind. Further, the battle had an immediate precursor which, although not officially recognized by the Battle Nomenclature Committee as being part of the Second Battle of Ypres, is integral to the fighting in front of Ypres in the spring of 1915. This is the fighting that took place at Hill 60 during April and May 1915, and which commenced with the capture of Hill 60 some five days before Second Ypres is officially recognized as starting. It is included in the discussion of the Second Battle of Ypres for a number of reasons, not the least of these being that Hill 60 is on the south-eastern edge of the Ypres salient and was considered as an important point in both the defence of, or assault on, the salient. Further, the fighting for that infamous piece of Flanders continued well into the Second Battle of Ypres and became the southernmost part of the fighting as the entire salient was engulfed in shot and shell. Also, the units holding the Hill became involved elsewhere in the salient throughout the battle as they were moved around to meet the German threat. Thus, the fighting at Hill 60 is not entirely separated from that of the Second Battle of Ypres, and an understanding of it aids the overall picture of the struggle for the Ypres salient in the spring of 1915, since a breakthrough at this point would have been likely to produce the outcome that the Germans desired – the removal of the salient and the capture of Ypres. The Second Battle of Ypres falls into four phases: the Battle of Gravenstafel Ridge; the Battle of Saint Julien; the Battle of Frezenberg Ridge and the Battle of Bellewaarde Ridge. Each of these phases is dealt with in some detail to indicate the changing nature of the battle as the fighting progressed. It should be remembered throughout this discussion that the Second Battle of Ypres was influenced by issues that were affecting the Western Front as a whole and also by the local issues that were, perhaps, of minor importance in the great scheme of things. All the various features come together to produce a story that is sometimes sad, often gallant and always fascinating.

Notes

1. See *Kitchener. Portrait of an Imperialist,* p291.
2. Italy was technically a German ally as part of the "Triple Alliance". This was ended on 26th April 1915 and Italy declared war on Austro-Hungary on 26th May 1915 and therefore entered the war though did not actually declare war on Germany until 28th August 1916.

CHAPTER TWO

Hill 60
17th April 1915

Some months prior to the German assault on Ypres, the British themselves had been looking at the possibilities of gaining some ascendancy
in the Ypres salient. They were hoping to achieve this by the capture of
Hill 60 on the south-east flank of the salient. The fighting for this scrap
of Flanders was particularly ferocious and overlaps with the main
fighting of the Ypres salient in the spring of 1915. It thus becomes so
intimately woven into the history of the defence of the salient that the
telling of its story relates to most of the fighting of the Second Battle of
Ypres.

Flanders has a generally gentle landscape in the area of the salient
comprising low rolling hills and shallow valleys with slow moving
streams – to some used to more rugged scenery this part of Flanders
would seem to be almost featureless. In this landscape any low hill or
mound gives panoramic views over the patchwork of fields, farms and
small villages. The military advantage of such elevations is obvious
today and it was obvious to the military commanders of 1914. During
the fighting around Ypres in the autumn of 1914, the Germans were able
to occupy most of the high ground in the immediate vicinity of the town
and with it they won the prize of good observation. In particular they
had gained significant parts of the ridge which runs from Passchendaele
to Messines in a broad sweep to the south and east of Ypres. In the
southern part of this ridge was a high point that in 1915 was to become
the epitome of the horrors of the Great War. That high point was known
as Hill 60 by virtue of the fact that its crest was enclosed by the sixty
metre contour on the large scale maps that the military were using.

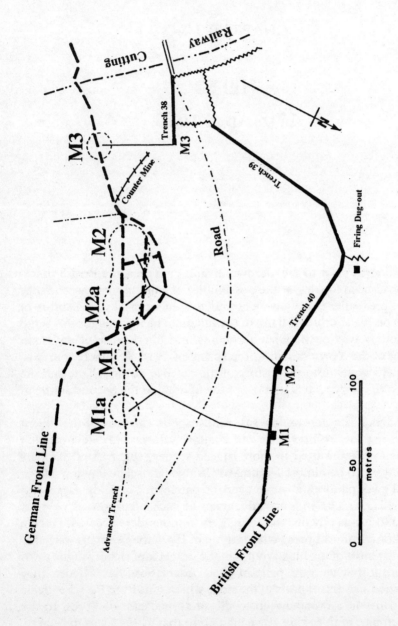

THE MINES OF HILL 60 APRIL 1915

Hill 60 was not a natural hill at all but had been formed during the construction of the Ypres-Comines Railway from the spoil excavated from the cutting through the Messines Ridge which had been deposited to the north-east of the railway between it and the Klien Zillebeke road. This was the highest of the spoil heaps formed by the excavation of the cutting; the other two, the Dump and the Caterpillar, were situated on the other side of the railway line. All three spoil heaps provided extra height to the natural topography but it was Hill 60 that dominated the others and gave good observation of the town of Ypres and its salient. Before the war the hill had been important for another reason, as its name of "Lovers Knoll" (*Cotes des amants*) implies. By the end of 1914 there was precious little love in the vicious fighting that took place on and around the hill as it became immortalized by the deaths of thousands of young men. In the spring of 1915 it was to become important to the British war effort as it was to be their first successful effort at offensive mining.[1]

The offensive nature of tunnelling had been realized for some time. The origins of such warfare lay in the siege tactics of earlier centuries and, on the Western Front, these siege tactics had been used by both the Germans and the French almost from the outset of trench warfare. The adoption of tunnelling showed that both sides had accepted early in the war that all hope of open warfare had vanished. They set about destroying each other's bastions by other methods. The idea behind tunnelling was simple. All that was needed was a tunnel under the enemy's lines with a suitable charge of explosives which, when detonated, would take the line away and defenders with it. The practicalities of mining, as it was called, were more complex and required specialists. In the winter of 1914 there had been some defensive mining, for instance, in the 4th Division sector near Le Touquet where a party of miners from the 2nd Monmouths successfully mined a German position and, in so doing, lay claim to the first successful mining operation carried out by the British army in Flanders.[2] However, in the early days of the war this kind of work was carried out, for the most part, by the Royal Engineers. By the start of 1915 it had already been realized that the Royal Engineers would have plenty to occupy them on the Western Front without taking on yet another specialized role. For mining to be a success it was necessary for the usual Field Company structure of the Royal Engineers to be modified. Under pressure from John Norton Griffiths MP (later Lieutenant Colonel) it was decided that specialist units should be raised for the sole purpose of tunnelling work. It was also decided that these units should consist of men who were familiar with working underground.

To the men of the coal mining areas of Britain, underground work was second nature and during the early months of 1915 many regiments such as the Monmouths, the South Wales Borderers, the Durham Light Infantry and so on had their ranks scoured for men with suitable mining experience. To these soldiers volunteers were added who had a thorough knowledge of sewer construction or underground railway tunnelling where the experience was mostly gained in tunnelling in clay and soft ground. These men were known as "clay kickers" because the method they used to take the clay from the working face required them to kick at their "grafting tool"[3] whilst supported on a timber framework which was known as "the cross". Men with mining experience from the various regiments were sent to form the Tunnelling Companies in readiness for this new warfare. The first to be formed in France was the 171st Tunnelling Company which originated when a party of 1st and 3rd Monmouths were attached to the Northumbrian Field Company. This group of men was given the task of demonstrating to the military hierarchy the effectiveness of military mining, and to do so they were ordered to work on two projects. The first of these at the Mound near St. Eloi was dogged with bad luck as the miners failed to sink a suitable shaft through exceptionally bad ground, and it was temporarily abandoned to allow them to concentrate on the work at Hill 60, which was to prove beyond doubt the value of the Tunnellers.

The sector including Hill 60 had been defended by the French. They had captured the hill on 10th December 1914 but lost it again a few days later in heavy fighting resulting in serious casualties to both sides. Early in 1915 the sector became a permanent feature of the British front line. The ground was littered with the decaying bodies of long dead Frenchmen and any digging around the hill was a nightmare, as poorly buried bodies were constantly being exhumed. In these conditions it became the task of the Tunnellers to tunnel from the British line through the spoil heap that was Hill 60 and under the German line, a distance of approximately 100 yards. The initial sites chosen for the shafts proved to have exceptionally bad ground conditions with soft clays and loose running sands and it became a necessity for a survey of the site to be carried out. This was accomplished by a party of the Monmouths under the most difficult conditions, as almost any movement attracted fire from the German lines. Levelling, to establish the relative heights of the hill and trenches, was carried out using a simple instrument known as an Abney Level and, though no one expected to achieve a high degree of accuracy, it was the best that could be done under the adverse conditions. Eventually the decision for the siting of the shafts fell to Lieutenant W.M.B. Burnyeat (1st Monmouths) who had been a mining engineer before the war. The sites picked for the two shafts, known as M1 and M2, were in Trench 40, and a third, M3, was sited in Trench 38 which was some fifty yards closer to the German trenches. Work on the shafts began on the 8th March. At first it was a very grisly business. The work began in daylight and on the site of M3 it was only a matter of minutes before the partially decayed body of a Frenchman was discovered. The sappers tried to lift the body out of the way but it fell apart in their hands. After seeking instructions the body was placed in a sandbag and removed to one side for reburial. Three other bodies in a similar condition were found in quick succession. All four unidentified Frenchmen were buried in quicklime that same night. Lieutenant W.P. Abbott, of the 3rd Monmouths, was to recall in later life that nothing brought back the horrors of Hill 60 more readily than the smell of quicklime.[4]

However, in spite of all this and the frequent shelling the area suffered, the shafts were eventually sunk to the required depth of approximately sixteen feet. It was determined by the officer commanding the miners, Major D. Griffith of the RE, that the tunnels should rise towards the German trenches with a gradient of 1 in 144, thereby allowing the free drainage of water away from the working face to a sump at the base of the shaft. From here the water was hauled to the surface in buckets. The gradient also meant that the charges could be placed at no greater depth than thirty feet below the German lines.

Conditions for the miners were very bad. At that depth it was not the decaying bodies that the sappers were up against but the soft clayey ground conditions. This meant that nearly every inch of the tunnel had to be shuttered with timber which was cut from the nearby woods. The timbers were simply butted together and every chink in the wooden tunnel armour was exploited by mud which squirted into the tunnel, adding to the miners difficulties. As if that was not enough the working space was very small. M3 was the smallest, with dimensions of three feet by two feet inside the timbering. M1 and M2 were a little larger at four feet by three feet six inches, though after about half way that was reduced to three feet two inches by three feet! These dimensions meant that no more than two men could work at the face at any one time. The miner clawed out the clay with his grafting tool, bayonet or bare hands and passed the spoil to his mate who then bagged it and tied it to a rope to be dragged out by other men. The bagged soil was used in repairing or improving trenches and any surplus was got rid of on ground that was "dead" to the enemy's observation.

A further problem throughout this work was one that was familiar to miners everywhere, that is ventilation. At first ventilation was achieved by the use of some antiquated fans. However, they proved to be so noisy that they had to be replaced by a bellows attached to a stout tubing which led to the face. Even then the air was bad. Candles and matches

15

would scarcely burn and in these conditions the men could only work for short periods. In no time at all men became exhausted and were glad to get away from the face to be able to breathe again. Some men were permanently affected by this experience. It has been said that one Sergeant David Evans, of the 1st Monmouths, known as "Dusky" because of his colouring, became white haired within six weeks[5].

The work was hard and dangerous. Most of the work had to be carried out in near silence. The men were aware that the Germans would be listening for them and there was no need to encourage counter mining activities. On top of all this the men usually finished their shift of eight hours soaked in sweat and muddy water. There were no dry clothes and no decent billets. For the six to nine days they were in the line the miners worked and slept in wet clothes and survived as best they could. To help stave off the chill the Army provided a tot of rum for each miner as he came from the mine; a small comfort gratefully received in those brutal times. After their turn in the line the miners were allowed three days rest in Ypres and most of them took full advantage of it by getting drunk on the plentiful supplies of beer and cognac. At that time Ypres was not the deserted ruin it was to become later in the war and it served to breathe life back into the subterranean fighters.

In the face of these enormous hardships the mines progressed slowly but surely and that fact alone is a great credit to the men and their leaders. The average drivage was ten feet a day – remarkable in such primitive conditions. At that time Lieutenant Burnyeat carried out an experiment to show that the workers of the Monmouthshire Regiment were at least as good as those men who had been specifically taken on for mining. During the experiment the mine was driven sixteen and a half feet, entirely by Monmouths, a figure never bettered during the time the mines of Hill 60 were being excavated in early 1915. The reasoning behind this test was not explained by Lieutenant Burnyeat but it may have had something to do with the confusion over the rate of pay for the miners. The "clay kickers" had been engaged at a princely sum of six shillings (30p) a day, an unbelievable figure for the soldiers of 1915. A sapper's rate of pay was a mere two shillings and two pence (11p) and an infantryman could expect even less. Perhaps Burnyeat was trying to show that his men were as good and cheaper, or that his men were worth more than the so called "specialists". This kind of confusion was to be the biggest problem with the Tunnelling Companies as men doing the same work were often paid quite differently and it stayed with them as long as they existed. However, on the whole, morale in the 171st was good during the mining of Hill 60.

As if the miners did not have enough problems, they were also called on to fight as infantrymen, as one of the Monmouths was to record:

16

On March 12th the enemy exploded a mine in the vicinity of our abandoned mines. Anticipating a rush, the men were withdrawn from the mines to assist the Liverpool Scottish repel the attack. The experience gained in first aid in the Welsh mines now stood the miners in good stead, as they were able to render yeoman service to the stretcher bearers in attending the wounded, thus we fought and worked alternately.[6]

Two days later there was the bad news from St. Eloi that the Germans had succeeded in exploding a mine below the British trenches which they had then captured. The resolve of the tunnellers at Hill 60 deepened and there was a new determination to complete the job successfully. Even then the Germans seemed to be making other plans. On 16th March it was confirmed that the Germans were counter mining and in response to this:

Three shifts were arranged, and the situation made clear to the men. This put us all on our mettle and we put forth every effort to get there first.[7]

The race was on and the stakes were high. Within two days of rearranging the shifts and flat out work commencing, a change of command was forced on the tunnellers when Lieutenant Burnyeat was wounded in the thigh and his position was filled by Lieutenant L. Hill. Lieutenant Hill was a mining engineer who took to his task with some vigour and, it is said, took a very keen interest in the welfare of his men, doing all he could to improve their working conditions, and although there was little he could do, his efforts were appreciated by the men. The work progressed well though all the time there was the threat of the German countermining operations. The work became desperate and "the men worked like Trojans" as they listened to the work of countermining.

In early April two sappers working in M3 actually broke into a German tunnel.[8] The two sappers reported the incident to Second Lieutenant T.L. Black, whose immediate action was to enter the gallery with the sappers. The small party was fired upon by a German they discovered in the gallery who had entered via the breakthrough. The British miners withdrew and, after a pause to reconsider his course of action, Black took the sappers back into the gallery. This time they discovered and disconnected a small German charge of 250 lbs of guncotton which was rewired so as to be fired if enemy activity was detected. Work ceased on the mine, but fortunately it had progressed far enough forward to be useful, though the intended powder chambers were never completed. Eventually the guncotton was doubled in preparation for firing. The incident reflects the continual danger experienced by the miners and also goes some way to explaining why the eventual charge placed in M3 was rather small.

By 10th April all works on excavation had been completed. M1 and

M2 were driven a total of 110 yards each, bringing them below the German lines. One miner described this period as "the most exciting period of my life, coupled with anxiety".[9] All that remained to be done was to charge the mines. The amount of explosives to be used was calculated by Major D. Griffith. The formula for the calculations which he had at his disposal was old fashioned, and was based on the use of gunpowder, which was an inefficient explosive by the standards of the day. Further, the formula required more precise information as to the depth of the powder chambers than Griffith had available to him. It should be remembered that the survey work had been done under fire and hence some of the levels, and therefore depths arrived at, were little more than approximations. With so many unknowns in the equation Major Griffith decided to assume that M1 was twenty feet below the surface, M2 was fifteen feet and M3 twelve feet. To form a substantial crater of approximately sixty feet diameter Griffith found that the following charges would be required:

M1 2,700 lbs. of gunpowder in each of two chambers
M2 2,000 lbs. of gunpowder in each of two chambers
M3 500 lbs. of guncotton laid directly in the sap.[10]

Orders were given and Lieutenant Hill began to organize the miners to charge the mines. The gunpowder was provided in 100 lb. sacks and each sack had to be carried to the trench and manhandled to the powder chamber of the mine. One soldier who was involved in the work has left the following account:

The nature of our work may be better realised if I state that a Regiment going into the trenches to relieve another considered themselves fortunate if they didn't lose more than 50 men. The approaches to our communication trenches were being continually shelled, and a few points were under machine gun fire. The officers carried the detonators in their pockets, and the men the explosives on their shoulders. One mishap, and we should all be hurled to eternity.[11]

In actual fact the officers carrying the detonators were probably in the greatest danger but, for all that, charging the mines was a nerve-racking job for all concerned. The following days were filled with a tense work-frenzy as the miners struggled back and forth to the line with their explosive cargo. By 15th April the mines were charged. The charges had been laid in waterproof boxes and each had double fused electrical detonator circuits. In case of some incredible accident, each mine was double fused with primitive burning fuses also. Four firing systems would make sure of detonation. All three mines were to be detonated from one dugout. Each powder chamber was sealed with a wall of sand-

18

bags. To increase the upward explosion, the first sandbag wall was followed by two more with an air gap of ten feet between each, a technique known as tamping. After these preparations all that remained was for a date to be set for the detonation and, with the German's counter-mine being very near to M3, that date needed to be as soon as possible.

There then followed a period of tense waiting:

> During the period of waiting for the orders the mines were zealously guarded, the wires and the fuse were examined every two hours. This meant a man having to get into the mine, thereby running the risk of being buried alive in the event of the enemy finding our mines and exploding them. We could now hear them working overhead which made us anxious to see our mines off.[12]

The War Diary is a bit more matter of fact over the continual checks that were carried out at this time:

> 13.4.15. Electric leads for mines tested in position and found satisfactory.
>
> 15.4.15. Tested resistance of mine circuit with P.O. Box and also tested capacity of exploders. Results satisfactory and within 2 Ohms of calculated resistances.[13]

On the 17th April at 7 pm the mines were detonated by Major D. Griffith, Lieutenant L. Hill and one other officer. At first it seemed as though nothing had happened but in fact they had all exploded in rapid succession. The War Diary records:

> Mines fired at Hill 60 7 pm weather very fine and clear. One of powder charges hung fire for 2 seconds and then some black substance appeared in centre of column of earth possibly damp and unexploded powder. Our own trenches undamaged. Craters about 25% larger than calculations led to expect.

The job of capturing the hill following the firing of the mines had been given to the 1st Royal West Kent. C Company of this battalion was to be the assaulting force and it had spent all day in trenches 39 and 40 in front of the hill. They were to be supported by B and C Companies of the 2nd King's Own Scottish Borderers, who were stationed in the communication trenches immediately to their rear. The remainder of both battalions were held in support in trenches some way behind the lines, the 2nd KOSB in trenches in Larch Wood with the 1st Royal West Kent between there and the front line. The tasks given to the main assaulting force were clear: C Company of the West Kents was to rush forward and capture the hill while the 2nd KOSB were to act essentially as pioneers for them, in so far as they were to start consolidation works immediately and form such carrying parties as would be necessary for the continued effort on the hill. The day had been a relatively quiet, fine, warm spring day during which the skies were patrolled by British airmen to help to keep the Germans from getting too much information of the impending attack. The War Diary of the West Kents gives the following details:

> There was not much noise, but the whole ground round shook as if there was an earthquake and a few minutes afterwards, bricks, Germans and all kinds of debris were hurtling through the air in all directions . . . C Company as the storming party rushed forward from trenches 39 and 40 in eight columns each headed by men armed with axes to deal with any entanglements which may remain in front of the enemy trenches.

The West Kents met little opposition as they moved forward with a party of sappers from the 1/2nd Home Counties Field Company RE. The wire had vanished and the German garrison of the 172nd Regiment had been so severely shaken that they found barely fifty men holding the hill. Some of these men offered some resistance and were bayoneted as the West Kents were carried forward in their rush. Some tried to escape down their communication trenches and were bombed by the bombing parties from the West Kents. The remainder, amounting to two officers and seventeen men, were taken prisoner. The West Kents had suffered only seven casualties. One of the prisoners was to comment:

> The British mines exploded with tremendous effect and must have killed a great many men. It was just like an earthquake and my whole platoon must have been wiped out.[14]

Soon the Germans had recovered enough to begin shelling the area, and although at first the firing was inaccurate since their guns had not been registered on their own lines on the hill, it did not take them long to achieve the range they required, and the hill came under a heavy shell-fire. That made the task of consolidation of even greater importance, as the need for some kind of cover grew. The War Diary of the West Kents states that the line taken up by C Company was more or less the line that had been held by the Germans, and in part that was on the British side of the craters that had been formed by the mines. Major J.F. Joslin soon appeared on the scene and grasped the importance of holding the opposite rim of the craters and at once ordered a new line to be constructed that could encompass the furthest rim of the craters. Whilst this was being done, communication trenches were being run back to trenches 39 and 40 by the working parties of the KOSB under the super-vision of the Royal Engineers. The Germans were by that time shelling the hill vigorously and the work became hampered by enfilade fire from the German lines across the railway cutting, on the flanks of the Caterpillar. This had been considered to be a problem and was one of the reasons why many officers had considered the capture of the hill alone was far too narrow an objective for an assault. The effect on the KOSB was that C Company, who were working on the right, that is nearest the railway cutting, were unable to make the progress that they would have wanted, and when B Company on the left had finished and were able to withdraw a little to relative safety, C Company needed to remain to complete their work. It was, however, completed.

During the consolidation of the former enemy line, a German mine was found. Under questioning, a German prisoner revealed that their sappers had planned to detonate their mine under the British forward positions in Trench 38 just two days later, on 19th April. Thus, it had been a victory by a very narrow margin. One account of the events of the day reads:

> The mines undoubtedly produced a great moral effect. Debris flew 200/300 feet in the air and up to 200/300 yards away, but all the men had been warned and only one accident occurred – to a man, who against orders, watched the effect over the parapet. The infantry were warned not to go down into the crater for at least half-an-hour after the capture, owing to the danger of poisonous fumes remaining there. The two craters at M2 were each about 90 feet across and together formed an enormous pit, the inside of the hill being literally blown out, the depth of the craters being about 30 feet. The crater formed by M3 was about 30 feet across. The success of the mines was unquestionable.[15]

Some of the men who were involved in the consolidation works on that first night on the hill reported the smell of gas and it has been suggested that this was because the Germans were actually using gas shells. If that is indeed the case then it would be the earliest record of that particular weapon. The Official History[16] points out that the smell may have resulted from German gas cylinders that had been installed ready for use and had been destroyed by the mines, and there is some evidence in the form of eyewitness accounts to suggest that some unusual cylinders were in fact seen during the capture of the hill. This is, to some extent, born out by the German account quoted in the Official History, which states:

> On the evening of the 17th April, Hill 60 in the sector of XV Corps was captured by the British after an explosion of mines. The fear expressed at the time that some of the gas cylinders dug in on Hill 60 had fallen into the hands of the enemy seem to have been groundless.

Of course, if gas cylinders had been found on Hill 60 it might have given the allies some indication of the German intentions for the coming weeks and might have made the higher command sit up and take more notice of the information they had received on its use from other sources. If this had happened then the discovery on Hill 60 may have had an impact on the whole conduct of the Second Battle of Ypres. However, it appears that the gas was in such small concentrations that it did not result in casualties, and so little attention was paid to the reports. Two days later two sappers were asphyxiated when they were overcome by "fumes" after descending into the craters against orders. Again little notice was taken of this since it was assumed, possibly correctly, that these gases were the result of the detonation of the mines.

Hill 60 had been captured by a combined effort. Holding it was to be the infantry's responsibility and that was a totally different matter. The capture of Hill 60 produced a small but pronounced salient in the British line. Without the capture of other heights, such as the Caterpillar, the holding of Hill 60 would be very difficult. Many of the field officers had recognized this and had advised against its capture, favouring an attack in the form of a large-scale raid which would have required the Germans to garrison the hill in strength, and thus expose them to artillery fire which could then be brought to bear upon the hill. However, on 17th April it had been shown by the 171st Tunnelling Company that mining could be successfully carried out. They had proved their worth and almost immediately the command of the Company passed from Major Griffith to Captain E. Wellesley and a specialist unit of "tunnellers" became firmly established, though many of the infantrymen who had worked on the tunnels in the hill were returned to their units soon after the mine had been fired. Some of these men were to take part in the severe fighting around Ypres that was to develop through the coming weeks.

For their part the infantry were to be severely tested over the next few days, and the wisdom of the capture of the hill was to be held to the closest scrutiny as they bore the brunt of some of the fiercest fighting so far experienced during the war.

Notes

1. The railway cutting is formed in the strata of the Paniselian Formation which comprise sands and clays. The three high points mentioned are formed from the spoil of these strata. It is also this formation that was excavated by the miners and produced such difficult working conditions: see Doyle, *The Geology of the Western Front*, p13.
2. See Dixon, *Out Since '14*, p28.
3. The grafting tool was a kind of small pointed spade – see Grieve and Newman, 1936, *Tunnellers*, p34.

4. See Dixon and Dixon, *With Rifle and Pick*, p74 and Barrie, *War Underground*, p49).

5. Hughes and Dixon, *Surrender be Damned*, p71.

6. Dixon and Dixon, op.cit., p76.

7. ibid. p77.

8. Barrie, op.cit., pp56–57.

9. Dixon and Dixon, op.cit., p77.

10. The figures quoted here may be found in several sources but seem to derive originally from the War Diary of the 171st Tunnelling Company RE.

11. Dixon and Dixon, op.cit., p78.

12. ibid.

13. P.O. Box – The Post Office Box: an instrument whereby the resistance in any given circuit can be balanced and hence measured.

14. Cave, *Hill 60*, p28.

15. This account from *On the Western Front* is derived from *The Work of the Royal Engineers in the European War. Military Mining.*

16. Throughout, the Official History refers to *Military Operations. France and Belgium 1915 Vol. 1.*

CHAPTER THREE

Hill 60

18th to 21st April 1915

In the early hours of 18th April, Hill 60 was a veritable inferno of high explosives and flying metal as the Germans trained guns of all calibres from, it is believed, as many as forty-four different batteries that they had within its range. By that time, C Company of the 1st Royal West Kents had been reinforced by its own B Company in the front line on the crest of the hill; while B and C Companies of the 2nd KOSB were still in support. At approximately 2.30 am the Germans launched the first of three counter attacks on the line held by the Royal West Kents. These were considered as being "small" attacks and they were not pressed with any great aggression, so that the defenders were easily able to beat them off with concentrated rifle fire. It was only in the last of the attacks that any of the Germans managed to reach their parapet in small numbers and these were immediately dispatched. Shortly afterwards the two front line companies were relieved by A and D Companies of the 2nd KOSB, though Second Lieutenant E.B. Walker's section and Second Lieutenant. H.A. Poland's platoon were unable to get away during the relief. To add weight to the support the remaining two companies (A and D) of the Royal West Kents were sent forward to the base of the hill. Whilst the fighting had ceased briefly to allow these changes to take place, the shelling did not subside at all and the Germans shelled the front line and supports as far back as Larch Wood with equal vigour.

It was approximately 4 am when the Germans launched a more deter-mined counter-attack against the hill which soon involved everyone in a fierce and extremely vicious hand-to-hand combat that resulted in

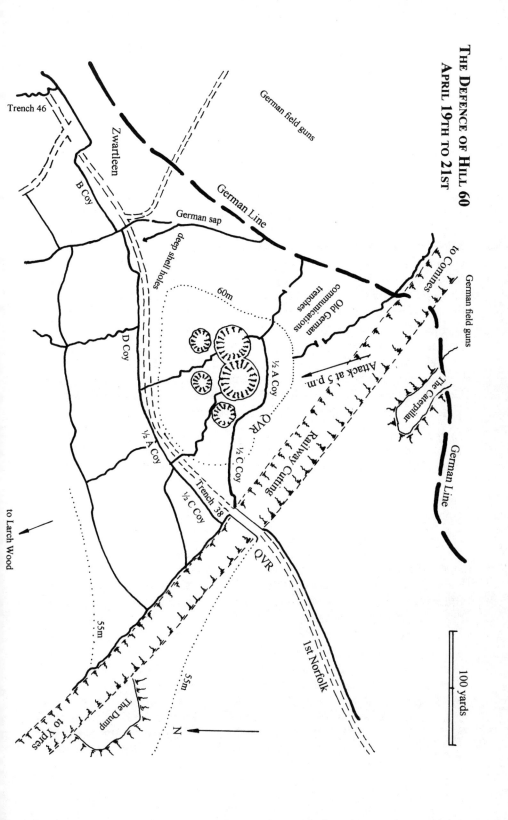

THE DEFENCE OF HILL 60
APRIL 19TH TO 21ST

Trench 46

German field guns

Zwartleen

B Coy

German Line

German sap

deep shell holes

60m

D Coy

Old German communications trenches

½ A Coy

to Comines

German field guns

The Caterpillar

German Line

Attack at 5 p.m.

QVR

½ A Coy

½ C Coy

Railway Cutting

Trench 38

½ C Coy

QVR

to Larch Wood

1st Norfolk

55m

55m

The Dump

to Ypres

N

100 yards

many casualties for both sides. The KOSB came under particular pressure, as described in their War Diary:

> A and D Coys. relieved the two coys. of the RWK regt. holding the hill. Owing to these coys. not having seen the place by daylight they were unable to take in the situation at once, consequently they did not guard certain areas where the enemy could crawl up unseen. The enemy made a counter attack and threw hand bombs and drove our men back a little.

During the fighting the 2nd KOSB were forced to give ground, retiring on the right to the line behind the crater there and leaving the Germans in charge of part of the crest. The fighting had cost them considerable casualties in officers and men. Lieutenant H. Malet was among those killed, and one of his men spoke highly of the gallantry displayed by the young officer as he led them to "find the Germans". Unfortunately for Malet he was a victim of the bulge in the lines caused by the attack when he was killed by German fire that was coming from the rear. As for the two small parties of the Royal West Kents, under Second Lieutenants Walker and Poland, which had remained on the hill when the KOSB arrived, they were entirely wiped out, not one man surviving the fighting of the early hours of the morning of 18th April. At one stage in the fighting, Second Lieutenant Doe of the West Kents was sent to reinforce his beleaguered comrades and his account gives a good impression of the overall conditions on the hill that morning:

> I was ordered forward to reinforce the left crater with my platoon about 4 am on the 18th. On reaching the Hill I found 2nd Lieut. Walker and 2nd Lieut. Poland and about 20 of our men with some K.O.S.B. 2nd Lieut. Walker was shot through the face about a moment after my arrival. Capt. Tuff was lying dead in the crater. In order to keep away the German bomb throwers (advice given by 2nd Lieut. Walker) I ordered a good fire to be kept up. This proved successful but after about an hour firing it was found that nearly all the rifles were out of order owing to the heat.[1]

It had been a difficult morning for those men on the hill but, although some ground was conceded, the line had held and, in spite if the shelling, there was a great determination to hold the line and not to concede yet more ground.

Even before the German counter-attack of 4 am had developed, help was on the way in the form of the 2nd Duke of Wellington's which had been held in reserve. At 3 am they were ordered forward from their positions near Zillebeke, A Company moving immediately, followed at 6 am by the rest of the battalion. The purpose of the move was to provide relief for the 1st Royal West Kents, which had by that time suffered very heavy casualties and, at 8.30 am, A Company took over the forward Royal West Kent positions and those of the 2nd KOSB by 11.30 am.

26

The fighting continued throughout the day and presently the 2nd Duke's were also suffering casualties including the company commander, Captain R. Milbank, who was so seriously wounded that he died some days later. During the late morning Lieutenant Colonel Turner and his HQ staff actually toured the front line trenches so that they could get first hand information on the situation on the hill, since one of the first things to suffer from the shelling had been the telephone wires. On his return to Battalion HQ he ordered B Company to support the company already committed, together with a platoon from each of C and D Companies. B Company had barely reached the trenches when their commander, Captain T.M. Ellis, was killed. This manoeuvre, however, appears to have stabilized the situation somewhat because for the next few hours there were no significant advances made by the Germans. They did, however, continue to shell the hill and its environs, making it extremely difficult for anyone to be absolutely clear about the situation on the hill and for bringing forward supports and material needed for the continued defence of the ground gained. This was to become a particular problem as the day wore on, and supplies of ammunition on the hill gradually dwindled as a result of the continued fighting.

Meanwhile the 4th battalion of the 13 Brigade, the 2nd King's Own Yorkshire Light Infantry, was being ordered from Ypres to take part in the action and moved forward at 7 am to occupy the position that had recently been vacated by the 2nd Duke's. Within a short time of their arrival in the early afternoon they were informed that they would be taking part in a counter-attack that was intended to recapture that portion of the hill that had been lost to the Germans in the morning. The plan for the attack, as issued from 13 Brigade Headquarters, was straightforward. Three companies of the 2nd Duke's were to make a frontal assault on the hill supported by two companies of the 2nd KOYLI, with a third acting as a local reserve and a fourth acting as a consolidating company. A Company of the 2nd Duke's had already been in action and were to be held as a somewhat battered and weakened reserve to that battalion. Thus in the front line of the assault, the 2nd Duke's placed B Company (Captain C.E.B. Hanson) on the right with C Company (Captain B.J. Barton) in the centre and D Company (Captain Taylor) on the left. Behind these in trenches 39 and 40 were B and C Companies of the 2nd KOYLI, commanded by Captain Alt and Captain Kent respectively. D Company (Captain Palmer) was positioned in the communication trenches immediately behind, while A Company waited next to the railway cutting in communication Trench 38 with spades ready to commence consolidation works as soon as any ground was captured. The scene was set and, at 6 pm under the cover of artillery fire directed on the hill, the attack started. B Company, 2nd Duke's, moving along the right flank had the most cover and were able to reach their objective quickly. C Company immediately came under heavy machine-gun fire and suffered very heavy losses as they worked forward, and only Captain Barton and eleven men managed to reach the German trenches;

> They, however, were sufficient to kill, capture and put to flight the German garrison of it. Pte. Behan and Dryden reached the right extremity of the trench, killed three Germans, captured two and drove away the remainder. Pte. Behan recommended for the V.C. Pte. Dryden for the D.C.M.[2]

Private B. Behan was awarded the DCM for his bravery as was Private C. Dryden, who was killed on the hill in the fighting of early May.

The situation for D Company was every bit as bad, for as they advanced all their officers became casualties and for a moment there was a little hesitation, then, supported by the companies of the 2nd KOYLI pressing on from behind, they reached their objective. The crest was once again in British hands and ferocious hand-to-hand fighting ensued as both sides struggled for supremacy of the hill. The 2nd KOYLI War Diary sets the scene vividly:

> The Germans also counter attacked continuously using hand grenades and bombs and furious combats took place in the craters made by the explosions of the mines which soon became a shambles filled with killed and wounded. The crater on the left we were unable to hold so we entrenched ourselves a few yards behind it our trench passing in front of the remaining craters. The Germans high explosive shells gave off blinding and suffocating fumes which caused great distress amongst the men but they hung on. Rifles got jammed from the heat of firing and grenades and ammunition were difficult to get up owing to the block of wounded in the communication and fire trenches and if it had not been for the stacks of German rifles and ammunition left behind which our men used in stead of their own it would have been very difficult to maintain our position on the hill.

The 2nd KOYLI and the 2nd Duke's did hold on to their gains amongst the hell of shell and rifle fire on the crest of the hill. The fighting throughout the rest of the day was brutal and at close quarters, as every scrap of the hill was fought for over and over again and the ground became covered with dead and wounded of both sides. It had not been an imaginative counter attack, as it was full frontal against the German positions, but this was, in part, exacerbated by the limited objectives of the initial attack on the hill. The artillery offered what help it could but in the end it was up to the infantry who needed to cover the ground, to engage the enemy, and the assaulting companies suffered heavy casualties accordingly. By the end of the day the 2nd Duke's, who had first entered the area on the morning of 18th April, had lost seventeen officers and 406 other ranks. The 2nd KOYLI, who had been brought forward specifically for the attack, had suffered fifteen officers and 225 other ranks killed, wounded and missing. With such numbers falling as a result of the counter attack it may have been prudent to examine the objectives more thoroughly. The hill was clearly of great importance in terms of observation, but that importance needed to be weighed against the cost of winning and holding the hill which, by itself, had very little strategic importance. It was, perhaps, time to cut the losses and surrender the hill once again to the Germans – or to take a wider view of the battle by engaging the Germans on a larger front. However, as will become clear, British interests were concentrated more towards the south as the planning for the Battle of Aubers Ridge was progressing, which made a widening of the objectives around Hill 60 impossible. Bearing these factors in mind it is difficult to understand the persistence shown by certain elements of the command in requiring that Hill 60 should remain in British hands. But that was the way it was to be, for on the morning of 19th April both battalions which had been in such heavy fighting on the hill throughout 18th April were relieved by the 1st Bedfords (15 Brigade) and the 1st East Surreys (14 Brigade attached to 15 Brigade), and the defence of the hill became their responsibility for a short time.

Although there had been heavy fighting for over twenty-four hours, the situation on the hill was far from clear and far from resolved. The attack of the British on 18th April had established a presence on the hill, but the line was far from complete and the position was somewhat precarious as the 1st East Surreys took over the positions. The crest of the hill was dominated by the three mine craters that had resulted from the detonation of the mines. The left (M1) and the middle (M2) craters, each formed by the detonation of two charges placed by the tunnellers, had coalesced to form a kind of deep figure of eight whilst the smaller crater (M3) on the right was separated from the others by approximately thirty yards. On the right of the position a trench ran from the railway cutting towards the right hand crater from whence there was a gap in the line. The forward trench occupied by the British ran in front of the two main craters, and was in fact an extension of the old German support line. These positions, from railway onto the crest and around to the left crater, were occupied by C Company of the 1st East Surreys commanded by Captain A.H. Huth. The remainder of the battalion was positioned in the trenches roughly following the road at the base of the hill. A Company held the right as far as the communication trench, completed by the 2nd KOSB to the left crater; D Company was in the section immediately to the left of this, and B Company occupied the left section that carried the line into the village of Zwarteleen. Near the junction of these latter two companies a length of trench stuck out into no man's land for a short distance at right angles to the main line. It appears that this trench had once been a continuation of a German trench that had been blocked off during the earlier fighting for the hill. The Germans had taken the opportunity to use as much of it as possible and had turned a sap away from the block towards the British line. The short length of trench occupied by the East Surreys was partly hidden from the right by two ruined houses in Zwarteleen which also obscured a full view of the battlefield for its occupants.

To the right of the East Surreys, on the other side of the railway cutting, were the 1st Norfolks (15 Brigade) and near to the bridge was the machine-gun section of the Queen Victoria's Rifles, who had been in the line to offer support since the first attack on the evening of 17th April. To the left and holding the line through Zwarteleen were the 1st Cheshires, also from 15 Brigade. The 1st Bedfords were in support in the trenches around Larch Wood, some five hundred yards behind the front line.

The German line ran around the base of the hill on the southern side and across the railway to the Caterpillar. To the left of the left-hand crater was the trench mentioned above which extended out from their present front line and into no man's land. This sap brought the Germans into close proximity with the British front line, not far from the junction of B and D Companies of the East Surreys. Between the head of this sap and separating it from the British front line was an area of ground that was heavily and deeply pock-marked by shell fire. Two old communication trenches ran from the German line across no man's land towards the crest of the hill and the centre crater. The trench on the right had been blocked well away from the German positions. The trench on the left branched so that it led to both the left and middle craters. This too had been blocked in no man's land and both branches had been blocked in their approaches to the craters. From this description, and by reference to the sketch, it is clear that on 19th April the situation for the British was far from satisfactory. Their forward line was incomplete and the left flank of the forces on the hill was completely in the air. It can also be seen that Germans in the sap could also fire onto the backs of the defenders in the craters.

The 19th April passed in relative quiet, though for Hill 60 that meant that the position was shelled continuously throughout the day, but there was no infantry attack. During the course of the day every effort was made to improve the trenches and keep them repaired, under the continuous shellfire which limited the amount of movement possible on the hill. In the absence of any infantry attack the opportunity was taken, wherever possible, to get the wounded away, of which there were many caused by the fighting to that time, not to mention the shelling of the day. At about 5 pm there was a furious bombardment of the position which suggested that the enemy infantry were preparing to attack, but after about half an hour the shelling died away and there was no assault. At 10 pm the 1st East Surreys adjusted their line with half of A Company, under Lieutenant G.R.P. Roupell, relieving half of C Company in the trenches immediately in front of the left and middle craters, with Second Lieutenant W.A. Davis and his men on the left and Lieutenant G.L. Wilson on the right. Meanwhile the half of C Company remaining in the forward positions attempted to extend their line to fill the gap between the right and the middle craters. Captain Huth was killed while supervising this improvement work. Each company had one platoon in the front line trenches and a further platoon in the trenches in immediate support.

The early hours of 20th April were quiet for those men of A and C Companies in the forward line. To the left, in front of D and B Companies, the Germans were seen to be attempting to improve their positions in the sap extending from their lines. The East Surreys tried to discourage this work by throwing bombs from their most forward position in the short length of trench in no man's land, but in this they were unsuccessful. The Germans continued work in the sap and succeeded in building a strong point at its end which they were able to loophole for the use of snipers and into which later in the day they were able to bring two machine guns. It was almost impossible for B Company to dislodge them, although they were only about twenty yards away, for each time one of the East Surreys raised himself above the parapet to attempt to fire on the Germans he was greeted by a rifle bullet, though this did not stop many of them trying. The East Surreys suffered a number of casualties in a short space of time as a result of the Germans' activity in the strong point at the end of the sap, but at that time there was very little that they could do about it.

At 11 am the Germans opened a very heavy bombardment on the entire area and much of the work that had been carried out improving the trenches was lost in a matter of minutes as guns of all calibres plastered the hill with explosives. The trenches were destroyed and men were buried alive as parapets collapsed under the weight of the incessant shelling. Major W.H. Paterson and Captain D. Wynyard left Battalion Headquarters for D Company sector so as to be able to assess the situation for themselves and they found much of the trench in a very bad state. It was while helping to get wounded men clear of the shattered trenches in this sector that Captain Wynyard was killed. Both B and D Companies suffered heavy casualties during this period as the day became a trial of grim survival in the face of the enemy's superior artillery. On both flanks the Germans had brought up field guns to very advanced positions, firing from immediately behind their front lines, and it is little wonder that the British infantry were suffering so badly.

By about 3 pm the Germans clearly believed that their artillery had created enough havoc to allow them to begin moving their infantry into attack. This they commenced to do, beginning with probing the lines of B and D Companies from the fortified position in the sap. The German snipers in their loopholed position were able to keep the British pinned down in their trench while yet more moved forward into the deeply shell-pitted ground between the trenches. At this point Private E. Dwyer took matters into his own hands. Dwyer did not fancy the prospect of being made a prisoner if the Germans managed to get into his trench, in fact he appears to have been more bothered by the thought of that than of being killed. Dwyer calculated that his best chance was to jump up on the parapet and begin hurling bombs immediately, thereby keeping the Germans' heads down long enough for his comrades to man the fire step and to lay down some fire on those Germans that were advancing toward the shell-pitted area and those in the strong point. It is recorded that Dwyer had managed to collect about 300 grenades (Hales grenades – a small grenade with a long handle) into the trench near him. He then leapt upon the parapet and proceeded to throw his bombs with some considerable accuracy. It is amazing that standing in full view of the enemy he remained uninjured throughout the action; possibly the accuracy of his bomb throwing had done much to prevent the snipers in the strong point from reacting. It is certain that the bombing of the enemy was not as accurate and Dwyer's action had prevented the Germans from making any significant advance, and his trench was saved. For his bravery that day Private Dwyer was awarded the Victoria Cross and at nineteen years of age he became the youngest winner of the award to that date.

At 4 pm the Germans made a very determined attempt to regain the hill as they increased their artillery effort. A Company, on the crest of the hill, suffered particularly badly from the guns firing in the vicinity of the Caterpillar as shells tore through their parapets and wrecked their positions:

> The bursting of shells was incessant and the noise was deafening. The little hill was covered with flame, smoke and dust, and it was impossible to see more than ten yards in any direction. Many casualties resulted, and the battered trenches became so choked with dead, wounded, debris and mud as to be well nigh impassable. Every telephone line was cut and all

communications ceased, internal as well as with sector headquarters and the artillery, so that the support offered by the British guns was necessarily less effective.[3]

The 1st East Surreys' Battalion Headquarters, situated near the junction of the communication trench to the middle crater and the support line, also came under fire, receiving a direct hit which put everyone there out of action and killed the commanding officer, Major Paterson. In A Company's forward trench only a handful of men remained, and Lieutenant Roupell ordered up his reserve platoon to reinforce his position. Even this manoeuvre was difficult, for the trenches were in such a bad shape from the shelling that the reserves almost had to dig their way forward, more or less repairing the trench as they went. There were many casualties amongst this platoon, but they eventually reached Roupell and his small band to give the reinforcement he had asked for. A Company hung on grimly to their task as the shelling continued until 5 pm , at which time it lifted on to the supports and reserves at the rear of the hill, which to all concerned indicated quite clearly that there was to be an infantry assault by the enemy. The rear areas were shelled so that it became almost impossible to get men or equipment forward in quantities needed to render much assistance to the defenders in their exposed forward positions on the hill. Shortly after their artillery had lifted, the Germans moved across the open ground in front of the Caterpillar and into the railway cutting to assault the trenches occupied by C Company. At this point the 1st Norfolks and the Queen Victoria's Rifles machine-gun section were able to give some assistance, firing from the trenches to the right of the hill, but the Germans pressed on. In the C Company trenches the shelling had produced heavy casualties, but one of the battalion's five machine guns was positioned there. Almost all the gun crew were dead but Corporal F.W. Adams, although wounded and with part of his jaw shot away, manned the gun alone and poured a hail of bullets at the oncoming Germans which broke up the German attack. Corporal Adams remained with his gun, giving what assistance he could, until he was shot through the head and killed. His name was put forward by the battalion for the Victoria Cross to mark his gallantry and sacrifice, but the award was not forthcoming on a day when the men of the East Surreys carried out many acts of bravery.

In A company's sector the Germans brought pressure to bear by crawling along their old communication trenches as far as they could, so as to bomb the British front line. According to the accounts of the day, this was particularly difficult to respond to, for the British bombs (the Hales bomb) were fitted with such long handles that they were almost impossible to throw with any great force from the narrow front line trench. The East Surreys managed to hamper the Germans' progress with some very dangerous improvisation, as some men threw back any German bombs that landed in the trench, while others used rapid rifle fire in an attempt to break up the attack and prevent the Germans moving further up the old communication trench. It was a successful answer, at least in the short term, but things on the left flank were not going well. Here the Germans were making moves against B and D Companies in their trenches on the left and towards the communication trench to the left crater. Their objective was clear – to cut off A Company from all assistance from that quarter and gradually surround them. Fortunately, a platoon of D Company had occupied the communication trench and the Germans were caught in a crossfire from the two trenches. For all that, the communication trench was not a healthy place to be, for by that time the Germans had brought up two machine guns into their sap and were able to cause problems in both the communication trench and in the crater on the crest of the hill where men were suddenly coming under heavy fire from their rear.

By this time the 1st Bedfords, under Lieutenant Colonel C.R.J. Griffiths, had moved up from their positions in the Larch Wood area and, seeing the problems at the crest, proceeded in that direction. Lieutenant Roupell assessed the situation and realized that his position was becoming grave, so he requested the company of Bedfords closest to him to move to the left crater to offer some flank support to his precarious position. This they did immediately, though they suffered heavy casualties in this manoeuvre. Meanwhile, Lieutenant B.H. Geary, in charge of the platoon of C Company in reserve, heard of Roupell's request for support and started out with his men. There was no way through the trenches, which were full of dead and wounded, and so Geary led his men over the open to join the Bedfords in the left crater, and it is said that his arrival in the position was greeted with a hearty cheer from the Bedfords. For the next couple of hours A Company, and its reinforcements, were able to beat off repeated attacks which were usually accompanied by a hail of bombs followed by assaulting infantry. Roupell was, by this time, the most senior officer on the crest of the hill and he needed to get more information on the situation around him. Of course, this was to prove difficult since the German shelling had disrupted all telephone communications with rear areas and adjacent units. Roupell was left with little option but to attempt to make his way back to sector headquarters himself. In spite of being wounded in eight places he made his way back through the fighting to get instructions and to stop long enough to get his wounds dressed. He then returned to his command on the hill, and though he admitted to feeling faint from the loss of blood, he continued to organize the defence for the next three or four hours.

At 8 pm the Germans were making progress along the left hand extension of the most forward part of the line. The line in that portion of the defences did not have any traverses, and it meant that it was easy to fire along its length to prevent the Germans moving along it. Of course, this also meant that the British could not reoccupy it fully either, since the Germans were also able to fire along its length so that the trench became a narrow extension of no man's land. The Germans were not content with assaulting in one direction, and started to work their way around the blocks in their old communication trenches and into the left crater. These were spotted by Lieutenant Geary, who collected up a number of rifles and, with Private White to load them for him, kept the Germans at bay with rapid rifle fire. Geary's men in the crater had started to come under fire from the rear, so he arranged his force within the crater to limit this by putting men all around the rim. He then sent three messengers to attempt to make contact with Lieutenant E.G.H. Clarke of D Company to his left and then set out himself to clarify the situation in the A Company position. None of his messengers got through to D Company but he found the situation in A Company under control, though the garrison was severely reduced and becoming short of ammunition. He was able to discuss the situation with Second Lieutenant Davis, since Lieutenant Wilson had been killed by this time, and an officer of the Bedfords in A company's trench, and the three men decided that there would be no surrender of the hill until it was absolutely clear that there could be no reinforcement. The time was a little before midnight, and Roupell was already on a mission to bring up more of the Bedfords with which he returned shortly after midnight. As Geary returned to his position in the crater, there was news also that reinforcements in the form of the Queen Victoria's Rifles were being brought forward to the assistance of the East Surreys and A and D Companies, Major P.T. Lees and Captain G.B.J. Fazakerly-Westby, were already moving to the right hand side of the hill, towards trench 38 and the right hand crater. The Victoria's had started out at about 9.30 pm but because of the heavy fire on the hill, it had taken them a good two hours to reach their destination, which was little more than 200 yards distant. Geary and Lees met on the battlefield and agreed to act in conjunction to clear the enemy from the left of the line, and some organization was put in place for this small-scale counter-attack, including Geary digging his men into a position so that they could command the middle crater more effectively. He also set about trying to establish communications with his rear, which had become increasingly difficult throughout the night. The Germans tried to move forward from the left for the second time, but Geary spotted them and, from his new trench, was able to bring sufficient fire to bear from his rifle, once again loaded by a private, to prevent them making progress. Geary was still expecting to attack with Lees' men but this did not happen, because the Germans had withdrawn slightly from the position on the left of their own accord. They remained close enough to the British line to continue to bring harassing fire on the defenders throughout the rest of the night. By that time, in the early hours of 21st April, a party of Victoria's had arrived carrying ammunition, and Geary immediately directed them to the men in the crater where the shortage of ammunition had become critical. While the arrival of ammunition had helped to ease the situation somewhat, Geary still wanted to rein-force his line and so he set off to find Major Lees to bring forward more of the Victoria's; however, during this time he was severely wounded in the head and his part in the fighting for Hill 60 was over.

On the right, the Victoria's had managed to get A and D Companies into position in trench 38 and the line running up to the right hand crater, but both companies were suffering from the shellfire that continued throughout the night. At a little after midnight, Sergeant E.H. Pulleyn and his sixteen men were ordered to fill a gap near the crest of the hill. Although they made it into position, there had been five casualties and the position could not be held, so Pulleyn and the remainder were forced to withdraw. The shelling of the Victoria's position was terrific, the fire coming from field guns near the Caterpillar, at ranges of between 300 and 500 yards. The effects on the trenches and defenders was devastating as trenches collapsed and casu-alties rose. By the early hours of the morning Major Lees and Captain Fazakerly-Westby had been killed,[4] and all other officers in the trenches, together with about 100 other ranks, had become casualties. It was at this time that Lieutenant G.H. Wooley came forward and took command of the right hand trenches and became the senior officer in that part of the defences. The young lieutenant used the Hales grenades to break up the attacking Germans, and his men responded to his action with rapid rifle fire. Soon the Hales bombs ran out and Wooley was reduced to using jam tin bombs, for which he had to borrow matches from Lieutenant D.L. Summerhayes, which on his own admission were much less effective, and he was relieved when more of the grenades arrived on the scene. His defence of this section of the hill was supported by Sergeant Pulleyn and Corporal Peabody, and both men were to receive the DCM for their bravery during that awful night. With the death of Lieutenant Summerhayes, Wooley became the only officer in charge of the defence of that portion of the line which extended from the right towards the middle crater. Wooley was lucky to escape injury

36

himself when a small German "egg" grenade exploded on his head and, although he was temporarily stunned, it did little more damage than rip his cap. The Victoria's had suffered badly by this time and it was probably no surprise to Wooley when he was ordered, both verbally and in writing, to bring back his small command. Wooley refused, stating that there were very few defenders on the hill and to withdraw his men would leave only small groups of the Bedfords and East Surreys there, and he was not prepared to abandon the regulars to their fate. At 2 am the East Surreys were relieved by the 1st Devons on the left of the hill, and this battalion had orders to extend their front around the hill which would then allow Wooley to withdraw. Wooley was ordered to go back to assist in bringing up the remaining Devons and in so doing he came across a party of sixty bombers of the Northumberland Fusiliers, with a plentiful supply of bombs, who were waiting in communication trench 38 to move forward into the action. They had lost their officer and had been waiting for instruction for some hours, and immediately Wooley ordered fifteen of them forward, with their bombs, to support the defenders of the craters. At dawn the relief of the Queen Victoria's Rifles was complete and Wooley brought out his small command of fourteen other ranks. Rifleman Sidney Seymour, who had survived the action, gave an account to the newspaper that was very frank, and in the course of it he says:

> It was a bad day for us as the Company at roll call numbered 26 men and one officer. Corporal Peabody did fine work attending the wounded. I had an awful shock next morning as he did not turn up for some hours after we were relieved. When he did turn up he broke down just as we all had done. The strain was awful and to see your pals go one by one adds to the horror. We cried like children and were completely broken up.[5]

It had indeed been a very bad time for all those battalions that had been involved in the fighting. The 1st East Surreys had suffered very heavy casualties, with fifteen officers and 264 other ranks falling during their stay on the hill. Lieutenant Roupell and Lieutenant Geary were also awarded the Victoria Cross to add to that won by Private Dwyer earlier in the day. Likewise, Lieutenant Wooley was also awarded the same honour for his part in the defence during the hours of darkness and for his courageous decision to stay and fight after he had been ordered to withdraw. Lieutenant Wooley's award was the first such award to be made to an officer of the Territorial Force. It had been a terrible day of fighting and the British had just about held the hill. Lieutenant Ince, adjutant of the 2nd Duke of Wellington's, was to comment later:

> What our troops withstood can to some extent be realized if it is remembered that the space fought over on the four and a half days between April

17th and 21st was only 250 yards in length, about 200 in depth. On to that small area the enemy for hours on end hurled tons of metal and high explosives, and at a time the hill top was wreathed in poisonous fumes. And yet our gallant infantry did not give way. They stood firm under a fire which swept away whole sections at a time, filled the trenches with dead bodies, and so cumbered the approaches to the front line that reinforcements could not reach it without having to climb over the prostrate forms of their former comrades.[6]

It had been a severe test for all those involved, but by 21st April the British were holding the hill and they continued to do so until the end of the first week of May. It is interesting to note that this heavy fighting was dismissed in less than three lines in the dispatches of Field Marshal Sir John French covering the period, when he stated:

On the 20th and following days many unsuccessful attacks by the enemy were made on Hill 60, which was continuously shelled by heavy artillery.[7]

What horrors and bravery those few words hide!

The days immediately following the heavy fighting on the hill were to see British attention and effort directed elsewhere as they fought off determined German attacks, aided by the release of poisonous gas, further to the north in what was to become known as the Second Battle of Ypres.

Notes

1. Second Lieutenant Edmund Basil Poland was killed while using a machine gun to stem the German attack. This account appears in the RWK War Diary.
2. 2nd Duke's War Diary.
3. See Cave, op.cit., p34.
4. Captain Fazakerly-Westby was commemorated on the Menin Gate; recently it has been demonstrated to the satisfaction of the Commonwealth War Graves Commission that his body rests in 1/DCLI Cemetery. The headstone has been appropriately marked. See Reed, *Walking the Salient*, p87.
5. See Cave, op.cit., p48.
6. See Cave, op.cit., p31.
7. French, *Complete Despatches*, p361.

CHAPTER FOUR

The Battle of Gravenstafel Ridge
Day 1 – 22nd April 1915

The fighting at Hill 60 had raised the suspicion in some minds that the Germans had been preparing to use poisonous gas as a new weapon, but the thought had been dismissed because the area was full of fumes of one sort or another from the exploding of the mines and the high explosives. There had been some other indications of what may have been about to occur in the salient but there was some problem of linking the information together and in assigning it the appropriate importance.

The use of poisonous gas or other such substances had been a possibility for years and military leaders were aware of the potential. It had been the subject of the Hague Declaration of 1899 and the Hague Convention of 1907 which had been signed by the European powers of the early twentieth century and which expressly forbade the use of gas in the event of war. In the earlier draft both Britain and the United States had refused to become signatories but in later versions they followed the rest of the major powers. It is not entirely clear that the treaty had anything to do with humanitarian reasons, for most of the senior military figures of the day had argued that the effective use of gas was too dependant on wind to be of any great importance. However, at the outbreak of war the use of gas was effectively "outlawed" and was generally seen as not "playing the game".

By early 1915 the stalemate of the Western Front had led both sides to consider new weapons and technology to assist in the breakthrough that could bring about the end of the war. To the Germans' aims this was essential, because it had become clear to them that they would not

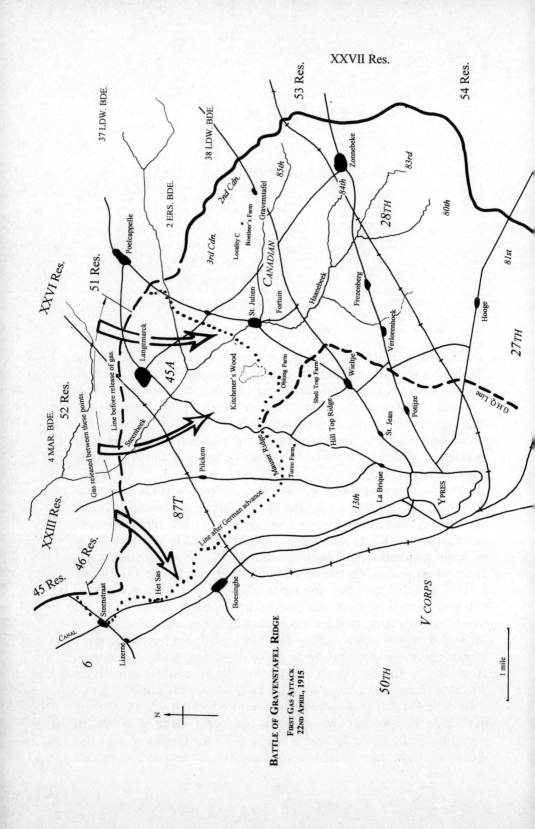

BATTLE OF GRAVENSTAFEL RIDGE

FIRST GAS ATTACK 22ND APRIL, 1915

XXVII Res.

XXVI Res.

37 LDW. BDE.

38 LDW. BDE.

2 ERS. BDE.

2nd Cdn.

3rd Cdn.

51 Res.

52 Res.

4 MAR. BDE.

XXIII Res.

46 Res.

45 Res.

6

53 Res.

54 Res.

85th

84th

83rd

80th

81st

28TH

27TH

CANADIAN

45A

87T

13th

50TH

V CORPS

Poelcappelle

Langemarck

Steenbeck

Plickem

Steenstraat

Het Sas

Lizerne

Boesinghe

St. Julien

Fortuin

Locality C

Boetleer's Farm

Gravenstafel

Zonnebeke

Haanebeek

Frezenberg

Verlorenhoek

Hooge

Kitchener's Wood

Oblong Farm

Shell Trap Farm

Wieltje

Potijze

St. Jean

La Brique

Hill Top Ridge

Mauser Ridge

Turco Farm

YPRES

Line before release of gas.

Gas released between these points.

Line after German advance.

G.H.Q. Line

CANAL

N

1 mile

be allowed to bargain from a position of strength, since the Allies had clearly shown that they would do all that they could to drive them from the soil of Belgium and France. It would appear that during the early months of 1915 the Germans had begun to stockpile quantities of chlorine with the express purpose of using it to produce an effective breakthrough on the Western Front.

On 14th April 1915 Private August Jager of the 234th Infantry Regiment, 51st Reserve Division, deserted to the French and took with him clear indications that gas was to be used. He indicated, under questioning, that an attack had been planned for 13th April but had been postponed, and he was able to give details of how the gas was to be delivered from cylinders via forty metre tubes and on to the battlefield. He also had in his possession a pad large enough to cover the mouth and nose and which could be fastened at the back of the head with tapes. He informed his interrogators that it needed to be soaked in a "special solution". The men of the French 11th Division had no doubt of the truth of the deserter's words and General Ferry passed on the information to his superiors who promptly dismissed it as nonsense. For all the horrors the Germans had visited upon Europe, it was thought to be inconceivable that they would stoop so low as to use this awful weapon to wage war. Further, the French commanders considered that Jager knew just a little too much about the whole matter, and it was believed that he had been primed as a decoy to cause fear amongst the troops and to prevent any forces being removed from the area to assist in the build up of troops further to the south for the Allied attacks planned there. Also, the military leadership simply could not see how sufficiently large quantities of gas could be delivered efficiently. The information was, nevertheless, passed on to the British[1] and their attitude was much the same – it simply was not the way war should be waged and therefore they did not believe that it could be waged in that manner. Nevertheless, the British did attempt to do something in so far as they asked for aerial reconnaissance which showed nothing of significance, and they shelled the German lines with heavy artillery in a vain attempt to search out the cylinders. This latter was ineffective if only because there was so little in the way of ammunition, so that a thorough bombardment could not be instigated. It was paying lip service to the warning but it should be remembered that for pre-1915 soldiers the term "gas" was meaningless since they had nothing in their experience with which they could understand the concept beyond, perhaps, the exploding of a high-explosive shell.

Further evidence came to the British, via the French, on 16th April from Belgian sources behind the German lines which stated that:

41

> ... the Germans have manufactured in Ghent 20,000 mouth protectors of tulle, which, the men will carry in a waterproof bag 10 cm by 17.5 cm. These mouth protectors, when soaked in a suitable liquid, serve to protect the men against the effects of asphyxiating gas.[2]

Were these the same protectors as carried by Jager? Was this supporting evidence? If it was, then it was largely ignored by the commanders in the area. The dismissal of the threat became complete when the attack which had been reported as planned for 16th April did not take place – it did not occur to anyone to check to see if the wind was in the appropriate direction to assist such an attack.

The French 11th Division took the threat seriously and had even begun to prepare some protection in the form of small pads of moist straw. The Division was replaced by the 45th Algerian Division and they saw no need to carry on the preparation for an attack that *Grand Quartier Général*[3] did not think was possible. No one seems to have thought of asking a chemist for his opinion about the truth of Jager's words – chemists were civilians and no one in the military was thinking of compromising security by getting a civilian involved, at least not yet!

Even the Germans themselves had not been happy about the use of gas but it gradually gained acceptance and some saw it as the only way to eliminate the Ypres salient,[4] which had been earmarked for the trial of the gas. The troops chosen to carry out the trial were those of Duke Albrecht's Fourth Army and the commander of its XV Corps, General von Diemeling, also had his reservations and commented :

> The mission of poisoning the enemy as one would rats affected me as it would any straightforward soldier – I was disgusted.[5]

Disgusted or not he was the commander who put the wheels in motion for the first poison gas attack of the Great War. Throughout April he had been patiently waiting for the situation to be exactly right so that the experiment with poisonous gas could commence.

In spite of all the indications, outlined above, that gas was about to be used by the Germans, the Allied High Command refused to accept it as a possibility. The consequences of this lack of belief, no matter how well considered, were to be felt on 22nd April 1915, which marked a new phase in the warfare of the Western Front and officially marks the beginning of the Second Battle of Ypres. The day was recorded as being a beautiful spring day, during the morning of which the Germans had bombarded Ypres with their heavy howitzers, including a 17-inch gun, the shell of which was reported as arriving with the "sound of an express train". This was the beginning of the wholesale destruction of the medieval town, as over the next few weeks Ypres slowly but surely became a victim of the war. At about noon this bombardment ceased

42

and the area fell quiet for most of the afternoon. The beautiful spring day had spoiled German plans, for they had hoped to release their gas much earlier in the day. A still day was of no use to them and it was 4 pm before a suitable breeze arose for their purposes. At 5 pm the Germans opened a furious bombardment of the entire area with their heavy howitzers and simultaneously released two clouds of gas on the north eastern flank of the salient. It should be noted that their field guns remained silent until 5.10 pm so as to allow the undisturbed dispersal of the gas towards the Allied lines. With the release of the gas cloud the first phase of the Second Battle of Ypres, later to be known as the Battle of Gravenstafel Ridge, commenced.

The sector of the salient which the gas was to affect first was that area manned by the troops of the French 45th Algerian and 87th Territorial Divisions. It has been said that these divisions were of poor quality but nonetheless they were to bear the brunt of the first gas attack of modern warfare. As might be expected, at first, the French soldiers were not unduly perturbed by the greenish mist they saw rolling towards them across the Flemish countryside, being driven by the gentle north easterly breeze that had sprung up in the late afternoon. They had no cause to be concerned, since no one had encountered gas used in this way and no one had any idea of its effects – even the Germans who had released it. It was not long before all this changed for as the gas reached the French troops they soon began to feel their eyes and throats burning and it was not long before they all experienced difficulty breathing. It was enough for the French divisions and they withdrew rapidly from their trenches in any manner they could – many succumbed to gas poisoning in those first few minutes as their lungs filled with fluid and they choked painfully in the gas filled trenches. Whilst it may be true that the quality of the French troops in the front line was not of the highest, it is also true to say the surprise use of gas, at least to those soldiers in the trenches, left little option but withdrawal. For the divisions to have remained in the trenches without any clear idea of what they were facing, or how to defend against it, would simply have resulted in more gas casualties – and dead soldiers offer no defence. There was a school of thought which suggested that if a soldier was to stand on the fire step and face the gas, he was less likely to be affected than if he sat in the bottom of the trench. Also, it has been suggested, probably correctly, that by fleeing, the French had actually increased the effectiveness of the gas in individuals. The remedy for the latter was to stand still in the trench and allow the gas to pass over the trench which it would do in a matter of minutes. It is worth noting at this point the effects of the gas upon the human body as detailed by the Official History:

43

Chlorine, the gas employed, has a powerful irritant action on the respiratory organs and all mucous membranes exposed to it, causing spasm of the glottis, a burning sensation in the eyes, nose and throat, followed by bronchitis and oedema of the lungs. Frequently, there is evidence of corrosion of the mucous membranes of the air channels and of the cornea. Prolonged inhalation or exposure to a high concentration of the gas will cause death by asphyxia, or, if not fatal, produce cardiac dilatation and cyanosis (blueness of the skin) as a result of the injury to the lungs.[6]

Whilst these effects are clear, and there may be some truth in the benefits of standing still in the trench, since the gas is heavier than air and is dispersed by the wind, it was also knowledge gained after the event and the French soldiers were not in a position to make such a judgement in the field. Consequently, as unfortunate as it was to turn out, the French would appear to have acted instinctively in the only manner they could and they withdrew leaving behind many of their comrades.

Whether or not there is justification for the French withdrawal, the effect on 22nd April was that by the time it was complete at about 6.45 pm there was a breech in the defences to the north-east of Ypres which was eventually recognized as being approximately 8,000 yards wide. Into this gap the German infantry was advancing as quickly as it could, now supported by its field artillery, to capitalize on the effects of the poison gas. For the next few hours or so the Germans had what was probably their best chance of wresting Ypres from the Allies' grasp. It is, perhaps, fortunate for the Allies that the gap was not larger – for some reason, which has not been explained, the gas cylinders in two critical areas of the front line were not opened. Opposite the Canadian portion of the line, at their junction with the French right flank, and those in the Belgian portion, at their junction with the French left flank, gas was not released. Thus the effects of the gas in these areas was minimal; the troops stood their ground and as the battle developed the importance of this was to be fully realized. Can it be that the dispersal mechanism had malfunctioned on the two flanks, or was its failure to be released simply because the orders had not been received to commence the operation? Whatever the explanation it was to prove fortuitous for the Canadian troops on the left flank of the British line.

In the British sector of the line it was some time before anyone realized that anything was going on. Even the sound of the French guns that had opened up as soon as their troops began withdrawing did not cause undue worry. The British were well aware that a new French division had just moved into the area and at first it was simply assumed that the divisional artillery of the new arrivals was "shooting themselves in". However, it was not long before the effects of the gas were being felt by

44

British soldiers thousands of yards west of Ypres, and even in other parts of the salient soldiers reported a strange sickly smell and stinging eyes and throats. As far away as the southern flank of the salient such effects were being felt, but the officers and men alike had no explanation, though some thought it may have something to do with the fumes produced by the German high-explosive shells which they were firing at the time.[7] It soon became clear to all concerned that something serious had taken place on the northern flank of the salient, and this too was soon to become reinforced by the sight of hundreds of French troops streaming back into areas west of the Yser Canal, all suffering, more or less, from the effects of gas poisoning. The situation was not helped by the loss of French officers from the Colonial units without whom it was difficult for any order to be maintained. One of the battalions to witness this withdrawal through the area immediately west of Ypres was the 2nd Battalion, the King's Own Yorkshire Light Infantry, who had only recently been involved in the fighting on the south flank and were preparing to return to that portion of the line. Their War Diary states:

> At 7 pm the Battalion marched out with the intention of relieving the Dorset Regt. in Sector C. As soon as we reached the Ypres-Poperinge road we were met by a continual stream of refugees coming from Ypres, followed by French Algerian troops and transport of all sorts which completely blocked the road and our further march forward. We then learnt that the Germans had used asphyxiating gases on the French Algerian troops trenches between the Yser Canal and Saint Julien and that they had left their entire line of trenches and that the Germans had broken through and were advancing on Ypres. Also that the retirement of the Algerians had left the Canadian line in the air and that they had been compelled to retire.

Although the last statement was not entirely true, the situation was slowly becoming clear to the troops in the area immediately behind the salient, and it was clear to all that something would need to be done and done quickly if Ypres was not to fall into the hands of the Germans.

To the left of the French was the Belgian Grenadier Regiment commanded by Colonel Lodz. One of the grenadiers, who had been part of a nine-man listening post, commented on the initial effect of the gas:

> All was so calm that we no longer thought about the war . . . when suddenly around 5.30 pm we saw a thick cloud rising above the German trenches opposite ours. Surprise and curiosity riveted us to the ground. None of us suspected at that moment what was going on. As the cloud of smoke grew thicker we thought that the German trench had caught fire. The cloud moved slowly towards us, but because of the wind we saw it was being carried towards our right flank and on to the French line.

45

Only the edge of the wave of gas reached us. It was less thick here but gave off a singular odour and seized me and affected my throat with such severity that for a moment I believed I was going to suffocate. Suddenly I heard cries around me "An attack! The Boches are there".[8]

Thus began the defence of the Belgian portion of the line as they, with rapid rifle and machine-gun fire, began to form a flank to their right as the French division continued to withdraw.

To the right of the French was the 13th Battalion Canadian Infantry (Royal Highlanders of Canada). The afternoon had been as quiet for them as everyone else in the front line, and the sight of the gas and the sound of rapid firing had caused some surprise to the men in the front line:

At first we thought it was just the intense musketry that was causing this yellow haze and then it began to come to us, and the French on our left . . . started pouring into our trenches, coughing and bleeding and dying all over the place.[9]

Thus throughout the salient it was becoming clear that the Germans had released asphyxiating gas and all the warnings that had been dismissed out of hand by commanding officers in both the French and British armies in the weeks preceding the attack were finally being realized. The following twenty-four hours were to dictate whether or not those ignored warnings would have a significant effect on the outcome of the battle. Immediately following the release of the gas and the realization that "something serious" was happening there were calls from all levels of command for the defence to commence and with these there were calls for assistance to accomplish it. There was a will to get things moving so that the defence of the salient could commence immediately. Unfortunately there was precious little information as to the situation at any point in the area to be defended. The quality of information was worsened, for instance, by the fact that many reports made were misleading or simply wrong, or had even been overtaken by events. A good example of this is the report made at 5.25 pm by the 3 Canadian Brigade to Divisional Headquarters, which ran as follows:

Situation quiet. Left section reports observing at 5.00 pm a cloud of green vapour several hundred yards in length between the French trenches to our left and those of the enemy. Firing is very heavy at that place also.[10]

By the time this report had been issued, the 3 Canadian Brigade had already begun its defence of the salient and suffered its first gas casualties. Events were happening so quickly that even at Brigade Headquarters, Shell Trap Farm,[11] there was a confused picture of what was going on immediately to the north and east of it. That being the case it is hardly surprising that at the headquarters of the 1st Canadian Division, at Château des Trois Tours near Brielen, there was even more confusion as to exactly what was happening and what actions would be necessary to improve the situation for the defenders. Fortunately, some of the senior officers, including Lieutenant General E.A.H. Alderson of the 1st Canadian Division, had decided to find out for themselves what was happening. Collecting intelligence in this manner was going to take time and between 5 pm and 6 pm that evening the situation in the salient was nothing less than critical as the Germans, and their gas, swept almost everything before them, eventually penetrating to a maximum depth of 5,000 yards before coming to a standstill.

Initial reports of the opening exchanges were confusing to the generals trying to direct operations, since there had been originally a belief that there were still French troops east of the Yser Canal. Thus, although the situation was recognized as being bad, the gravity of the situation had not been fully grasped. This erroneous belief had led Lieutenant General Sir Herbert Plumer, commanding V Corps, to assess the situation as being one where the area from Shell Trap Farm east to the front line was thinly defended. Westwards from Shell Trap Farm he estimated a gap of 3,000 yards between his defenders and the French, whom he believed were still east of the Canal. In the absence of the latter, a point which was not finally clarified by Plumer until 9 pm, the gap between his defence east of Shell Trap Farm and the west Canal bank, where the French could be found, was more like 8,000 yards. The situation was, indeed, very grave, for had the Germans chosen to pursue their advance on the evening of 22nd April, then it is possible that one Canadian and two British divisions would have become completely cut off in the salient. That this disaster was avoided at all is due to two main factors. The first of these is that the Germans chose not to continue their advance beyond the low ridge south of Pilkem, known as Mauser Ridge. The second was that there was a rapid deployment of available British and Canadian forces in parts of the area attacked, which is likely to have helped dissuade the attacking German troops by giving, at least, a show of force.

As early as 5.55 pm, that is less than one hour after the initial release of gas, Lieutenant General Alderson had issued orders to the commander of the 3rd Canadian Brigade, Brigadier General R.E.W. Turner VC, that he should deploy his forces to assist the battered Algerian Division. It would seem that Brigadier General Turner had already commenced to do that and, realizing there had been a break-through, had ordered his 13th Battalion to begin to turn a flank along the Poelcapelle – Saint Julien road, which then was faced approximately north-westwards into the breech in the line made by the

German advance. At the same time Lieutenant General Alderson impressed upon the 2 and 3 Canadian Brigades then holding the line to remain where they were – there was to be no withdrawal. To assist in this Alderson placed the divisional reserve, the 10th and the 16th Battalions, at Turner's disposal, though because of the congestion of the roads it was some time before the 10th Battalion was actually able to report to Turner. Further assistance for Turner was given by the arrival of the 7th Battalion from 2 Brigade reserve. Meanwhile further confusion was caused by 3 Brigade Headquarters issuing alarming reports:

> 6.25 pm. Left of our subsection is retiring.
> 6.30 pm. Your wire to us is down. Our left driven back, and apparently whole line forced back to Saint Julien.
> 7.10 pm. We are forced back to GHQ Line, attack coming from west. No troops left.[12]

These highly mistaken reports of the fighting can have done little to help Alderson assess the situation, and it was not until 8.25 pm that Turner was able to reassure his commander that his original line still held, but with a protective left flank thrown back along the road as mentioned before. How such mistaken reports came to be issued from Brigade Headquarters is not clear, but they serve to indicate the conditions prevailing on the battlefield in so far as it was a very confused and confusing situation to grasp for all involved, not least for those who were responsible for directing reserves of troops to assist the defence. It also suggests that perhaps the staff work at the Brigade Headquarters was not as well organized or as thorough as it should have been and may reflect the limited experience of the officer concerned. It should be remembered, however, that this was the first time that the Brigade had been called upon to act under such circumstances and it was, in effect, learning its trade as the battle progressed – under these conditions it would have been highly unlikely for mistakes not to have occurred.

In the 3 Canadian Brigade the 13th Battalion on the left of the line began turning their flank almost as soon as Alderson issued the order to do so. Lieutenant Colonel F.O.W. Loomis, CO of the 13th Battalion, was at Saint Julien at the time the order was given and he was becoming increasingly concerned for his command as it became clear that the Germans were advancing rapidly. He began securing what reinforcements he could and organized them such that they could make contact with the flank now being turned to his north-east. All through this period the battlefield was being swept by artillery and machine-gun fire from the encroaching Germans. In fact the artillery fire was said to be so strong that many of the small villages and farms in this area of the salient were simply wiped off the map. Amongst the reinforcements available to the Canadians were the only two units of the French divisions that had not withdrawn. These were the 1/1st *Tirailleurs*, supported by the 1/2nd *bis Zouaves*. These units were on the immediate left of the Canadians and it would seem that they had escaped the full effect of the gas, since they were near to the area where the cylinders had not been opened, and were prepared to hang on to support the Canadians for as long as they could. During the next few hours these "poor quality" French troops held their position and were to give valuable assistance to the hard pressed Canadians.

The defence put up by the Canadians was, as might be expected, stern. The line could not be more than thinly manned but the Canadians fought hard and sold each scrap of land and each casualty dearly to the advancing Germans. In one instance two platoons of the 13th Battalion were completely wiped out by a superior force of Germans which was, however, held up thanks to the sacrifice of the Canadian platoons. It is to the 13th Battalion that the distinction goes for the award of the first Victoria Cross for the Second Battle of Ypres. This award was made, posthumously, to Lance Corporal Frederick Fisher, who used his machine gun to great effect in front of the grave-yard in Saint Julien and so helped to prevent the Germans pressing on to that village. The citation for this award will be found in Appendix II. Similar actions were witnessed all along the Canadian line, and in one instance the 10th Battery of the Canadian Field Artillery was almost lost near the village of Keerselaere when the Germans closed to about 200 yards and attempted to surround them. Major W.B.M. King, a commander of some years' experience, ordered two guns of the battery turned round and then proceeded to fire at the Germans over open sights until they eventually withdrew to look for easier prey. It was a lucky escape for one battery, though during the day the Germans had captured French batteries in their initial rush and had overrun the 2nd London Heavy Battery as they captured Kitchener's Wood. For his action in saving his guns that day and for holding up the German advance in his area, Major King was awarded the DSO.[13]

The fighting continued well into the evening as the Germans pressed forward wherever they could. On the left of the thinly manned, turned flank the 1/1st *Tirailleurs* were attacked in force at a little before 9 pm and began to give way. About 200 of them were rallied and were attached to six platoons of the 13th Canadians and together they were able to resist the attack. It is at this point in the proceeding that Colonel A.D. Geddes makes his first appearance. Geddes was commander of the 2nd Buffs who had begun to move from the 28th Division reserve to support the Canadians. Brigadier General Turner sent a request to Geddes asking him for his assistance. Geddes, who later was given a makeshift brigade to command, complied immediately by sending one company of the 2nd Buffs, under Captain F.W. Tomlinson, to assist the 13th Canadians though they did not come into action until early on the following day. The Buffs' War Diary comments as follows on this period as it was preparing to move into the line:

> Meanwhile French Zouaves and Turcos were (streaming) down the road towards YPRES. It was an astonishing sight to see the British troops standing nonchalantly in the main street of Saint Jan and the Canadians marching calmly N & NE the direction from which the Frenchmen were retiring the latter exclaiming as they passed "*nous sommes trompes*", "*tout est perdu*" etc.[14]

To the north the news was a little more encouraging for the British commanders. The Belgians, under the command of General de Ceuninck, who held the canal bank from Steenstraat to die Grachten, a distance of some two miles, had completely held up the German advance in their sector and had successfully turned a flank on their southern boundary with the French. They had also prevented the Germans crossing the canal in the area and from capturing the bridges nearby. Such was the success of the Belgians that de Ceuninck was able to offer to lend the French three of his own battalions to assist in the counter attack they were, by that time, proposing.

Almost as soon as the French had realized that their forces were withdrawing, they began talking of regaining the lost ground. Since the two divisions in the area had been routed it was going to take considerable skill to arrange any kind of counter attack. Even so, a little before 8 pm, less than three hours after the first release of gas, the French notified Lieutenant General Alderson that they were going to counter-attack and requested his assistance on the right of their proposed attack. Alderson was not slow to react to the request and ordered his 3 Canadian Brigade to make an attack through Kitchener's Wood, so recently captured by the Germans. The orders were issued at 8.25 pm and thus, by the time all preparations had been made, the attack could never be other than a night attack. In itself this was likely to be a difficult operation, but the ground to be fought over had not been fully reconnoitred or appraised, and to make matters worse there was precious little artillery available to prepare the way or render support. Nevertheless, Alderson undoubtedly believed that in offering such support to the French he was aiding in the defence of the salient, and hence Ypres. In view of the difficulties surrounding the proposed attack, the events that followed demonstrated the immense skill, courage and self sacrifice that was present in the Canadian battalions charged with the duty as they pushed home the attack, in the face of mounting problems, on an enemy still flushed with his initial successes.

By this time of the evening, with the fighting continuing all around the northern and eastern portions of the salient and with reinforcements from the other divisions in the area still being gathered together, it was necessary for the attack on Kitchener's Wood to be carried out with the nearest and strongest reserves. Two battalions were earmarked for this job, the 10th Canadians of the 2 Brigade and the 16th Canadians of the 3 Brigade who had both been acting as divisional reserve. These units were ordered to report to the 3 Canadian Brigade Headquarters at Shell Trap Farm, which itself was now coming under threat from the German advance. The 10th Battalion, under Lieutenant Colonel R.L. Boyle, had been sent with a note from their Brigadier General, A.W. Currie, to suggest that they should be used in a defensive role to improve the line eastwards in front of Saint Julien and towards the 13th Battalion, who were still holding their old front line. Events had somewhat overtaken Currie since Brigadier General Turner had been ordered to attack Kitchener's Wood immediately. Turner expressed some regret at deploying the 10th Battalion in the van of his assault but this was probably because they were not from his own brigade and because it was necessary for him to ignore Currie's request. However, the 10th had arrived first and so were deployed first in a field to the north of Brigade Headquarters and facing their objective. The deployment showed little imagination. The attack had been planned as being on a two-company front with each company providing two ranks with thirty yards between each. The 16th Battalion, under Lieutenant Colonel J.E. Leckie, were deployed similarly, immediately behind the 10th. This deployment meant that the two battalions were to attack in a close packed formation towards the wood, suspected to be heavily defended by a buoyant enemy, over unprepared ground. It was, perhaps, a naïve plan, but in view of the circumstances and the urgent need to support the proposed French attack it was, unfortunately, the best that was available. As the 16th Battalion deployed they were spoken to by Canon Frederick Scott, at that time chaplain to the 3 Canadian Brigade, who had accompanied them in their march to the front line:

> The men were told that they had to take the wood at the point of the bayonet, and were not to fire as the 10th Battalion was in front of them. I passed down the line and told them that they had a chance to do a bigger thing for Canada that night than had ever been done before. "It's a great day for Canada, boys", I said. The words afterwards became a watchword, for the men said that whenever I told them that, it meant that half of them were going to be killed.[15]

51

Once the battalions had been moved to their position there was one further error of judgement, when Lieutenant Colonel Boyle decided not to send a party to take out the German machine guns known to be in Oblong Farm to the left of the direction he was assaulting. In fairness to Boyle he had been given specific orders to attack the wood and, as such, assumed that the clearing of Oblong Farm was the responsibility of others – and since there was little time for questioning or confirming orders he decided that he should carry on by following his orders exactly.

By 11.45 pm on 22nd April all was ready for the attack to begin and, in good order, with fixed bayonets, the Canadians moved forward. The adjutant of the 10th Battalion, Major D.M. Ormond, wrote in the war diary as follows:

> Not a sound was audible down the long waving lines but the soft pad of feet and the knock of bayonet scabbards against thighs.[16]

The attack began some 500 yards from the wood. As the two battalions moved off there was little reason to believe that the enemy had any knowledge of their approach though there was some, apparently random, rifle fire from the wood. The distance closed without incident until about 200 yards from the wood, when the attackers encountered a hedge which had not been anticipated – the result of not allowing time for even limited reconnaissance of the ground to be covered. Whilst the hedge was not a huge obstacle it was soon discovered that there was a thick strand of barbed wire running through it. Nonetheless, the Canadians began to force their way through as best they could. The noise of breaking twigs and equipment scraping against the barbed wire was enough to alert the German defenders. As the first wave of the 10th Battalion emerged from the hedge and began to reform, the Germans sent up a flare which bathed the area in near daylight, exposing the Canadians and their intentions to the soldiers in the wood. Immediately the enemy began to fire, and the almost reflex reaction of the Canadians was to throw themselves flat. Major J. Lightfoot of D Company of the leading battalion was heard to say, "Come on boys! Remember you're Canadians". With that the men rose to their feet and with a yell began to charge the wood. Sergeant Matheson was to record later:

> The wood seemed to be literally lined with machine guns and they played these guns on us with terrible effect. Our men were dropping thick and fast.[17]

It was not only from the wood that the waves of assaulting Canadians were taking fire but also from Oblong Farm, which had not been neutralized by others. In the words of another survivor:

KITCHENER'S WOOD
22ND/23RD APRIL 1915

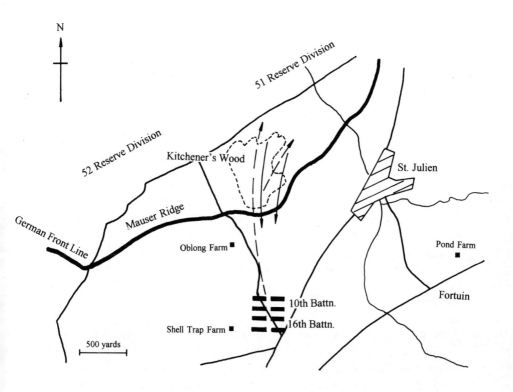

Instantly the word was given to charge, and on we rushed, cheering, yelling, shouting and swearing straight for the foe. At first the Germans fired a little too high and our losses until we came within fifty yards of them were comparatively small. Then some of our chaps began to drop, then the whole front line seemed to melt away, only to be instantly closed up again.[18]

In no time at all the Canadians were amongst the Germans in the wood and a terrible hand-to-hand battle ensued, as some of the survivors were to recall:

We fought in clumps and batches, and the living struggled over the bodies of the dead and dying. At the height of the conflict while we were steadily driving the Germans before us, the moon burst out. The clashing bayonets flashed like quicksilver and the faces were lit up as by limelight.

Cheering and yelling all the time we jumped over the bodies of the wounded and tore on. Of the Germans with the machine guns not one escaped, but those in the wood stood up to us in the most dogged style. We were so quickly at work that those at the edge of the wood could not have got away in any case. Many threw up their hands and we did not refuse quarter.

I vaguely saw some Germans and rushed at the nearest one. My bayonet must have hit his equipment and glanced off, but luckily for me, another chap running beside me bayoneted him before he got me. By this time I was wildly excited and rushing into the wood up a path towards a big gun which was pointed away from us.[19]

In that initial rush the Canadians had recaptured the guns of the 2nd London Heavy Battery but the 4.7-inch guns were too big to be manhandled in the midst of a battle and although teams were sent for to retrieve them, the Canadians fought on past them. The guns had already been the scene of one fierce struggle for one of the Canadian officers recorded that they were piled high with dead "British, Turcos and Germans".

Soon the Canadians were taking prisoners and as they did so it became obvious that the attack had struck at the junction of two German units, the 2nd Prussian Guards and the 234th Bavarian Regiment; that may have assisted in their advance through the wood, as the two units tried to organize a unified defence of ground they themselves had only recently captured. In no time at all the Canadians had burst through the wood and had reached the line of a hedge some fifty-five yards or so beyond it. Here they proceeded to dig in, but that proved to be no easy task since the ground was reported as being so hard that even bullets ricocheted off it. The reason for the soil of Flanders being so hard in the spring of 1915 has not been satisfactorily explained by the historians of the battle for, in springtime in Flanders, it would be expected that the soil would normally be quite soft and suitable for digging at least shallow cover. In the early days of the fighting there is some evidence to suggest that there was a sharp frost at night and this may have hampered the Canadians. In any event the Canadians had problems digging any sort of cover but, nonetheless, made every effort to establish a line on the northern side of Kitchener's Wood. This advance through the wood had taken little more than fifteen minutes. Just after midnight the Canadians had reached the furthest extent of their counter-attack – but holding the wood was going to be a totally different matter. In the rush through the wood, the 10th and 16th Battalions had become thoroughly mixed up, and the first task for the remaining officers was to sort out the men such that the 10th Battalion held the left hand part of the line and the 16th the right hand portion.

Whilst this was taking place Major Ormond had returned through the wood to report to Lieutenant Colonel Boyle, but instead found a group of men from his battalion trying to clear a German strongpoint at the south-western corner of the wood. They were not having any success and he, together with Lieutenant W. Lowry, attempted an outflanking manoeuvre:

For a few moments all was quiet, the Germans not firing a shot nor throwing any flares. In the redoubt I distinctly heard the levers of machine guns being worked backwards and forwards testing their action.

Then we opened fire, and the bomb throwers commenced throwing their bombs. I could see that these were falling short. Our rifle fire was ineffectual and weak owing to the jamming of the bolt in our rifles by the use of British ammunition issued to us.[20] The Germans opened a murderous fire on us with their rifles and machine guns. Yet with a yell and "at 'em Canadians" we charged, but before we could reach half the distance to the redoubt, practically all our men were mown down. Of my party I think there was only one man besides myself who was not bowled over. It was useless to go further. I made my way back to the other trench in the blazing light of German flares and rifle fire.[21]

The small-scale action had brought about another twenty or so casualties for the Canadians and they could ill afford to lose more men. Ormond decided that he would not risk any more lives, and ordered that a trench be dug at right angles to the redoubt which would at least prevent enfilade of the trench at that part of the wood. Moments after this Lieutenant Lowry was seriously wounded but did not seek medical attention until he had made his way back to Shell Trap Farm and reported the situation to Brigadier General Turner. There was little that Turner could do at this time, shortly after midnight; his reserves had not all arrived and could not be deployed to assist the two battalions engaged in the wood.

It was at about this time that the 10th Battalion lost their CO, Lieutenant Colonel Boyle, to a burst of machine-gun fire – he was not to live long enough to regret his decision not to attack Oblong Farm and neutralize the machine guns there. Even this incident is surrounded by speculation, since some reports suggest that Boyle had been foolish enough to flash an electric torch onto his map to locate his position and was fired at instantly. This would seem to be a very careless act for a soldier such as Boyle, since he had plenty of experience and was not given to careless actions. The command fell briefly upon Major MacLaren, but he too became a casualty when he was wounded in the leg, and was last seen that night trying to help the seriously wounded Boyle back to a dressing station. In this confusion the command finally came to Major Ormond, the adjutant, and he was left with the sizeable problem of maintaining the attack in the wood and holding the ground won with an ever diminishing command at his disposal.

The Canadians were, at least at one stage of the attack, very optimistic, since Lieutenant Colonel Leckie of the 16th Battalion had even sent out patrols to attempt to link with the 13th Battalion who were still manning the old front line. These patrols, not unexpectedly, met with no success, for the 13th Battalion was well over a mile away from the wood. This being the case it soon became clear to the officers in the wood that they had little in the way of flank cover on the right, and it was known by that time that the French had made no move to cover their left flank. Added to this they had little in the way of artillery cover, and it was recognized that it would only be a matter of time before their position was untenable.

The tenuous grasp that the Canadians had on the wood was becoming increasingly threatened and at about 2.30 am on the morning of 23rd April Lieutenant Colonel Leckie of the 16th, as senior officer on the field, decided it was time to withdraw. Even in that the Canadians did not have an easy time of it because, as the most forward groups began to withdraw, those behind fired on them in the darkness, believing them to be advancing Germans. The Canadians brought a number of prisoners with them out of the wood, and would have liked to have brought the guns of the 2nd London Heavy Battery out with them. Unfortunately the teams that had been requested had not arrived and, under the circumstances, they were in no position to do anything but destroy the stockpiled ammunition and abandon the guns. Slowly but surely, they withdrew from their costly won gains in the wood and headed for the trench at the southern edge which they had overwhelmed in the first rush of the fighting only hours before, where they established a line and waited for the reinforcements which arrived in the form of the 3rd Battalion, commanded by Lieutenant Colonel R. Rennie. It then became possible to extend the line towards Saint Julien.

It had been an expensive night's work for the Canadians. At roll call at 6.30 am the 10th Battalion were to realize just how expensive, for they were able to muster only five officers and 188 other ranks. The battalion had gone into the attack 816 strong. The 16th Battalion had fared little better for when their roll was taken they mustered five officers and 263 other ranks. Sergeant C. Stevenson, of the 10th Battalion said:

> I looked back across the field we had crossed the previous night and I could see what havoc had been wrought on our boys, for all around were the dead bodies of men who, a few hours before, had been singing Canada's national song. They died with it on their lips, but their memory will live for many a day and year to come. For they made a name for the Dominion that will live in history.[22]

With the withdrawal of the Canadians from Kitchener's Wood in the early hours of the morning of 23rd April, the fighting of the first day of the Second Battle of Ypres can be said to have ended. In under ten hours of fighting there had been a massive French withdrawal and staunch Canadian defence – and there had been heavy casualties on both sides. The value of the attack on Kitchener's Wood may, quite rightly, be questioned since, on the face of it, the plan was ill conceived and ill prepared at brigade level. However, perhaps it should be accepted that neither Alderson or Plumer had much choice but to order the attack since both men recognized that something had to be done and done quickly. On the other hand the execution of the attack cannot be faulted. The two Canadian battalions had carried the wood with amazing dash and ferocious fighting. For the success of the operation to have been complete they needed support, particularly from the French, who had asked for a supporting attack to be made in the first place. Further, the Canadians could have used efficient artillery cover. The French were not able to match their wishes with action, and in the event were unable to organize any form of counter-attack in their sector, remaining resolutely in their trenches to the west of the Yser Canal. Perhaps this is not surprising, bearing in mind the rapid withdrawal they had only recently made – but the Canadians had made every effort to comply with their orders and the French inactivity had cost them dearly. As far as artillery support was concerned, it was a general weakness in the defence of the salient at the time. There were neither the guns nor the ammunition to assist as much as anyone would have liked, but to the credit of those artillery units involved they did all that they could to ensure that the guns available offered all the support they could. That this was insufficient for the night attack on Kitchener's Wood is not so much to do with the artillery as the overall state of the army at the time. These shortages in artillery, particularly in heavy guns and artillery ammunition, were to become even more obvious, and critical, as the Second Battle of Ypres progressed. In spite of these adverse factors the Canadians had done everything that they could to bring the fight to the advancing enemy and in so doing had probably given him something to think about. While they were thus engaging the enemy there, they bought some time to allow the limited reserves in the salient to be mobilized into some sort of order that allowed them to be brought effectively into the fight in the coming hours.

Notes

1. The relevant report, as quoted in the Official History, on the threat of gas can be found in Appendix VI.
2. See *Official History 1915 Vol. 1*, p165.
3. The French equivalent of General Headquarters.
4. The Germans knew the salient as the "Ypres Bridgehead".

5. See Moore, *Gas Attack*, p17.
6. See *Official History 1915 Vol. 1*, Footnote p177.
7. See Bourgoyne, *The Bourgoyne Diaries*, p188.
8. McWilliams and Steel, *Gas! The Battle for Ypres, 1915*, p50.
9. ibid. p51.
10. See McWilliams and Steel, op.cit., p56.
11. During the battle this farm was most often referred to as "farm in c.22.b" to give it its map reference. Many of the battalion histories use the name Shell Trap Farm which was not popular with the staff for obvious reasons and it became known subsequently as Mouse Trap Farm. Throughout this account the earliest name, Shell Trap Farm, is used.
12. See *Official History 1915 Vol. 1*, footnote p179.
13. King was later promoted to Brigadier General CRA and commanded the 4th Canadian Divisional Artillery.
14. "we are deceived, all is lost".
15. Scott, *The Great War as I saw it*, p37.
16. See Dancocks, *Gallant Canadians*, p29.
17. See Dancocks, ibid., p30.
18. See McWilliams and Steel, op.cit., p67.
19. ibid., p67.
20. This is the first record of many instances during the battle when the Ross Rifle used by the Canadians failed to perform.
21. See Dancocks, op.cit., pp32–33.
22. ibid., p34.

CHAPTER FIVE

The Battle of Gravenstafel Ridge
Day 2 – 23rd April 1915

The conditions for the defenders of the salient were critical as the dawn of 23rd April broke. The stern defence offered by the Canadians by turning a flank in the apex of the salient and the counter-attack through Kitchener's Wood had done little enough to stabilize the situation but had, perhaps, brought some respite and bought time in which some kind of organized and unified defence could be established. At 2 am with the battle raging at the front, Canon Frederick George Scott, who had marched to Shell Trap Farm the night before, found himself in a dressing station near Wieltje:

> The wounded were brought in from outside and laid on a table, where the doctor attended them. Some ghastly sights were disclosed when the stretcher bearers ripped off the blood stained clothes and laid bare the hideous wounds . . . There were many Turcos present. Some of them were suffering terribly from the effects of the gas. Fresh cases were being brought down the road and laid out on the cold pavement till they could be attended to.
>
> About two in the morning a dispatch rider arrived and meeting me at the door asked if I could speak French. He said "Tell the Turcos, and everyone else who can walk to clear off to Ypres as soon as they can – the Germans are close at hand." Indeed it sounded so because the rifle fire was very close. I went into the room and delivered my message, in French and English, to the wounded men. Immediately there was a general stampede of all those who could possibly drag themselves towards the city.[1]

The situation was far from clear at this stage of the day and there was still much fighting before any semblance of a true defensive line could

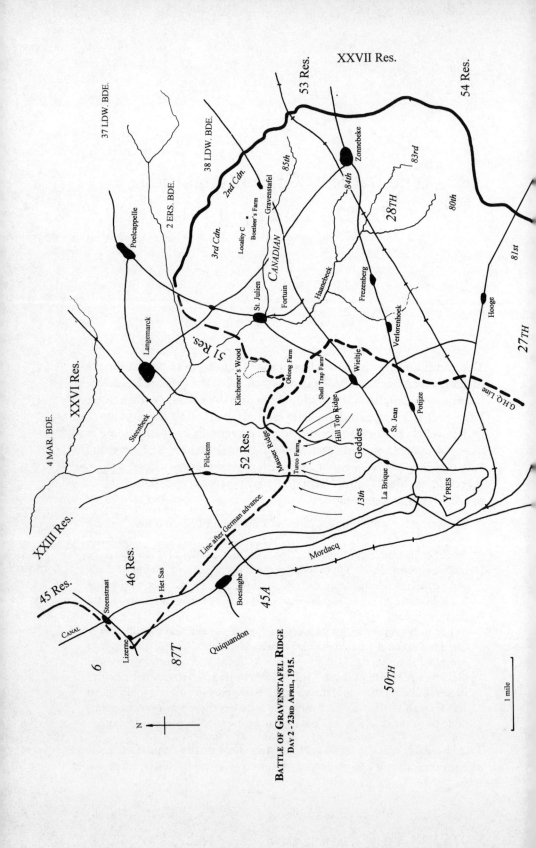

XXVII Res.

37 LDW. BDE.

38 LDW. BDE.

53 Res.

54 Res.

2 ERS. BDE.

2nd Cdn.

3rd Cdn.

85th

Zonnebeke

83rd

84th

28TH

80th

Poelcappelle

Locality C

Boetleer's Farm

Gravenstafel

81st

Langemarck

51 Res.

St. Julien

Fortuin

Hannebeek

Frezenberg

Verlorenhoek

Hooge

27TH

XXVI Res.

Steenbeek

Kitchener's Wood

Oblong Farm

Shell Trap Farm

Wieltje

Potijze

G.H.Q. Line

CANADIAN

4 MAR. BDE.

Pilckem

52 Res.

Mauser Ridge

Turco Farm

Hill Top Ridge

Geddes

St. Jean

St. Jean

XXIII Res.

Line after German advance.

La Brique

Y PRES

13th

Mordacq

45 Res.

46 Res.

Het Sas

Boesinghe

45A

6

Steenstraat

CANAL

Lizerne

87T

Quiquandon

50TH

N

1 mile

BATTLE OF GRAVENSTAFEL RIDGE
DAY 2 - 23RD APRIL, 1915.

be established. The forces on the north flank of the salient as dawn broke were as follows: the 13th and 15th Canadians held the old front line and the 13th had turned a defensive flank northwards; the line from there to Keerselaere was thinly held by the Canadians and some 200 men of the 1st *Tirailleurs*; from Keerselaere to Kitchener's Wood was a gap, in front of Saint Julien, though by the continuing movements of troops of the Canadian Division efforts were being made to close it and to close it quickly; the 16th and 10th Canadians were in front of Kitchener's Wood, but from there to the Yser Canal the line was almost non-existent with only small parties of men, notably the 3rd Middlesex, the 2nd Buffs and men of the 3rd Canadians which were available for the defence of the area from Shell Trap Farm westwards. The nearest French troops were those of Colonel Mordacq's 90 Brigade (45th Algerian Division) in positions along the canal to the north-east of Brielen.

The disposition of the German forces at this time was completely unknown and it was one of the tasks of the commanders to obtain as much intelligence as possible concerning that. As part of this exercise aerial reconnaissance was used. Lieutenant Louis Arbon Strange left his airfield before daybreak, flying a BE2c, so as to be over the battlefield as soon as there was sufficient daylight for observation:

> . . . I was up in the air before daybreak, taking Capt. Harold Wyllie over the salient in order to ascertain what had happened during the night, as soon as there was sufficient light to see by. To our amazement we could find no troops in the usual trenches, but soon discovered a new front line of trenches about four or five miles nearer Ypres. Whether these were occupied by French or Germans it was impossible to tell from the heights, but as soon as we dropped down low enough we obtained ample evidence that this new line extending from Boesinge to Saint Julien was held by the enemy. Wyllie hastily sketched it in his map, and then we hurried back; by 8.30 am we were at GHQ, where we expressed our apprehension of the fact that we had failed to discover any traces of British troops confronting the Germans in their new positions. We wondered why the latter had taken the trouble to dig themselves in, when as far as we could see, there was nothing to prevent them continuing their advance.[2]

The situation was bad; it took most of the rest of the day to improve the defence of the northern flank, but in so doing many British and Canadians became involved in ferocious fighting and before the day was over casualties had become very heavy for all the units engaged.

When the battle had commenced many of the units in the general area had deployed more or less without orders from the senior officers – there were many experienced units around Ypres and it was not long before most of them expected to be involved in the fighting on the north of the salient. The 2nd Buffs and the 3rd Middlesex were already in the Wieltje area anyway and late on the evening of 22nd April, Colonel A.D. Geddes of the 2nd Buffs was assigned four battalions to form a makeshift brigade. This brigade comprised the two battalions mentioned, both from the 85 Brigade, and the 5th King's Own and the 1st York and Lancaster from the 83 Brigade. The first of these was already near Saint Jean but the latter were in billets in Ypres and so did not join what was to become known as Geddes' Detachment until the morning of 23rd April. Although moves were already being made for Geddes to take over the command of the detachment almost immediately the attack had begun, the first orders issued by Geddes were not until early on the morning of 23rd April, by which time he was beginning to pull his command together, but with precious little in the way of staff to assist in the controlling of the assembly of what was becoming a large body of men. One of the first acts that Geddes carried out on the evening of the 22nd April was to detach B Company of his own battalion under Captain F.W. Tomlinson to assist the Canadians holding the extreme eastern portion of the line. Also, two companies of the 3rd Middlesex were detached to form a guard for the bridge over the Yser Canal east of Brielen. That was at 9.30 pm on 22nd April and thus even before his force was completely assembled Geddes was being asked for support. With the promotion of Geddes, albeit temporarily, to the command of a makeshift brigade, his own battalion came under the command of Major R.E. Power, who remained in command of the battalion for the next phase of the Battle of Gravenstafel Ridge.

Geddes' Detachment was placed at the disposal of Lieutenant General Alderson commanding the Canadian Division, and Geddes was instructed to give all the support possible with his band of fighters that was assembling in the early hours of 23rd April; it was very soon after that he was called upon to take part in a counter-attack which had been largely instigated by the French. The French had been given a bloody nose on 22nd April and there was a feeling, particularly amongst their senior commanders, that this situation should not be allowed to continue – they wanted to regain all the ground they had surrendered to the Germans as soon as possible for it was a matter of military pride. As early as 1.30 am on the morning of 23rd April General Putz, the commander of the French troops in the area, had issued orders to the 90 Brigade, under Colonel Mordacq, and the 87th Territorial Division, commanded by General Roy, for an attack to take place at 5 am. Mordacq was ordered to advance to capture Pilkem whilst Roy was ordered to force a crossing of the Yser Canal between Boesinge and Lizerne and to occupy the second line of trenches in that area. It was, to say the very least, an optimistic order. The 87th Territorial Division had only recently been chased out of the trenches by the Germans and the morale amongst the middle aged territorials cannot have been very high. Mordacq's troops, on the east of the Canal, were hardly better placed to carry out such an order. Remember that the Algerian Division to which his brigade belonged had also been chased off by the Germans and their gas, and it would have been quite a problem to reassemble all the men he needed in the short time he was to be allowed to prepare for the counter-attack. As if to sweeten the bitter pill for the French soldiers Putz indicated that the British 28th Division and a Canadian Brigade would be joining in the fighting. The French reaction to this is not recorded and it can only be guessed at with reference to their conduct during the remainder of the second day of the battle.

The extent to which these French orders had the blessing of the British Commander-in-Chief is not entirely clear. Sir John French was mindful that he needed to support the French commander and if possible allow him the opportunity to regain the ground lost during the initial German onslaught. Therefore, it can be assumed that the orders had the tacit approval of Sir John French and if, at this stage, he had any misgivings about the French Army's ability to regain the ground, he did not voice them to the French. Indeed, it is true to say that for several days of the battle Sir John French was swayed more by the persuasiveness of General Ferdinand Foch than by the needs of his own troops. Of course, this may also be seen as Sir John French carrying out his orders to act in a subordinate role to the French commanders. This meant that he had very little room to manoeuvre and could only acquiesce to the French plans whether he believed in them or not.

The dispatch of Sir John French covering the incident concerned, throws some light on the way the Commander-in-Chief was thinking but it, too, is vague in its detail:

> I fully concurred in the wisdom of the General's (Foch) wish to re-establish our old line and agreed to co-operate in the way he desired, stipulating, however, that if the position was not re-established within a limited time, I could not allow the British troops to remain in so exposed a position as that which the action of the previous twenty-four hours had compelled them to stay.[3]

Unfortunately Sir John French's "limited time" was to develop into a moveable feast which he amended as necessary, allowing the British troops to stay in an exposed situation far longer than was really necessary. Even if French was mindful of his subordinate role it was his vacillation in the early days of the battle, perhaps more than anything else, that may suggest that he was not the right man for command of the British Expeditionary Force.

In any event the request for support was passed to General Alderson by 3.45 am and he immediately issued an order to Brigadier General M.S. Mercer of the 1 Canadian Brigade:

> At 5 o'clock two French battalions are to make a counter attack against Pilkem with their right resting on the Pilkem – Ypres Road. You will co-operate with this attack at the same time with your left on the road.[4]

It was 4.15 am before Mercer was able to read this order and it left him precious little time to get organized. Once again the counter-attack was to be over unprepared ground with little precise knowledge of the disposition of the enemy. Some minutes after Alderson had sent the message to Mercer he sent a similar message to Geddes suggesting that if it was at all possible he should connect and cooperate with the attack. The time scale for the attack was very tight and both Mercer and Geddes must have recognized the fact that to comply with Alderson's wishes, and those of the French, was likely to be impossible. Nevertheless, both men began working to put troops in the field to support the intended French counter-attack. For Geddes that meant ordering his own 2nd Buffs and the 3rd Middlesex to take up positions on the southern flanks of Hill Top Ridge to the north of La Brique. Mercer, by that time, had the 1st and 4th Canadians at his disposal. These troops had been released from Army Reserve by General Sir Horace Smith-Dorrien at 8.15 pm on the evening of 22nd April for just such a contingency. At about 1.30 am on 23rd April Lieutenant General Alderson ordered them forward to take place in the attack then under preparation. Prior to this both battalions had been in billets in Vlamertinge some four miles away, and once they had received orders there was still some distance to cover before they could be got into position on the east of the canal to the north of Ypres, from where they would take part in the counter attack.

Whilst all this was going on Brigadier General Turner of the 3 Canadian Brigade was receiving reinforcements that really would have been of more use to him some two or three hours earlier. At 2 am the 2nd and 3rd Canadians arrived at his headquarters ready for deployment as needed. At that time Turner had no indication of the success of the attack on Kitchener's Wood or of the continuing struggle to hold on to it. Nevertheless, he decided that, with the information at his disposal, he should rush reinforcements in to the fighting in the wood. He ordered three companies of the 2nd Canadians into the area of the wood. It was proposed that one company would reinforce the right of the 16th Canadians on the right in front of the wood; one was to reinforce the centre and deal with the troublesome redoubt that was causing the 10th Canadians so many casualties; the third was to take out the machine guns at Oblong Farm which were enfilading the positions of the Canadians in front of the wood. For A Company the task was going to be a difficult one for it would be necessary for them to cover the ground over which the 10th Canadians had charged the previous night. By the time the three companies were in position it was daylight, but there was no thought of halting, and they went forward over the corpse strewn approaches to the wood. As A Company moved off they came under intense machine-gun and rifle fire. The effect was devastating for, in a matter of minutes, the 2nd Canadians had suffered well over 200 casualties, and only about fifteen men from A Company even reached the trench held by Major Ormond and the remnants of his 10th Canadians. However, and probably purely by accident, this charge at the redoubt had created somewhat of a diversion and both flanking companies completed their tasks with far fewer casualties. With C Company capturing Oblong Farm, the Germans' ability to bring flanking fire to bear on the fighting in the wood ceased. It is sad to consider what could have been the effect if Lieutenant Colonel Boyle had neutralized the machine guns in the farm the night before. It may have saved Canadian lives, if not that of Boyle himself. The tragedy of the 2nd Canadians shows a further example of the Canadians being thrown into the assault without adequate staff work; there was no time for all the details to be arranged if the flank of the salient was to be saved. But the loss of life during the attack, and others throughout the battle, was to diminish the already limited and hard pressed resources still further, and ultimately was to lead to the eventual shrinking of the salient much closer to the ramparts of Ypres itself. It was as much to do with the tenacity and bravery of the soldiers in the front line as anything else that the salient held at all in those early days of the 1915 battles for Ypres. Whether or not the orders were misguided meant little to the Canadians in the shallow trenches in front of Kitchener's Wood, because for the rest of 23rd April they had to endure heavy shell fire and machine-gun and rifle fire knowing that there was little that they could do by way of answer, and throughout the day the casualties continued to rise in the battalions that had been shot to pieces even before the day had begun.

The story for the 3rd Canadians was similar, as two of its companies (C and D) were sent to the right of Kitchener's Wood to plug the gap there between the wood and the 14th Canadians in front of Saint Julien. The two battalions had casualties as they moved forward and still more throughout the day as they slowly extended their flank, in part, at least, thanks to the tenacity and leadership of Lieutenant W.J.P. Jarvis[5] of C Company, who was able to extend his line although many of his platoon became casualties in the process. This brave officer then reported to Lieutenant Colonel F.W.O. Loomis of the 13th Canadians to obtain reinforcements for his line, which was then extended to the Haanebeek.

As 5 am approached there was no sign of movement from the French along the canal bank. Lieutenant Colonel A.P. Birchall, commanding officer of the 4th Canadians and in charge of the two Canadian battalions for the attack that morning, was puzzled by the apparent lack of movement as the zero hour passed. By about 5.25 am he had everything ready, with the two battalions deployed in seven waves in front of La Brique, ready for the advance. From this position, Birchall assumed that the French had started to attack but that they had remained out of his direct view behind some of the low hedges along the canal bank. The fact that there was little or no firing from, or indeed to, that area does not appear to have concerned him and he decided that he had to make a move. This he did and the waves of men moved off towards the crest of Hill Top Ridge and over the top onto its forward slope, into a storm of rifle and machine-gun bullets. Birchall's small command advanced in short rushes but was losing heavily as it proceeded. The two battalions kept on going and managed to make contact on their right with the men of the 3rd Middlesex, who were already putting up some fire from shallow trenches in the depression between Hill Top and Mauser Ridges (this later became known as Colne Valley). The Middlesex had advanced and as they did so they had tried to establish contact with the 2nd Buffs, who they knew were their flanking battalion on their right. The Middlesex were unsuccessful in this but continued to advance, even though they were unsure of their right flank. To their relief the Canadians had come up on their left flank but, by that time, both Canadian battalions were thoroughly mixed up.[6]

> At about 6.20 am the Canadians and the Middlesex advanced to attack the position and advanced to a bank between 600 and 800 yards from the enemy's trench under heavy sniping. Colonel Stephenson then conferred with an officer of the Canadians who said he had received orders from the brigade to dig themselves in. As no support had arrived and the enemy's fire was getting very heavy the Battalion remained under cover of the bank awaiting reinforcements – our right side being *en l'air*. The battalion was shelled very heavily for about 4 hours and was nearly suffocated at times with fumes from the shells.[6]

The account of the Middlesex War Diary gives a clear picture of the situation in the early hours of the morning of 23rd April. It is worth noting that the suffocating effects of the shells during the long bombardment they endured has been credited to the use of a percentage of lachrymatory shells. It is further recorded that during the advance of the Canadians and the Middlesex, the British artillery shelled Turco Farm so effectively that the Germans abandoned the position just below the crest of Mauser Ridge. The advancing troops soon occupied the remains of the farm but were entirely frustrated in their efforts to consolidate the position when it was discovered that there was no way of calling the accurate artillery fire off their prize. The combined force then withdrew and had to make do with digging cover at the base of the ridge, which was far from satisfactory since the ground was very wet, making the trenches shallow, muddy affairs.

Although the 2nd Buffs had not been contacted by this part of the advance during the morning they had, nevertheless, been moving forward and were trying to extend to the right to join up with the Canadians that they believed to be there. The 2nd Buffs War Diary gives an account of their part in the action:

It was after 4 am and in broad daylight before the battalion was collected and had got under way. Major R.E. Power was in command and put out an advanced guard under Captain Barnard. About 800 yards N of Wieltje some dug outs and trenches were reached, these were occupied by the Canadians. These trenches were screened by a hedge under cover of which the battalion closed up. Beyond was open country so the battalion at once deployed and was immediately subjected to a furious machine gun and rifle fire from the enemy who were entrenched in two parallel lines about 1200 and 900 yards distant on rising slopes to the north. Moving at the double platoon followed platoon in quick succession in the open many casualties occurring. Two companies soon reached a farm 400 yards on while the remaining company took advantage of the frail cover afforded by a fence 150 yards behind the farm around which were a few Canadians from which Major Power ascertained that there was a space of 200-300 yards of open ground to the east only lightly held. On it were three parallel lines of trenches facing N with their right resting on the GHQ wire. Major Power ordered the battalion to advance half right and occupy the forward of these trenches. In the trench were found a few men of the 1st Zouaves. The regiment therefore advanced by rushes across the open and lost heavily.

Once again the advance had been met with a hail of bullets from the Germans holding Mauser Ridge and, although they had managed to make contact with the Canadians, it had been at some cost, since they lost over eighty men and two officers in their dash over the open ground. The farm mentioned would appear to have been Shell Trap Farm which, by the time the 2nd Buffs had arrived, had not been vacated by the Headquarters of the 3 Canadian Brigade, though it was by that time perilously close to the front line. It had not been a successful morning; such gains that were made were at the expense of significant casualties to the battalions concerned, though the position was improved slightly simply because the Buffs had made contact with the Canadians, and because the Middlesex had acted in conjunction with the 1st and 4th Canadians. This had allowed a more or less continuous, though thin, line to be established between the old front line to a point about 1,200 yards from the canal. By this time the defenders had a total of ten and a half battalions in the line with a further seven in reserve with which they faced a total of forty-two German battalions. The general strength of the Germans in the area became apparent as the day wore on and aerial reconnaissance became possible.

On the negative side the French had failed to make any noticeable movement, though some firing was thought to have originated from Mordacq's 90 Brigade, which had made some effort at deployment in readiness for the counter-attack. The most action offered by the French was by the 1st *Zouaves*, who had remained in the trenches during the withdrawal of the previous day, such as those who had been absorbed into the 2nd Buffs for some hours on 23rd April near Shell Trap Farm. The lack of French action, after they had asked for support, should not have been unexpected, bearing in mind the recent history in the salient. It was, however, unacceptable and at this point Sir John French should have been seriously questioning the motives of his French allies. But more lives were to be thrown away by British commanders before the day was out, to demonstrate their commitment to a cause which, on the face of it, the French already believed was lost. Perhaps the most useful thing to arise out of the sixteen hours of fighting and counter-attacks was that the British had demonstrated to the Germans that the salient would be defended, and that they were prepared to defend it at some considerable cost. It is, perhaps, worth noting at this point that French felt himself to be in a difficult situation. He was supposed to cooperate fully with his ally and that much had been made clear to him on previous occasions. He knew that to cooperate was likely to be costly for him and his troops. It appears that French did little to resolve this situation and became more convinced that the constraint that these orders placed on him were designed to hasten his own downfall.

The Germans, for their part, had halted at the end of the first day when the gap in the defences was largest; possibly because they had expected a general withdrawal of the British Divisions in the salient. That this did not happen must have surprised them and the ferocious defence of the north flank, when all seemed lost did much to confuse them. In fact through much of the second day the Germans made little effort to advance, contenting themselves with shelling British lines and improving their own positions wherever that was necessary. It is likely that the Germans' advance had exceeded all their expectations and a short pause was necessary to allow them the time to establish lines of supply and communication. It is in the light of "limited objectives" that the Germans' approach to the battle should be seen. At each stage everything needed to be in place before the next step was taken. To ascribe the pause to their ammunition being "exhausted", as had been suggested in some quarters,[7] was to misunderstand the German tactics completely. There is more reason to believe that the Germans themselves feared the effects of their gas, and had hesitated in their forward rush to avoid any effects associated with gas lingering on the battlefield. Whatever the reason for the pause it would appear to have been a serious error of judgement on their part, for it was also of use to the defenders of the salient.

Whilst all this action was taking place further movement of available reserves into the area was being made. Two battalions of the 27th Division were on the move to the area. The 2nd Duke of Cornwall's Light Infantry (82 Brigade) and the 9th Royal Scots (81 Brigade) arrived in the area around Potijze at 3 am and 4.30 am respectively and were held in Corps reserve, until they were temporarily attached to the Canadian Division and were sent to the 3 Canadian Brigade, commanded by Brigadier General Turner. Also the 13 Brigade of the 5th Division was detached from its division to be sent across Ypres from the area of Hill 60 to take part in the defence of the northern flank. The Brigade was commanded by Brigadier General R. Wanless O'Gowan and began to arrive in the area to the east of Brielen in the early afternoon of 23rd April. It consisted of mostly regular battalions with considerable experience of the fighting in the salient; these were 2nd King's Own Yorkshire Light Infantry, the 1st Royal West Kents, the 2nd King's Own Scottish Borderers, the 2nd Duke of Wellington's, with the addition of the 9th London (Queen Victoria's Rifles) Regiment from the Territorial Force. All but the 2nd Duke of Wellington's, who were held in reserve, were to see action before the day was out.

During the morning, whilst all the fighting and movement was going on around Ypres, Sir John French left his headquarters in Saint Omer to visit General Foch in his headquarters in Cassel. Although it would appear that Sir John had gone to the meeting to insist that the line around Ypres be shortened to allow for the withdrawal of the French troops, it did not take long for Foch to convince him that the French Army would act to regain all the ground lost as a result of the gas attack. This Sir John accepted but not without some reservation. The main point that French stressed was that should the French be unable to retake all the ground they had lost he would act to shorten his line accordingly. Whilst it is said by some historians that French had gone to see Foch determined to shorten his line, the account of the Official History makes no reference to this.[8] The ease with which he was apparently swayed by his counterpart is seen as indicative of weakness in French. Whilst this may be true it is, perhaps, understandable, in the light of the British Government's expectations of him,[9] that he should want to act in conjunction with his ally; early in the morning of 23rd April things were far from clear in the salient so there may have been a good reason for French to acquiesce to Foch's request. Perhaps the questions on the conduct of French during this battle should not be asked at this point, but his conduct throughout will be examined in more detail later. Whatever the reasoning behind Sir John French's actions that morning, it is clear that the French commander had persuaded him that there were sufficient troops in the area to mount a significant counter-attack against the Germans on the north flank of the salient. Although the outcome of this meeting would appear to reflect badly on French, he left it not only intending to support the French ambitions with the troops at his immediate disposal but also to order up any available reserves, including the infantry of the 50th Division which were newly arrived in France and which he placed at the disposal of General Smith-Dorrien.

At 9.15 am reports from the 3 Canadian Brigade, still holding much of the old front line and a refused flank, did little to alleviate the anxiety of the commanders. These reports were to the effect that the Germans were able to enfilade much of the left of the Brigade front from captured French trenches, and in crossing the Poelcappelle-Saint Julien Road, the Germans were able to fire at the backs of those holding the original front line. Further, it was reported that Saint Julien itself would become untenable unless moves were made to recapture the old French front line. Lieutenant General Alderson suggested that a new line be dug behind the most forward positions so as to blunt the angle which had been formed by the German advance, and moves were put in place immediately to achieve this. Until this could be achieved the 13th and 15th Canadians held on throughout the day, though food and water were short and ammunition was running out. Before the day was out both battalions were forced to use their iron rations, since there was no hope of making a supply line to their present precarious position.

It was as a result of the meeting between French and Foch that later that day General Quiquandon was to issue an order, timed at 1.20 pm, to the French 45th Algerian Division, who were supposed to carry out the counter-attack to alleviate the situation in the salient. The order was based on certain assumptions and incorrect intelligence of the overall situation. For instance, the order states that, "The Germans appear for the moment to have exhausted their ammunition".[10] There were no grounds for such an assumption, and if anyone had taken the trouble to get the story from the front line troops the fallacy of such a statement would easily have been recognized. When a similar order reached Brigadier General Turner he angrily put a line through it and commented on the quality of the information coming from the rear! Such a statement can only be explained if it is assumed that the Germans had paused because of a shortage of ammunition and not for some other reason, such as to regroup ready for a further attack. Clearly this thought had not crossed the mind of Quiquandon, who was painting as rosy a picture as possible. Whatever the reasoning behind the order, Quiquandon was to place the responsibility for the attack that afternoon on Mordecq's 90 Brigade once again, with the instruction that he should advance towards Pilkem with his right flank on the Ypres-Pilkem Road, and should act in concert with the British, advancing east of the same road towards Langemarck. This part of the order showed some considerable lack of appreciation of the situation in the area after the fighting of the morning, and it was to lead to considerable confusion before the afternoon was out. Despite the fact that the order was in error in some places and had been prepared with some haste, it was sufficient to put the French 90 Brigade on standby and to set the wheels in motion for the expected British support. Simultaneously, the French 87th Division was ordered to continue fighting in the Steenstraat – Lizerne sector, thereby throwing some weight to the French left flank to assist in the operations near Ypres. The attack was ordered to commence at 3 pm.

Lieutenant General Alderson was soon in a position to issue an order, timed at 2.40 pm, to organize the support for the French. The task he gave his command was to cross between 500 and 800 yards of more or less open ground to close with the enemy. The 13 Brigade, now assembling ready to cross to the east of the canal, were expected to attack between the canal and the Ypres-Pilkem road with the 2nd KOSB on the right and the 1st Royal West Kents on the left, supported by the 2nd KOYLI and the 9th London – that is, the Brigade was to attack across the area that the French had already been told to attack. The resulting confusion must be put down to a lack of coordination between the two command structures involved. Geddes' Detachment, for the purpose of the attack under the command of the 13 Brigade, was to attack to the east of the Ypres–Pilkem road with four battalions (the 2nd DCLI on the right supported by two companies of the 9th Royal Scots, with the 2nd East Yorks, and the 1st York and Lancaster successively on the left), with a fifth (the 5th King's Own) in support who were, in the event, moved early to fill the gap developing between the 2nd

71

DCLI and the 2nd East Yorks. As they advanced over the ground fought over earlier that day by the 1st and 4th Canadians and the 3rd Middlesex, any survivors were to be collected to add weight to the attack. When the orders were issued there was little enough time for the battalions to be sorted out in time for the 3 pm attack, and so it was delayed until 4.15 pm. The order issued to the East Yorks and the York and Lancaster by Geddes details their part in the action; timed at 3.20 pm, it runs:

> The 13 Brigade crosses by the pontoon bridge at 3 pm and advances to the attack at 3.45 pm with its right on the Ypres-Pilkem Road. First objective Pilkem. O.C. East Yorks. will send an officer at once to report to Gen. O'Gowan at pontoon bridge C19c. The East Yorks. and York and Lancs. will co-operate with this attack east of the Pilkem-Ypres Road, East Yorks. with left on that road and maintaining touch with the 13 Bde. York and Lancs. will move on right of East Yorks. Two battalions of 27th Div will co-operate in the attack on the right of the York and Lancs. Buffs and Third Middlesex will hold their present line. 5th KORL[11] (less 1 company) will follow the attack in reserve moving with its left on the Pilkem-Ypres Road. Each Bn. will move on a front of 500 yards. HQ will remain for the present at Wieltje where reports should be sent.[12]

The plan was quite clear even if the objective of Pilkem was ambitious, but its realization was to be a different matter altogether, particularly since things started to go wrong almost immediately. Unfortunately, the available artillery to support the attack was not informed of the alteration of the 3 pm start time for the attack. This was partly because the various parts of the artillery had not established suitable communication lines, and partly because the infantry commanders were not keeping the artillery commanders fully appraised of the situation as it developed. At a little before the original 3 pm start time the artillery opened up with a three minute preparatory bombardment of the German lines and then it fell silent. There was no infantry advance at this stage and the artillery had depleted its already meagre ammunition reserves. There was to be no further preliminary artillery bombardment, though when the attack eventually commenced the artillery did all it could to support the assaulting troops. Eventually, however, everything was ready for the advance, with each battalion involved formed up in five or six lines, but once again the start time had been missed and it was not until 4.25 pm that it commenced, with the right of the attack, led by Lieutenant Colonel H.D. Tuson of the 2nd DCLI, not starting until 4.55 pm.

The 13 Brigade, who had already come under shell fire as they crossed the canal, moved forward and immediately came under shell, rifle and machine-gun fire as they moved off, but in spite of this they maintained the advance. The 2nd KOSB War Diary records the events of the advance:

> Position of enemy unknown until Battalion came to trenches occupied by the Canadians about 300 to 400 yards from enemy position. Casualties very heavy during the advance of over 700 yards. About 30 men chiefly of C Company with a few of A advanced under Capt. Bland beyond the trenches occupied by the Canadians and established themselves in an old support trench about 100 yards forward. In attempting to press beyond this the party was wiped out. Capt. Bland[13] was killed trying to pull a wounded man into cover.

It was not a good start for the attack but the 2nd KOSB consolidated such ground as they had gained as best they could and waited for their relief. The story for the 1st Royal West Kents on the left of the Borderers was even worse, in so far as the movement of the French to their left created a huge problem for the advance of the Kent battalion:

> . . . it was soon apparent that the French Algerian troops on our left would crowd out our firing line as they were coming across our front. In consequence of this the supporting lines were held back under the cover of the canal bank and low ground and only one platoon at a time pushed up to support the firing line.[14]

The movement of the 7th *Zouaves* was the only one made by Mordacq's 90 Brigade, but for some inexplicable reason they had chosen to move more east than north, succeeding only in pushing the Royal West Kents from their northerly movement and on to the flank of the 2nd KOSB who were trying to maintain a steady advance. The War Diary remarks that, "This was fortunate for the battalion as it saved many casualties". It had, in all probability, saved many casualties in the Royal West Kents because they had been unable to deploy their men as ordered, but it had also succeeded in adding a further element of confusion in a situation that was already difficult for senior officers to understand and control. To make matters worse, the French troops advanced just far enough to cause confusion and then withdrew again to their trenches – it was the only movement made throughout the afternoon by the French troops in the area. It is worth noting at this point the comments made in the War Dairy of the 1st Royal West Kents when referring to the orders that had been issued to them:

> All the time these operations had been going on it was never apparent exactly what line the enemy were holding, the only fact which was very evident was that they occupied a very strong entrenched position which any way without artillery preparation and strong reinforcements it would be madness to assault.

At least one battalion officer had made a reasonable assessment of the situation from his position under the enemy guns, but for those directing the operations the full truth of the situation was not to become apparent until the casualties for the day were counted, and the lack of any substantial progress against the Germans on Mauser Ridge was fully realized.

For Geddes' Detachment, to the right of the KOSB on the east of the Ypres-Pilkem road, the story was not too different. To begin with, Geddes' command had been somewhat depleted by the departure of two companies of the 9th Royal Scots to support the Canadians near Saint Julien, and although these were ordered to rejoin their battalion they did not arrive in time to take part in the action. Thus the 2nd DCLI, with the remaining companies of the 9th Royal Scots in support, were commanded directly by Lieutenant Colonel Tuson of the 2nd DCLI for the duration of the attack. In his first wave Geddes had ordered the 2nd East Yorks to maintain contact with Tuson's command, and for the 1st York and Lancaster to move with its left flank on the Ypres-Pilkem road, that is, in touch with the 2nd KOYLI of the 13 Brigade. Geddes held the 5th King's Own in reserve but it was not long before this unit was called upon to fill the gap which opened between the 2nd East Yorks and the 2nd DCLI as the attack developed.

The 1st York and Lancaster made progress from the area of La Belle Alliance, a farm on the western flank of Hill Top Ridge, and as it did so it came under very heavy rifle and machine-gun fire. Using all the available cover the battalion made every effort to continue the advance by moving one platoon forward at a time and avoiding exposing any one company to the hail of bullets. However, the scant cover of hedges and such like was insufficient to allow the battalion to gain much ground, and as they emerged into the open they suffered heavily from shell and small arms fire. During the first rush over open ground many officers and senior NCOs were killed or wounded, but the remainder pressed on until they had lost so heavily that to have continued the assault would probably have resulted in the complete destruction of the battalion. As it was, Lieutenant Colonel A.G. Burt and his adjutant, Captain E.S. Bamford, were killed[15] and another dozen officers were wounded, whilst the casualties amongst the other ranks mounted to over 400. The remains of the battalion had to be satisfied with holding the forward position it had reached until it was safe to withdraw, and with the deployment of their machine guns in relatively safe positions some 1,000 yards from the enemy, where they were able to bring harassing fire to bear and to provide some much needed support.

The 2nd East Yorks fared little better, with most of the battalion getting no closer than 100 yards of the enemy by which time the ranks had been so badly thinned that the attack halted. The War Diary notes:

> Superb courage was displayed throughout by all ranks. The spirit and tenacity of the men is shown by the fact that a party of men, under Corporal Hall, who for some unaccountable reason did not receive the order to retire, actually entrenched themselves within 30 yards of the enemy, where they remained undisturbed by the Germans for over 48 hours without food or water.

But casualties had been heavy in the battalion and although the attack had been carried out with "great energy and dash", the East Yorks had little to show for it when the fighting subsided.

To the right of the 2nd East Yorks were the 2nd DCLI, who were deployed for the start of the attack between English Farm and Wieltje Farm to the west of Wieltje. As the attack progressed they too suffered heavily from the enemy fire from Mauser Ridge. The DCLI pushed home a very determined attack and came to grips with the enemy around Turco Farm, where there was severe hand-to-hand fighting. For a short while they were able to hold the farm, but because of a break-down in the organization of the attack and lack of support, those who had fought their way to the farm were ordered to withdraw. For the second time in the day Turco Farm had been wrested from the Germans to be given up because of insufficient weight in the attack.

For the men of the 2nd Buffs and 3rd Middlesex, together with the 1st and 4th Canadians, the afternoon attack was merely an extension to that which they had carried out in the early hours of the morning, barely twelve hours before, but they were now expected to push forward once again as Geddes' Detachment moved through their positions. The Middlesex War Diary gives the following details:

> The attack recommenced somewhere about 4.30 pm. The majority of C Company under Major Large advanced with the first line whilst one platoon of A Company under Col. Stephenson followed in the second line about 150 yards in the rear. The advance was conducted by rushing over extremely open country for about 250 yards where the 1st line suffered very heavy losses. Col. Stephenson took one platoon of A Company up to reinforce the firing line. About five Maxims swept these companies from right front and 2 or 3 from left front and practically everybody in that portion of the line was killed or wounded within 3 minutes.

The attack had failed all across the front attacked. There had been little gain and much loss of life for the British and the Canadians. By about 7 pm the attack had been completely broken by the Germans and there was little that could be done but to break off the fighting. A line was established from Kitchener's Wood through Hampshire Farm to Colne Valley beneath Turco Farm to the Yser Canal at South Zwaanhof Farm, and there contact was made with the French. The French attack in the north between Steenstraat and Lizerne had also made little progress and it had become a very dismal afternoon for the Allies.

When darkness fell at about 9.30 pm, further movement and reliefs became possible. A new line was organized by Brigadier General Wanless O'Gowan and Colonel Geddes at what had been termed the "high water mark" of the attack, but which was basically sited in Colne Valley, some 600 yards from the enemy. It was not an ideal spot since it was partially overlooked by the enemy, and as it was at a low point in the countryside, water was found at about two feet down, so that it was impossible to dig deep trenches. To add to the miseries of the survivors of the afternoon's gallant attack there was very little chance of supplying them with food, though some units, no doubt as a result of the efforts of their own quartermasters, received some bacon and bread. Very little ammunition could be brought forward during the hours of darkness. At 11.30 pm the first reliefs took place as the Middlesex and their Canadian comrades in arms were withdrawn into support and reserve of the 13 Brigade. The 4th Rifle Brigade also arrived to reinforce the 13 Brigade. This Brigade had now suffered such severe losses since the start of the war that there was hardly an officer or man left who had fought with it at Mons, or, to put it another way, in eight months of front line duty the entire personnel of approximately 4,000 men had been replaced. These kinds of casualty figures were, unfortunately, to become commonplace, particularly amongst the divisions that were frequently involved in heavy fighting. During the day the 1st York and Lancaster had casualties amounting to fourteen officers and 411 other ranks; the 2nd East Yorkshires, fourteen officers and 369 men. The 2nd KOSB had over 200 casualties whilst the 2nd DCLI and the 5th King's Own had over 300 casualties between them. Similarly the 3rd Middlesex had lost all but twenty men of the two companies that had been engaged throughout the day. The 1st and 4th Canadians, who had started the day fresh from reserve at Vlamertinge, had sustained casualties of eleven officers and 393 other ranks, and eighteen officers and 436 other ranks respectively. Lieutenant Colonel A.P. Birchall of the 4th Canadians, who had taken charge of the two Canadian battalions' advance, was among those killed.[16] He had been wounded twice during the action but had continued to lead his men from the front. His bravery went unrewarded, though he was posthumously recommended for the award of the Victoria Cross. If Foch had any doubt about the British commitment to his support he need only have looked at the casualty figures for the day. The casualties had so thinned the ranks of those units involved that late in the night of 23rd April, Major General E.S. Bulfin ordered the 150 (York and Durham) Brigade, so recently arrived in the battle arena, to support the 13 Brigade should they be required to do so. During the day other reinforcements had been brought up, including the 1st Cavalry Division, which had succeeded in reaching Woesten unopposed and was thus in a position to support the French should there be a further German attack on their front. This division was to be joined later by the 2nd and 3rd Cavalry Division, who were by the night of 23rd April in the region of Poperinge. Infantry reinforcements were also on the move and one of the first to be ordered in to the area was the 10 Brigade, (4th Division) under Brigadier General C.P.A. Hull, and it was not long before the remaining brigades of this division were brought up to defend Ypres.

As these troop movements were carried out on the north flank of the salient, the Canadians, still holding part of the old front line in the north-east corner, were making moves to shorten their line and hence blunt the angle in the defences that had arisen as a result of the German breakthrough to their left. The 3rd Canadian Brigade, with the company of the 2nd Buffs commanded by Captain Tomlinson, withdrew successfully to a line to the east of the Poelcappelle-Saint Julien road, to join Lieutenant Colonel W.F.H. McHarg and his 7th Battalion. This movement was completed without casualties, though the shelling of the line by the Germans as the withdrawal took place did much to speed its completion. Fortunately the Germans did not realize the withdrawal was taking place, and the shelling did not include the new line, leaving the defenders to dig their trenches in relative peace.

Whilst throughout the day there had been a slight improvement in the situation on the north flank, it had been at some cost, as many of the available reserves had been used on hastily prepared attacks without clear objectives or the necessary support. The comments in the war diaries clearly show that the advancing battalions did not have an idea of where the German line was until it was far too late, and an officer of the West Kents was to describe the attack as "madness", but the battalion carried on as best it could under the circumstances. For all the sacrifice of the battalions involved, the situation in the salient was, at nightfall, still considered to be perilous. Thus it was with some relief that the British commanders heard that the Belgians north of Steenstraat had been able to close a 700 yard gap between themselves and the French, and had even been able to offer reinforcements to aid the French, so it was felt that this had gone some way to stabilizing the situation in the north. However, the conditions in the French sector were still cause for grave concern, since they still had so few troops east of the canal, and the Germans had at least partial control of no fewer than seven bridges across the canal. It appears that, at this stage, the Germans were considering using their bridgehead to force a crossing of the canal, thereby making a breach between the French and the Belgians and then destroying the French completely. The consequences of such an action on the British forces in the salient would have been catastrophic and would certainly have meant the surrender of the last major Belgian town to the Germans.

No one in the Allied command could have been satisfied with the conduct of the battle during its second day. They had stalled the Germans, but it had been achieved by the expenditure of gallant lives and not necessarily due to their leadership. The Battle of Gravenstafel Ridge was a two day battle in which much should have been learned. There had been thousands of lives lost in three fruitless counter-attacks during the two days, and at the end of all this fighting the line was no more further advanced than it would have been if they had simply ordered an advance after nightfall. Such a manoeuvre would have resulted in fewer casualties and the final line established would have been much the same. With the establishment of the line on the night of 23rd April, Sir John French had demonstrated his commitment to an ally who remained resolutely within his defences on the west side of the Yser Canal. This must have been a worry to French as he considered his options for the next phase of the battle.

Notes

1. See Scott, op.cit., p38.
2. See *Fifty Amazing Stories of the Great War*, p248.
3. See French, op.cit., p365.
4. McWilliams and Steel, op.cit., p82.
5. Lieutenant Jarvis was killed later in the day's fighting.
6. See 3rd Middlesex War Diary (WO95/2279). The story told in *Canada and Flanders* is somewhat more successful.
7. See McWilliams and Steel, op.cit., p91.
8. *Official History 1915 Vol. 1*, p201.
9. French had clear instructions from Kitchener to the effect that he was to do everything in his power to support the French. It appears that French did not have the wholehearted support of Kitchener since he had already offered the French commanders the opportunity to replace French. This had been turned down. (see Holmes, *The Little Field Marshal*, pp 167–195.)
10. McWilliams and Steel, op.cit., p91, quoted from an order issued by General Quiquandon which had arisen as a result of the meeting between Foch and French.
11. 5th King's Own (Royal Lancaster) Regiment.

12. See 2nd East Yorks and 1st York and Lancs War Diaries (WO95/2275).
13. Capt. Charles Ernest Edward Bland DSO is commemorated on the Menin Gate. He was a veteran of the Boer War and had been awarded the DSO for bravery during the First Battle of Ypres.
14. 1st RWK War Diary (WO95/1553).
15. Lieutenant Colonel Burt is buried in New Irish Farm but Captain Bamford is buried in Poperinge Old Military Cemetery.
16. Lieutenant Colonel Arthur Percival Dearman Birchall is commemorated on the Menin Gate.

CHAPTER SIX

The Battle of Saint Julien
Day 1 – 24th April 1915

The details of the fighting of the two previous days that had reached the Commander-in-Chief were such that he felt he was in a position to authorize a memo issued by Lieutenant General Robertson to his Second Army commander, General Sir Horace Smith-Dorrien, on the morning of 24th April, 1915. In part it reads:

> Evidently not much reliance can be placed on the two French Divisions on our left. We do not know where the division ordered from Arras is at present but it ought to be in action by noon somewhere NE of Poperinge.
> It is of course of the first importance that our left should not be turned, and your dispositions should be such as to safeguard the left . . . The Chief thinks that vigorous action E of the Canal will be the best means of checking the enemy's advance from the line Lizerne to Boesinge.[1]

It is interesting to note that this memo was timed at 9.30 am, by which time the need for "vigorous action E of the Canal" had been pre-empted by more than five hours by the Germans' desire to carry on with their attack on the salient. It is also of interest to note that even at this early stage of the fighting the Commander-in-Chief had some doubts on the reliability of the French, but was not even fully appraised of their deployment in the north of his own sector of the front line.

The Germans had started the day by bombarding the Belgians in the north near Steenstraat and the French in Lizerne. They followed up the bombardment with an infantry attack against the Belgians by which they hoped to outflank them and thereby drive a wedge between them and the French. In this they were unsuccessful and were completely

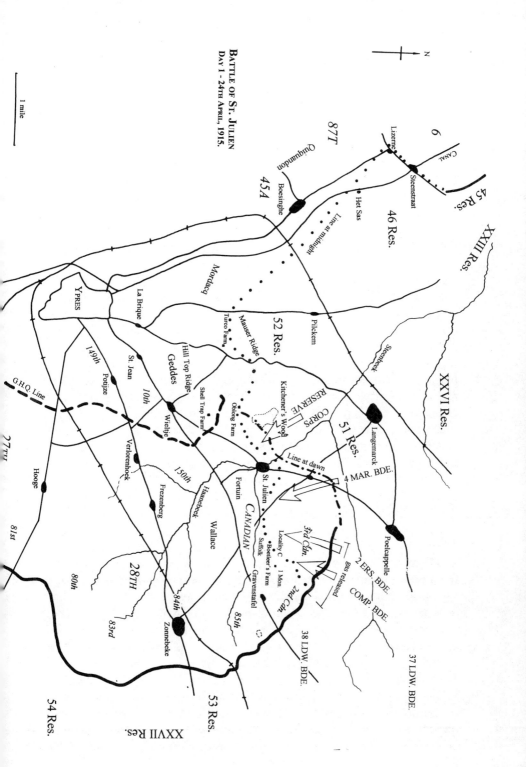

BATTLE OF ST. JULIEN
DAY 1 - 24TH APRIL, 1915.

1 mile

N

6
45 Res.
CANAL
Lizerne
Steenstraat
Het Sas
87T
Quiquandon
Boesinghe
45A
46 Res.
Line at midnight
XXIII Res.
52 Res.
Plickem
Mordacq
La Brique
YPRES
Turco Farm
Mauser Ridge
Steenbeek
XXVI Res.
149th
St. Jean
Potijze
Hill Top Ridge
Geddes
Shell Trap Farm
Oblong Farm
Kitchener's Wood
RESERVE
CORPS
51 Res.
Langemarck
G.H.Q. Line
10th
Wieltje
27TH
Hooge
Verlorenhoek
150th
Frezenberg
Line at dawn
St. Julien
Fortuin
4 MAR. BDE.
Poelcappelle
81st
Hanebeek
Wallace
CANADIAN
3rd Cdn.
Locality C
Boetleer's Farm
Suffolk
1 Mon.
2 ERS. BDE.
gas released
COMP. BDE.
80th
28TH
84th
83rd
Zonnebeke
85th
2nd Cdn.
Gravenstafel
38 LDW. BDE.
37 LDW. BDE.
54 Res.
XXVII Res.
53 Res.

81

out-manoeuvred by the Belgians, who threw their flank out to enclose Zuydschoote, thus outflanking the Germans, and once again made contact with the French. At the same time the Germans were throwing forces into an attack at Lizerne to push out the French and establish a firm position west of the canal. After fierce hand-to-hand fighting in the village the French were forced to retire. However, the French were not prepared to leave it like that, and took the initiative by attacking Lizerne with part of the 87th Territorial Division, commanded by General Codet. Codet had been given the task by his superiors, although his division could scarcely be considered strong after the gas attack of 22nd April, and so he was forced to use the freshest troops at his disposal – the 418th Infantry Regiment. This regiment comprised mostly raw recruits and was probably not the best for the kind of action envisaged, but supported by the 3rd Battalion of the Belgian 2nd Regiment of *Carabiniers* the attack was set in motion. This attack, at 8.30 am, like the one that followed at 2.30 pm, did not succeed in forcing the Germans out of Lizerne, but did succeed in enclosing the village on three sides, thus making it very difficult for the Germans to make any real progress in the area. The troops of the 418th Regiment performed well in the fighting and advanced steadily in the face of heavy German fire, but could not take Lizerne. Although this must be considered as, at least, a partial success for the French, elsewhere they made little headway. However, the German commanders must have looked upon their operation in the northern sector of the battlefield as being a failure, since they had not moved one step closer to isolating the French from the Belgians and had expended some considerable effort to achieve almost nothing. Further south opposite Brielen, at 1.30 pm, the *Zouaves* of Colonel Mordacq's Brigade advanced from the Canal bank to pass through the 4 Rifle Brigade (13 Brigade) in a vain attempt to bring pressure to bear on the German line in front of Pilkem. After five hours of fighting they had not succeeded in closing with the enemy but had established a line in front of the 4 Rifle Brigade between the Canal and the Ypres-Pilkem Road. It was little more than a costly gesture, but it did allow the British troops the opportunity to be relieved from their former front line positions should that become necessary.

In the Canadian sector of the salient between Kitchener's Wood and Gravenstafel, the Germans chose to adopt a different approach. After a preparatory bombardment lasting an hour, gas was discharged over a 1,000 yard portion of the front line, held by the 15th and 8th Canadians immediately north of Gravenstafel. The release of gas had been dictated by the breeze that morning which was blowing from a north-north-east direction towards the Canadians. Undoubtedly the release of gas on a favourable breeze was designed to allow the attacking troops of the

German 53rd Reserve Division all the time they needed to exploit the gains which must have been anticipated following the collapse of the French line on the evening of 22nd April. The Germans were to find out that the Canadians were made of sterner stuff, especially now that the initial surprise that had acted so favourably for them had gone. Also, since the first release of gas there had been many suggestions on how to cope with it and the Canadians were aware, by the time they were attacked, that a wetted rag of some kind would offer at least some measure of protection. Thus as the gas reached them they wetted all kinds of rags with just about any form of liquid they had at hand and with these wrapped around their mouths and noses they waited, if somewhat apprehensively, for the German assault that they knew would follow. The use of the wetted rag seems to have had varying success, since some veterans insisted that they saved their lives whilst other believed they had little beneficial effect. One thing is certain, however, and that is that the wetted rag could offer no protection for the eyes which began streaming to such an extent as to partially blind many of the men in the line that day. It is difficult today, perhaps, to imagine how these men felt as they waited for the pall of gas, which rose to a height of fifteen feet, to reach them. It is just as difficult to imagine the courage it required for them to stand quietly and wait, knowing full well that even if the gas did not kill or disable them they would be required to face up to a frontal attack from the Germans. Nevertheless, the Canadians of the 8th and 15th Battalions did just that in the early hours of the morning of 24th April.

The German attack followed quickly on the gas. They were met by rapid rifle fire from the Canadian trenches and suffered heavily. The Canadians' problems continued as the Germans pressed, when the Ross rifle they used began to jam with frightening regularity and with it there was a reduction in the rate of fire that the Canadians were able to put down. The Ross rifle was the standard issue to the Canadians, and although it was supposed to be of the same calibre as the Lee Enfield used by the British Army, it soon became apparent that under the rigours of trench conditions the Ross would not perform satisfactorily with the British ammunition with which the men had been supplied:

> Men cursed the rifle and threw it away to grab a fallen one and try again. I have seen strong men weep in anguish at the failure, with a useless rifle in their hands and the enemy advancing.[2]

Men were instructed to release the bolt by giving it a sharp blow with the handle of their entrenching tool or by placing the butt of the rifle on the floor and kicking it open with the heel of their boot. These methods had a measure of success but the Canadians' fire power was greatly reduced by the fact that the weapon was not as reliable as the Lee Enfield, though the specification was almost identical to the weapon supplied to the British troops. Whilst the Germans suffered heavy casualties as they pressed home the attack in the north-east portion of the salient, there can be no doubt that their casualties would have been substantially greater had the Ross rifle been up to the task asked of it on that morning.

The weight of the German attack eventually took its toll on the gallant Canadians and soon there was a gap created on the left of the 8th Battalion as A Company of the 15th Battalion all but ceased to exist. Here the effect of the gas attack had been horrendous and dead and dying men scattered the area they had once defended – they had had little success with their wetted rags – and throughout the first hours of the attack many men succumbed painfully as their lungs filled with fluid from the effects of the gas. It is unfortunate that these brave men facing gas and heavy artillery could expect little in the way of support. Both the 8th and the 15th Battalions had sent urgent requests for artillery support but tragically the artillery, as weak and short of ammunition as it was, was too far away from the critical point developing between these two battalions to render any assistance. Many of these men would never be aware of the fact that the artillery had been moved to cover the break in the line from earlier fighting, and could not be moved rapidly enough to assist those battalions now fighting for survival in the apex of the salient.

The flank to these battalions, facing north-west after the fighting of the previous two days, was the next point in the line to be attacked as the Germans made an effort to pinch out the apex of the salient. Here the line was held by B Company, the 2nd Buffs, the 13th, 7th and 14th Canadians, as far as Saint Julien, and then by the 3rd Canadians up to the eastern edge of Kitchener's Wood, where the 10th, 16th and 2nd Battalions could be found. Here the effects of the gas were not great since it had tended to drift to their south-east almost parallel to their trenches. However, the trenches were beginning to fill up with wounded and gassed from the battalions already engaged. The Germans struck the flank over open ground in the daylight of the early morning. They attacked in a series of waves of the 4th Reserve Ersatz Infantry Regiment and each wave was met with as much sustained fire as the Canadians could muster. Canadians who survived the day were to remark on the discipline showed by the advancing waves of German soldiers as they marched on the Canadian lines in a purposeful and steady manner, never faltering as the Canadians met them with as much fire as they could lay down. In those days of the Second Battle of Ypres a grudging respect for the enemy was to develop on both sides of the line. By the time this attack was under way the Germans had brought approximately twenty-four battalions onto the field to attack eight, mainly Canadian, battalions defending the route towards Ypres. In this area the artillery of the II Canadian Artillery Brigade were able to offer substantial support to the 2 and 3 Canadian Brigades, and assisted in breaking the attacks made on those brigades early in the day.

Within about half an hour of the Germans' infantry attack falling on the apex of the salient, and with the enemy's numerical superiority clearly evident, it was realized that the battalions in the front line would need reinforcements if there was to be any hope of holding the line. Reinforcements would be necessary also if they were to withdraw in safety to a new position. It was at about 4.30 am that Major Ormond, now commanding the 10th Canadians, received a telephone call. He was to hand over his portion of the line in front of Kitchener's Wood to the 2nd Battalion and move to strengthen that portion of the line around the 15th Battalion, which was in danger of falling. It was not possible for Ormond to comply in the time available since the situation in the area had changed since the order was issued. Ormond was directed towards "Locality C", a high point on the Gravenstafel Ridge, and there his battalion was to provide reserves for those battalions already heavily engaged in the fighting. The 10th Canadians were already severely thinned by the previous two days of fighting but, nevertheless, they moved to comply with the order as Major Ormond described:

> It was broad daylight, we were within one hundred yards of the enemy machine guns and had to go over a low ridge in full view of the enemy.[3]

The men filed into a communication trench which gave some cover for part of their journey to the rear, under the covering fire of the 16th Battalion who were themselves about to be withdrawn to act as reserves, but eventually they had to make a dash across open ground as Private Sydney Cox was to relate:

> We had to run about fifty feet, jump into a cabbage patch or wheat field, or something or other there, and you would see three or four men run and they would get one – and then you'd think "Well I'll crawl" and then you would see three or four crawl and they would get one. "No, I'm going to run". You had to make your mind up which way you wanted to be hit.[4]

It was not a good way to have to move but the 10th Battalion obeyed the order and made a dash for it. One man, Private Charles Bloxham, actually carried out a wounded comrade and then went back to bring in some stragglers. He was later awarded the DCM. However, because the Canadians had moved in small groups they managed to minimize their losses as they moved out from Kitchener's Wood. Nevertheless, by the time Major Ormond was able to report to the 2 Brigade forward headquarters at Pond Farm, his command was only three officers and 171 other ranks – the 10th Battalion had been reduced to less than a company in just over one day of fighting. Brigadier General A.W. Currie, commanding the 2 Brigade, had not realised that the reinforcements he had sent for were going to be so few. On the night of 22nd April he had loaned the battalion to Brigadier General Turner and since then had received little information on the battalion's involvement in the fighting. Although Currie appears to have appreciated what the 10th had been through, he had no choice but to order them back into the line to support the 7th Battalion who were, by that time, attempting to defend the approaches to Locality C.

By 5.30 am the 10th Battalion was in position at Locality C. Almost without time to prepare their defences, in some old and poorly constructed French trenches, they came under an infantry attack which they were able to beat off as described by Major Ormond:

> We stood up on our parapet and gave them three ruddy cheers and shook our fists at them. We gave them everything we had and they figured it wasn't worthwhile, and they just turned round and went back. They did it again and we did it again. We were quite happy about it. So then they did it a third time. When they went back a third time we thought we had won the war.[5]

The fact that Major Ormond's Canadians had beaten the Germans back at all is even more remarkable when the effects of the Ross rifle are taken into account. Ormond says that only two or three rounds per minute could be fired when twelve or fifteen would have been more like rapid fire. Once again soldiers were reduced to kicking open the bolts but before long they began to throw away their unreliable Ross rifles and take up the Lee Enfields of fallen British soldiers that soon began to litter the battlefield. To have sent such courageous men as the Canadians into battle with such a weapon as the Ross rifle is just one of the many tragedies of the Second Battle of Ypres.[6]

Whilst this manoeuvre was going on, the Germans succeeded in making a breakthrough on the front of the 15th Canadians who fell back to the second line near Locality C. However, the two platoons on the left of the battalion and the adjoining company of the 2nd Buffs stood their ground and held on to the original line for all they were worth. It was after 9 am when, with most of the officers killed or wounded and nearly all the ammunition gone, they were forced to surrender to the enemy.

Meanwhile the Germans continued their attack on the north-west flank and, if only because of the weight of numbers, they began to have some success with their frontal assault against the 13th Battalion. To make matters worse, the Germans were, by about 7 am, beginning to work around to the rear of that battalion on its right flank as the 15th Battalion began to give way under the sustained pressure. This left Major V.C. Buchanan, commanding the 13th Battalion, no choice but to withdraw his men to the reserve line to the west of Locality C. This withdrawal was accompanied by heavy shell fire and the 13th Battalion lost heavily. The effect of this withdrawal was to leave the right flank of the 7th Battalion very much exposed, and the Germans continued to batter at their defences. The men of the 7th stood their ground and were more or less totally overwhelmed. In the words of one of those who was made a prisoner on that day; "We stayed too long".[7] Things could have been even worse but for the bravery of two men who manned the battalion's two Colt machine guns. Lieutenant E.D. Bellew and Sergeant H.N. Peerless refused to give up without a fight and maintained the fire from the guns after the crews had become casualties. As they poured accurate machine-gun fire at the enemy he was forced to falter, at a range of no more than 100 yards, in his forward rush. Eventually Sergeant Peerless was shot dead and with ammunition running out, a wounded Lieutenant Bellew destroyed his gun and was captured by the oncoming Germans. When he was released in 1919 it was announced that he had been awarded the Victoria Cross.

It is hardly surprising that, with the troops of the north-eastern apex of the salient fighting for survival, there was some time lag between the events occurring and the senior commanders receiving the news. As early as 6 am the Canadian Division's headquarters had received information that the Germans had entered the 15th Battalion's trenches, but these reports were not confirmed to Lieutenant General E.A.H. Alderson until 7.20 am, when Brigadier General Turner asked for support for his beleaguered 3 Brigade. There was not a lot that Alderson could do since he had very few troops at his disposal that he could use in a supporting role. Nevertheless, he ordered two battalions of the 150 Brigade forward from the Canal bank to man the GHQ line to support both the 2 and 3 Canadian Brigades. The 4th East Yorkshire and the 4th Green Howards, the two battalions concerned, were new to the front, having arrived in the area a matter of days before. Unfortunately for them there was little time to get used to trench service, as they were plunged into a highly charged critical position immediately behind the Canadians, who were fighting for their existence. The other two battalions of the brigade (5th Green Howards and 5th Durham Light Infantry) were then detached from the 13 Brigade and ordered to rejoin their own, with the idea being that all four battalions would be used to relieve the 3 Canadian Brigade.

News of the breakthrough reached the higher echelons of command at V Corps headquarters some twenty minutes after Alderson had received it, but it was almost four hours before the confirmation was received by Plumer and his staff. Acting on this belated information, Lieutenant General Plumer issued orders to the Canadian Division "to take instant action to reconstitute the line". It is difficult to understand the logic in such an order, bearing in mind the intense fighting that had been continuing all morning. Plumer, however, was unaware of the precise situation and acted in the only manner he could. Unknown to him, he was many hours too late, for since about 6 am the Canadians had been fighting to "reconstitute" the line at the apex of the salient. At that time what the Canadians really needed was some reinforcement, but Plumer had none at his immediate disposal. He had already ordered the 151 Brigade, also newcomers to the front, to support the Cavalry Corps, which was in reserve to the left flank on the west of the Yser Canal and offering support to the French divisions fighting there. He had already promised Alderson the 10 Brigade and the 149 Brigade, the only other troops that were immediately available, but unfortunately they had not yet arrived in the area so that there was little else that Plumer could do apart from issue an order, which, on the face of it, appears to be stating the obvious. At least it showed he was aware of the situation that was developing in his V Corps area.

After suffering heavy losses at the hands of the Canadians all along the line of their attack, the Germans paused briefly to sort out the situation and to regroup their forces that had become thoroughly mixed up during their convergent attack on the north-west and north-east of the apex of the salient. They had not succeeded entirely in pinching out the salient as quickly as they would have liked, but all along the front, in the line held by the Canadians from in front of Gravenstafel to beyond Saint Julien, things were becoming increasingly difficult for the defenders as their losses mounted. At this stage of the battle the troops forming on Locality C were next to be targeted by the Germans, as this point became the focus of their fierce bombardment and renewed attacks. The Germans clearly believed it was necessary to take control of the higher ground as part of the next phase of their operation, and they began their assault again on Locality C at a little before 11 am. The conditions there deteriorated rapidly, as shell fire and enfilade rifle fire screamed around the defenders. Major Percy Guthrie, who was then with the 10th Battalion, wrote:

The air was absolutely full of whistling bullets and shrieking, whistling and crashing shells. I had men on each side of me shot dead – at practically the same instant I saw six men blown to bits a few yards away. I saw arms and legs torn off by shell explosions all along the line. I saw men with eyes protruding, arms dangling and otherwise mangled on all sides of me. In every sense of the word war is indeed Hell.[8]

Guthrie was one of the lucky ones, for he survived to tell the tale, but this kind of attack could not be borne indefinitely and most of those present knew it could only be a matter of time. It was not long before the 3 Canadian Brigade was forced to give ground and finally an order was issued at noon to do just that. As they retired they fought all the way back, selling each piece of ground as dearly as their dwindling numbers and ammunition would allow. The withdrawal took the Canadians down the reverse slope of Gravenstafel Ridge and Major Ormond was to comment:

> We decided we'd better pull back and let him come up onto the skyline and then we'd get our own back.[9]

Unfortunately for the Canadians the Germans were able to shell them all the way with, in particular, their 5.9-inch howitzers, causing terrible damage as they withdrew. The artillery available to the Canadians was still in short supply – there was no more they could call upon – and the shell shortage did not help matters. For all that, the artillery of the Canadian Division and that of the 27th and 28th Divisions did all they could to support their infantrymen in the firing line. The rationing of shells which, for instance, limited the 18-pounder field gun to no more than three shrapnel shells per day, was completely ignored as the gunners fought their guns with all the ammunition that the divisional ammunition columns could get to them. In the Canadian Division they were firing on average as many as 150 shells per gun per day throughout the Battle of Saint Julien. So, whilst the artillery was outnumbered and short of ammunition, the gunners did all in their power to assist in the defence of the salient in those critical hours of the first day of the battle and it is in no small way due to them that the Germans did not push on through the 3 Canadian Brigade at a more rapid pace.

The immediate reaction of Lieutenant General Alderson to all the problems arising around Locality C was to commit the only troops he had left at his disposal to the battle. He ordered forward the 4th East Yorks and the 4th Green Howards (150 Brigade), already in the GHQ line, and put them under the command of Brigadier General Turner, suggesting that they should be used to counter-attack "with energy" and thereby stop the Germans in their tracks. As this order was issued a column of German troops, mounted and artillery, were spotted moving on to Saint Julien. The two fresh battalions were redirected to help the 3 Canadian Brigade to form a defensive line in front of Saint Julien. This area was now developing into a critical point in the day's fighting since most of the available reserves had already been committed and, whilst up to that point some semblance of a line had been maintained, it was recognized that if the enemy could get sufficient reinforcements forward the chances of holding him were likely to be small.

At this time (approximately 11.30 am) it was becoming clear to V Corps that a closer control of the troops in the forward areas was desirable. The headquarters of the 27th Division were at Potijze and it was considered that these could be used to direct the Corps reserves should there be any breakdown in communications. With that in mind General Plumer put Major General Snow, commanding officer of the 27th Division, in charge of all reserves in the area, to be used at his discretion should communication lines be interrupted. Fortunately, Snow and Alderson had a history of working together and that made the situation somewhat easier since Snow was able to anticipate the needs of the commander of the Canadian Division. Snow was then able to send some additional support to Turner in the form of the 1st Royal Irish Regiment, or rather the remains of it, for it could muster no more than 356 men to send into the battle. Meanwhile the Germans were capturing the western end of the Gravenstafel Ridge and sweeping all the remains of the Canadian defenders before them.

Thus the situation by noon of 24th April had worsened considerably, as the Germans had battered at the defences of the salient and had forced the 3 Canadian Brigade to evacuate the first line trenches and then Locality C. Added to these problems were the shortages of reinforcements and the lack of adequate artillery support. It is readily appreciated that the senior officers had a difficult situation which they would be required to resolve as the afternoon progressed. As they were all well aware, time was not on their side. The fight for the afternoon was to be for the possession of Saint Julien, which had remained in Canadian hands up to midday as a result of some fierce fighting. One such incident occurred to the left of Saint Julien on the eastern edge of Kitchener's Wood, in the defence of a farm which was to become known by the Canadians as Doxsee's House. Lieutenant William Doxsee,[10] who was later killed, of the 2nd Canadians, and a gun crew of the 10th Canadians, held off the Germans during the better part of a day of fierce fighting by the efficient use of their Colt machine guns. During this fighting the casualties gradually mounted and the ammunition became short but the small garrison continued to hold off, one after another, the Germans' attacks. Lance Corporal George Allan manned his gun with great skill and bravery until he was killed. He was recommended for a Victoria Cross, but his gallantry was recognized by the posthumous award of the DCM.[11] Eventually the defenders of Doxsee's House were overcome, and few escaped as the Germans stormed on their way to Saint Julien.

At Saint Julien the situation was becoming desperate as noon approached. The garrison of B Company of the 15th Canadians, on the left, and the 14th Canadians on the right, together with an assortment of stragglers, had been under fire throughout much of the morning. They had begun the day outnumbered by about 10 to 1 and the shelling throughout the morning had done nothing to improve the situation for the defenders. At 11.30 am Captain Wilfred Brotherhood of the 14th Canadians was to send the last message from the stricken village:

> Enemy have shelled us out and are advancing from our left and front. Will hold every traverse if we have to retire along line to our right. Captain Williamson killed.[12]

Once again the Canadians had started to fight a fierce rearguard action as they slowly surrendered the village to the Germans. Even as they retired through the village the guns of the II Brigade Canadian Field Artillery were at work to help the defenders get out as best they could. In some cases the small groups of men soon became surrounded and were forced to surrender. Private W.C. Thurgood of the 7th Canadians was to comment on his capture:

> Though we held our hands aloft and were now unarmed, the cold-blooded crew started to wipe us out. Three of our men were bayonetted before an officer arrived and saved the rest of us. Even then our rough captors struck us with their rifle butts and kicked some of our men who were unfortunate enough to be laid up with wounds.[13]

Perhaps the actions of the Germans reflected the losses they had suffered as they attacked the Canadian lines, but it was not the only example of such behaviour to be reported before the end of the Second Battle of Ypres and was probably not exceptional behaviour for either side.

It was as this stage of the attack on Saint Julien developed that the two battalions of the 150 Brigade had first reached the battlefield and it was the movement of the Germans that had brought about their change in orders and their redirection to support Brigadier General Turner's 3 Canadian Brigade. Turner had been instructed by his division to hold his line, but in this order there was some ambiguity and room for misinterpretation. When Turner received this order a little after midday he was not holding anything that could be easily described as a defensive line, since his brigade had been so badly mauled that the "line" was little more than groups of men fighting desperately and barely hanging on. Turner, therefore, assumed that the order referred to the GHQ line and proceeded to organize his defence on that. Turner even spoke to the divisional staff before the movement was completed, but the misunderstanding continued. The net result of this failure of communications was that a gap of approximately three miles was left in the line from the original front line to the GHQ line, with only a small party remaining at Boetleer's Farm to the south east of Locality C. Meanwhile, under the direct orders of Turner, the two battalions of the 150 Brigade and the remnants of the 2nd, 3rd, 14th, 15th and 16th Canadians began to form up in a defensive line from the Saint Jean – Peolcapelle road southwards. Whilst the GHQ line was the next prepared line of defence, it was mostly east facing and as such hardly suitable to bear the brunt of any attacks from the north or north-east, where the Germans were concentrating their efforts in the early afternoon of 24th April, 1915.

At about 2.15 pm Major General Snow, commanding the 27th Division, realized that the situation on the left of the salient was becoming dangerous and that he had little in the way of reserves he could offer to the Canadians, since he had dispatched the 1st Royal Irish Regiment already. He thus proceeded to order the 1st Suffolks and the 12th London (Rangers) Regiment, both of the 28th Division, into reserve positions in support of the hard pressed Canadians. He placed Lieutenant Colonel W.B. Wallace of the 1st Suffolks in charge of both battalions. He took this unusual step of using another division's reserves without any reference to Major General E.S. Bulfin of the 28th Division because, in his opinion, there was no time to be lost and in so doing he had, at least, found some reserves to help out the Canadians. At the same time he ordered the 8th Middlesex and the 2nd Gloucesters of his own division to act as support for Wallace's detachment, which he then directed to Fortuin and towards the gap created by the withdrawal of the 3 Canadian Brigade. He also sent the following message to Turner:

> The enemy's advance from Fortuin must be stopped at all costs. You must move every man you have to drive him back. I have directed two battalions under O.C. Suffolks from Frezenberg against Fortuin. I am also sending you up the Royal Irish Regiment from here and have directed them on cross roads in C23c.[14] You will get in touch with these troops and take command in that part of the field and drive the enemy northeastwards. I am issuing these orders as I am on the spot and communications appear to be dislocated and time is of the highest importance. Act with vigour.[15]

Turner chose not to act with vigour, and it would appear that he chose to ignore the order altogether as he continued to form his defences around the GHQ line. Nevertheless, a quarter of an hour later Alderson, his divisional commander, was also urging him to hold on as help was arriving, and he informed the Brigadier General that he was sending the 4th Canadians, the 2nd KOYLI and the 9th London (Queen Victoria's Rifles) Regiment of the 13 Brigade in to the area. Turner probably saw no problem with holding on in the GHQ line, but it was not this line that Alderson was talking about, which became clear when these two battalions arrived on the scene. At 4.35 pm Alderson sent a further message to Turner to confirm that the battalions already mentioned, together with the four fresh battalions of the 150 Brigade, were in and around Wieltje, or about half a mile behind the GHQ line. Alderson also acknowledged, somewhat surprisingly, that he "had no exact knowledge of your situation at the present moment, but hope that you are still blocking Saint Julien". It was to be some hours before Alderson was fully aware of the situation but, nevertheless, he was trying to direct Turner to action through a muddle which was worsened by the "fog of war". The movement of these various bodies of men into the area did not go unnoticed by the Germans, who soon began to shell their approach. Anthony R. Hossack of the Queen Victoria's Rifles told of his experience of the advance to the line:

A detonation like thunder, and I inhale the filthy fumes of a 5.9 as I cringe against the muddy bank. The German heavies have got the road taped to the inch. Their last shell has pitched on our M.G. teams, sheltering in a ditch on the other side of the road. They disappear, and all we can hear are groans so terrible they will haunt me for ever. Kennison, their officer, stares dazed, looking at a mess of blood and earth . . . More and more of these huge shells, two of them right in our midst. Shrieks of agony and groans all round me. I am splashed with blood. Surely I am hit, for my head feels as though a battering-ram has struck it. But no, I appear not to be, though all about me are bits of men and ghastly mixtures of khaki and blood.[16]

All of this was happening as the battalion was approaching the main area of the battle in what the Battalion War Diary simply calls "operations E. of the Canal". The area to which they were being sent was, by that time, becoming crowded with men and there was little cover except what they could dig for themselves. The two battalions of the 13 Brigade found the GHQ line was so badly crowded that they chose to lie out in the open behind the line. The War Diary of the 2nd KOYLI explains:

At 12 noon the Battn. got sudden orders to proceed at once to assist the 10th Canadian Bde. (sic) in retaking the lost line NE of Wieltje. We marched at once followed by the Q.V. Rifles and on approaching Saint Jean were subjected to a very heavy shell fire which followed us until we eventually reached our allotted position in part of the G.H.Q. line of trenches 500 yards NE of Wieltje where we had to crowd into a trench already filled with Canadian Highlanders. Owing to bad Staff arrangements by the Canadian Divn. this line which should have been empty and ready for occupation was so crowded with troops of different Regts. that our companies had to lie out in the open fully exposed to the enemy who opened a heavy shrapnel fire on us killing Lieut. Hunter and many men and wounding Lieut. Webb and many more.

The confusion over the line being defended by Turner should have been realized at that point. These two battered battalions had been sent up in support, but the first Canadians they came across were in the trenches which, at that time, were considered support trenches. The officer responsible for the War Diary entry clearly recognized the problem that had been allowed to develop as a result of the confusion between Brigade and Division staffs.

At the same time as the 2.30 pm order Alderson also redirected the two companies of the 3rd Middlesex, guarding the Canal bridge, to rejoin Geddes' Detachment, thereby strengthening the north flank immediately west of the Ypres-Pilkem road. Geddes' Detachment remained in the line all day, and whilst not directly involved in the heavy fighting to their right flank, were forced to endure periods of heavy shelling throughout it.

Whilst all this was going on the men of the 8th and 5th Canadians were still holding the old front line in the east of the salient. The 8th, on the left, were aware that they had no flank since the withdrawal of the 3 Brigade and were awaiting reinforcements with which to form a flank, or orders to withdraw. At about 1.15 pm came the news that the battalions wanted to hear. The 3 Brigade were to counter-attack to restore the situation supported by two battalions of the 150 Brigade. The news was greeted with cheers, but sadly these men had all been misled for by the time that it had reached them, the 3 Brigade were already falling back to the GHQ line. Once again there had been a breakdown in communications. Brigadier General A.W. Currie, commanding the 2 Canadian Brigade, realized quite clearly that he needed to do something quickly to protect the left flank of his brigade, and hence save the 8th and 5th Canadians, who were spread too thinly to efficiently man the line they already held, thus making it impossible for him to extend them any further to the left to help close the gap that had formed. Early in the day Currie had been informed that the two battalions of the 150 Brigade were being brought up to act as support for his brigade, but it was noon before the first of these battalions even appeared in the area. At this point a further confusion arose which really should have been avoided. The battalions arriving in the area had been directed to support the 3 Canadian Brigade now moving into the GHQ line, and not Currie's 2 Brigade. Currie was still expecting them to be his support and tried to order them to do just that. The commanding officer of the battalion concerned, believed to have been the 4th Green Howards, refused to move to support either until his orders had been clarified. It is difficult to understand what could have possessed the CO of the Green Howards to make such a stand in the heat of battle when he knew that the communications were so poor – did he need to see the Germans attacking before he took action? On the other hand, his battalion was fresh to the salient, had received no trench training and it is perhaps understandable that he did not want to have his men badly used and without clear orders. Currie may well have been frustrated by this stance but in all probability it was correct, for Currie could not countermand the orders of his superiors without reference to them. In the event, the 4th East Yorkshires and the 4th Green Howards remained attached to the 3 Canadian Brigade and, as was pointed out to Currie, the order for a counter-attack which he wanted them to carry out had been cancelled anyway. The situation was not clarified for Currie, however, for he still had his brigade in the line with no left flank and without any realistic support to improve the situation, Currie felt, quite rightly, that he was in danger of losing his battalions. General Snow was not about to change his mind on the matter since he was of the belief that it would be necessary to strengthen the area immediately around Fortuin to the south of Saint Julien. It would appear that he too had not fully grasped the situation insofar as it would be pointless to reinforce the area of Fortuin with the Canadian 2 Brigade in such peril and their 3 Brigade already in the next line of defence behind Fortuin. There was a need at this stage for some kind of unified action to stabilize the line, but unfortunately for the soldiers fighting out this fierce battle that was not to be.

As this mix up was progressing, the situation for the 2 Canadian Brigade was worsening as the Germans began to make their way through the gap between the left flank and Locality C. Nevertheless, it was decided by Lieutenant Colonel Louis James Lipsett (8th Canadians) and Lieutenant Colonel George Tuxford (5th Canadians) that they were going to stay put. Both officers realized that if they began to withdraw then the flank of the 28th Division would be put under threat, which might lead to further withdrawals along the front of the salient – a situation which both officers wanted to avoid if at all possible. The decision was made in the absence of Currie, Lipsett taking on the mantle of the Brigadier General, who could not be located but was, in fact, personally searching for the reinforcements to support his brigade in their stand. It was an action which brought some criticism from

Snow, who considered that he should have remained at his Brigade Headquarters to make just such a decision.

The artillery for their part had been fighting their guns hard all morning, but after noon Lieutenant Colonel J.J. Creelman of the II Brigade Canadian Field Artillery realized that, with ammunition running out, he had better make plans for his own evacuation. He decided that all the ammunition he had left could be fired by six guns, so he ordered two and a half batteries of his brigade to be withdrawn and at 2.45 pm this is exactly what he did – an action which was witnessed clearly by the Germans who were now in possession of the high ground of Gravenstafel Ridge. Creelman, like all other artillery commanders, had ignored the shell rationing and on 24th April it is recorded that his 7th Battery fired 1,800 rounds. This was mainly as shrapnel shells fired over open sights into the masses of the German attacking the 8th Canadians at ranges of as little as 900 yards. At the same time as Creelman began the withdrawal of his guns, Wallace's detachment was making an appearance on the scene and Wallace at once agreed to attempt to fill the gap to the left of the 8th Canadians, and planned his move by 4 pm. It was unfortunate that by that time the Germans had complete control of most of Gravenstafel Ridge and Saint Julien had fallen at 3.30 pm, so that Wallace's detachment came under heavy fire from the advancing Germans. To make matters worse the Allied artillery had not been made aware of troop movements in the area and continued firing while Wallace advanced. The 1st Suffolks, who were leading, had 280 casualties whilst the 12th London lost over sixty men including their commanding officer, Lieutenant Colonel A.D. Bayliffe, who was wounded. The advance of Wallace's detachment reached the Keerselaere-Zonnebeke road and stopped – the gap to the left of the Canadians was still open. Wallace was aware of the desperate plight of the Canadians and when they appealed for a further effort to be made he dispatched two companies of the 1st Suffolks, under Lieutenant S. Bradley,[17] to Boetleer's farm where they were later to be reinforced by the remains of the 10th and 7th Canadians dispatched there by Currie.

To the left and a little in front of Saint Julien were C and D Companies of the 3rd Canadians. Their position had become vulnerable from about noon as the defenders of the village began to become overrun. Soon the companies were locked in a struggle as they tried to maintain their position and protect their flank against Saint Julien while they waited for the counter-attack that had been cancelled. It was a one sided battle and by 3.30 pm the Germans were entering Saint Julien from the north-west. Few men of the two companies of the 3rd Canadians survived; C Company was left with no more than

96

forty-three men and most of these had been wounded in the fighting.

To the left of this, in front of Kitchener's Wood, were the 2nd Canadians, less their A Company, which had ceased to exist in the fighting of the previous day. Now under command of the 3 Brigade, their commanding officer had asked Turner to allow them to try to hold their line until nightfall. That was not to be, for at 1.40 pm Turner issued an order for them to retire to GHQ line, and there ensued another rearguard action in which the Canadians inflicted heavy casualties on the Germans but lost heavily themselves. Strongpoints, such as Oblong Farm to the west of the wood and Hooper's House and Doxsee's House to the east of the wood, held on for hours, but it was inevitable that they would be required to withdraw. Few Canadians managed to make it back from these positions. At the end of the day the 2nd Canadians had lost the equivalent of two companies in the fighting in front of Kitchener's Wood in less than forty-eight hours.

As Wallace's two battalions turned north-eastwards to face the enemy, the two battalions of the 150 Brigade were also beginning to move. This move was directed by General Snow although he had placed them under the direction of Turner. This fact has caused some consternation amongst some Canadian historians who suggest that Snow was creating a muddle and was exceeding his authority. Whilst there may be some truth in the former, since conditions in the battle-field were becoming very confusing, there can be no question of the latter. He was the senior officer in the field and had been given the authority to direct Corps reserves as he saw fit in the event of a breakdown of communications. Thus if he saw fit to attach units to the Canadians he could, just as readily, detach them for another purpose as the situation on the battlefield changed. Further, it would appear that Turner had ignored Snow's order earlier in the day because he was unaware of the authority that had been given to Snow. Clearly there were problems with the command structure during this phase of the battle, and it was necessary for Snow to take some action on the northern flank since Turner had withdrawn his brigade and was by that time facing mostly east – the wrong way to defend effectively against any attack coming from the north, which was where the Germans were directing their efforts at that time.

Whatever the military protocol of the situation, the 4th East Yorks and the 4th Green Howards were marching into battle near Fortuin and to their right was the 1st Royal Irish Regiment. In their advance Lieutenant Colonel G.H. Shaw commanding the East Yorks was killed and Lieutenant Colonel M.H.L. Bell of the Green Howards took command of both battalions and attacked the Germans that were seen to be advancing south-west out of Saint Julien. The advance by the

Yorkshire men and the Irishmen, assisted by two sections of Lieutenant Colonel Creelman's II Brigade CFA and the guns of Colonel Rundle's CXLVI Brigade of the 28th Division, succeeded in pushing the Germans back on Saint Julien, finally coming to rest under heavy rifle and machine-gun fire on the banks of the muddy Haanebeek. Subsequent to the attack the Germans withdrew from Saint Julien, leaving its corpse-strewn streets for the ridge to the north, and for the moment Saint Julien was effectively in the middle of no man's land.

The afternoon had been a long one of confusion and furious fighting in which the conditions had deteriorated rapidly from the Allied point of view. However, the attack by the 150 Brigade had at least halted the Germans on the north flank, although the situation on the north-east still remained dangerous, with a gap remaining between Currie's brigade and Boetleer's Farm and from there to Wallace's battalions, who had paused on the Keerselaere-Zonnebeke road to the east of Fortuin.

As darkness fell there were further troop movements in an attempt to stabilize the line such as it was. The Yorkshiremen and the Royal Irish were returned to reserve at Potijze, and Wallace's detachment was moved back to a slightly better position on the Fortuin-Gravenstafel road. The Canadians were still in need of support, and throughout the evening this was sought from the 28th Division which proceeded to do all they could to help the hard pressed Canadians. It had been suggested that a force consisting of one and a half companies of the 2nd Northumberland Fusiliers, two companies of the 2nd Cheshires and one company of the 1st Monmouthshires, all of the 84 Brigade and commanded by Major E.M. Moulton-Barrett, could be used. This force had been directed at 5 pm to dig trenches under shellfire to establish a line across the Zonnebeke-Langemark road to the south-east of the cross-roads between Fortuin and Gravenstafel and then to occupy and hold it. At 8.30 pm, after a request from Lieutenant Colonel Lipsett, Moulton-Barrett moved his mixed party forward to take up position westwards from Boetleer's Farm. The line was then extended to the left by the 10th and 7th Canadians and by two half companies of the 8th Middlesex as far as the Haanebeek. The 1st Monmouths were on the right of this line and throughout the evening and the early part of the night they tried to make contact with the left flank of the 8th Canadians. They were unsuccessful because of the heavy rifle and machine-gun fire in the valley of the Stroombeek which continued at least until 10.30 pm. By that time the gap was much shorter, but it had not been completely filled.

Other reinforcements were also beginning to arrive in the area as a result of the arrangements being made as the fighting continued. The

149 Brigade (50th Division) reached Potijze at about 10.30 pm, whilst from the same division the 151 Brigade began arriving in Potijze from about 7 pm. The 10 Brigade (4th Division) had been on the move for some hours during the day and had reached Vlamertinge by about 3 pm, where they were told to wait until midnight before entering the battle area.

It had been a long day for the defenders of the Ypres salient. When the day had begun it seemed as if there was some form of order on the battlefield after two days of fighting, and although the situation was far from good it rapidly became clear that it was going to get very much worse during the course of the day. As the day developed, the confusion caused by the Germans' ferocious assault on the north-eastern portion of the salient grew and ultimately almost brought about the complete collapse of the command structure, as generals started to question the orders issued by their superiors and attempted to change the orders of some of the units moving in the main part of the battlefield. It is difficult to make a judgement on who was wrong and who was right – the situation was never that clear cut. However, it can be seen that the generals concerned were all being ruled by different priorities, and whilst it may be possible to suggest that Snow had caused some problems when he assumed command in the salient, he had in fact been directed to do so under specific conditions which he considered applied. Similarly it may be possible to demonstrate that Currie should not have left his brigade headquarters to look for support but communications were very poor in the salient and he was left with little alternative, especially since he saw his priority as making every effort to save his Brigade. Paradoxically his absence could have brought about the loss of the Brigade, if it had not been left in the competent hands of the likes of Lieutenant Colonel Lipsett. The loss of his brigade could have had catastrophic effects on the defence of the salient, as the 28th Division would then have been exposed at the heart of the defence of the salient. In turn, the refusal of Turner to obey the order issued by Snow could have been very serious. His inability to communicate his exact actions as he withdrew to the GHQ line, when Alderson believed he was holding a line much further forward, was equally serious. Once again his priority was to save his Brigade, which had been severely battered in the early morning attacks, but in so doing he had compromised the safety of adjacent units and had seriously jeopardized the defence of the salient. Thus there were mistakes made in the direction of the battle but there were mitigating circumstances by which they can be understood, if not totally excused.

Perhaps the biggest error of all was not one which is directly related to the command structure, but the fact that the Canadians had been allowed to go in to battle with weapons that were not really up to trench warfare. The Ross rifle was a good enough rifle and continued to be used throughout the war by snipers because it tended to be more accurate than the Lee Enfield. It was not, however, up to the punishment that it could receive in action in the trenches. Whether or not this was the result of the use of unsuitable ammunition is to some extent irrelevant, since if it could not use the Lee Enfield ammunition it should not have been in use anyway. It is a common tale to read the accounts of survivors of the battle bemoaning the sad performance of the rifle – most believe they could have done more with a rifle which could maintain a steady rate of fire. Similarly the Colt machine gun was not a suitable weapon. It was heavy and awkward to handle, it needed special ammunition and frequently became jammed. It says much about the Canadians that they were able to mount any sort of defence on 24th April under these circumstances – but they had, and it is in no small way due to their gallantry and dedication to their cause that the north flank of the salient did not collapse with the release of gas in the early hours of the morning. One wonders at the outcome of the day's fighting had the brave men of the Canadian Division been equipped with a more suitable rifle, let alone a more reliable machine gun!

Throughout the afternoon, whilst all the fighting had been going on, there had been many messages flying back and forth between the senior commanders of the Allies, in which aspects of the conduct of the battle were set out. Lieutenant General Plumer, and for that matter General Smith-Dorrien, were well aware of the need to hold the line to allow the French the opportunity to regain the lost ground – they both realized the folly of trying to hold the narrow salient for too long if the French failed to make any progress. At 4.15 pm Sir John French notified his subordinates of his views:

> Every effort must be made at once to restore and hold the line about Saint Julien or situation of the 28th Division will be jeopardised.[18]

This indicated that French expected his generals to take the necessary action to recapture the ground they had lost in the day, and not simply hold onto the line to which they had been forced to retire. The note set in motion the train of events that were to unfold on 25th April. The initial reaction of Plumer was to inform Lieutenant General Alderson of the Chief's wishes. Alderson received the order at 6.30 pm and it meant that he was then required to rethink his plans for the next few hours. He had already been given the 10 and 150 Brigades, and had planned to use them to relieve the 3 Canadian Brigade and Geddes' Detachment, but these plans had to be abandoned as he proceeded to work on the attack requested by his superiors. Besides the units mentioned he had a further six battalions at his disposal: the 2nd KOYLI, the 9th London, the 1st Suffolks, the 12th London, the 1st Royal Irish Regiment and the 4th Canadians. All of these units had already been in action and were not fully up to strength, but they were to be added to the attack. Alderson decided to place Brigadier General C.P.A. Hull of the 10 Brigade in charge of the attack and issued orders accordingly. The order, issued at 8 pm ordered the attack to commence at 3.30 am on 25th April and stated, in part:

> The first objectives of the attack will be Fortuin (if occupied by the enemy), Saint Julien and the wood in C10 and 11 (Kitchener's Wood). After these points have been gained, General Hull will advance astride of the Saint Julien-Polecappelle road and drive back the enemy as far north as possible. All units holding the front line of trenches will follow up the attack and help to consolidate the ground gained.[19]

Whilst Hull began to work on a plan, there was no time for thorough reconnaissance or preparation; he had insufficient staff to control the fifteen battalions in his command, he had no divisional troops and he did not have any thorough intelligence on the position of the enemy. He was not even sure if he could contact all the battalions concerned in sufficient time to gather them for an attack and, to make matters worse, it was raining. It soon became clear to Hull that an attack at 3.30 am was unlikely and it was delayed to 5.30 am to give his troops time to assemble, by which time it would be daylight and the enemy would have the benefit of full observation of the attacking troops.

From the German point of view the day was probably viewed with some disappointment. The progress against the French and the Belgians had not developed and they had not really managed to obtain any firm position on the west of the Canal. Against the British and Canadians they had made some gains but, following the success of the release of gas on 22nd April, the results of the day's fighting can hardly have been what they were expecting. Instead of delivering a decisive blow to the defenders of the salient and cutting off the retreat by outflanking the French, the Germans had only succeeded in making a large dent in the line. This line had been battered by artillery, subjected to the use of poison gas and numerous infantry assaults but had not been completely broken. This must have come as a bit of a surprise to the Germans, and it is possible that, with the surprise of the use of gas no longer with them, time was also running out if they were to flatten the salient and secure the line of the Yser Canal as far as Ypres. Nevertheless the 51st Reserve Division, supported by the 52nd, were placed on alert in readiness for a further attack on 25th April, with the objective of capturing the ridges to the north of Wieltje and Frezenberg and striking at the heart of the defence of the salient. It had been decided that they would not waste any more time or effort in fruitless attacks against the French or the Belgians in the north of the area.

Thus at the end of the day both sides had already set the wheels in motion for another day of heavy fighting in the salient, and a day which had started with some hope for both sides was looking less positive for all concerned by its close.

Notes

1. See *Official History 1915, Vol 1*, Appendix 22, p394.
2. McWilliams and Steel, op.cit., p104.
3. Dancocks, op.cit., p36.
4. ibid.
5. ibid., p37.
6. The Ross rifle was considered to be superior in some respects to the Lee Enfield and saw continued use during the war as a sniper rifle indicating its superior accuracy.
7. McWilliams and Steel, op.cit., quoting L.C. Scott, p117.
8. Dancocks, op.cit., p38.
9. McWilliams and Steel, op.cit., p118.
10. Lieut. William Doxsee is commemorated on the Menin Gate.
11. see Dancocks, op.cit., p40; Lance Corporal Allan is commemorated on the Menin Gate.
12. McWilliams and Steel, op.cit., p121.
13. ibid., p122.
14. These are the cross-roads about 1,000 yards north-east of Wieltje near von Hugel Farm.
15 McWilliams and Steel, op.cit., p133.
16. See *Fifty Amazing Stories from the Great War*, p83.
17. Lieut. Stephen Bradley was killed in action during the fighting for Bellewaarde Ridge on 25th May 1915.
18. See *Official History, 1915, Vol. 1*, Appendix 23 p394.
19. See *Official History, 1915, Vol. 1*, Appendix 24 p395.

CHAPTER SEVEN

The Battle of Saint Julien
Day 2 – 25th April 1915

Brigadier General Hull had his orders. He was to attack with his own Brigade of five battalions plus another ten that had been placed at his disposal. He was to attack immediately and with as much "vigour" as his fifteen battalions could muster. His objective was to capture Saint Julien and Kitchener's Wood and occupy Fortuin. This was a fairly clear statement of purpose, but since no one was entirely clear as to the extent of the German advance it was going to be a very different matter to make the actions fulfil the desire. A consequence of this was, of course, that Hull had no clear idea of where his Brigade might first come in contact with the enemy and his planning for the attack was of necessity somewhat approximate. As he worked out his plan it began to rain, and his troops moved into position and took what little shelter they could from the weather and waited. For some the wait was short. Hull had delayed his attack from 3.30 am to 4.30 am and then, finally, 5.30 am simply to allow his forces sufficient time to get through the gap left in the GHQ line wire and to begin deploying themselves. The manoeuvre was all carried out in something of a rush; a rush with which Hull could not have been happy. He had not had time to prepare a plan properly – he had not even seen the ground in daylight, for his Brigade was just coming into the battle zone. He did, however, continue making his plans to get his over-large, if not unwieldy, command into action. It was not a satisfactory way to start a counter-attack. The change of zero hour was to create further difficulties, as some units remained uninformed of the change and commenced their movements early. Initially this was to have the effect of the artillery firing the preparatory bombardment early

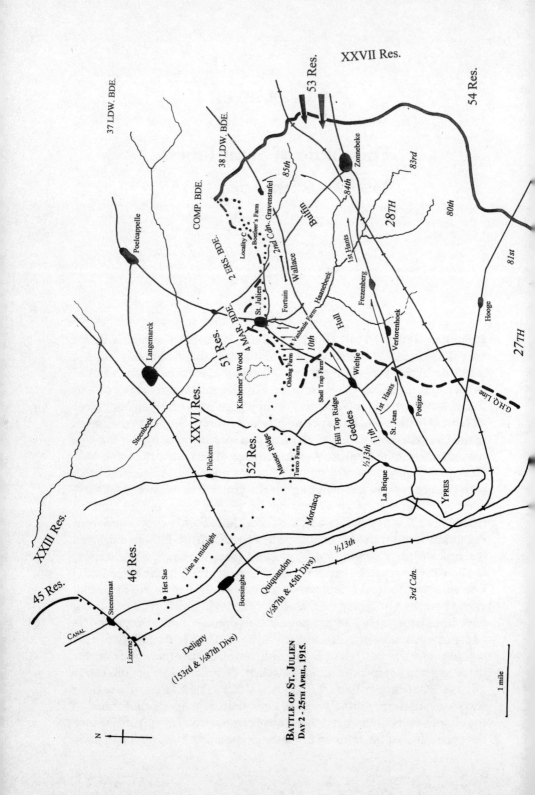

XXVII Res.

53 Res.

54 Res.

37 LDW. BDE.

38 LDW. BDE.

COMP. BDE.

Poelcappelle

85th

Zonnebeke

83rd

28TH

80th

2 ERS. BDE.

Locality C

Boetleer's Farm

2nd Cdn. Gravenstafel

Wallace

Buffin

1st Hants

4 MAR. BDE.

St. Julien

Fortuin

Vanheule Farm

Haanebeek

Frezenberg

81st

51 Res.

Langemarck

Kitchener's Wood

10th

Hull

Verlorenhoek

Hooge

Oblong Farm

27TH

XXVI Res.

Steenbeek

Shell Trap Farm

Wieltje

G.H.Q. Line

52 Res.

Mauser Ridge

Turco Farm

Hill Top Ridge

Geddes

1st Hants

Pilckem

½13th

St. Jean

Potijze

11th

Mordacq

La Brique

Y PRES

XXIII Res.

46 Res.

Line at midnight

½13th

45 Res.

Steenstraat

Het Sas

Boesinghe

Quiquandon

3rd Cdn.

CANAL

Lizerne

(⅓ 87th & 45th Divs)

Deligny

(153rd & ⅓ 87th Divs)

N

1 mile

BATTLE OF ST. JULIEN
DAY 2 – 25TH APRIL, 1915.

once again – the gunners did not receive any notification of the change in orders until it was far too late for them to do anything else. During the fighting that followed other consequences of the delay became apparent.

The Germans abandoned Saint Julien as the previous day's fighting had died away. They were of the impression that upon their withdrawal to the heights above the village it had been occupied by the Canadians – it had not. This point was clearly confirmed to them by the Royal Artillery when they started firing the preparatory bombardment into Saint Julien. As soon as the shelling ceased the Germans began moving their firepower into the battered remains of the village ready for the attack they now knew was coming. Unfortunately, there was little that Brigadier General Hull could do about the lack of communications with the gunners – it was difficult enough for him to find and inform his own Brigade to let it know of the situation, not to mention the various units that had been attached to him. In fact, three battalions – the 2nd KOYLI, the 9th London and the 1st Royal Irish Regiment – did not receive orders to say that they were to be part of the attack until it was far too late for them to act. The otherwise detailed War Diary of the 2nd KOYLI simply records:

> At 3.30 am an attack to retake Saint Julien commenced headed by the 10th Brigade. The KOYLI, now only 250 strong remained in reserve.

Thus even one of the units which was supposed to be involved in the attack was unaware of what had happened, or that the time for the attack had been changed from 3.30 am, when the Diary entry for 25th April was being made. The loss of these three units, though all had already suffered casualties, had seriously reduced the power of the counter attack, as all three remained, effectively, outside Hull's control, firmly in reserve in the trenches of the GHQ line. To make matters worse, the battalions of the 150 Brigade, under Brigadier General J.E. Bush, had not received notification of the change of the zero hour for the attack. This meant that at 3.30 am the 5th Green Howards and the 5th Durham Light Infantry advanced, unopposed, for some distance towards their objective, but when it was realized that their flanks were exposed and that no other troops appeared to be advancing, they withdrew once again to await orders. It should be remembered that these two battalions, like those from the same brigade used the previous day, were new to the battlefields of France and Flanders. They had arrived barely a week before and, until they were marched into the battle zone of the Ypres salient, had not even seen a front line trench. They had not been given the "trench training" which was afforded to all new units coming into the line. It is to the credit of both officers and men of these units

105

that they remained steady in an exceptionally trying situation, which must have played heavily on the minds of the young men awaiting their first taste of battle on the Western Front. For all their steadiness, the lack of communication between the brigades meant that Hull's force was effectively reduced by a further two battalions and, perhaps more importantly, the flank cover he was expecting did not materialize immediately which then led him into other decisions to prevent the situation from further deterioration.

Eventually, as 5.30 am approached, Hull was beginning to see the deployment of his own Brigade taking place. On the right facing Saint Julien were the 1st Royal Irish Fusiliers and the 2nd Royal Dublin Fusiliers, whilst on the left, facing Kitchener's Wood, were the 2nd Seaforth Highlanders and the 1st Royal Warwickshire Regiment. Supporting the left was Hull's Territorial battalion, the 7th Argyll and Sutherland Highlanders. Hull's Brigade was, for the most part, a first class Regular unit with regiments with long traditions of service to the Crown and much was expected of them.[1] At this stage of the Second Battle of Ypres there was one thing which was, perhaps, of greater importance, which was that Hull's Brigade was up to strength. He had at his disposal approximately 5,000 of the most disciplined and best trained soldiers that remained available to the Commander-in-Chief at this stage of the war. Time was short if the attack was to go in by 5.30 am, and so as the battalions arrived they were deployed and ordered directly into the advance. At first there was little by way of opposition, but as a result of the premature artillery bombardment the Germans were well aware that something was happening. It was, by this time, almost full daylight and any advantage of moving while under the cover of darkness or the early dawn had long since disappeared. It was not long before the advancing troops began to take casualties from snipers lying out in the fields in advance of the Germans positions. Soon this fire intensified as the four leading battalions moved steadily forward. For those advancing on Kitchener's Wood, machine guns began to rattle from the direction of Oblong Farm, now back in German hands, and Juliet Farm, both about 400 yards south of the objective. For those advancing on Saint Julien, there was intense fire from the direction of the village as the German machine gunners got on with their deadly work. Marching forward with the 1st Royal Warwicks was Second Lieutenant Bruce Bairnsfather:

> Bullets were flying through the air in all directions. Ahead in semi-darkness, I could just see the forms of men running out into fields on either sides in extended order, and beyond them a continuous heavy crackling of rifle fire showed me the main direction of the attack. A few men had gone down already, and no wonder – the air was thick with bullets.[2]

The leading lines of the attack managed to advance about a quarter of a mile into this hail of bullets, but the attack was destined to fail. The wording of the Official History shows the severity of the situation:

> A few men tried to crawl back into cover, but the majority of those in the leading lines never returned; mown down, like corn, by machine guns in enfilade, they remained lying dead in rows where they had fallen.[3]

The attack was not proceeding well and under such circumstances it took all the training, discipline and courage of those involved not to break and simply run for cover. One officer of the 2nd Royal Dublin Fusiliers wrote:

> One unforgettable scene remains in the writer's memory; one company, which had lost all its officers and which had been ordered to retire, was doing so in disorder, when the small untidy figure of Colonel Loveband, clad in an ancient "British warm" and carrying a blackthorn stick, approached quietly across the open making, as he walked, the lie-down signal with the stick. The effect was instantaneous and for hundreds of yards along the front the men dropped and used their entrenching tools[4].

Captain J.M. Dickie, also of the Royal Dublin Fusiliers, who also took part in the attack commented:

> Captain Tobin Maunsell with Corporal Lalor and a few men, got into the village up a ditch but the rest of the company under me was mopped up trying to get there in extended order. Young, French and Salveson were killed next me and Elsworthy wounded close to the village. I was hit but managed to carry on for half an hour and arrange the defence of the last farm on the road up to the village.[5]

The few men under Captain Maunsell were, apparently, the only soldiers to get even close to the enemy that morning. The bodies of Lieutenant C.S. French and Second Lieutenant E.M. Salvesen were never recovered and they are commemorated on the Menin Gate in Ypres, along with many of their comrades, whilst Lieutenant N.C.N.R. Young is buried in Hazebrouck. The farm referred to here is thought to be Vanheule Farm, which is about 600 yards south-west of Saint Julien.

The War Diary of the 1st Royal Warwicks, who were on the left of the attack, gives detail of the action:

> The Brigade attacked at 4.30 am (sic). We attacked Wood on the left of the line with the 7th Arg. and Suth. Highldrs in support. The Sea Highldrs, the R. Irish Fus. and the R. Dub. Fus attacked on our right on Saint Julien. Owing to the German trenches being insufficiently shelled and supports unable to come up the line retired at about 7 am to trenches

near the farm and consolidated our position. Our casualties were very heavy, 15 officers and 500 other ranks killed wounded and missing.[6]

The 1st Royal Warwicks had suffered badly and the lack of artillery preparation is clearly mentioned in the entry, but it does not mention the fact that the point at which they were to form up was actually already in German hands. This was left to the War Diary of their support battalion, the 7th Argyll and Sutherland Highlanders:

The Battalion first came under fire on reaching C23c[7] north, the point where the R. War. Reg. had been told to form for attack being in the hands of the enemy. A good few casualties occurred here. A Company moved to the SE corner of C17c[8] followed by B Company to reach which point they had to cross ground swept by rifle and machine gun fire. A message asking for reinforcements on his left being received from the O.C. R. War. Reg., A Company went forward in small parties. The ground was very open and swept by a heavy fire, few of them succeeded in reaching the firing line. B Company was moved under cover more to the east and pushed up to the triangle of trees in the north part of C17c[9] from which point it was easier to get reinforcements up to the firing line. C and D Companies were also directed on this point. The battalion became a good deal mixed with the 2nd Seaforths and some of the R. War. Reg. and the principal casualties occurred here as it was not only under close rifle fire but was also heavily shelled by field and heavy guns. Reinforcements were sent forward with fewer casualties from this point but most of the first line was withdrawn and a position taken up running from N point of Farm in C22b[10] through farm in C17c[11] to farm in C17d[12] to stream in C18c[13]. There was no preliminary bombardment, a few shells being dropped in the road.

During the brief period that this part of the entry for the day covers (approximately 4.30 am to 6.30 am), the 7th Argyll and Sutherland Highlanders had lost twelve officers and 425 men. Very little had been achieved.

The battalions of the 10 Brigade had suffered terribly in advancing on their objectives, but as their advance came to a bloody and grim halt the Germans ceased firing, and it was possible for at least a short while for some rescue of the wounded to be carried out. Lieutenant Walter Critchley of the 10th Canadians witnessed the scene from his position further to the east and was so moved that he wrote:

I have never seen such slaughter in all my life. They were all lined up – I can see it now – in a long line, straight up, and the Hun opened up on them with machine guns. They were just raked down.[14]

It had been a disciplined assault but it had been very costly. In about twenty minutes of intense and accurate German machine-gun fire the

10 Brigade had lost seventy-three officers and 2,346 other ranks. That is, about half the Brigade had disappeared in a hail of machine-gun bullets and most of these highly trained soldiers of the Regular army were considered to be more or less irreplaceable. The Brigade dug in where they were stopped, and they were able to secure a line from Shell Trap Farm through Vanheule Farm and then in echelon back to the Haanebeek. It was a small gain, but it was at a terrific cost. Perhaps more important than the ground that was gained was the fact that they had been able to establish a line they could now defend, and in so doing had helped to stabilize one portion of the northern flank of the salient.

Whilst his own Brigade was being slaughtered, Hull became aware that he had no right flank to his attack because the portion of the 150 Brigade that had come under his command had not received the revised orders to carry out the necessary movement. Hull realized that it was probably too late to get them to move as originally planned, and hence ordered forward the 4th and 7th Northumberland Fusiliers of the 149 Brigade (Brigadier General J.F. Riddell), which had been placed under his control by Lieutenant General Alderson. Hull now wanted them to form the right flank to his attack by supporting the battalions in that part of the battlefield and thickening his line in that area. The two battalions of the 149 Brigade immediately set out to the right, but instead of thickening his line in the area east of Saint Julien, began extending to the right (east) and in so doing came in for very similar treatment to the main attack of the 10 Brigade. There was a gap on the right of the attack as far as the battalions of Wallace's Detachment and although to close this gap would have been the ideal situation, it was simply too far for two battalions, under fire, to be extended. It was not until much later in the morning, at 10 am, that Hull finally made contact with the battalions of the 150 Brigade, who appear to have been acting under the orders of Brigadier General Currie of the 2 Canadian Brigade. By this time the 5th Green Howards and the 5th Durhams had already moved forward into the position to the left of Wallace's Detachment, so as to fill the gap that remained in the defences to the west of Saint Julien.

The attack on that morning had failed to gain any of the objectives – it had even failed to close to a distance of less than 100 yards with the enemy. To some extent the poor result of the attack must be related to the hurried preparation. The confusion in the orders, the premature artillery support and the lack of proper reconnaissance of the enemy positions all played a part in the destruction of the 10 Brigade. The artillery fire had been mistimed as a result of the delay in new orders reaching the gunners, and when fire was able to support the attack it was not directed at Saint Julien, because it was mistakenly believed that a party of Canadians, numbering 200, were still holding a portion of the village – they were not, but the German machine gunners were. When the error was realized, Saint Julien was shelled very heavily from about 10.40 am until 11 am when it is estimated that a total of 960 shells fell in the village. It was too late by some five hours for the 10 Brigade, as its casualties now lay in rows in front of the German occupied Saint Julien. This attack of the 10 Brigade was another example of the outcome of a hastily prepared attack, which although carried out with great courage and determination was destined to failure. That it was carried out so hastily reflects badly on those senior commanders who required it to be done and, in particular, it reflects badly on Sir John French who, at least on the face of it, had placed the needs of his allies before those of his own army. It can be argued that the Commander-in-Chief was acting directly on his orders from Kitchener by supporting the French in the manner he had. Although that may be true it does not excuse his part in the slaughter that had occurred during the day. It would appear that in an effort to buy the French more time and to show his own willingness to help, Sir John French chose to ignore the potential effects of the mechanized war of the Western Front. He had been prepared to act too quickly with a poorly prepared plan and virtually no artillery support with which to carry it out. It was not the only example of poor judgement during the Second Battle of Ypres. The casualties of the 10 Brigade on the morning of 25th April can be put into context when it is considered that on the same day, on the Gallipoli Peninsula, the Anzacs had sustained fewer casualties in landing on the beaches.

By 6.15 am, the advance of the 10 Brigade had been totally halted and the situation was becoming clear to Brigadier General Hull. He made his report to Plumer at V Corps headquarters by 9.15 am in which he concluded that the attack should not be continued, though Hull had nothing left with which to continue the attack in any case. By that time, however, V Corps had other things to worry them, as the news of the morning's attack by the Germans on the 85 Brigade front was just beginning to reach them – there was much more fighting to be endured before Sunday, 25th April came to an end.

It has been suggested that the German attack on the 85 Brigade and the 2 Canadian Brigade in the apex of the salient was designed as a subsidiary attack, whilst the main weight of the effort was to be through Saint Julien. The latter had been pre-empted by the advance of the 10 Brigade which, although unsuccessful in gaining its objectives, had the effect of deflecting the Germans' energy into defence rather than assault. The attack on the line to the west of Gravenstafel may have been designed as subsidiary but it did not lack any ferocity since, as the 10 Brigade was beginning its assault, some three miles east of Saint Julien the Germans opened an intense shrapnel bombardment. It was to last four hours and the area was swept backwards and forwards with shrapnel until 9 am. This was then followed up with high explosives and gas shells which lasted for a further four hours before there was any sign of an infantry assault. It was in response to this heavy shelling that the 4th Green Howards and the 4th East Yorks had been moved forward although, unknown to them, they should have been supporting Hull's abortive attack on Saint Julien.

The 5th Green Howards and the 5th Durham Light Infantry had a very difficult time during the morning as they were moved around the battlefield, mostly under shellfire and often without any real idea of what they were trying to achieve. In spite of the difficulties these units, new to the Western Front, managed to get into the line between the right of Hull's attack and Wallace, and spent much of the day under the heavy bombardment that was preparing for, and supporting, the attack in the apex of the salient. An account by Second Lieutenant S.E.G. Corry of the 5th Green Howards gives an idea of the conditions during their approach to the front line positions:

> The same evening (i.e. the 24th) we moved our position, going towards Ypres, where the Canadians had taken their positions. We advanced in the open without cover, under an absolute hurricane of shellfire. For so long that night we remained where we were until the order came to advance. We took up another position also in the open – and I think most of the chaps were asleep when we were hurriedly roused up. We changed our frontage towards the position that was being held by an Irish Regiment. We remained the whole day under heavy fire. That was where the Adjutant, and Captain, Grant-Dalton was wounded.[15]

It had been a harrowing introduction to life on the Western Front for the two Territorial battalions. It is recorded in the Official History that the total casualties for these two battalions that day were four officers and 284 other ranks – and they had played largely a supporting role. Whilst they had not suffered as much as many of the other units, such as those in the 10 Brigade, they had carried out their duty fully and were justly proud of their performance in their first action, and in the part they had played in the defence of Ypres.

During the hours leading up to the commencement of the German shelling, the situation in the line had remained far from clear for the commanders. Plumer had little idea at V Corps headquarters as to what was going on – how could he? There were men much closer to the action than Plumer who were completely in the dark. Plumer attempted to get some control of the situation, and ordered Alderson to send someone forward to handle the situation in his sector and to attempt to get to grips with the dispositions of the troops involved. Plumer, no doubt, acted correctly. He could not have been expected to do otherwise than to attempt to gain information. Alderson sent Lieutenant Colonel G.C.W. Gordon-Hall to Wieltje to Brigadier General Turner's head-quarters. Here, although he was unable to contact Turner, he directed Currie to extend his left flank south-west towards the northern stream of the Haanebeek, using the 7th and 10th Canadians which had already been seriously thinned in the fighting of the previous days. Brigadier General Mercer was instructed that, with the help of the 1st and 4th Canadians, also seriously undermanned, he was to use his 1 Brigade to extend westward from Currie's brigade to the Zonnebeke-Langemarck road. Brigadier General Bush of the 150 Brigade, then supporting the Canadians, was instructed to form a line from there to the southern stream of the Haanebeek. It is worth pausing at this point to consider these instructions. Currie was already concerned that his Brigade was in a precarious position, and although he had the assistance of the 7th and 10th battalions, their manpower of 300 was hardly likely to be sufficient to carry out the order properly. Mercer was instructed to use one battalion, the 4th Canadians, which had already suffered losses on 23rd April, and which had already been assigned to Brigadier General Hull for his attack that morning. Is it possible that Lieutenant Colonel Gordon-Hall was unaware that Alderson had already ordered this unit elsewhere? If not, then why was the order being countermanded to allow the unit to be sent elsewhere? Brigadier General Bush had already lost half of his command which had been sent forward to assist the defence of the northern part of the salient on the 24th April. Now his remaining two battalions, which had, incidentally, also been assigned to Hull, had been given yet another task to complete. The 4th Green Howards and the 4th East Yorks had already moved forward once that morning and, completely unsupported, had been forced to withdraw. Bush cannot have been satisfied with the orders he was receiving and, like the other two brigadiers, must have wondered how he was to carry out the instruc-tions and, if he did, how long it would be before someone else came forward from the Division and changed them again. It was a very unfortunate situation that was developing even as the Germans were laying their guns and preparing for the attack. The confusion in the rear areas was, to some extent, compounded by the actions of those in the forward areas. As mentioned above, Lieutenant Colonels Tuxford and Lipsett had been trying to get support for their battalions (5th and 8th Canadians respectively) and had appealed to Moulton-Barrett and his mixed detachment of trench diggers for help, which was gladly given.

The consequence of this was that the switch line that they were preparing, to join the line established running roughly east-west in front of Saint Julien with the old front line, was not completed. This meant that if a withdrawal from the now very precarious apex became necessary there was no prepared line on which it could be made. Of course, Alderson was unaware of this and in all probability so was Currie, who must have thought that his two battalions were fighting on in isolation. The fact that both Tuxford and Lipsett were trying to save the line and as much of their depleted battalions as they possibly could is praiseworthy, but it had done nothing to help clarify the dreadful command confusion that was developing. It was going to get worse as the day progressed, and the situation in the apex of the salient was to come perilously close to total collapse before the day was out and the fighting had subsided once again.

The initial infantry attack on the 85 Brigade (28th Division) came at 1 pm, after eight hours of artillery preparation of the forward trenches and their supports. On the front of the 2nd East Surreys the Germans were just seventy yards away. They were soon upon the defenders and succeeded in breaking through the line in several places. On the right there was vicious hand-to-hand fighting, but the East Surreys succeeded in holding their trench, capturing one German officer and twenty-eight men in the process. The rest of the Germans who had entered their trench were killed or driven off. The centre of this thousand yard sector was also held intact where, with the help of a company of the 8th Middlesex, the East Surreys were successful in driving off the enemy. To the left of the sector they were unable to do likewise, a fact which has been in part put down to the fact that all the officers there became casualties and the direction of the defence was lost somewhat. At 3.30 pm, and again at midnight, attempts were made by Lieutenant Colonel R.J. Bridgford, commanding two companies of the 2nd King's Shropshire Light Infantry, to drive out the Germans. Both were unsuccessful and the Germans retained possession of approximately sixty yards of the trench. The East Surreys then isolated the Germans by digging a trench around three sides of the captured trench to prevent the further progress of the enemy. In the area of the 3rd Royal Fusiliers the trench lines were about 200 yards apart, and the Germans failed to cross no man's land and to enter the trenches there.

Further west in the 2 Canadian Brigade area there had been efforts to relieve the battered remnants of the 5th and 8th Canadians. Lieutenant Colonel J. Turnbull of the 8th Durham Light Infantry (151 Brigade) had been ordered to take his fresh battalion forward to be prepared to assist the 85 Brigade. However, it appears that Lieutenant Colonel Tuxford (5th Canadians) persuaded Turnbull to assist in supporting his men and, where possible, to relieve them. Turnbull agreed to do this and his inexperienced men, new to the Western Front, filed into the Canadian trenches and began taking over from Lipsett's 8th Canadians. There were some of the Canadian soldiers in the trench who felt that they should not be leaving the fight to such "green" youngsters. Nevertheless, they had been in the thick of things long enough and had a lot of casualties and were grateful for the assistance offered. When daylight broke and the shelling of the area began, all but one of Lipsett's companies had been relieved. That company had to remain with the defenders of the apex for the rest of the day. This area was now defended by a mixed bag of units which included the 5th Canadians, one company of the 8th Canadians, the 8th DLI and one company of the 1st Monmouthshires, whilst Boetleer's Farm was still manned by Lieutenant S. Bradley and his two companies of the 1st Suffolks. It was to be a very miserable day for all the units involved as both rifle fire and shellfire increased in intensity throughout the day. Along this portion of the line the shellfire became so heavy between 9 am and noon that between forty-five and sixty-eight shells were falling every minute! With the arrival of the 8th DLI on the scene, Major Moulton-Barrett concluded that his direct assistance in reinforcing the Canadian's flank had ended, and he withdrew his Northumberland Fusiliers and the Cheshires attached to him to the line along the Gravenstafel-Fortuin road that he had been preparing the night before. C Company of the 1st Monmouths remained behind. A report appended to their War Diary gives the following details:

> Just before daylight the Company received orders from Major Moulton-Barrett that it was to return and occupy the line previously dug – this order, however, was cancelled. Capt. Perry went to Major Barrett for orders and was killed.
> Capt. Stanton took command and found that Major Barrett with his remaining companies had returned to the line dug during the night. Capt. Stanton moved up to support the 8th Durhams who required help.[16]

This short account clearly shows that even at battalion level confusion was developing, and that there was a tendency for battalion or company commanders to act independently. At this stage some kind of unified command structure would appear to have been necessary. That it was not available was not the fault of the company officers who took it upon themselves, in the absence of firm orders to the contrary, to give assistance as their reading of the situation saw fit. Some such as Captain B.L. Perry of the 1st Monmouths paid for their gallant decisions with their lives. It is also clear from this short account and the account in the War Diary entry that Captain Stanton had assisted the 8th DLI "until he felt that the Durhams could hold their lines". The 1st Monmouths had been overseas for only two months but considered themselves to be seasoned troops compared with the 8th DLI.

The fighting on Gravenstafel Ridge, around Boetleer's Farm in particular, continued well into the afternoon, but gradually the Germans were gaining the upper hand. At 3.30 pm the Germans launched an attack from the north and west simultaneously, but in spite of heavy fighting they failed to take the farm from the tenacious defenders. An hour later, the pressure on the area became so great that ground in the vicinity of the farm was given up as some of the defenders were forced to retire. The 8th DLI withdrew from Boetleer's Farm in good order, fighting all the way, and accounted for a number of the enemy as they did so. It was, nevertheless, a withdrawal, though only a small one, and as steadily as it was completed it could have placed the right flank of the 2 Canadian Brigade in jeopardy if it had continued; the line faltered and the Germans began to look like breaking through. It was at this point that the confused command structure on the battle-field was about to have an almost catastrophic effect. On hearing that there was a withdrawal of the 8th DLI in progress, Brigadier General Currie assumed, quite wrongly, that his position in the apex was becoming untenable. His belief was further reinforced when he received the information that the 151 Brigade, originally assigned to support his Brigade, had now been sent to replace Wallace's Detachment so that these troops could be returned to the 28th Division. Currie assumed that the switch line was completed and had been occupied. The result of this erroneous information was that, late in the afternoon and appar-ently without reference to the brigade commanders on either side, Currie ordered his troops to withdraw. It was still daylight and Tuxford argued with his brigadier that it would be madness to retire, but the order stood – Currie was not going to lose his Brigade if he could do anything about it. Tuxford and Lipsett set about trying to extricate their commands from the fight in broad daylight. It was somewhat easier for Lipsett because his Battalion had been partially relieved by the 8th DLI and were in support anyway. Tuxford had a bigger problem, but he succeeded in preparing the covered withdrawal of two of his companies, while the two remaining would follow as soon as they could. The with-drawal up the forward slope of the eastern end of Gravenstafel Ridge in broad daylight cannot have been easy since they would have been retiring over ground swept by the enemy fire, but nevertheless Tuxford had obeyed the order and succeeded in disengaging his men from the enemy and in maintaining good order as he did so. Neither Tuxford nor Lipsett had been happy with the order, which had clearly placed adjacent brigades in peril and had given ground to the enemy.

To the left of his brigade the men of Currie's 7th and 10th Battalions fought on through the day, although they were continuously under heavy enemy fire. The battalions were so weak that they were combined under Major V.W. Odlum of the 7th Battalion and numbered no more than 300 men. The shellfire west of Boetleer's Farm was just as heavy as elsewhere along the line that morning. During the morning Odlum was to ask Currie on more than one occasion for support since they were becoming isolated, and had not been able to make contact with the adjacent 1st Canadian Brigade. To be fair to Currie he had no support he could offer; the artillery had been withdrawn and was out of range, and every time Currie thought he was going to get help it was diverted elsewhere. As the day wore on and their numbers began to decrease even further, Odlum attempted to get new orders as his command had diminished to no more than 200 men. Whilst Odlum was away from his command, attempting to assess the situation and obtain orders, the 7th and 10th Battalions reformed and the 10th Canadians came under the command of Major Percy Guthrie. It was about this time that Currie had issued the order to retire, but the runner carrying the order to the 10th Canadians did not get through. Guthrie was not the sort of man to retire without a direct order and although he seems to have been aware of other units around him retiring he was prepared to hold his ground. He did, however, make every effort to ascertain whether the order applied to him and even set out to look for instruction. In the end it was Lieutenant Walter Critchley who contacted brigade and brought the order for retirement through to Guthrie – it was then a little after midnight. Major Guthrie wrote:

> Without this order I would have maintained my position and been anni-hilated.[17]

The withdrawal was successfully completed and, as reported by the 7th Battalion:

> The enemy knew nothing of their movement. They made a successful withdrawal although at the time completely isolated and outflanked.[18]

Whilst all this was happening on the left flank of the brigade, it soon became apparent to Lieutenant Colonel Lipsett that there had not been a general withdrawal from Boetleer's Farm. He immediately organized his 8th Canadians to turn them around and back into the fray to give what support they could to the 8th Middlesex, the 8th DLI and the 1st Monmouths, who were still hanging on determinedly. Lieutenant Colonel Tuxford was not slow to follow – both battalion commanders had been unhappy about the order to withdraw. Their departure was leaving other units in considerable danger and they felt that the only option was to go back into the line – they were, however, disobeying a direct order from Brigadier General Currie. Further, Lieutenant Colonel Turnbull of the 8th DLI had received the order to retire from Currie, but was unsure if his Battalion was actually under the Brigadier's control, so he decided to remain in his trenches around the Farm and wait for support. The 3rd Royal Fusiliers to his right had not received orders to retire and would hold their ground until they did.

For Tuxford's part he was keen to return if only to render assistance to the two companies that he had left behind when he began the retirement. He turned his C Company around and took them back up the reverse slope of Gravenstafel Ridge, by this time being swept by enemy fire from the left. The colonel was to comment later:

> During the journey up the hill which was swept by machine gun and artillery fire I remember seeing the Battalion Cook, Purvis, a bright young fellow, who always appeared to be in the best of spirits, plodding steadily along, with his cap stuck jauntily on one side of his head, and the man looking across actually winked at me![19]

As they reached the crest of the ridge they witnessed the companies retiring slowly up the hill and fighting all the way. It was a steady, controlled withdrawal and the Canadians on the ridge were now able to give a measure of cover whilst coming under fire themselves. To the left Lipsett had not been so fortunate as to rescue his remaining company, for at about 6 pm the Germans rushed its position and completely overwhelmed it – only forty-two men from the company made it back to the lines that evening. The order to withdraw had effectively ended resistance in the area of Boetleer's Farm. It had been issued under a misconception of the battle at the time and had almost brought about a full scale withdrawal. Fortunately, there were a number of very steady men in charge of the situation at the front and it is probably down to them that the situation did not become any worse. The action of Lipsett and Tuxford[20] was in direct contradiction of the order they had received, but their action and that of Turnbull of the 8th DLI had no doubt done much to steady the situation and dissuade the Germans from pushing forward too quickly, and probably prevented a major breakthrough in the line. The net effect, though, was that Boetleer's Farm fell to the Germans on the evening of 25th April. With the situation steadied somewhat, Tuxford and the other battalion commanders were able to establish a better position in a makeshift switch line, which carried to the left flank of the 3rd Royal Fusiliers via Berlin Wood in the original front line of the 85 Brigade, and for a while the Fusiliers were able to enfilade the Germans on their left flank. The gap had been closed again, but it was no thanks to Currie and his hasty order to withdraw.

Boetleer's Farm had fallen but the embattled troops had been able to hold the line in a desperate day of fighting in the area. As they settled into their new defensive positions those battalions and companies who had defended the left flank of the 28th Division knew they would have to sit tight until more reinforcements could be brought forward. They had struggled all day against almost overwhelming firepower, but no one could tell them with any degree of certainty when, or if, the reinforcements could be expected. Night did not bring the end of the problems for the defenders, as German snipers, now occupying the farm buildings so recently vacated, remained active. The 1st Monmouths attempted a raid on one farm (possibly Boetleer's Farm) to get rid of the snipers:

> On the night of the 25th the line was being badly sniped from a farm in a gap between two trenches. A weak platoon under Lieut. Lones was sent to investigate and surround the farm. Lieut. Lones and his sergeant tried to enter the farm, but both were shot at. The men were heavily bombarded with grenades and had to retire.[21]

Lieutenant Ralph Lones and Sergeant B. Abbott were both wounded and made prisoners but both survived the war. The Germans continued active sniping from their vantage point for the rest of the night.

On the left of this area, to the west of Saint Julien, where Shell Trap Farm now formed part of the front line, it was finally decided that the 3 Canadian Brigade headquarters should evacuate their forward position. Since the attack of early morning and the establishment of the 1st Royal Warwicks in a line immediately in front of the farm, the head-quarters had come in for some heavy treatment at the hands of the German artillery. Enclosed within the farm buildings was the advanced dressing station of the 14th Canadian's Medical Officer, Captain F.A.C. Scrimger. He had been working non-stop since the battle had started on the evening of 22nd April and it was he, in all probability, whom Canon Scott had witnessed hard at work when he had visited the forward area on that evening. Scrimger and another MO, Captain Haywood, managed to evacuate all but the most seriously wounded and then returned repeatedly to ensure their safety. For Captain H. MacDonald it was fortunate that Scrimger was on the scene. In an account of the action, published in the *Montreal Star* MacDonald reported:

> I was in front of the Canadian Headquarters Staff on the 25 April, which was the third day of the terrific Saint Julien fighting, when I was hit in the neck and shoulder. I was dragged into a building where Capt. Scrimger dressed my wounds. A few minutes later German shells found the building and set it on fire. The staff were forced to abandon the

building and left me there as an apparently hopeless case. But Capt. Scrimger carried me out and down to the moat fifty feet in front, where we lay half in the water. Capt. Scrimger curled himself around my wounded head and shoulder to protect me from the heavy shell fire, at obvious peril of his own life. He stayed with me till the fire slackened, then got the stretcher bearers and carried me to the dressing station.[22]

For his bravery on that terrible afternoon at Shell Trap Farm, Captain Scrimger was awarded the Victoria Cross – the fourth such award to be made to the Canadians in the fighting of Second Ypres.

As darkness fell across the blasted landscape of the battlefield it was clear that, although the line had held, it was very thinly held by groups of tired soldiers without any unified command and, sometimes, not in contact with the groups on their flanks. It was clear to Plumer at V Corps headquarters that there was an urgent need to get the command structure sorted out to avoid the confusion that had dogged the operations to defend Ypres over the previous three days. As early as 2.30 pm on the afternoon of 25th April Plumer had started the process with an order, to take effect from 7 pm, that was to place Major General E.S. Bulfin (28th Division) in charge of the 11 Brigade, then coming into the area, the 2 Canadian Brigade, the 150 Brigade and the 8th Durham Light Infantry (151 Brigade); that is, Bulfin was to take charge of troops amounting to about two divisions. Similarly, Lieutenant General E.A.H. Alderson was to take charge of the 1 and 3 Canadian Brigades, the 10 Brigade, the 13 Brigade, the 149 Brigade and Geddes' Detachment; also approximately two divisions. This was thought to be necessary because so many units had been rushed to the area and divisions and brigades had been broken up and sent to where it was felt they could best serve. By placing Alderson in charge of all the troops from the junction with the French to Fortuin, and Bulfin in charge of all troops from Fortuin to his own 28th Division in the old front line, it was considered that a step in the direction of a unified command structure had been taken. It was a very different matter, under the conditions of the battlefield on that day, to let all the different units concerned know of this reorganization and Plumer was to urge that both generals clarified the leadership to all concerned. He further notified them that any units not immediately required were to be sent to Major General Snow (27th Division), who was to remain in charge of the Corps reserve. It was fortunate for the defenders of the salient that the Germans had no idea how thinly held the line was, or how disorganized certain parts of it had become, but the Germans did not press their infantry attacks as night fell and remained in their trenches or consolidated the ground won during the day of heavy fighting.

Whilst all the fighting was going on east of the Canal, troop movements were continuing to the west of Ypres to ensure that all available reinforcements were in the area ready, should the Germans be able to mount an attack of sufficient strength to breach the line as they had done on 22nd April. By noon on 25th April Brigadier General J. Hasler's 11 Brigade (4th Division) had arrived in Vlamertinge. Shortly afterwards Hasler was told that he would, on reaching the battlefield, take command of all troops between Fortuin and the left flank of the 28th Division; that is, the 11 Brigade, the 2 Canadian Brigade, the 150 Brigade and the 8th DLI. In view of the order issued by Plumer that afternoon it is presumed that Hasler was to remain subordinate to Major General Bulfin. Hasler was further instructed that his Brigade would go into the line in the evening, on the left of the 28th Division, thus allowing the 2 Canadian Brigade to be relieved. He was to commence the movement immediately to get his Brigade to Saint Jean by dusk, and to continue to the line under the cover of darkness. The 1st Hampshires, commanded by Lieutenant Colonel F.R. Hicks, set off first, a half an hour in front of the Brigade, because Hasler had sent them to make contact with the 28th Division in the apex of the salient. The main body of the Brigade set out at 10.30 pm and they were to attempt to make contact with the 10 Brigade and thence to extend right to contact the Hampshires, on their right flank. By this stage of the battle the conditions in Saint Jean were appalling, and for one member of the 5th London (Private V. Hember) it was to leave a lasting impression:

> In parts the smell was terrible . . . It is impossible for anyone to understand the awfulness of an absolutely ruined village. The tremendous holes in the road, ruins, dead horses and, perhaps, dead bodies . . . I for one was feeling rather anxious[23].

All the time the brigade was being deployed that evening it came under shellfire, and as they marched along the road towards Wieltje conditions became worse – the infantry fighting may have finished for the day but the German gunners did not let up. Private A. Pumphrey of the 5th London was to record:

> Here again more shells bursting on either side of the road to show up in their blinding flashes the forms of marching men so that for an instant every detail of their equipment stands out clearly against the flame and they appear to be marching literally, as they indeed are metaphorically, into an inferno . . . hurriedly taking up a line along hedges just behind the crest of a ridge, digging in feverishly began. Crouching behind their meagre supports the men wait expectantly the renewed fighting of the coming day.[24]

The 11 Brigade had arrived on the scene and it was clear to all concerned that the task ahead of them was going to be a very difficult one indeed. Conditions in the area were far from clear as a result of the day's fighting, and there was no firm idea of the exact location of all the units Hasler was to relieve or, indeed, where the firing line was actually situated. Aerial reconnaissance late in the afternoon had suggested that there was an unbroken British line; but it was going to be difficult to find this, if indeed it existed, in the darkness that was by then covering the battlefield. The 1st Hampshires were fortunate enough to locate the 3rd Royal Fusiliers as instructed, but there was no one to guide them to the area in which they were to deploy. Colonel Hicks' battalion dug in facing north, only to discover with dawn that they were only about 400 yards from the 3rd Royal Fusiliers and were too close to be helpful since they had been expected to extend to the left to look for the rest of the brigade. Under the cover of an early morning mist Hicks was able to extend his position almost to the village of Gravenstafel, forming a line that was to prove to be very useful as the day wore on. The main body of the 11 Brigade was not so fortunate in their march to the front that evening, and failed to contact any of the troops that they were supposed to. Brigadier General Hasler had been notified of enemy patrols on the roads around Saint Julien, and he decided to move his column south of Fortuin where they eventually dug in for the night on the Zonnebeke Ridge. It is difficult to understand how several thousand men can be missed in a battlefield as crowded as the Ypres salient was becoming, but none of the battalions in the line made contact with Hasler as he marched his men through the night. When dawn broke Hasler was to discover that the main body of his Brigade was dug in some 700 yards to the south, that is behind Wallace's Detachment, and situated in a difficult position for the relief or reinforcement of that unit should that be necessary during the coming daylight hours.

Other troop movements during the hours of darkness came as a direct result of the order issued by Plumer in the early afternoon. Alderson reorganized his forces accordingly by relieving those units who had been in the line the longest. Geddes' Detachment was relieved by Brigadier General Wanless O'Gowan's 13 Brigade, and their place defending the bridges across the Yser Canal was taken by the now sadly depleted 1 Canadian Brigade. The three reserve battalions that had been attached to Geddes' Detachment remained in reserve at Potijze.

Although there had been much troop movement both in and out of the line as the generals tried desperately to organize the best defence they could around Ypres, there were still some noticeable gaps as the dawn of 26th April approached. The first such gap was about a quarter of a mile wide, and lay between the left flank of the 3rd Royal Fusiliers and the right of the 1st Hampshires, the latter of whom had just entered the line to the east of Gravenstafel. Another gap of about a half a mile was present between the left of the 1st Hampshires and those companies defending the area near Boetleer's Farm on the other side of the village of Gravenstafel. Finally, there was a gap, the largest, of about 1,000 yards between the latter units and Wallace's Detachment in front of Fortuin. These areas had been the scene of bitter fighting, and although all the attacks had been beaten off there was still a need for consolidation before the troops in the area could withstand any heavy German assault.

It was fortunate for the French that during 25th April the Germans had abandoned all plans to continue their effort along the Yser Canal. The French were trying to get their reserves and reinforcements into the area, but only one regiment of the 153rd Division had reached it during the day. General Putz saw fit to reorganize his forces so that the 45th Division and half the 87th Division, under General Quiquandon, would hold the south of his sector whilst the 153rd Division, when it had finally arrived, and the other half of the 87th Division, under General Deligny, were to hold the north. Putz remained optimistic and even returned the cavalry loaned to him by Smith-Dorrien the day before, though he did request to keep the horse artillery. However, since all his replacements had not arrived in the area, Putz was not in the position to make any substantial effort at regaining lost ground – in fact, holding the line was probably about the best the British could expect for the time being. However, as the day wore on and more troops arrived, the optimism in the French camp grew, and it was proposed that a counter-attack could be launched the following day using the divisions already in the area plus the 18th and 153rd Divisions that were now arriving. Naturally, the French turned to the British for support in the venture and the Commander-in-Chief agreed to this request. To assist in the defence of the salient the Lahore Division of the Indian Army had arrived in the area. Sir John French now put these troops at the disposal of Sir Horace Smith-Dorrien and his Second Army to assist in the support of the French attack. The French had proposed that the attack should commence at 5 pm the following day. Smith-Dorrien recognized that it was likely to be difficult to achieve a joint action of this type in such a short period of time – he also recognized that some action on the part of the French was going to be necessary if he was not to lose his own forces in the salient. Therefore, he agreed to the French request and, with only minor changes to the French proposal, he set to work preparing his forces for the counter-attack whereby the French were supposed to regain much of the ground they had lost three days before.

Immediately, officers from the Indian division were sent into the salient for reconnaissance, particularly to find the best way of getting the Division to the assembly point around Wieltje in the short time that was available. However, not for the first time since the fighting had begun, the French began to have second thoughts about the proposed attack, and eventually cut the attack to using only part of the 18th Division and those units already in the line. This meant that they were not putting enough weight into the attack and were, perhaps, relying too heavily on the effort that Smith-Dorrien could muster in his Second Army. To make matters worse they insisted that the start time was moved forward to 2 pm. Smith-Dorrien was astonished by such a proposal and angrily reported the situation to his Commander-in-Chief. Not unexpectedly, Sir John French informed him that he must support the French although Smith-Dorrien pointed out that there simply was no time for him to organize such an attack if it was expected to be successful. French took no notice and instructed Smith-Dorrien to carry on with the preparation. It must have been with some foreboding that Smith-Dorrien continued with the work of preparation. It was 2.15 am before his headquarters were able to issue the operational orders for the attack and formalize the plan that had been discussed during the afternoon of 25th April. After all the effort and sacrifice that had gone into the defence of the salient on 25th April, it began to look as if yet another hastily planned attack was going to be set in motion long before it had been thoroughly prepared – it was not a very auspicious start to another day of defending the salient.

Notes

1. See Appendix III for Order of Battle.
2. See *Bullets and Billets*, Bairnfather, p95.
3. See *Official History, 1915 Vol. 1*, p242.
4. See Wylly, *Crown and Company*, p41.
5. ibid., p40.
6. The wood spoken of here is Kitchener's Wood, 2nd Lieut. Bruce Bairnsfather was one of the wounded officers. See War Diary of the 1st Royal Warwicks.
7. SE of Shell Trap Farm.
8. Cheddar Villa Area.
9. About 500 yards SE of Oblong Farm.
10. Shell Trap Farm.
11. Woodland Farm.
12. Vanheule Farm.
13. Probably the Haanebeek.
14. See Dancocks, op.cit., footnote p41.

15. See Marsay, *Baptism of Fire*, p117.
16. See Hughes and Dixon, op.cit., p33.
17. See Dancocks, op.cit., p41.
18. ibid., p42.
19. See McWilliams and Steel, op.cit., p175.
20. Lieutenant Colonel Lipsett was later promoted to Major General and was commanding the 4th Division when he was killed in action on 14th October 1918. Lieutenant Colonel Tuxford became a Brigadier General and survived the war.
21. See 1st Monmouths War Diary.
22. See Batchelor and Mateson *VCs of the First World War*, p74.
23. See Mitchinson, *Gentlemen and Officers*, p65.
24. ibid., p66.

CHAPTER EIGHT

The Battle of Saint Julien
Day 3 – 26th April 1915

The situation for the front line troops defending the salient on the dawn of 26th April was not good. True, it had been improved somewhat by the movements of 25th April, but the continual narrowing of the salient was making life very difficult, since the German forces ranged around it were able to fire to just about any point within it. Also there were still gaps in the line and before this day was out, these were going to cause problems and add to the confusion. It was in response to these difficulties that Smith-Dorrien had agreed to cooperate with the French, though with a clearly stated reluctance, particularly after the French had decided that their attack was to commence some three hours earlier than they had originally planned. The organization was hurried but at 2.15 am the Second Army headquarters was able to issue Operation Order No.8 (see Appendix IV) detailing the proposals for a joint operation with the French to take place at 2 pm that afternoon. In the course of the order it states:

> That portion of the 2nd Army facing North will assume the offensive, in conjunction with the French, in order to drive the enemy away from the position he now occupies.[1]

The order goes on to refer to that mixture of troops falling mainly under the control of Lieutenant General Alderson and includes only one fresh brigade – the 11 Brigade – which had arrived on the scene during the evening of the previous day. The rest of the units involved had all been in action and many had suffered substantial casualties. The staff of the Second Army headquarters, in all fairness, were well aware of this,

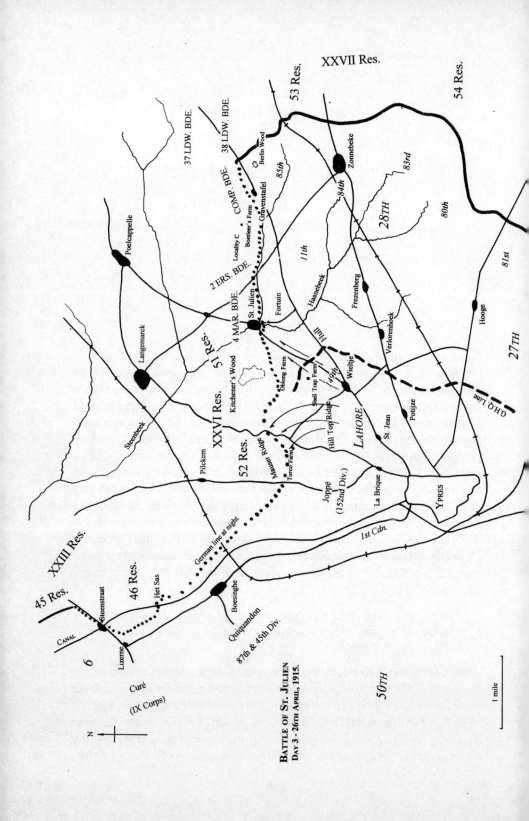

XXVII Res.

54 Res.

53 Res.

83rd

80th

81st

Zonnebeke

28TH

84th

Berlin Wood

85th

11th

Haanebek

Frezenberg

Hooge

27TH

37 LDW. BDE.

38 LDW. BDE.

COMP. BDE.

Gravenstafel

Verlorenhoek

Boetler's Farm

Locality C

St. Julien

Fortuin

IIIH

Wietje

Potijze

2 ERS. BDE.

4 MAR. BDE.

149th

St. Jean

GHQ Line

Poelcappelle

Kitchener's Wood

Oblong Farm

Shell Trap Farm

LAHORE

51 Res.

Langemarck

Hill Top Ridge

XXVI Res.

Mauser Ridge

Turco Farm

La Brique

YPRES

Pilckem

52 Res.

Joppé
(152nd Div.)

Steenbeek

German line at night.

1st Cdn.

XXIII Res.

46 Res.

Het Sas

Boesinghe

45 Res.

Steenstraat

Quiquandon

CANAL

6

Lizerne

87th & 45th Div.

50TH

Curé

(IX Corps)

N

BATTLE OF ST. JULIEN
DAY 3 - 26TH APRIL, 1915.

1 mile

though perhaps not fully aware; to add weight to the attack they added the Lahore Division from the Indian Army Corps to those forces already in the salient. Its officers had already begun to reconnoitre the ground for the approach in the hours of daylight during the evening of 25th April. At 10.30 am V Corps issued its Operation Order No.12 outlining its expectations (see Appendix IV) and gave the following arrangements for the Lahore Division:

The Lahore Division is assembling as follows:
Jullundur Brigade on right,
Ferozepore Brigade on left assemble about Wieltje and Saint Jean and will be deployed ready to begin an advance by 1.20 pm from an east and west line from Farm in C28a *(Wieltje Farm)* to Ypres-Langemark Road. The Sirhind Brigade will be in reserve about Potijze.[2]

The objectives of the attack by the Division were to support the movement of the French, whilst at the same time assaulting the German line in front of Kitchener's Wood and Saint Julien, with a view to forcing the enemy back on Langemarck. Just how wishful the thinking was for this attack will become clear shortly but first it is necessary to discuss the French proposals for their attack on the left, which the Second Army was supporting.

Immediately to the left of the Second Army the French had rearranged their command structure such that General Joppé, commanding the 152nd Division, was to take charge of that portion of the attack nearest to the British sector, with the addition of Mordacq's Brigade of *Zouaves* from the 45th Division. His objective was to push the enemy northwards on Pilkem and Langemarck in the area between the Yser Canal and the Ypres-Langemarck road. The 152nd Division had only recently arrived in the area and was more or less at full strength and there was much optimism in the French camp as to the outcome of the impending attack. Further north the French 153rd Division and part of the 18th Division, commanded by Generals Deligny and Lefèvre, both recent arrivals in the area, were to assault Lizerne to wrest this village from the German grasp and force them back across the Canal. The Germans had not pressed their attacks in the area on 25th April and this probably assisted the French greatly in their preparations. This northern attack, commanded by General Curé, the French IX Corps commander, was then to be directed towards Steenstraat, Bixschoote and Het Sas and was to be supported by the Belgians on its left. In the centre of these two attacks General Quiquandon, commanding the rest of the 45th Division and the 87th Division, was to take advantage of the successes on his flanks to drive the Germans from the western bank of the Canal. Once again the

127

French seemed determined to regain lost ground and, for the first time, they were prepared to use reasonably fresh troops to try and achieve this. But, even before details were finalized by the British command for their support, the French had reduced the weight of the attack to no more than the seventeen battalions that were already in the line. They were not prepared to commit any more troops to increase the chances of success to an attack with objectives that must have looked difficult to achieve to the British commanders, even if the French used everything at their disposal. It did not matter that Smith-Dorrien had complained to his chief – he was told in no uncertain terms that he was to carry on with his hasty plans to cooperate fully with an ally that appeared to be, at best, only half hearted in its commitment to the attack and at worst over ambitious.

To add to all this activity there had been reports, totally incorrect as it was to turn out, that there had been a breakthrough on the 11 Brigade front in the area of Gravenstafel Ridge. As a consequence of this the 2 and 3 Canadian Brigades were ordered forward once again. These battle scarred units marched back through shellfire towards the line before the error had been realized, then they were ordered to dig-in as support and were forced to endure yet another day of shelling though, thankfully, it resulted in few casualties. The scare had arisen as a result of the Germans trying to make their way through the quarter of a mile gap between the 1st Hampshires and the 3rd Royal Fusiliers under the cover of an early morning mist. It has been recorded that one party of the Germans even shouted, "We are the Royal Fusiliers", as they advanced, but an officer of the Hampshires noticed that the accent was other than it should have been for the Londoners of the battalion concerned, and he ordered his men to open fire.[3] The Germans rapidly dispersed, but for the rest of the morning they shelled the area from that of the 85 Brigade all along the Gravenstafel Ridge in an attempt to dislodge the defenders, whilst attempting to use their infantry to make the best advantage of the gaps in the British line. The situation in this part of the line was that the 3rd Royal Fusiliers had turned their left flank around Berlin Wood to try and contact the Hampshires but a gap remained, whilst a larger gap to the left of the Hampshires was at least partially covered by a party consisting of two companies of the 2nd King's Own Shropshire Light Infantry and the 6th Durham Light Infantry, under the command of Lieutenant Colonel R.J. Bridgford. This party had been sent to relieve Moulton-Barrett's Detachment which, following the wounding of Major Moulton-Barrett, was by that time under the command of Captain R.T.K. Auld, also of the 2nd Northumberland Fusiliers. This command was further reinforced later in the day by one company of the 1st Welsh from the 28th Division. As the early morning hours passed, the Germans made progress with their attacks developing from Locality C, and by 4.30 am they had succeeded in driving the remaining British forces from the crest of Gravenstafel Ridge. By 6.30 am the Germans had succeeded in reaching the cross-roads 1,500 yards south-west of Gravenstafel[4] but they could not proceed further. The British line, though still with some gaps, held once again and as the time wore on the situation was steadily improving, as the available troops were being utilized in the defence of the salient. It was, however, a very trying day, if only because of the shellfire. Wallace's Detachment was by that time almost cut off and so heavily shelled that everyone thought that they would have to fight to the finish. It did not come to that end, and at nightfall the weary remains of the Detachment were relieved by the 5th Green Howards and 5th Durham Light Infantry of the 150 Brigade, who had spent a very wearing day under shellfire in the support lines after their initiation into the battle the day before. Private Jim Stevenson of the 5th Green Howards summed up their day :

> Dawn – another thick mist all round. Stuck in the trenches all day – 'A' Company suffered many casualties from the shelling and the continuous sniping. Left the trenches at 8.30 pm for the second time to dig more trenches – it was a quiet night, except for occasional shellfire. We later moved forward with the 5th Durhams to relieve the London Regiment.[5]

The fact that the Germans did not follow up their intense shelling by more vigorous infantry attacks during the day is perhaps significant. It has been said that Duke Albrecht's 4th Army, comprising the five Army Corps and five Brigades in front of Ypres, was itself nearing exhaustion after four days of continual fighting. It had undoubtedly suffered badly at the hands of the defenders of the salient and its losses were high. However, it had not suffered the intense artillery bombardments that the British and Canadians had and it was still numerically superior. Whilst it is probably true to say that the Germans were feeling the effects of the fighting, it is also true that they were conserving their forces for later efforts. Nevertheless, the attack which swept them as far as Kansas Cross, south-west of Gravenstafel, was to mark the end of their infantry's advance in the Ypres area for the month of April 1915. At the beginning of the attack they had sought to flatten the line around Ypres and to capture the Yser Canal as far as Ypres. In so far as it would have been difficult to capture the Canal without the town it must be assumed that the capture of Ypres was also considered important. In this respect, at least, their objectives had been thwarted since the release of gas four days earlier.

Meanwhile, the preparations for the attack of the Lahore Division continued. The two front line brigades made their way to the form-up positions and at 1.20 pm the artillery commenced its preparatory bombardment of the German positions. There had been little time for the Lahore Division's artillery to prepare; some of the guns had been left on the west bank of the canal, and only those required for the close support of the infantry had accompanied the Division eastwards. There the guns were sited as best they could be, though there was no chance for them to register any suitable German targets, and in many cases their guns were placed in the open, clearly visible to the Germans and open to counter battery fire from the start. Elsewhere the artillery was ordered to support the Division, and such artillery that was not needed for the support and protection of the 28th Division was also ordered to join in the preparation. The bombardment lasted forty minutes and at 2 pm it opened a five minute rapid fire at which time the French, British and Indian forces began their assault.

East of the Langemarck-Ypres road the Ferozepore Brigade was deployed with three battalions in the front line; the Connaught Rangers were on the left; the 57th Wilde's Rifles were in the centre, while the 129th Baluchis were on the right of the Brigade. To the right of this brigade was the Jullundur Brigade which had also deployed three battalions in the front line, with the 47th Sikhs on the left, against the Ferozepore Brigade; the 40th Pathans were in the centre and the 1st Manchesters on the right flank of the Brigade. The attack was to take them over the corpse littered ground that had been travelled by the Geddes' Detachment three days earlier; that is, generally north and east in the direction of Saint Julien and Kitchener's Wood. The soldiers of the attacking brigades cannot have been very inspired by the sight of so many corpses littering the battlefield in the direction they were to assault. However, they were quickly out of their trenches and advancing in a very determined and thoroughly disciplined manner along the southern flanks and towards the crest of Hill Top Ridge. As the movement into the open ground commenced, the Germans opened up a fire with their 5.9-inch heavy field howitzers that was both heavy and accurate. On the right of the attack the heaviest casualties occurred as the battalions crested the ridge and the artillery took devastating effect, with the medium calibre shells ripping huge holes in the advancing ranks. In some cases whole platoons were knocked out by a single shell and the British and Indians fell in heaps.[6] It was not the only problem the advancing troops had to contend with, for they were also subjected to a very intense machine-gun and rifle fire which crackled along the line and cut them down as if:

. . . a scythe (was) being drawn across the legs of the troops as they advanced. At one moment they were moving forward as if nothing could stop them, the next second they had simply collapsed.[7]

The attack was being destroyed as both artillery and machine gunners took advantage of a target of massed troops advancing in daylight. From left to right of the attack the story was the same. The Connaught Rangers' advance had been slowed by a number of hedges which they had to pass through, all the time hampered by heavy fire. The battalion fell a little behind as a result of this but soon met the full ferocity of the German fire and managed to close to within about 120 yards of the enemy. To do this they had lost fifteen officers and 361 other ranks. The 57th Wilde's Rifles advanced more quickly, but in a matter of minutes they had taken heavy casualties, losing no fewer than seventeen officers as they advanced to within eighty yards of the enemy front line. Among the officers to fall was Captain P.D.A. Banks who, with his orderly, Bhan Singh, also wounded, two other wounded officers and an NCO, had taken cover from the murderous fire in a ditch. Banks ordered his small party to dig-in whilst he did his best to cover them, though he must have been fully aware that there was little he could realistically offer. Banks was then mortally wounded by a gunshot wound in the head, and although there was little hope for the officer, his orderly remained with him throughout the rest of the afternoon in the storm of shellfire and raking machine-gun bullets. At nightfall, although weak from his own wounds, Bhan Singh carried Banks out in an effort to get help. By the time he was back in the British lines Banks was dead. For his devotion to duty throughout that long afternoon and the effort he made to save the officer, Bhan Singh was awarded the DCM.

As the 129th Baluchis (Ferozepore Brigade) crested Hill Top Ridge, machine-gun fire from a farm (Canadian Farm) to their right, at the head of the shallow valley, began to force them left and into the 57th Wilde's Rifles who suffered heavy casualties during the day. This was also to effect the Jullundur Brigade, with the result that they were also forced to the left. At that moment the attack had lost direction and was beginning to move away from its objectives. At about this time the 40th Pathans machine-gun officer, Lieutenant F.L.R. Munn, was trying to get his gun forward to aid in the support of the attack. Most of his crews became casualties and the guns ended up in the Zwaanhofbeek. It was with considerable difficulty, and the bravery of Sepoy Haidar Ali and Sepoy Muktiara, that a machine gun of the 40th Pathans (Jullundur Brigade) was rescued from the Zwaanhofbeek between Hill Top and Mauser ridges, as the Pathans managed to carry their advance closest to the enemy.[8] Then to the frustration of the surviving machine gunners they found that the machine gun was jamming repeatedly, apparently damaged by its immersion in the muddy waters of the Zwaanhofbeek. That day the 40th Pathans, who were in their first battle since arriving in France at the beginning of April, got as close as anyone to the enemy with their bombing officer, Lieutenant R.J. Thornton, reaching a point about forty yards in front of the German wire. Once wounded, Thornton was forced to remain where he was with virtually no cover, except that offered by the manure piles, for the remaining hours of daylight. The fact that the 40th Pathans were able to close with the enemy at all must be in no small way down to the leadership of its officers such as Captain J.F.C. Dalmahoy of whom John Buchan was to write:[9]

> The 40th Pathans were amongst the chief sufferers. The Colonel fell, and nearly all the British officers were killed or wounded. There died Captain Dalmahoy, a soldier of exceptional gallantry and skill, who still led on his men after he had been six times hit.

The commanding officer, Lieutenant Colonel F. Rennick, was mortally wounded during the attack and was one of five commanding officers who became casualties that afternoon in the Lahore Division.

To the right of the attack, the 1st Manchesters got to within sixty yards of the enemy, but by that time most of the officers were casualties and sergeants took control of the depleted companies and privates commanded platoons. It had been a dreadful half an hour or so for the advancing battalions, which can be put into some kind of context when it is realized that three batteries of the German Guard Cavalry Division fired 2,000 rounds against the attack, that is, something over 150 rounds per gun. It was a devastating fire which the Germans were able to put down even though they were themselves partially enfiladed from the direction of Boesinge. The Manchesters lost 289 officers and men in that short space of time including their commanding officer Lieutenant Colonel H.W.E. Hitchins. The 47th Sikhs suffered even greater casualties when all but one of their British officers became casualties. The command of the battalion then devolved to the surviving officer, Lieutenant A.E. Drysdale.

> He rose most nobly to his task, cheering men forward and leading then under an infernal fire to a point within seventy yards of the enemy, where he held on . . .[10]

However, by the end of the fighting the 47th Sikhs could muster no more than ninety-six officers and men having sustained almost 350 casualties during the advance.

To the left of the Lahore Division General Joppé had launched his attack promptly at 2 pm and at first it seemed to be making good progress. At 2.20 pm, at about the same time as the British and Indian units were closing on the German wire, the French were halted as the enemy discharged gas immediately in front of them as a defensive measure. The experience of 22nd April had left the French very cautious of gas and they hesitated, and although the gas blew across their front towards the Lahore Division, the French finally withdrew to their support line between La Belle Alliance and South Zwaanhof Farm. In the Lahore Division the gas had the immediate effect of halting the attack in its tracks. These soldiers had not encountered anything like this but the warnings they had been given did help them as they began to wet rags and handkerchiefs with which they covered their faces. Some of the Indian troops had no means of protection and were forced to fall back, but the Connaught Rangers, the 1st Manchesters, the 40th Pathans and the 47th Sikhs held their positions under both the gas and the very heavy fire. This is clearly explained by the historians of the Indian Corps:

> The troops were quite unprovided with any means of warding off the effects of the fumes. The most they could do was to cover their noses and mouths with wet handkerchiefs or pagris, and, in default of such poor resource, to keep their faces pressed against the scanty parapet. It was of little avail, for in a few minutes the ground was strewn with bodies of men writhing in unspeakable torture while the enemy seized the opportunity to pour in a redoubled fire.[11]

The gas had provided the desired effect on both the French and British sectors of the front.

The release of gas does not seem to have been planned as a defensive action. It appears that the cylinders had been dug into position ready for an attack that the Germans were planning themselves. The pressure that the German front line had been placed under by the combined French and British attack had persuaded local commanders to release the gas or, at least, some of it. The German account of the event runs:

> Incidentally during an enemy counter attack on the 26th April in the area south-east of Pilkem, the detachment of the gas cylinder batteries released gas from a few cylinders for defensive purposes; with good results as far as can be gathered from the records.[12]

Some authorities, including the Germans themselves, suggest that the decision had been made by the men of the gas battery acting under their own initiative. This is to some extent born out by the fact that the breeze that afternoon appears to have been westerly or north-westerly since the gas was blown from the French to the British and Indian front. This is unlikely to have been thought to have been the appropriate direction for the release of gas except perhaps as a kind of last ditch measure, as it appears to have been used here. However, the net effect of the release of gas from some of the cylinders dug-in to the German front line was to be satisfactory for the Germans, since it stopped the advance in its tracks, and allowed them even more time to use their superior artillery to wreak even greater havoc amongst the troops who were then trying to dig-in to gain what little cover they could.

During this attack Jemadar Mir Dast of the 57th Wilde's Rifles took charge of his platoon after all the officers had been put out of action. He rallied the men and steadied them through the discharge of the gas and then completed his day's work by rescuing eight battalion officers who were lying wounded on the battlefield. This was made even more remarkable by the fact that during his rescue mission he was wounded himself. For his actions throughout this awful afternoon he was to be awarded the Victoria Cross. In a similar manner Acting Corporal Issy Smith of the 1st Manchesters rescued a number of injured men whilst under the heavy fire put down by the Germans and he, too, was awarded the Victoria Cross.[13] It was a just reward for two of the many acts of gallantry during the attack of the Lahore Division which otherwise went unrewarded. For instance, Major H.R.C. Deacon, of the Connaught Rangers, and a mixed party of about 100 British and Indian soldiers refused to give up the fight or, indeed, any of the ground they had gained during their advance. The Germans stormed their position and in fierce hand-to-hand fighting Deacon's party was slowly forced backwards. This went on until the mixed band of fighters had been pushed back about eighty yards when the Germans withdrew. Presumably the enemy had driven them far enough away from the trenches so they could not be a great problem. Deacon and his party remained at the spot, about 100 yards in front of their original line, until after dark when it was recognized that the position was hopeless and they withdrew. Deacon was never recognized for his stubborn leadership that day though he did go on to be awarded a DSO and Bar before the war finished. In spite of all the bravery it had been a black day for the division, which had suffered 1,829 casualties to all ranks, including two battalion commanders killed and another three wounded. They had not been able to gain any ground that they could hold and by nightfall the British line was back more or less exactly where it had started.

The considerable casualties suffered were the effect of a hastily drawn up plan for the Lahore Division, but to its right the effects were every bit as devastating, if not more so, on the 149 Brigade. The Brigade, commanded by Brigadier General J.F. Riddell, had been in reserve in the vicinity of Wieltje. During the morning Riddell had released the 5th

Northumberland Fusiliers to be used in the Fortuin area, where it had been wrongly reported that the Germans had broken through one of the gaps in the British line. Therefore Riddell's Brigade was only three battalions strong (the 4th, 6th and 7th Northumberland Fusiliers) when at 1.30 pm he received Lieutenant General Alderson's orders to move forward to take part in the attack which had, in fact, already begun with the shelling of the Lahore Division's objectives. Riddell had to act and he had to act quickly for his divisional commander, or more correctly at this time Alderson, would have expected him to be moving into action already in any case, since the "Operation Order No.1" (dated 26.4.15, see Appendix IV) had been issued from Alderson's headquarters at 12.30 pm. This order stated in part that:

> The Northumbrian *(sic. should read Northumberland)* Brigade will attack Saint Julien and advance astride the Wieltje-St. Julien road at the same time as the Lahore Division moves forward.[14]

This dreadful mix up has been seen by some historians as another example of the breakdown in staff work during the battle, but this criticism should be mitigated by examining the train of events that brought about the situation where a Brigadier General could receive orders requiring him to attack after the attack had already started on his flank. In the first place Smith-Dorrien had pointed out that there was insufficient time to get all the elements of the attack ready by the 2 pm start time. He had been ignored – no fault in staff work there. Second, the staff had worked out a plan and issued orders, although hastily drawn up, by 2.15 am. The lack of time that had been allowed necessitated their brevity, but the Second Army staff should not be blamed here. Third, the V Corps orders were issued at 10.30 am, less than three hours before the 149 Brigade were expected to move, and in that time the V Corps orders had to be disseminated through, and digested by, the divisional commanders, including Alderson, before it could even reach Riddell at the 149 Brigade headquarters on the battlefield itself. The fact that Riddell actually got the order at all an hour after it had been issued by Alderson is perhaps an indication that the staff had functioned reasonably well. If the attack had commenced at 5 pm as had originally been supported by Smith-Dorrien, then there was, perhaps, some time for Riddell to deploy his Brigade and examine the ground, albeit briefly. It had taken some time for the order to filter downwards but it should be remembered that this was a battle situation in which communication was, at best, difficult. Telephone lines were frequently disrupted and the only way to the front by foot was through Ypres, or across one of the canal bridges close to the town, all of which were more or less continuously under fire. Taking all of this in to account it is not sufficient to say that the delay in the issuing of orders was down to a lack of staff work; there may have been faults on their part and the plan was certainly hurried, but it should be remembered that they were being pressurized by the French on the one hand and the Germans, who were dominating the battlefield with their artillery, on the other. There can be no doubt that issuing an order to Riddell at 12.30 pm and expecting him to act upon it inside the hour was very optimistic to say the least, and it would seem to be likely that Alderson's staff were well aware of this, but the British were in a position where they had to cobble together an almost makeshift plan to accommodate the requirements of the French and their own Commander-in-Chief. If, indeed, there were any major failings in the staff work then perhaps they should be levelled at Smith-Dorrien who should have refused to acquiesce to Sir John French's wishes to keep the French commanders happy. Fortunately, Sir Horace Smith-Dorrien was far too good a soldier not to realize that if he did raise too many obstacles, French would simply replace him with someone who would do his bidding. Smith-Dorrien undoubtedly recognized the difficult position he had been placed in, and in turn the trouble that his orders were likely to cause to the front line units, but as a truly professional soldier he got on with trying to organize the best possible plan he could in the time allowed, recognizing that it was likely to prove to be insufficient against an enemy who was by that time well entrenched around the north flank of the Ypres salient. The fault of the situation that was developing as the battle progressed should, without question, be placed at the feet of Sir John French and the attitude he adopted, against any advice and military sense, to keep his allies, and in particular General Foch, happy though, perhaps, some of that blame should be shared by Kitchener for placing French in a position he was incapable of handling.

All of this could not have been of any interest to the man on the ground, in this case Brigadier General Riddell, for he still needed to get his men moving. He acted immediately and sent his three remaining battalions into action as soon as he received the order. The first problem that Riddell needed to overcome was that of getting his battalions to the starting point, and to do this it was necessary to feed them through the limited gaps in the wire protecting the GHQ line. Such was the haste with which the brigade was put into motion that they did not even have time to collect extra ammunition, but by 1.50 pm they were all moving to the start position. As they filtered through the GHQ line the battalions began to suffer heavily from shellfire but this brigade, like the others of the 50th Division new to the front, remained steady and advanced in artillery formation either side of the Wieltje-Saint Julien road towards their objective of the latter village. As they advanced, diverging from the main direction of attack of the Lahore Division, a unit of the 10 Brigade was supposed to move forward to fill the gap that was forming. After the events of 25th April, Brigadier General Hull did not have the troops to spare and he had informed Alderson to that effect. Nevertheless, Hull went forward personally to inform the 7th Argylls that they were to leave the trenches to form a support battalion as the attack of the Lahore Division developed against Kitchener's Wood. However, as discussed already, the Lahore Division was forced left, the attack did not develop on Kitchener's Wood, and the 7th Argylls, therefore, did not leave their trenches. None of this can have been known to Riddell as his brigade moved forward diagonally across Kitchener's Wood with their left flank exposed to machine-gun fire from that direction. The 149 Brigade advanced steadily and, as the first Territorial Force Brigade to go into action in its own right, it set a very high standard for others to follow. It did, however, suffer terrible losses from both shellfire and machine-gun fire as it did so, and consequently it did not advance very far in front of the British front line before it was stopped. The Divisional History comments:

> Just when the 6th Battalion had reached its furthest point in the direction of Saint Julien, i.e., at 3.45 pm, their Brigadier met his death. General Riddell (accompanied by his Brigade Major), for the purpose of getting into close touch with his battalion commanders, left the support trench in which he had established his headquarters at about 3.30 pm and proceeded towards "Vanheule Farm". At about 150 yards south of this farm he received a bullet through the head and fell dead.[15]

The death of Riddell was no surprise to his Brigade Major since he was well aware that Riddell would want to lead from the front:

> I did all that I could to stop him going into what I knew was almost certain death, but it was of no avail, as he was too brave a man to think of self under the circumstances.[16]

Riddell had, apparently, got close enough to be seen by the men of his Brigade and he stepped out in front with a stick in his hand to lead them. One eyewitness is recorded as saying that even the wounded rose to their feet to follow him. It was one tragic loss amongst the many the Brigade was to suffer that day.

With casualties mounting the Brigade came to a halt and dug-in where it was – there was no thought of retiring. However, it soon became clear that the fact they had not paused to collect extra ammunition was going to become a problem. Lieutenant Colonel A.J. Foster of the 4th Northumberland Fusiliers tried to contact brigade headquarters to remedy the situation, only to be told of Riddell's death and that he now commanded the Brigade. He then ordered the Brigade to dig-in and stay where they were. They held their line, slightly forward of the original British front line but still some way short of Saint Julien, until early the following morning when Foster and Hull decided that their position was untenable and they were withdrawn. This abortive, largely unsupported and hurried attack on Saint Julien had cost the three battalions of the Brigade a total of forty-two officers and 1,912 other ranks, killed, wounded and missing, or about two thirds of their strength.[17] It was, perhaps, the most appalling counter-attack to be undertaken in those vicious days of the Battle of Saint Julien.

Before the day had ended there was one further movement of troops on the left of the British line. The French decided that they should regain the trenches they had lost when the gas had been discharged early in the afternoon. To that end the 4 Moroccan Brigade, forming part of General Joppé's 152nd Division, moved forward and took the unoccupied Turco Farm completely unopposed. The 8th *Tirailleurs*, of the same brigade, also moved forward at about 7 pm to occupy the trenches they had abandoned in the early afternoon. The Official History notes that they did so

> . . . with such noise and shouting that they early drew fire. They came nearly abreast of the Lahore Division but they went no further.[18]

This movement was accompanied, if not fully supported, by three battalions of the Sirhind Brigade (15th Sikhs, the 4th Gurkha Rifles and the 1st Highland Light Infantry) of the Lahore Division, who were moving up to relieve the battered Ferozepore and Jullundur Brigades on the left of the British sector. At nightfall there was a suggestion that these relatively fresh troops would make an attack on the German defences. Lieutenant Colonel J. Hill, commanding the 15th Sikhs, went forward with his battalion and the Gurkhas to establish the full situation. It was a fruitless exercise, as it took some time simply for Hill to locate groups of the most advanced men. He eventually contacted Major Deacon who was, as already mentioned, hanging on to a trench with an ever-dwindling party of British and Indians. From this trench and with the information supplied by Deacon, Hill was able to assess the situation more completely. He then reported the situation to his brigadier,[19] with the recommendation that the attack on the German lines be abandoned. Hill considered it would have been pointless to attack at night, when it was clear to him that the German wire was still intact. Fortunately the brigadier concurred with Hill's assessment of the situation and consequently Hill withdrew his party and brought out Major Deacon and his group at the same time. The Sirhind Brigade then proceeded to consolidate the position in the original front line with the help of the 3rd Sappers and Miners and the 34th Sikh Pioneers.

Through the history of the Great War the term disaster has been frequently used and often with less reason than could be applied to the counter-attacks of 26th April 1915; it had been a truly disastrous day for the British in the salient. The casualties for the day had been heavy, with approximately 4,000 being sustained by the Lahore Division and the 149 Brigade alone on a front of little more than one mile. There had been casualties all across the front including those resulting from the Germans' attack on the 11 Brigade and 85 Brigade at the eastern end of the salient. It is one thing to lose men in the defence of a position but 26th April should remembered as the day when men were lost in totally fruitless and ill-prepared attacks against an enemy that was reasonably well prepared and was superior in numbers and artillery. Whilst the plan may have had some merit, that is, to drive the Germans back and regain a more stable and wider salient, it had been conceived hurriedly and it had been paid for with the lives of brave men from Indian and Northumbrian Divisions. That night the main activity was one of rescue as groups of men went out into no man's land to attempt to recover the wounded. Whilst the Germans were not particularly active they did maintain a nervous and sporadic fire throughout the night. There was also much use of flares by both sides throughout the hours of darkness which hampered the recovery of casualties as would-be rescuers were illuminated to provide targets for the German machine gunners. Nevertheless the Germans too had been affected by the killing of the day and one soldier (Binding) was to write:

After fresh attacks a sleeping army lies in front of one of our brigades; they rest in good order, man by man, and will never rise again . . .[20]

It was a scene of carnage that the would-be rescuers picked over that evening, as the worst day of the battle for the Allies so far came to a close.

Elsewhere the Germans had not had it all their own way. In the area of Lizerne the 46th Reserve Division (XXIII Reserve Corps) was gradually forced back by the strong French effort. A German account of the day notes:

In the late evening Lizerne was taken by the French after heavy artillery bombardment; a breakthrough was feared, and a counter attack to recapture the place was ordered, but the 204th Reserve Infantry Regiment would not attempt it; "The infantry again evidently lacks the right offensive spirit" (war diary of the XXIII Reserve Corps). The enemy seemed superior in numbers so the corps commander decided to retire the front line.[21]

This comment is interesting since it highlights the refusal of an infantry regiment to counter-attack and also includes the comment from the corps war diary. These suggest that, at least in some places, the conditions on the battlefield were every bit as misunderstood by the German commanders as they were by the British or French commanders. The Germans, too, had suffered heavy casualties since the battle had opened and the casualty figures show that, by the end of April, the XXIII Reserve Corps and the XXVI Reserve Corps, who had been most heavily engaged, had suffered 6,761 and 6,231 casualties respectively. Whilst the Germans had initiated the battle and had won all the ground they had not, most certainly, had it all their own way. It is, therefore, to be expected that the battalions fighting in the northern part of the salient were becoming depleted and battle weary, and if the commander had been fully aware of the situation then the comment in the war diary would not have needed to have been made. Whilst the Germans had given ground around Lizerne it had been very slowly, but the French attacks between Lizerne and Het Sas had met with no success.

It is difficult to assess the French effort during this day of the Battle of Saint Julien, since it had been one of mixed fortunes for them. In the north they had captured Lizerne and it had been at some cost to the divisions involved. It had made some difference to the line but it was a long way short of re-establishing themselves across the canal as they had intended, and they had come nowhere near the objective of the day, which had been Bixschoote. Whilst the success was limited and qualified, the French, for the first time since the battle commenced, had made a real commitment to the fighting. They had even taken a number of prisoners and guns which had done something to restore the morale of the French in that area. This limited success could not be repeated in the ground immediately adjacent to the British. Once again the release of gas, one of the rare occasions when it was released for defensive purposes, had produced confusion in the French ranks, and although they had regained their start line, by the end of the day they had not made any progress towards any of their objectives. An indication of the level of commitment shown by Joppé's force is the fact that his Moroccans had relatively light casualties, with two officers and fourteen men being killed with about 200 wounded and missing. Many of the missing appear to have headed for the rear as soon as the gas was discharged but they rejoined the ranks later. Set against the almost 2,000 casualties in the 149 Brigade, the French would appear not to have been included in the battle in this area! In the central area General Quiquandon was unable to make any headway since his progress depended on the success of the actions on his flanks which did not occur.

At the close of 26th April nothing had been achieved for all the loss of life. For the defenders of the salient it must be looked upon as a day when they managed to keep out the Germans but at enormous cost. Even for the Germans the day would perhaps be seen as one of limited success for they had made but small gains against the brigades defending Gravenstafel Ridge. In what was an ostensibly offensive battle for them their greatest success for the day was in a defensive role, as they stayed within their lines and slaughtered British and Indian forces with some ease.

The line that existed by nightfall was, to say the least, precarious, and the salient had continued to narrow under the pressure of the Germans at its eastern extremities. It was now manned by French, Indian and British troops and was still supported by two Canadian Brigades. There had been some reorganization of the command structure on the previous day, but there was still room for improvement as these units were still difficult to control on a battlefield that was becoming crowded as the Germans continued to pressurize the northern flank. All of these matters were issues that would need to be faced by the French and the British before the fighting of the Second Battle of Ypres was finished; some hard decisions still needed to be made, as the commanders of both armies were forced to recognize some hard facts about the way the battle was being conducted.

Notes

1. Quoted in the *Official History 1915 Vol. 1* – see Appendix 26, p397, for full transcript.
2. Quoted in the *Official History 1915 Vol. 1* – see Appendix 27, p398, for full transcript.
3. See the account of the incident in Atkinson, *Regimental History: The Royal Hampshire Regiment Vol. 2*, p58.
4. This crossroads is shown as Kansas Cross on later trench maps of the area.
5. See Marsay, op.cit., p31.
6. See McWilliams and Steel, op.cit., p191.
7. ibid., p190, see also Merewether and Smith, *The Indian Corps in France*, p295.
8. Lieutenant Munn received the MC for his part in the action. Sepoy Haidar Ali was awarded the Indian Distinguished Service Medal and Sepoy Muktiara was awarded the Russian Medal of Saint George 4th Class.
9. Quoted in *The Bond of Sacrifice Vol. 2*, p117.
10. Merewether and Smith, op.cit., p297. Lieutenant Drysdale was awarded the MC for his part in this action.
11. ibid., p304.

12. Quoted in the *Official History 1915, Vol. 1*, p267.

13. The citations for both these awards can be found in Appendix II.

14. This order is as quoted in the *Official History 1915 Vol. 1*, p399. It should be noted that this is the second "Operational Order No. 10" issued in two days. The Northumbrian Division (50th) comprised the 1/Northumberland, 1/York and Durham and 1/Durham Light Infantry Brigades.

15. Quoted in Davies and Maddocks, *Bloody Red Tabs*, p102 (extract from Wyrall *The History of the 50th Division*).

16. Quoted in *The Bond of Sacrifice* Vol.2, p394.

17. It is worth noting that the casualties are comparable to those of the Lahore Division.

18. *Official History 1915, Vol. 1*, p261.

19. Brigadier General W.G. Walker VC.

20. Quoted in McWilliams and Steel, op.cit., p197.

21. Quoted in the *Official History 1915, Vol. 1*, p268.

CHAPTER NINE

The Battle of Saint Julien
Day 4 – 27th April 1915

The lack of success for the Lahore Division prompted Sir Horace Smith-Dorrien to pen a long and clear letter to Lieutenant General Sir William Robertson, Chief of the General Staff. In this letter[1] he sets out his concerns over the conduct of the French Army and the manner in which its commanders had approached the problem of regaining the ground lost to them on the opening day of the fighting. The French were still making noises about counter attacks but, in the mind of Smith-Dorrien, they were still proposing attacks which were under resourced in both manpower and artillery support. He did, however, recognize that the continued support for the French effort, such as it was, would be necessary – without support, both moral and material, the French were unlikely to do anything, and that would influence the British Army's defence of the northern part of the salient. It was, no doubt, with these factors in mind and to lend support to the French, that he had ordered the Lahore Division to cooperate in the French attack planned for 1.15 pm on Tuesday 27th April, 1915. But he also points out his reservations:

> I fear the Lahore Division have had very heavy casualties, and so they tell me have the Northumbrians, and I am doubtful if it is worth losing any more men to regain this French ground unless the French do something really big.[2]

It is quite clear that Smith-Dorrien had recognized two issues which were causing him problems and serious doubt. The first is that the French had not, to that time and after five days of heavy fighting, shown

143

themselves capable of living up to their grand ideas. The second was that, in allowing the French to continue with their rather half-hearted attempt he was sacrificing the troops he had at his disposal, and it should be said that these were, for the most part, well trained, experienced men of regular regiments, not to mention such Territorial Force troops who had been sufficiently well trained to fill the gaps made by the earlier fighting of the war. It was clear to him that the battle was becoming no more than a waste of life and, at a time when there was little chance of success, it was a waste of a precious resource to any army – its trained and experienced manpower.

It was also in this letter that Smith-Dorrien pointed out what he considered to be the consequence of the French inactivity, which was the withdrawal to a shorter, more defensible line closer to Ypres. The line he considered to be most suitable was the GHQ line:

> This, of course, means surrendering a great deal of trench line, but any intermediate line, short of that will be extremely difficult to hold, owing to the loss of the ridge to the east of Zonnebeke, which any withdrawal must entail.

At this point he detailed the line that he considered to be appropriate for a withdrawal and stated:

> I intend tonight if nothing special happens to reorganize the new front and to withdraw superfluous troops west of Ypres.

There was a lot of sense in the argument put forward by Smith-Dorrien. Whilst his resources were diminishing in terms of the assaulting infantry available, the narrowing salient was becoming overcrowded with all sorts of units besides infantry, such as the artillery, the Royal Engineers and other ancillary troops. The more crowded the salient became, the more difficult it was to control, and the greater the risk the forces were placed under in the event of a breakthrough by the Germans at, for instance, Lizerne or Het Sas. It was, perhaps, the vulnerability of his army in the salient that was of the greater concern to Smith-Dorrien, rather than the French regaining the ground that they had lost. Whilst it would probably have been useful to regain the ground lost, to establish a wider salient and to push the Germans away from the walls of Ypres, Smith-Dorrien was well aware that with the present commitment this was highly unlikely. For this reason he considered it important that this message was conveyed to the Commander-in-Chief so that an informed decision could be made at the very highest level. In so doing he had effectively terminated his own military career as the events of the day were to prove. In spite of the warnings which are inherent in his letter Smith-Dorrien went on:

It is very difficult to put a subject such as this in a letter without appearing pessimistic – I am not in the least, but as an Army Commander I have, of course, to provide for every eventuality and I think it is right to let the Chief know what is running in my mind.

The Chief's attitude to what was running in his mind will become clear later, but it was less to do with military sense than with politics and personal enmity between the two men. The politics of the situation were emotionally charged. First there was the obvious concern of Sir John French to be seen to be acting closely with his ally as he had been instructed by the War Office in London. The problem was, it would appear, that French was so beguiled with Foch's attitude that he was almost incapable of questioning the Frenchman's ideas and beliefs concerning the conduct of the battle. Second, there was, perhaps, the more emotive issue of surrendering yet more Belgian soil to the invader. Britain had, at least on the face of it, entered the war to defend Belgian neutrality and by the spring of 1915 was defending the last town of any real size that had not fallen in to German hands. To some extent the war had been "sold" to the people of Britain, not to mention neutral countries, on the basis of this defence. Therefore, it was considered possible for any withdrawal, no matter how tactically prudent, to be seen as yet another setback in the defence of "Gallant Little Belgium". Even if this issue was not uppermost in Sir John French's mind he would have been aware of the calls on him and his forces, and the defence of the salient was seen as a necessary fact of the conduct of the war – a fact that remained with the British Army until almost the end of the war. It was not the attitude that was being adopted by the French, which was set out quite clearly in an official document entitled *Franco-British Operations in France and Flanders*:

> The greater part, and the best, of the available shock troops were assembled in the region of Arras in view of the principal offensive to be launched at the beginning of May. This explains why the neighbouring sectors, themselves drained of troops, were unable to lend sufficient reinforcements in spite of the urgency. This is similarly the explanation of the momentary artillery inferiority on the Flanders front.[3]

General Foch had clearly come to the conclusion that the loss of ground around Ypres would need to be treated as a local setback and would need to be borne so that other issues could be addressed, not the least of these being the proposed offensive planned to the south of Ypres for May 1915. It also appears that Foch saw the loss of ground in Ypres as being more of a problem that the British would have to deal with, especially since there had been plans to relieve all the French divisions from the Ypres area. That this did not occur was a function of the need for troops in the Gallipoli landings,[4] but Foch did not consider that, since he had more or less written off the French part in the defence of the salient anyway.[5] The dilemma facing the British in the defence of the salient is clearly set out in the Official History:

> To resume the offensive vigorously before Ypres without serious rein-forcements was to invite failure and run the risk of heavy casualties without any compensatory success; while to make a really serious effort with large forces to recover all the lost ground might react adversely on the planned offensive further south and would to that extent be playing into the enemy's hands.[6]

Unfortunately for the Lahore Division it was the former course of action that was to be followed as the British Army commanders attempted to support half-hearted French ambitions. During the morning of 27th April, General Putz, the commander of the *Détachement d'Armée de Belgique*, issued an order for a further attack. A preliminary artillery bombardment was to commence at 12.30 pm, to be followed by an infantry attack at 1.15 pm. It was to support this attack that Smith-Dorrien had ordered the Lahore Division into action for the second time in two days. Initially the infantry to be used by the French was to be of no greater weight than on the previous day but, at a request from Smith-Dorrien, General Putz ordered General Joppé to use all of the fresh brigade he had at his disposal and not keep one regiment in reserve. The net effect of this, and the other alterations the French made, was that there were only two extra battalions available for the French attack. Smith-Dorrien was not happy with this, since any movement made by the British depended upon the French maintaining the left flank so that the stronger their force the happier he could feel. There was nothing more he could do, however, and to comply with the wishes of his own commander he ordered the Lahore Division to provide support to the French attack. He made it clear that it was not to move until such a time as the French had advanced sufficiently to secure the left flank along the Ypres-Langemark road, which was to remain as the boundary between the two forces. At this stage it is clear that Smith-Dorrien was unprepared to throw away any more troops on the dreams of the French and becoming less inclined to cooperate and, increasingly, more inclined to consider a withdrawal to a line which could, at least, be defended in numbers should the Germans continue their assault. It was an attitude which was to have a considerable effect on the rest of the battle if not on the rest of the war. Smith-Dorrien's proposals to shorten the line may have been better received by almost any other senior commander except French on which it had the adverse effect of delaying the withdrawal which even French seemed to realize was not only

1. A pre-war photograph of the Cloth Hall and St Martin's Cathedral. Most of this was reduced to rubble during the fighting of 1915.

2. The action that won Second Lieutenant Geary the Victoria Cross. *(From* Deeds That Thrill the Empire*)*

3. Steenstraat. The French memorial marking the first use of poison gas in warfare. The original memorial was destroyed by the Germans in the Second World War.

4. The ground over which the 10th Canadians advanced on 22nd April to attack Kitchener's Wood. Nothing remains of the wood today but it would have been situated near to the crest of the gentle rise.

5. The memorial to the 10th Canadians at the site of Kitchener's Wood. A relatively new memorial to the Western Front but there can be none that is more deserved.

6. Shell Trap Farm as it is today. This was the farm where Canon Scott saw his first victim of gas and where Captain Scrimger won his VC. The land rises behind and to the left of the farm to a low ridge on top of which once stood Kitchener's Wood. This area eventually fell to the Germans on the last day of the fighting of Second Ypres.

7. Hill Top Ridge. The Indians attacked towards the crest parallel with the road and met the German artillery and machine-gun fire as they crested the ridge.

8. The grave of Brigadier General Julian Hasler at White House Cemetery.

9. Vancouver Cross. The Brooding Soldier Memorial to the Canadians who were killed in action during the fighting for Gravenstafel Ridge and St. Julien.

10. Frezenberg Ridge looking towards Zonnebeke. The British 28th Division held this portion of the ridge until 8th May when the Germans swept it aside.

11. Captain Alfred John Hamilton Bowen, 2nd Monmouths, winning the first of two DSOs.
(From Deeds That Thrill the Empire

12. *The Canadians at Ypres* – a painting by William Barnes Wollen. It captures the action of the Princess Patricia's Canadian Light Infantry at the Battle of Frezenberg.

(By permission of the Regiment)

13. The memorial to the "Originals" of the Princess Patricia's Canadian Light Infantry at Westhoek.

14. Bellewaarde Ridge – the British view. Railway Wood is on the crest of the ridge.

15. Bellewaarde Ridge – the German view. The attacking British forces would have climbed this rise to meet the German machine guns. The road on the right is along the line of the 1915 railway and Railway Wood is off picture to the right.

16. Lance Corporal W. Dixon, 3rd
Monmouths, a survivor of the
Frezenberg Ridge fighting was
later awarded a DCM for bravery
at Ypres.

17. Corporal J. H. Spencer, 1st
Monmouths and 171st Tunnelling
Company. He was one of the
party involved in the successful
mining of Hill 60 in April 1915.
He was killed in a later mining
operation at Hill 60.
(Photo: Ray Westlake)

18. Captain Charles Ernest William Bland DSO, 2nd King's Own Scottish Borderers. Killed on 23rd April. *(Photo: Southey)*

19. Captain Edward Henry Brocklehurst, King's. Killed in action at Hill 60 on May. *(Photo: Southey)*

20. Captain Gordon Cuthbert, 8th Middlesex. Killed in action 27th April. *(Photo: Southey)*

21. Captain Thomas Britain Forwood, 2n King's Own. Killed in action 8th May *(Photo: Sout*

22. Captain Alan Arthur Fowler, 2nd Cameron Highlanders. Killed in action 28th April. *(Photo: Southey)*

23. Second Lieutenant Dorrien Edward Grose-Hodge, 3rd Battalion the Suffolk Regiment attached to 1st Battalion. Killed in action 24th April. *(Photo: Southey)*

24. Captain Benjamin Lewis Perry, 1st Monmouths. Killed in action 26th April. *(Photo: Southey)*

25. Lieutenant Rowland George Pritchard, 1st Suffolks. Killed in action 24th April. *(Photo: Southey)*

26. Major William James Rowan-Robinson,
    2nd King's Shropshire Light Infantry.
    Killed in action 12th May. *(Photo: Southey)*

28. Second Lieutenant John Collet Tyler,
    Royal Artillery. Killed in action at Hill 60
    18th April.   *(Photo: Southey)*

27. Major Andrew Roddick, Essex Yeoman
    Killed in action 14th May. *(Photo: South*

29. Captain Cecil Francis Harvey Twining
    3rd Battalion the Hampshire Regimen
    attached to 1st Battalion. Killed in acti
    3rd May. *(Photo: Southey)*

30. Lieutenant Colonel Charles Augustus Vivian, 15th (Ludhiana) Sikhs. Killed in action 27th April. *(Photo: Southey)*

31. Sergeant William Pritchard and his son Private Reginald Pritchard, 3rd Monmouths. Both were killed on 2nd May 1915.

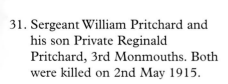

32. Second Lieutenant William Lucius Palmer, 3rd Monmouths. Nineteen-years-old. Killed during the bombardment of Frezenberg Ridge on 8th May 1915.
(Photo: RRW Museum, Brecon)

33. Lieutenant C. H. G. Martin, the machine-gun officer of the 3rd Monmouths. Killed on 2nd May 1915.   *(Photo: Southey)*

34. Captain I. E. M. Watkins, 2nd Monmouths. Killed in action on 7th May 1915.
(Photo: RRW Museum, Brecon)

35. Captain Alfred John Hamilton Bowen, 2nd Monmouths, in charge of C Company, on 8th May.

36. The dedication of the 1st Monmouths Memorial on Frezenberg Ridge. On the extreme left is Captain R. C. L. Thoms, seventh from the left is CSM R. Cheek and directly behind the stone is Lieutenant Colonel C. A. Evill – all suvivors of the fighting of Second Ypres. *(Photo: Len Jones)*

37. The Princess Patricia's Canadian Light Infantry return. Ceremony of remembrance in the Grote Markt in Ypres, 8th May 1985.

necessary but inevitable.[7] Ultimately it was to lead to the downfall of Smith-Dorrien and he never commanded an overseas unit again. This has been seen as a great disadvantage to the British War effort since Smith-Dorrien is seen by some as a very capable general whose involvement in the remainder of the war was sorely missed.[8]

The Sirhind Brigade, the freshest of those of the Lahore Division, was to be the main force to be employed in the British sector. The Brigade already had two battalions in the forward area, with the 15th Sikhs on the left against the Ypres-Langemark road and the 1st Highland Light Infantry to their right, in contact with the 13 Brigade positions. It was arranged that the 1/1st Gurkhas (Lieutenant Colonel W.C. Anderson) and 1/4th Gurkhas (Major B.M.L. Brodhurst) were to pass through these two units with the 4th King's in support, whereupon the 15th Sikhs and the 1st HLI would leave their positions to add further weight to the attack. The Ferozepore Brigade was to act to support the right flank of this Brigade, with the 9th Bhopal Infantry and the 4th Londons in the front line, followed immediately by the Connaught Rangers, then the 57th Wilde's Rifles and the 129th Baluchis. It was, in effect, a repetition of the attack of 26th April and there was no reason to suggest that there was any greater chance of success than there had been for that attack. It would appear that at this stage of the battle the British commanders were knowingly throwing away the lives of their soldiers with ill defined objectives in a desire to keep the French satisfied. They should have been questioning very closely, perhaps, the motives of the French, and should have been asking for a much bigger commitment than the French were prepared to offer. It was with these things in mind that Smith-Dorrien had written his long letter to Robertson. Nevertheless he had still ordered the Lahore Division to sacrifice itself in what he must have realized was most likely to be an unsuccessful operation.

It was unfortunate that this situation was muddied by the urgency of the situation and the political situation between Kitchener, French, Smith-Dorrien and their allies. In reality something needed to be done but each player in the scene saw a different mutually exclusive solution. Kitchener had left Sir John French in no doubt of his subordinate position to the wishes of Joffre and Foch. French felt he was being too tightly controlled and had become suspicious of practically everyone's motives, seeing his own career in peril in many of the actions of his own subordinates.[9] His compliance with the orders from London was mingled with distrust and suspicion of the French. Smith-Dorrien was not known for his even temper and although his long letter is very clearly reasoned and sensible he, too, probably recognized his own vulnerability and the need to tread carefully in dealing with his Chief.

As for the French there would appear to have been little love lost between them and Sir John and they expected him to comply with their request knowing that they effectively had the support of the British Government. It was under these circumstances that the counter-attacks were ordered. The responsibility for their failure and the loss of life must finally rest with Sir John French as the Commander-in-Chief but, more than the responsibility that came with command, he must take a large part of the shared responsibility for not trying to resolve the situation, that had arisen between him and the other parties since the start of the campaign in 1914.

At 12.30 pm, and exactly as planned, the artillery bombardment commenced. To take advantage of the cover afforded by the bombardment, Brigadier General W.G. Walker ordered his Sirhind Brigade to move, whilst at the same time the Ferozepore Brigade were moving out from their shelter trenches in the rear to take part in the advance. The action by Walker, undertaken under his own initiative, placed his Brigade in the most forward position; he had moved it long before any sign of French activity could even have been expected and prior to his right flank being protected by the Ferozepore Brigade of his own Division. This was against the express orders of Smith-Dorrien. In exactly the same manner as the attack on 26th April had been broken up, the Germans began shelling as soon as the Sirhind Brigade crossed the crest of the Hill Top Ridge and in no time at all the Brigade was suffering heavy losses though every attempt to use all the natural cover was made.

> In passing the ridge the attack came under severe frontal cross fire from rifles and machine guns, as well as from several other directions. The enemy had registered the range of every likely spot with great accuracy, hedges and ditches which would give any sort of cover had all been marked down, and casualties were heaviest in their vicinity.[10]

The leading battalions slowed and halted, but with the arrival of their supports, progress into the valley (later known as Colne Valley) in front of Canadian Farm was made, but there it stopped. A small party of the 1/4th Gurkhas managed to enter the farm but it was impossible for them to be reinforced until after 4 pm when the 4th King's, commanded by Lieutenant Colonel J.W. Allen, moved forward in support.

The Ferozepore Brigade, some little way behind, met with the same treatment as it too crested the ridge and a Brigade that had started the advance with only 1,648 rifles was thinned even further. Once again it persevered in its task and slowly and painfully moved forward until it was in touch with the Sirhind Brigade, at which point all movement ceased. Once more it sustained heavy casualties, the 9th Bhopals having over 100 casualties in the supporting movement. Likewise the 4th Londons were swept away by enemy fire though Second Lieutenant J.R. Pyper was able to use his machine gun to good effect though he had been wounded.[11] It must have seemed like a rerun of the events of the previous day where men were simply blown away with little or no consequence. It is interesting to note the entry in the war diary of the 1st Royal West Kents, who were witness to the attack from trenches further to the east:

> ... the attack was again resumed at 2 pm (sic) with much the same results as that of yesterday. A little more ground was gained and many more casualties were suffered.

It is a very matter of fact description of what had occurred. Nothing had been achieved.

Alarmingly for the advancing British troops, the French had not moved at all from their positions to the left of the Ypres-Langemarck road. The Official History states that the French were unable to move because they were pinned down by a heavy barrage as the infantry assembled.[12] Presumably it was the same barrage through which the Lahore Division had moved in its attempt to close with the enemy. In fairness to the French they had all the problems in their sector which had been experienced by the British, especially in the control of the mixture of units that had been thrown together in the days since the first gas attack. The mixture of regular, territorial and colonial units has been suggested as part of the cause for the lack of movement as all attempts at their organization for the attack failed. Joppé's 4 Moroccan Brigade had failed to move as planned at 1.15 pm but according to the 152nd Division's war diary:

> After a strong preparation by artillery, the Moroccan Brigade at 2.00 advanced to the attack but it was stopped and even gave way like the left of the Lahore Division (English) and the right of Mordacq's Detachment due to the release of asphyxiating gas. The troops were driven back, regaining the trenches which they had left.[13]

This would appear to be the only reference to the use of gas during the early afternoon; even the diary of the 4 Moroccan Brigade makes no mention of it though it does refer to the attack:

> The advance was difficult and very slow due to the presence of German machine gun fire which beat all the ground in front.[14]

Could it be that the entry in the 152nd Division's diary for 27th April was in error? It appears to describe the events that had happened on the previous day, with the release of the gas in particular, but as in so many other aspects the attack had been identical, perhaps the diarist could be forgiven for mixing up some of the minor details. The Lahore Division did not give ground in the manner described on either day. The history of the Indian Corps states that during the period from the start of the attack until 3 pm

> . . . the French had been steadily attacking, and, although losing very heavily, they still continued to form a firing line.[15]

It would appear that gas was not a problem at this stage of the attack. There is reference in this history to the release of gas on 27th April but much later in the day when it states that at 7 pm the French were driven from their trenches. It would appear that what little French movement there had been was small, small enough to have gone almost unnoticed by the adjacent British units. Perhaps it had been no more than the slow and difficult infiltration which had been indicated in the 4th Moroccan Brigade's war diary entry for that afternoon.

The lack of French determination probably had little influence on the outcome of the attack. It had been brought to a halt in the British sector and there is nothing to suggest that even a "vigorous" attack by the French would have achieved a great deal more. The fact that the French came under heavy fire and did not make any significant move suggests that the only thing a more vigorous attack would have achieved would have been even more casualties. It is, perhaps, just as well that the French did not make a move. The British effort was itself limited by the lack of fresh troops and there was some difficulty in finding any support for those troops already committed. A more vigorous and determined attack by the French would have required support from the already depleted resources at the disposal of the British commanders. With the lack of effort from the French, the British could feel justified in limiting their support to those troops already committed to the attack as planned. The attack had stopped in much the same place as the previous day but still more would be expected of the battered Lahore Division before the day was out.

Whilst this abortive attack was in progress, General Smith-Dorrien was to receive a telephone message from Lieutenant General Robertson, the Chief of the General Staff. It was Sir John French's response to Smith-Dorrien's letter. The message was recorded by Robertson in his own handwriting and it is worth reproducing in full because it is indicative as to how bad things had become between two of the most senior officers of the British Army:

> Chief does not regard situation nearly so unfavourable as your letter represents. He thinks you have abundance of troops and especially notes

150

the large reserves you have. He wishes you to act vigorously with the full means available in co-operating with and assisting the French attack having due regard to his previous instructions that the combined attack should be simultaneous. The French possession of Lizerne and general situation on Canal seems to remove anxiety as to your left flank. Letter follows by staff officer.[16]

It would appear from this record of the telephone message that Sir John French was overseeing a completely different battle to everyone else involved in the British sector. There was, on paper at least, an "abundance of troops", but what French appears to have failed to appreciate was that all the troops so far engaged had suffered heavily. It is all very well to suggest, for instance, that Smith-Dorrien had the 149 Brigade at his disposal – he did, but that Brigade had already been reduced by 2,000 as a result of a fruitless attack under the most terrible conditions on 26th April. It was the same story for most of the units that were included in French's "abundance of troops". Consequently, the same can be said of the reserves that were available. Most had seen plenty of action; for instance, two Canadian Brigades were in reserve, but they had been so greatly reduced in number during the earlier fighting that they numbered little more than a battalion each. This point is further illustrated by the fact that during the morning preceding the latest attack there had been an attempt to find a brigade to support the Lahore Division, and the best that could be found was a composite unit comprising the 2nd DCLI, the 1st York and Lancaster, the 5th King's Own and the 2nd Duke of Wellington's. This "brigade", to be commanded by Lieutenant Colonel Tuson of the DCLI, numbered 1,290 all ranks. So much for Sir John French's idea of "large reserves".

Further, whilst the French had made progress in the Lizerne area, the situation on the left flank of Smith-Dorrien's Second Army would hardly seem to warrant a lack of anxiety. In the preceding days the British had witnessed the reluctance of the French to make any substantial moves to stabilize the front there, which had continually placed the British left flank under pressure. There had been some progress at Lizerne but none along the Canal itself and that fact alone must have been enough to concern Smith-Dorrien. His left flank should not have been considered to have been properly formed, never mind safe. As he pointed out, he had to take into consideration the possibility of another German breakthrough in the French sector and the likely effect that would have on the British troops that would become trapped as the neck of the salient was pinched closed. Sir John French appears to have ignored these facts. There are perhaps two reasons for this. The first is the fact, mentioned before, that he did not want to be seen to be falling short of his commitment to support the French. The second, and possibly more important reason is one which should not have had a large influence on the professional soldier, which was his dislike for Smith-Dorrien; unfortunately this was not a unique situation in the command structure of the main armies involved. The apparent lack of understanding that French showed in that telephone message is laced with a personal enmity which had no place in a battle where thousands of men were dying every day. To his credit, Smith-Dorrien had identified the likely problems to his commander, but in recognition of his reading of the situation he was told to "act vigorously"; that message coming at a time when one of his divisions was being slaughtered on the crest of Hill Top Ridge.

With the message fresh in his mind, Smith-Dorrien had little option but to order General Plumer to take "vigorous" action. At 2.40 pm the composite brigade, commanded by Lieutenant Colonel Tuson, was placed at the disposal of Major General Keary to provide support for his by now seriously weakened Lahore Division. The plan was to attack again with the same tired depleted Division, once again in support of a French attack which was to begin with an artillery preparation at 5.30 pm. The most forward of the troops of the Lahore Division were still some 300 yards away from the enemy. The French advanced prior to the British troops being ready, once again failed to make any progress under the very heavy fire, and were halted even before they had drawn level with the left flank of the Sirhind Brigade. But in the French sector optimism remained high, as reports from General Curé indicated further progress in the Lizerne area with the capture of small numbers of prisoners and some minor amounts of equipment. It was a small success which enabled the French to justify further action on the left of the British and another joint effort was ordered for 6.30 pm. At that time Tuson's Detachment was ordered to attack to support the right of the Lahore Division. The war diary of the 5th King's Own explains the operation very succinctly:

> The battalion was ordered to support an attack on C15.[17] In moving up under heavy fire from shell, one shell killed 12 men and wounded five others. Dug in and remained under arms for the rest of the night.[18]

The entry briefly sums up the events. The attack was met with the same heavy artillery fire and simply stopped. The Official History considered that for a brief time there was a degree of hope that the German wire would be reached. It was not. Probably the troops that came the nearest to the wire were those of the 4th King's who had been supporting the main Sirhind Brigade attack. A small party, commanded by Major E.M. Beall, managed to get within 200 yards of the wire, but the heavy fire and realization that the wire was unbroken meant that further progress was halted. For his actions that day in leading the men forward, and for leading reinforcements forward to the line he had established, Major Beall was awarded the DSO.

At the same time as Beall was struggling to get his men forward, in the French sector the cry of "Gas" went up and once again the colonial troops turned and ran as they were bombarded with gas shells. There was such a rush for the bridges across the Yser Canal that General Putz appealed to the cavalry of the British V Corps to intervene and stem their flight. In the event the help was not required as French *Chasseurs*, who had been held in reserve, carried out the task and prevented a full scale rout of the French colonial troops. The situation was not quite as bad as it at first seemed, since not all the troops affected had withdrawn and part of the French line from Turco Farm to the Boesinge road was fully manned. Nevertheless the attack had come to nothing once again. The result was that the Sirhind Brigade was left in a somewhat forward position without satisfactory flanks. To remedy this the 1/1st Gurkhas made contact with the 13 Brigade to their right and, by turning almost at right angles, the 15th Sikhs, facing west, made contact with the French. Once again, as night descended on the scene of carnage, the Germans ceased their heavy fire and left the British, French and Indians to begin their rescue operations. The day's fighting had cost the Lahore Division a further 1,205 casualties. It had been another fruitless day.

Whilst all the fighting of the afternoon and early evening was going on, the difference of opinion between Sir John French and Smith-Dorrien had reached an inevitable conclusion. At 4.35 pm, as the Lahore Division was organizing for its second attack of the day, Smith-Dorrien received the following telegram from GHQ:

> Chief directs you to hand over forthwith to General Plumer the command of all troops engaged in the present operations about Ypres. You should lend General Plumer your Brigadier General, General Staff and such other officers of the various branches of your staff as he may require. General Plumer should send all reports direct to GHQ from which he will receive his orders. Acknowledge.[19]

Smith-Dorrien had effectively been relieved of his command of the Second Army in front of Ypres and it was the end of his military career. He remained in command of the Second Army in name only until 6th May but from this point on Lieutenant General Plumer was in control of it. Smith-Dorrien did not serve in an active capacity again during the war. The telegram was sent "in clear", that is to say that any operator would be able to know what had been sent from GHQ, and there can be no doubt that it had been done with the express purpose of humiliating Smith-Dorrien as much as possible, as he was stripped of his command and his staff. The removal of such a capable general at this stage of the battle shows, perhaps more than anything, Sir John French's lack of capacity to command. There was no other reason for the dismissal other than the enmity between the men. However, it is necessary for there to be trust between senior commanders and this had been noticeably absent between the two men since the Autumn of 1914. The comments made by Smith-Dorrien in the letter to Sir William Robertson had undoubtedly precipitated a situation that had been continuing for six months but there was nothing in the letter that was intrinsically incorrect or that would warrant dismissal. The events that followed were to more than justify the stance adopted by Smith-Dorrien as the Second Battle of Ypres progressed.

By 5.30 pm the command of all the British troops in front of Ypres had been transferred from Smith-Dorrien to Plumer, who from that time effectively controlled all the troops involved in the operations around Ypres under the title of Plumer's Force. The transfer was designed to be as smooth as possible so that staff work could continue uninterrupted, and to that end Major General G.F. Milne, Smith-Dorrien's Chief Staff Officer, and Major General J.E.W. Headlam, commanding the artillery of the Second Army, were also transferred to Plumer's staff together with four other General Staff officers (Lieutenant Colonel R.H. Hare, Major C.J.C. Grant and Captains W.G.S. Dobbie and R.J. Collins). The change in command was not likely to have a great effect since most of the troops in the salient had already come under Plumer, except the Lahore Division; however, from that moment on Plumer reported directly to the Commander-in-Chief rather than through the Second Army headquarters. Whilst this may appear to be a simplification of the command structure and perhaps of some benefit to the overall running of the battle, it must be remembered that Smith-Dorrien's removal had not been thought of in that way at all – he was dismissed because he could not agree with Sir John French and any benefits arising from that dismissal in the short term were nothing more than accidental. By 8 pm the new staff had been formed and was operating under Plumer. Shortly afterwards Plumer received written orders to consolidate the line held and to make it "more secure against attack". The second item of the order runs:

> You are also requested to prepare a line east of Ypres joining up with the line now held north and south of that place for occupation if and when it becomes advisable to withdraw from the present salient. Please report early as to the position of the line you select for this purpose. It should be such as to avoid withdrawal from Hill 60.[20]

Plumer was being asked to carry out Smith-Dorien's suggestion. It is quite clear from the correspondence between GHQ and the two generals concerned that Sir John French had not removed Smith-Dorrien for his lack of military ability. On the contrary, it was more probably because of his superior ability and his readiness to disagree with Sir John French that he was eventually sent home. French, however, insisted that it was because Smith-Dorrien had become "windy" and "pessimistic" and that sickness levels in the Second Army were unacceptably high. It was all a bit thin but it was sufficient to bring about the dismissal of Smith-Dorrien.[21] Plumer's opinions on the matter do not appear to have been recorded but he was probably not surprised by the events of the day since he knew both men very well. He would not have been surprised by the order to prepare for a withdrawal; after all, the situation was such that it made sense to shorten the line to a size that could be manned with the ever diminishing numbers at his disposal. Plumer simply got on with the job in hand and began his assessment of the situation for the report requested by GHQ. It is interesting to note that when French came to prepare his dispatch covering the battle there is no mention of the incident relating to the dismissal of Smith-Dorrien, and that the first time a withdrawal is mentioned he is at pains to give the impression that it had been his intention to do just that all along.[22]

In the east of the salient all of these matters must have seemed very far away. The line from the north-east corner westwards was held by the 85 Brigade, the 11 Brigade and the 10 Brigade almost as far as the Wieltje-Saint Julien road, as it had been on the previous day, though a number of mixed commands still remained. This portion of the line was shelled heavily all day but, as the Germans made no effort to assault with infantry, the line held. There were no further withdrawals and by the close of day the line was more or less the same as it had been the day before. Therefore, as darkness fell, it was considered to be an appropriate time to carry out some reorganization and relief of the forces in the area. The 11 Brigade took over all the line from Berlin Wood to Fortuin, the 10 Brigade took over from Moulton-Barrett's Detachment and the elements of 150 Brigade still in the line, and filled in all the gaps that were present. During the reorganization the Germans continued to shell the area and during the late evening Brigadier General J. Hasler of the 11 Brigade was killed. General Bulfin (28th Division) commented:

> I saw poor Julian Hasler at Saint Jean on the 27 April, the place was being heavily shelled – I sent him up Grogan and Le Preu, my GSO2 and 3, to help him, and some signallers, but all the lines were constantly cut so I ordered him to get out as soon as it was dark. He was killed about 9 pm that night – he could have got out at 6 pm but delayed.[23]

Hasler was the second Brigadier General to die in the defence of the salient and, like Riddell, it was because he had insisted on being as close to the front as possible.

Hasler's death was symptomatic of the problem that was going to be faced by the defenders of the salient: as it contracted, it was becoming increasingly vulnerable to shellfire from all sides. During the day Poperinge, some six miles to the west of Ypres had been shelled and Smith-Dorrien's advanced headquarters were lucky to escape damage. One soldier of the Transport Section of the 1st Monmouths remarked:

> On April 26, 27 and 28 about 5.30 pm Poperinghe was being shelled by a very heavy gun and, it appeared, quite close to our detail camp. It made a mess of this pretty place, but nothing of the gun has been seen.[24]

The gradual loss of the eastern and northern part of the salient was having the effect of pushing the war into those areas that had remained largely unscathed, and further withdrawals would only make this more and more likely.

At the end of the day, and subsequent to the reorganization of troops in the north-east of the salient, the command of the various units in the area was also amended. To begin with, Geddes' Detachment was broken up and all the battalions that had been attached since the early hours of 23rd April were returned to their brigades. General Snow was given back all the units of the 27th Division to his command, but still retained the Corps Reserve, which at that time amounted to no more than two battalions. General Bulfin was given the 11 Brigade, the 150 Brigade and the 151 Brigade to command as well as his own troops of the 28th Division. General Alderson was given 10 Brigade, the 13 Brigade and the 149 Brigade to add to his command. At the command level it had been a day of change, though whether or not all of these changes were necessary or for the better may still be open to some considerable discussion. On the battlefield very little had changed. There had been some improvement in the overall defence of the line, but the attacks of the Lahore Division had been yet another tragedy which had achieved nothing and, along with the French on their left, they were back in the same place as they had started, having paid a high price in casualties. In two days of fighting the Lahore Division had sustained nearly 4,000 casualties[25] or about one third of its bayonet strength. They had done everything that could have been expected of them but at the end of 27th April all they could do was rescue such wounded as they could from the battlefield and prepare for whatever calls that would be placed on them during the coming day.

At 9.15 pm General Putz's Chief of Staff, Colonel Desticker, went to V Corps headquarters to confirm the reorganizations that had taken place in the French sector and to indicate to Plumer that the French wanted to prepare for an attack. The attack was planned to begin the following afternoon, once the newly arrived artillery had time to register to its satisfaction. To those who were aware of this French plan it must have seemed that they had heard it all before as the French persisted with their, perhaps understandable, desire to regain all that had been lost. As part of the plan General Putz was requesting the support of the British on his right flank and, as before, this had already been agreed by Sir John French. The plan did not offer anything new and it looked as if more British soldiers would be sent into battle to assist the French in an enterprise that had little to recommend it.

Notes

1. See Appendix IV for full letter.
2. As quoted in the *Official History 1915 Vol. 1*, Appendix 29, p401.
3. See *Official History 1915 Vol. 1*, footnote p271.
4. The 29th Division, the last of the regular divisions to be formed, had been earmarked for this sector but was diverted to the Gallipoli landings.
5. See *Official History 1915 Vol. 1*, footnote p271.
6. *Official History 1915 Vol. 1*, p271.
7. See Holmes, op.cit., p283.
8. See Haythornthwaite, *The World War One Source Book*, p346.
9. See Holmes, op.cit., pp 272 ff.
10. Merewether and Smith, op.cit., p316.
11. Second Lieutenant Pyper was awarded the MC (see Merewether and Smith, op.cit., p320).
12. *Official History 1915 Vol.1*, p273.
13. Quoted in McWilliams and Steel, op.cit., p202.
14. ibid.
15. Merewether and Smith , op.cit., p321.
16. See *Official History 1915 Vol. 1*, Appendix 30, p402.
17. The Mauser Ridge.
18. War Diary of the 5th Royal Lancs (WO95/2274).
19. See *Official History 1915 Vol. 1*, Appendix 31, p403.
20. See *Official History 1915 Vol. 1*, Appendix 32, p403.
21. See Holmes, op.cit., p284.
22. See Sir John French's dispatch VII dated 15th June, 1915 in *Complete Dispatches*.
23. See Davies and Maddocks, op.cit., p71 quoted from PRO WOCAB45/140.
24. See Hughes and Dixon, op.cit.
25. Merewether and Smith, op.cit., p332.

CHAPTER TEN

The Battle of Saint Julien
Days 5 to 7 – 28th to 30th April 1915

The Battle of Saint Julien had been thus far one of continued fighting. The Germans had shelled the salient heavily and made assaults against the Allied line during the first few days of the battle. For the Allied part it was a battle that had seen determined, stubborn defence and, unfortunately, ineffective counter-attacks. To begin with the phase of the battle which commenced on 28th April appeared not to be significantly different. Early in the morning a minor counter-attack, comprising two companies of the 2nd King's Shropshire Light Infantry, to regain a stretch of the East Surreys' trenches near Broodseinde that had been lost three days before, was a complete failure and the Shropshires suffered heavy casualties from the close range small arms fire. However for the British troops this minor operation at 2.40 am on the morning of 28th was to mark the last counter-attack for a number of days, as it eventually became clear to all concerned that they were achieving nothing and were costing dearly.

Also early that morning, Geddes' Detachment was officially broken up following the order of the previous day to do so. It had served its purpose during a critical period of the battle and its units were to be returned to their respective brigades. Geddes, who had spent the night at the 13 Brigade Headquarters at Saint Jean, was about to leave for Potijze to rejoin his regiment when he realized he had lost his map. He asked Brigadier General Wanless O'Gowan for another and whilst the General had left the room to find a map for him a shell landed in the room, Colonel Geddes was killed and his two staff officers (Major H.C.M. Makgill, Royal Scots Fusiliers, and Lieutenant J. Nichols, 9th

158

London Reg.) were seriously wounded. It was an unfortunate incident that killed a soldier who had served so well under the most stressful conditions in the early days of the battle.[1]

Later the same morning a telegram was sent from General Headquarters to emphasize the reorganization of the command within the salient. With the removal of Smith-Dorrien from the immediate scene General Plumer was now in charge of most of the units that were actively engaged in defending the salient and he was answerable directly to the Commander-in-Chief, Sir John French. To that end V Corps, the Lahore Division, the 50th Division and three attached brigades were to become known as "Plumer's Force" from 7.50 am on 28th April. It was a large command, though all of the units had been engaged to a greater or lesser extent, and were depleted and suffering from the effects of the heavy fighting. Perhaps one of the major problems that was to face Plumer in the next few days was one of communication with his large and rather dispersed force, but it was a problem that had been a feature of the battle to this date and it was not likely to disappear with the reorganization of the command structure.

The losses already sustained by the British and the French during the battle had, as discussed in the previous chapter, suggested to Smith-Dorrien that it was time to consider a withdrawal to a line that was shorter and possibly more readily defended. In spite of Sir John French's apparent opposition to the manoeuvre, General Headquarters had already issued Plumer with a warning order to do just that and at 10 am on 28th April Plumer received a message from French's Chief of Staff stating that he, French, thought it would:

> . . . in all probability be necessary tonight to commence measures for the withdrawal from the salient to a more westerly line . . . take such preliminary measures for commencing retirement tonight, if in the C-in-C's opinion it proves necessary.[2]

This remarkable turn around in the space of several hours was the first of many to beset Sir John French during the coming days before the line was eventually shortened. It was fortunate for French and his beleaguered army that the Germans were not able to carry on with their attacks as plans to use gas again were thwarted by the weather, so that 28th April saw a pause in the fighting, or at least a cessation of infantry assaults. The German artillery, however, continued to shell the entire area heavily, concentrating particularly on the 85 Brigade, the Canal crossing and various roadways supplying the front line. The German superiority in artillery allowed this barrage to continue almost unabated for the next few days and the front line soldiers could not even hope for a reply as both guns and ammunition were conserved by the Royal

Artillery. A member of the 5th London (London Rifle Brigade) was to write of the experience in the trenches at that time:

> There is no need to recount in detail all the horrors and discomforts of the three days spent in that enfiladed trench shelled intermittently and unable to strike back, we lay at the mercy of the German guns on the Gravenstafel Ridge. Of the enemy we saw nothing . . . At last on the night of the 29th April, after some 170 casualties . . . we were ordered to quit the trench and move to the Saint Julien front . . .[3]

There did not need to be an infantry assault to cause heavy casualties as the German artillery was able to dominate the salient so completely. For all troops in the front line the real difference of the last days of April was that they did not have to suffer infantry attack. They were all well aware that they were in the middle of a battle and most would have realized that once the shelling stopped or lifted off the front line then an enemy infantry assault was likely to follow.

Meanwhile Sir John French had travelled from his headquarters to Cassel to meet with General Foch to explain to him the necessity of an immediate withdrawal from the most easterly, and exposed, part of the salient. Foch was opposed to any discussion of withdrawal and, in fairness, was able to put some strong arguments forward for maintaining the situation as it then was, for example:

> . . . the new position selected for the British Army is at the foot of the ridges, and will be more difficult to hold than the present one on the crest.[4]

He was able to set all his arguments out in writing for Sir John French (see Appendix V) and as part of one of his conclusions to his note he stated:

> The retirement should not be ordered for the moment; it should be forbidden. If the enemy infantry does not attack in the region under consideration it should not be provoked to one by a retreat.[5]

Besides his obvious displeasure at the suggestion of a withdrawal, Foch still wanted the opportunity to believe that his forces could regain all the ground that had been lost on 22nd April. He could not hope to achieve this if the British insisted in pulling back so soon, since he would not have any support for his right flank. Clearly his arguments were sound, provided that the French Army was capable of the effort and commitment required to produce a large-scale attack, which for a number of days looked increasingly unlikely. However, his arguments were at least strong enough to convince Sir John French, for on his return to his headquarters he ordered Plumer to act in cooperation with the French attack planned for the afternoon of 28th April – and to delay the withdrawal until its effects were known.

The French plan for the attack that afternoon was much the same as it had been since the ground had been lost some six days earlier. The left flank was to capture Steenstraat whilst the centre was to join in by crossing the canal at Boesinge, which would then be followed by the right flank pushing forward in a northerly or north-easterly direction and thereby forcing the Germans to give ground. It was in the last-mentioned part of this operation that the British would be needed to ensure the right flank of the French attack could be protected. It can only be imagined what the reaction to this attack was amongst the senior British officers. After all, the French had promised much and achieved so little in the earlier attacks, so why should this latest one be any different? It was decided, however, that if the French did not move then neither would the British. This was, finally, the tacit acceptance that the French had no real desire to expend significant effort in the area of the salient.

Whilst all this had been going on, General Plumer had been working on his plans for the withdrawal which he was able to present to Sir John French during the day. The line he had chosen ran from Hill 60 in the south to the front of Hooge, then across the Frezenberg Ridge, then to the east of Shell Trap Farm, and thence back to the Canal on more or less the line that then existed.[6] It meant giving up a sizeable portion of the salient with a maximum depth of about two and a half miles in front of Frezenberg. However, in his appraisal of the situation Plumer pointed out that, in his opinion, the line being held on 28th April could not be held permanently unless the French were able to gain all the ground they had lost. He also pointed out that the British could do little to improve the situation themselves without using a very large force which, of course, they did not have. In his opinion, also, the local attacks would cause further heavy losses without substantially improving the situation. Finally, he stated that the withdrawal would take four nights and that the longer it was delayed the more difficult and costly it would become to achieve the line he was proposing.

In spite of the clear picture that Plumer had drawn for French there was no option but to delay the commencement of the withdrawal to allow the cooperation with the French that had been agreed between French and Foch in their morning meeting. At 3.30 pm the French launched their attack as three French regiments, under the command of General Curé, attacked Steenstraat, supported by both Belgian and British artillery. This attack of the French left met with no success; the units concerned sustained heavy casualties without achieving anything. The German account of the attack states that it was stopped entirely by artillery fire. Meanwhile, the planned moves of the French centre and right had not happened, though both areas had put up a heavy fire. A consequence of the lack of movement of the French right was that the Sirhind Brigade also did not move and was, therefore, spared the heavy casualties that had been inflicted on the Division in the previous two days. During this attack the Germans did not make any effort to move other than to use their artillery to break it up. In fact, the Germans took the opportunity during the day to bring up more heavy guns to the Houthulst Forest, some eight miles to the north of Ypres, and to arrange for replacements to be brought up from Ghent. For them, at least, it had been a relatively quiet day as they sat patiently and waited for the wind to change direction so that they could use their gas once again.

It is strange to note that an order was issued to the Lahore Division, timed at 3.34 pm, that they were to consolidate the line they had held on 27th April. That is, within five minutes of the French starting their attack at Steenstraat it had been realized, or accepted perhaps, that the French right was not going to move and thus the British busied themselves in consolidation works. From a French point of view, and had they been immediately aware of it, this would probably have been taken as indicating the low level of commitment and cooperation of the British. Bearing in mind the losses sustained in previous attempts to support abortive French attacks, it was probably considered the best course of action that the troops in the line could take. The consolidation, to provide a line to coincide with the 13 Brigade, was to be carried out during the hours of darkness and, although that was still some hours off, the issue of the order clearly demonstrated that nothing was expected of the French effort. At the same time the 1 Canadian Brigade was placed at the disposal of Major General Keary of the Lahore Division to assist in this if necessary. Keary wasted no time in getting the Canadians to provide protection for his troops while this work was carried out. The majority of the work was carried out by two companies (20th and 21st) of the 3rd Sappers and Miners of the Lahore Division. Here it should be pointed out that a small gain in ground was actually achieved without the Division sustaining any casualties. Whilst reconnoitring the ground the sappers realized that it was possible to dig the line further forward, since there was an area of dead ground in the bottom of the shallow valley in front of them which was concealed from the German trench by the convexity of the rising ground on which it was situated. This line, dug as it was in the low ground between Hill Top Ridge and Mauser Ridge, was able to join up Shell Trap Farm and Turco Farm by way of Canadian Farm. It was completed and suitably wired during the moonlit night of 28th April and those involved were perhaps a little surprised that the Germans had not moved to prevent

162

its completion. During the works the Germans could be seen quite clearly moving about on the skyline about 500 yards distant as they carried out their own wiring in front of their line to improve its defences in the event of yet another counter-attack. Neither group fired on each other as the work progressed and when the British line was completed in the early hours of 29th April it was handed over to the 13 Brigade for their occupation from that time.

The day had seen a change, not only in the pattern of the fighting, but also in the attitude of the Commander-in-Chief. Sir John French had finally gone to his opposite number in the French army and put his case for withdrawal. Admittedly he had been persuaded to delay his plan, but nevertheless had instructed that preparations should be made for just that eventuality. To the soldiers in the trenches the effect of Sir John French's change of heart was that they had not been forced into yet another fruitless and expensive counter-attack, though they were still asked to hold on to a position that was becoming more perilous the longer the French delayed their efforts to regain the lost ground to the north of the salient.

The 29th April was destined to be much the same kind of day as 28th, in so far as the Germans still shelled the area and refrained from any infantry attacks. Early in the morning General Putz issued orders for yet another French counter-attack against the Germans in Steenstraat and on the west bank of the Canal. This attack was planned for noon but was postponed at 9.30 am since the newly arrived French artillery had not had time to register and was, therefore, likely to be less than adequate for the purpose of support for the infantry. Once again Sir John French agreed to hold the line as he had on the previous day to allow the French a chance to recover the lost ground – and all the time the German shelling of the salient continued. Foch was by this time insisting to French that a "simultaneous not successive" strike was necessary and his request for an "attack with the greatest energy" was conveyed to General Plumer. It is a pity that, at this stage, French was not able to stand his ground and point out to Foch that his troops had, on previous occasions, attacked "with the greatest energy" and that it was the French who had failed to make any significant contribution. As Commander-in-Chief, French should not have acquiesced so readily to the wishes of General Foch.[7] In theory, at least, Foch was correct in his desire to recapture the lost ground to attempt to maintain as large a salient as possible, and in opposing any withdrawal that was going to make the area into little more than a German artillery target. However, he should have accepted that after seven days of hard fighting, some of it against a weapon against which, at the time, there was little defence, it was highly unlikely that his troops could actually deliver what he

163

wanted. It is, at this distance, difficult to see what merit the two commanders saw in the repeated counter-attacks which showed little imagination and even less variation. Perhaps the sole merit in the whole plan to date was that both commanders were trying to operate together and in so doing present a defence that was as strong as possible to the enemy. That, however, could just as easily have been achieved by taking the joint decision to abandon the tip of the salient, and in so doing conserve the rapidly diminishing number of troops and material in their respective commands.

The day remained relatively quiet, apart from the continual shelling of particular targets by the enemy. This gave at least some opportunity to commence the relief of some of the battalions in the line that had seen much fighting over the last week or so. The 2nd Lancashire Fusiliers (12 Brigade) were brought into the area, as part of the deployment of the 4th Division from reserve, and had spent much of the last three days slowly moving into the battle zone. On 29th April they were sent to relieve the 1st Royal Warwicks, who had been so heavily involved since their arrival with the 10 Brigade some days before. The 2nd Lancashire Fusiliers' history comments on their arrival:

> The battalion received a warm welcome to the famous salient, being shelled almost all the way up from the Canal; Major Griffin was wounded in the head, though he was able to rejoin two days later, and three drivers and three horses of the transport were killed. Major Griffin at first refused to go to hospital, though he was bleeding profusely, and Tyrrell[8] had to invoke the regulation which provides that all combatant personnel on being wounded come under the orders of the medical service before he could enforce his views on his commanding officer.[9]

As was almost normal at this time, the relief was accompanied by confusion over the exact position they were to reach and the lack of guides and adequate maps, and it was 1.30 am on 30th April before the battalion was able to complete the relief. They had been on the move since 7.45 am on 29th, except for a short break near Vlamertinge in the early afternoon, and it must be imagined that it was a tired unit that arrived in the front line that night.

Similarly, the 2nd Monmouths, also part of the same Division, were being held in reserve at La Brique at a little distance from the main firing line but close enough for them to be well aware of the scale of the battle going on around them in this, their first, visit to the salient. Private C.P. Heare recorded:

> This is the real sight of the war, houses are smashed, food on table as if people run off having a meal, shells screaming all the time. One pitched in a party behind us, what an awful mess . . . the soldiers are lying about

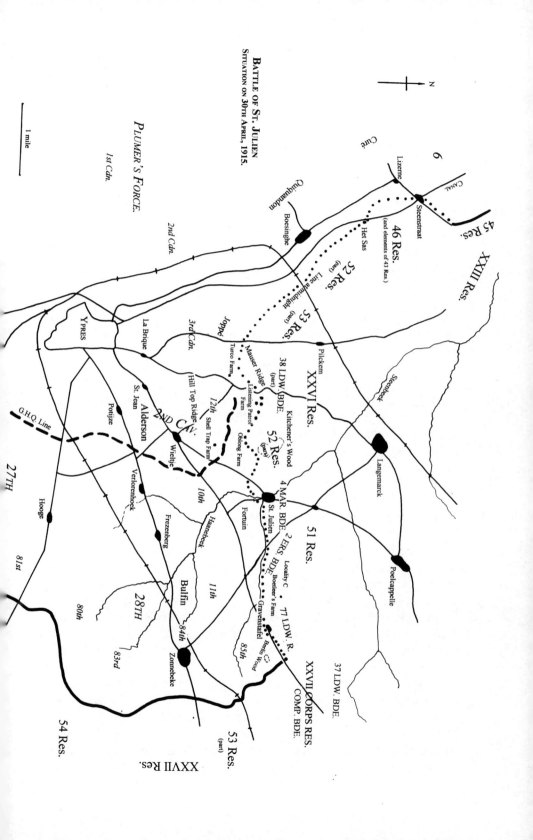

BATTLE OF ST. JULIEN
SITUATION ON 30TH APRIL, 1915.

1 mile

N

PLUMER'S FORCE.

1st Cdn.
2nd Cdn.
3rd Cdn.

Cure
CANAL
Lizerne
Steenstraat
Het Sas
6
45 Res.
XXIII Res.
46 Res.
(and elements of 43 Res.)
52 Res. (part)
53 Res. (part)
Line abandoned
Quiquandon
Boesinghe
Pilckem
XXVI Res.
Steenbeek
Langemarck
37 LDW. BDE.
Poelcappelle
YPRES
La Brique
Joppé
Turco Farm
Mauser Ridge
38 LDW. BDE. (part)
Listening Patrol Farm
Kitchener's Wood
52 Res. (part)
Oblong Farm
51 Res.
12th
Shell Trap Farm
2ND CAV.
Hill Top Ridge
St. Jean
Alderson
Potijze
Wieltje
Verlorenhoek
10th
St. Julien
4 MAR. BDE.
Fortuin
2 ERS. BDE.
Boetleer's Farm
Locality C
77 LDW. R.
Gravenstafel
85th
Berlin Wood
XXVII CORPS RES. COMP. BDE.
G.H.Q. Line
Hooge
27TH
81st
80th
83rd
28TH
Frezenberg
Haanebeek
Bulfin
11th
84th
Zonnebeke
54 Res.
53 Res. (part)
XXVII Res.

in the road screaming, groaning and swearing with wounds and gas . . .
The wounded on the road scream every time a shell lands. It seems no
one can live in this for long.[10]

Whilst these units were making their entry to the salient the French had
decided that they would attack after all. At 6 pm, and completely
independently, the French attacked Steenstraat once again and
succeeded in driving the Germans out of the village. They did not,
however, succeed in driving the Germans off the west bank of the Canal
and the attack was not extended to the French centre or right.
Therefore, the British forces were not called upon to provide flanking
cover and remained in their trenches.

During the evening of 29th April Plumer issued a preparatory order
for the withdrawal to his divisional commanders, in which he set out the
general arrangements for the withdrawal of all the British troops from
the eastern tip of the salient. It was to be a piecemeal retirement with
each stage carefully planned to maintain sufficient men in the front line
to allow the enemy to believe it was fully manned. The initial phase was
to remove those divisions (the Lahore, the 50th Northumbrian and the
2nd Cavalry) that were in the salient but not at that time manning the
line to the east of the Canal.[11] At the same time preparations were being
made for the construction of the new line of defence and in the construction of additional bridges to provide better access over the Canal, which
would greatly assist the movement of men and equipment to and from
the front. Unfortunately, this operation could not be carried out since
Sir John French had agreed to yet another postponement to await the
outcome of the attack planned by the French for 30th April – it would
seem that their minor success at Steenstraat during the early evening
had given them reason for optimism.

At 3 am on 30th April General Putz once more issued orders for an
attack to commence at 8 am. It was similar in its objective to all the
other attacks the French had ordered but Putz was mindful of the wind
direction which would have favoured the release of gas against the
Steenstraat area, and so he ordered the attack to develop from the right
flank northwards rather than in the manner of 28th April. The wind
may have favoured the Germans, though they made no attack, but the
early morning mist did not favour Putz and the attack was put back until
11.15 am. Plumer, in accordance with his Chief's wishes, issued orders
to the artillery to support the French and to the Sirhind Brigade to co-
operate with the right flank of the French attack. When the attack
commenced General Joppé's troops made some progress as they
advanced slowly along the east bank of the Canal, but the right of his
152nd Division did not move since the enemy wire remained uncut.

166

The Sirhind Brigade, therefore, did not move. On the French left at Steenstraat progress was slow and casualties were heavy. Once again the French had failed to live up to their own expectations.

It was not enough for Putz that this attack should fail, for even as his men were dying in the attempt to regain the ground, he approached General Plumer with a proposition for yet another joint attack to take place on 1st May. The plan was that the combined forces should attack Hill 29, the highest point of Mauser Ridge. It was a simple frontal attack and lacked any subtlety whatsoever. Plumer, of course, immediately referred the plan to General Headquarters and received the response that he could only support the French attack with fire, but that he was not to engage any of the infantry under his command in the assault. It would appear that General Headquarters was finally getting the message that there were no longer any troops to spare to go chasing the futile hopes of the French commanders whose hopes were much bigger than the wherewithal to fulfil them; the French had been every bit as profligate with their men's lives as had the British in the early days of the defence of the salient. It was perhaps with these facts in mind that Sir John French informed Foch, yet again, of his intention to withdraw from the tip of the salient. Foch was alarmed enough by this decision to travel immediately to Hazebrouck, to General Headquarters, to meet French whom he persuaded, yet again, to delay the withdrawal. For the third time in as many days the French commander had succeeded in swaying the decision of the British Commander-in-Chief and each time Foch exploited this element of indecisiveness in Sir John French, he was leaving the troops, mainly British, in extreme danger of encirclement and annihilation. But French agreed once again, and it is perhaps fortunate that the Germans had no idea of the weakened state of the defenders, for it could have been one delay too many.

Later in the evening of 30th April the 2nd Essex (12 Brigade) were marched into the salient and so completed the build up of the 4th Division in the area. The 2nd Essex historian commented on their arrival in the salient:

Frequent checks were made by transport blocking the roads, all under heavy fire, which caused twenty casualties to the Battalion, Lieut. R. Pierson being among the killed.[12] During the evening the Essex men went into the trenches, holding the left of the British line for upon their left was a French Moroccan Brigade.[13]

That evening they had been part of the relief of the 13 Brigade (5th Division). Perhaps none of the Essex had any idea of what had happened to the men they were relieving or gave any thought of what the future could hold for them. However, when the 13 Brigade was withdrawn its strength was a mere 1,400 all ranks. The French, however, still wanted a delay to the withdrawal, though in fact it was becoming increasingly inevitable. The only question that remained was whether it would be an orderly voluntary withdrawal or one forced upon the defenders by German pressure.

Notes

1. Colonel Geddes is buried in Ypres Reservoir Cemetery.
2. See *Official History 1915 Vol.1*, p278.
3. See Mitchinson, op.cit., p67.
4. See *Official History 1915 Vol.1*, p404.
5. ibid., p405.
6. See Appendix V for further details of the withdrawal.
7. French probably felt he was acting within his own orders – see for instance Holmes, op.cit.
8. Lieutenant W. Tyrrell RAMC was the Medical Officer to the Battalion. He was later to receive the DSO and Bar and the MC.
9. Latter, *The History of the Lancashire Fusiliers 1914–1918*, p38.
10. See Dixon, op.cit., p33.
11. See Appendix V for details.
12. Lieut. Roy Pierson is buried in Duhallow A.D.S. Cemetery, Ypres.
13. Burrows, *The Essex Regiment*, p125.

CHAPTER ELEVEN

The Battle of Saint Julien
Day 8 – 1st May 1915

After three days of vacillation, 1st May was to prove to be the day on which Sir John French was to get his wish to begin the withdrawal of his troops from the tip of the salient. Ironically enough it was another Frenchman who was able to tip the balance in French's favour, when General Joseph Joffre intervened to curtail any further discussions on the matter. The timing of the note from Joffre to French, sent via Foch, could not have been more opportune for the British, but for the French it was perhaps ill timed, coming as it did at a time when General Putz was still trying to recapture lost ground. Putz had planned an attack for 3.10 pm on 1st May and it had been agreed that the Sirhind Brigade would, if necessary, move to support the French. It was an optimistic plan, as were all those that had gone before, and made all the more so by the British commanders warning the 4th and 28th Divisions to move if the Sirhind Brigade actually made any progress. It must have been realized by most of the senior officers that this was not going to occur. There is evidence to support this in the history of the 2nd Essex, for instance:

> It was expected that the Essex would occupy the captured trenches if required, but the General commanding the Sirhind Brigade did not think they would be needed. And he was right as the attack was not pressed.[1]

Brigadier General W.G. Walker VC, commanding officer of the Sirhind Brigade, clearly understood the situation very well; the lessons of the days preceding this abortive attack would not have been wasted on commanders at all levels across the front. Nevertheless, the French remained optimistic even when the 3.10 pm attack failed to materialize, as the artillery opened fire and the French infantry stayed resolutely in their trenches. It is difficult to imagine what can have been running through the mind of General Putz at this stage. His men had failed to move as ordered and presumably were able to give him a satisfactory reason, perhaps the wire had not been cut or the assaulting troops were not all in position. Whatever the reason it must have satisfied Putz, because he simply rescheduled the attack for 4.40 pm, but once again the French divisions did not move. It was then reported by the British liaison officer with the French that, "the men were too tired for any further serious effort". In this statement can be seen the result of the continued efforts of the French to recapture the lost ground. As has been highlighted in earlier discussion, some of the French troops available were not of the highest quality and others had been rushed to the area to bolster the defence. All had been involved repeatedly in ill-planned, unimaginative frontal attacks, and there had been substantial casualties. Some had experienced the effects of gas and this had had a serious demoralizing effect on many of the poorer quality troops. It had been a mistake to continue to hurl gradually diminishing numbers of tired, demoralized men into battle in this manner when, even for the French, the sensible thing to have done would have been to consolidate what they had with such men as were available. Whilst their desire to regain the ground is understandable, the rather blinkered approach adopted by the French command towards its own troops, not to mention those of the British Army, is not excusable. The days of counter-attacking had achieved little.

It was with these matters in mind that Joffre had contacted Sir John French, even while the last attacks were meant to be under way, with a note which set out, from the beginning, the situation as Joffre saw it:

> In the present situation the principal object which the Command of the Allied armies has in view is the preparation of operations on the front Arras-Neuve Chapelle. The attention is to attack on that front and to act on the defensive about Ypres.[2]

Joffre had, effectively, written off the defence of the old Ypres salient. It had no major importance to him and he even suggested reducing the forces in the area so that more resources would be available for the attacks that were planned further south. Again, it is possible to see merit in Joffre's argument, but four or five days of wasted effort had done little to conserve resources – it is almost as if Joffre had also let it run to see if success could be achieved and then decided to stop the assaults when, and only when, it became apparent that they were squandering men and material. Perhaps, also, Joffre was mindful of the fact there had been

170

plans for all French soldiers to be released from the salient. The fact that they had not been was, at least in part, because the British troops earmarked for this job – notably the 29th Division – were sent to the Mediterranean to take part in the Gallipoli landings. To some extent Joffre saw Ypres as essentially a British problem and was happy to limit the French involvement in the fighting where he could.

Fortunately Joffre's approach fitted much more closely with the ideas of Sir John French, for although he had been opposed to the idea as proposed by Smith-Dorrien, he was eager to get on with the organization of the withdrawal. There can have been no reason to delay it further and certainly General Plumer had made it quite clear that he considered to delay was to invite unnecessary problems. In his response to Joffre, French pointed out to his ally that the continuing defence of the salient would still require a French involvement between the Langemarck road and the Yser Canal, that is the area already held by them. He went on to point out:

> . . . the troops should be of the best quality, in sufficient strength, and that adequate measures of defence should be taken.[3]

This comment would appear to be a direct reference to the collapse of the left flank of the salient on 22nd April when it had been manned by two inferior French divisions. French did not want his flank, even in the proposed reduced salient, manned by anything but the best troops that the French could find. There is some justification in the request since if these units had done more to hold their ground in the first place then the abortive counter attacks would not have become an issue. In fairness to those troops they had had the misfortune to stand in the way of the first poison gas attack and, although the Canadians had managed to stand firm on the flanks of the attack, it is no more than speculation to suggest that better units in the French sector would have actually made a better job of holding the line. However it may be that the collapse of the left flank would not have occurred. French would appear to have believed that this was the case and it was not unreasonable for him to ask for the best help that could be provided by his ally so that the line about Ypres could be maintained.

It did not take long for French to set things in motion. By 3.45 pm he was aware that the first French attack had failed and an order was issued from General Headquarters:

> You will begin tonight to carry out the withdrawal of your troops on the eastern part of the salient.[4]

By 4 pm Plumer had issued his orders to allow the withdrawal to commence at 8 pm that evening. In the first part of the manoeuvre

Plumer ordered the Lahore Division to leave the salient for billets in the region of Ouderdoum, to the south-west of Ypres. Also, as part of this initial withdrawal, much of the artillery was ordered either closer to Ypres or to the west of the Canal. These moves left the front line intact and there were still some reserves in close proximity should anything untoward happen on the coming day. The front line was now manned, from the left, by the 4th Division up to about Shell Trap Farm, the 28th Division in the centre about Zonnebeke, and the 27th Division on the right as far as the southern edge of Sanctuary Wood. The reserves comprised the 2 Cavalry Division at Potijze, the 50th Division distributed largely to support the 28th Division at Verlorenhoek and Frezenberg, and the Canadian Division, which was by this time situated west of the Canal at Brielen. Beyond Sanctuary Wood the line, which included Hill 60, of the south-eastern part of the salient was held by the 5th Division.

Plumer was finally able to put his plans for the withdrawal into operation and simultaneously he issued orders for the second phase of the operation to take place during the night of the 3rd–4th May. At 7.30 pm General Plumer moved his headquarters from Poperinge to Abeele. Poperinge had been shelled on numerous occasions during the preceding days but Plumer had refused to leave until he was ordered to do so by General Headquarters. In view of the shrinking salient and the fact that the Germans would soon be moving their guns forward it made sense to be somewhat further back. As it was, Major General Keary, commanding the Lahore Division, had a lucky escape. He supervised the withdrawal of his Division from his headquarters in Potijze and in the early hours of the morning vacated his quarters which were, within minutes, destroyed by shellfire. By the end of the night the first stage of the withdrawal had been completed without any significant problem, and all that remained was to ensure that the rest of the operation could be completed in a similar manner over the coming nights.

For the men in the front line the decision to begin the abandonment of the tip of the salient could not have come too soon, though at first few of them would have been fully aware of what was going on precisely. In the front line they had suffered another day of heavy shelling and this fact is remarked upon in many of the war diaries and battalion histories of the day, for instance that of the 2nd Essex:

> No advance was made beyond the trenches, owing to the fire of 11 inch howitzers from the Houthulst Forest, which had spent the whole day searching for the Essex, but, happily, did not get nearer to them than fifty yards. The Pompadours suffered somewhat heavily from shell fire, for they had 15 killed and 14 wounded, 2nd Lieut. P.J. Barrell being killed by a sniper.[5]

Whether or not the large calibre howitzer had been searching for the Essex in particular does not matter since the shelling all along the line was heavy throughout the day, and it should be noted that, although they had remained in the trenches, they had sustained thirty casualties, mostly as a result of the artillery fire. In a similar vein the 2nd Lancashire Fusiliers' historian commented on the failed French attacks and the Germans' response:

> . . . though this (attack) did not materialize the 12th Brigade received a good deal of the reply of the German artillery to the French guns' preparatory fire and the battalion lost 3 men killed and 28 wounded. The day was spent in strengthening the position by thickening the banks and building revetments and parados with sandbags. The night was calm.[6]

Throughout the salient men were still to be employed on fortifying their positions, for although the intention was to withdraw it was necessary that the defences were as sound as they could be should there be any attempt by the Germans to attack the front line. However, it would appear that the shelling, while heavy, did not affect all the front line, as shown by the experience of the London Rifle Brigade:

> On 1st May warning orders for the readjustment of the line were received, and the necessary instructions, which were to come into force on the receipt of further definite move orders, were issued at a conference of company commanders which was held in the open, so quiet were the enemy.[7]

At this time the London Rifle Brigade were holding the trenches along the Fortuin-Gravenstafel road and it is hard to imagine why a portion of the 11 Brigade front should have escaped the shelling which was so heavy on the 12 Brigade front. Perhaps, since the latter brigade was holding the junction with the French, the Germans may have been probing along that line searching for a weakness or a break. The London Rifle Brigade did not, however, escape the consolidation works and some "slip trenches" were dug to provide additional cover, while at dusk burial parties were found to bury the soldiers they had found in the field adjacent to their position.

Whilst the withdrawal was a necessary and welcomed plan of action, once it had started the line and the salient was at its most vulnerable and for the senior officers and men alike it was a very tense time. Disengaging with the enemy is never an easy manoeuvre, but to do it in a manner that the enemy would remain unaware of it until it was complete needed careful planning, cooperation of all involved and no small element of luck. If the Germans decided to attack in force at any time after the withdrawal had commenced the British troops in the salient would have been in a very difficult position. Even though the first phase had progressed satisfactorily, there were still two tense nights and two long days before it could be completed and during that time it was hoped that the Germans would satisfy themselves with bombarding the trenches, for although that may produce casualties it would require an infantry assault to take and hold the ground.

Whilst over most of the salient the Germans were happy to continue shelling the British positions, there was one area which had become something of a thorn in their side. As described earlier, Hill 60 had been captured by the British on 17th April and the Germans were not happy with the situation. There had been heavy fighting on the hill since its capture and at approximately 7 pm on 1st May the Germans decided to make a further attempt to wrest Hill 60 from the British grasp. On the morning of that day the 1st Dorsets had relieved the 1st Devons on the crest of the hill, the latter unit going into supports in the shelters at Larch Wood. To their left was the 1st Bedfords who had been in that position for five days. The Dorsets were organized such that A and C Companies were on the hill and B and D Companies were in support trenches about 100 yards behind. The hill was by that time a terrible sight, with the dead of the two nations lying all over the place. It was almost impossible to provide any burial parties to even begin to clear the ground, for since the area was swept by fire almost continuously any movement simply invited more casualties. Numerous accounts of the hill at this time state that it was impossible to dig a trench without uncovering the dead of the earlier fighting. The stench of death and decay gathered over the hill like a pall which can only be imagined by anyone who did not experience it.

The enemy opened his attack on 1st May with a fierce bombardment using everything from trench mortar to large calibre guns. Then after a few minutes the Germans released gas, and in no time it was on top of the Dorsets on the crest of the hill. Sergeant Major Ernest Shephard of the Dorsets commented on this new form of warfare:

We had just given orders guarding against the gases the Germans use. These orders had just reached one platoon (No.7) when the enemy actually started pumping out gas on to us. This gas, we were under the impression, was to stupefy only. We soon found out at a terrible price that these gases were deadly poison. First we saw a thick smoke curling over in waves from the enemy trenches on left. The cry was sent up that this was gas fumes. The scene that followed was heartbreaking. Men were caught by fumes and in dreadful agony, coughing and vomiting, rolling on the ground in agony.[8]

It was their first experience of gas and, although there was some information on how to deal with it, there would appear to have been some confusion over just how deadly it actually was. Within minutes no one in the Dorsets' trenches had any doubt!

As soon as the alarm for gas was raised Lieutenant Colonel E.G. Williams, of the recently relieved 1st Devons, called his men out and, completely under his own initiative led them into the gas to support the unfortunate Dorsets. When the Devons reached the trenches they found them to be full of men "choking and gasping for breath, some foaming at the mouth, in every degree of agony and distress".[9] The defence had been broken over a line of about 400 yards, except for Second Lieutenant R.V. Kestell-Cornish (1st Dorsets)[10] and a small group of men who had leapt onto the fire step, to some extent avoiding the full effects of the gas as it gathered in the bottom of the trenches, and opened fire on the Germans, who were by that time trying to close on the trenches of the gassed defenders. Major H.N.R. Cowie[11] of the Dorsets, reported to Brigade afterwards on methods of protection used during the day:

> 2/Lieut. Kestell-Cornish at first used a bit of rifle flannelette; at one time he appeared on the point of collapse, but the application of a hand-kerchief well soaked in water enabled him to carry on.[12]

Major Cowie also remarked that getting the men on the fire step immediately seemed to reduce the effects of the gas.

The Devons were able to offer great assistance in filling the gap in the line that the gas had caused:

> But the Devons arrived in time; as they reached the trenches they manned the parapet and started firing at the advancing enemy. Some men, though not trained machine gunners, managed to get the Dorsets' machine-guns in action, and in the nick of time the German advance was stopped.[13]

Further, their bombers were able to act to stop small parties of Germans who were attempting to work around the edges of the main craters and into the British lines. At about this stage there was a slight shift in the breeze, with the effect that the gas began blowing back on the Germans, who immediately withdrew as fast as they could. Sergeant Shephard wrote in his account that when this happened the surviving Dorsets wanted to charge after them, so incensed had they become at the sight of their own dead and dying caused by the gas. Of course they were prevented from doing so, since it was more important to re-establish the line that had nearly been overrun than anything else. The 1st Devons had acted promptly, and thanks to Lieutenant Colonel

Williams' reading of the situation they had helped the Dorsets at a crucial time; in fact, the Brigade Order recording the incident comments on the Devons' "resourcefulness, devotion to duty, cool temerity and endurance"[14] as contributing to the security of the hill on 1st May.

To the left of the Dorsets the 1st Bedfords had come in for some very similar treatment as the gas came over them and the shelling continued. Many of the men were overcome by the gas in the first few minutes of the attack, and soon a trench on the left of the area (Trench 46) could not be manned and was briefly abandoned. However, one soldier, Private Edward Warner, went back to the trench and manned it alone to prevent the Germans entering it. The Germans did not press the attack vigorously at this point, possibly because they too were feeling the effects of their own gas, and Warner was able to keep them out with accurate and sustained rifle fire. Efforts were made to send up reinforcements to Warner, but they all failed to reach him because of the concentration of the gas. Eventually, Warner, though affected by gas and nearing exhaustion after fighting in the trench alone, went back and brought up men himself and the trench that had almost fallen into the Germans' hands was held, and the attack gradually died away. Warner died shortly afterwards from the effects of gas poisoning; he was awarded a posthumous Victoria Cross for his gallantry that day.[15]

The German account of the fighting on 1st May suggests that they were attempting another experiment, and some sources record that there was no infantry assault. The accounts of those regiments involved in the heaviest fighting suggest otherwise. Indeed, if it had been an experiment it is difficult to understand what was hoped to be achieved by it. The Germans already knew of the effects of their gas – it had been used on the other side of the salient already and to some effect – and it can only be assumed that the experiment was in fact an effort to dislodge the British from Hill 60. In so far as the line had held it must be seen as an experiment that failed. Also, there must have been some increasing doubt in the minds of the Germans as to the effectiveness of the gas, especially since some of it appears to have blown back on the assaulting troops. For all that, it had been a very sharp action which had caused over 200 casualties in the 1st Dorsets, with most of those being from C Company which had been on top of the hill, while the Bedfords recorded 293 casualties by the time they were relieved at the end of the first week of May. The Devons, who had charged up so vigorously to fill the gap, were much luckier with only seven killed and thirty-one wounded. Sergeant Shephard summed up the fighting on the hill that day:

Hell could find no worse; the groans of scores of dying and badly hurt men, the chaos which, however, soon gave way to discipline, the fierce fighting and the anxiety.[16]

The fighting for the hill subsided by dawn on the 2nd May. It had been a vicious night at Hill 60, but to the north the rest of the salient remained untroubled by German infantry, and by dawn the first phase of the withdrawal had been successfully completed.

Notes

1. Burrows, op.cit., p125.
2. See *Official History 1915 Vol. 1*, p286.
3. ibid., p287.
4. ibid.
5. Burrows, op.cit., p125. Second Lieutenant Philip James Barrell is commemorated on the Menin Gate.
6. Latter, op.cit., p39.
7. Maurice, *The History of the London Rife Brigade*, p97.
8. Shephard, *A Sergeant-Major's War*, p40.
9. Atkinson, *The Devonshire Regiment, 1914–1918*, p79.
10 Captain Robert Vaughan Kestell-Cornish died of wounds 17th June 1918. By that time he had been awarded a MC and Bar and had been mentioned in despatches four times.
11. Major Cowie died of wounds 20th May 1915 and is buried in West Woodhay Churchyard, Berks.
12. *History of the Dorsetshire Regiment*, p68.
13. Atkinson, op.cit., pp 79–80.
14. ibid., p80.
15. Private Warner is commemorated on the Menin Gate.
16. Shephard, op.cit., p40.

CHAPTER TWELVE

The Battle of Saint Julien
Day 9 – 2nd May 1915

The withdrawal during the night of the 1st–2nd May left three regular divisions manning the main part of the salient, which was itself to be evacuated during the following nights. On the right, from the southern edge of Sanctuary Wood, was the 27th Division; in the centre of the salient from the middle of Polygon Wood to Berlin Wood, near Gravenstafel, was the 28th Division; from here to the junction with the French in the vicinity of Turco Farm was the 4th Division. The French completed the defences of the salient in the north by carrying the line to the Yser Canal, and thence along its west bank northwards to their eventual junction with the Belgian Army, at Steenstraat. In the south the 5th Division completed the defences from Sanctuary Wood to the vicinity of Saint Eloi. The coming days were to be of great importance to the Allies and their defence of Ypres. Whilst it had been recognized that to regain ground would have been the ideal answer to the German offensive (or experiment as they preferred to think of it), it was eventually also realized that this was not going to happen, and once the withdrawal had commenced the increased vulnerability of the salient made it even more important that those troops in the line behaved as near to normal as possible. To some extent this depended on the behaviour of the Germans. If they pressed attacks on to the somewhat weakened divisions during this phase of the operation, the men in the front line could hope for little support and could only fight it out. However, if the Germans remained relatively quiet, then it was hoped the withdrawal would be completed without the enemy becoming aware of the goings on in the British trenches.

178

Sunday 2nd May began quietly enough and at 10.45 am General Plumer issued the orders for the second stage of the withdrawal, which was to include the removal of the 2 Cavalry Division from reserve at Potijze and the 149 and 151 Brigades, which had been supporting the 28th Division. If all went well these troops and the remaining artillery would be removed on the evening of 2nd May; but a little over an hour after the order had been issued the Germans were to have something to say about the events of the day. At noon they opened a heavy bombardment along the northern flank of the salient from approximately Berlin Wood to Turco Farm, or along most of the front held by the 4th Division. It was a furious bombardment which had clearly been designed to do as much damage to the forward trenches as possible, and throughout the day they treated other sections of the line to the same kind of ferocity. This immediately suggested to everyone concerned that there was to be an infantry assault on the northern flank. This did not occur at first, though the shelling continued into the afternoon. Then, following a relatively quiet period, the Germans switched to gas shells at about 4 pm and followed this up with the release of cloud gas at 4.30 pm. At that point an attack looked imminent – the hours of shelling had been merely to soften up the front line ready for the infantry assault that was about to follow. Suddenly the hopes for the next phase of Plumer's plans for the withdrawal seemed to be at risk, as all along that part of the salient men steadied themselves in preparation for the inevitable assault.

At this stage it is perhaps appropriate to review briefly the arrangements that had been made for protection against gas. It was soon realized that the gas used by the Germans on 22nd April was chlorine, and it did not take long for it to be appreciated that some form of breathing apparatus would be required if men were to be able to hold the front line against this weapon. In its simplest form a defence against the gas could be a wetted rag pressed against nose and mouth, and although not suitable for long exposures to the gas it could be effective. During the days immediately following the first use of gas there was considerable activity to come up with a more satisfactory method to combat the gas. Following the capture of the German prisoner in mid-April, it was known that the German assaulting troops had been supplied with gauze pads which had been impregnated with suitable chemicals and which were to be strapped around the nose and mouth. It was to this method that the British Army first looked as its medical and scientific officers sought the best answer to minimize the effects of the gas on the front line troops. By the beginning of May the army had begun issuing "pads of compressed cotton wool", which had been impregnated with a solution of sodium hypochloride. The idea was that,

179

providing the pad, and thus the chemicals, were kept moist, they would neutralize the effects of the gas, at least in the short term, to allow the defenders to man the line as the gas passed over them. According to some accounts, such as that of the 2nd Lancashire Fusiliers, these "respirators" were issued in small quantities at first with no more than two per platoon being available to any battalion. It is difficult to imagine how the command could have considered it worth issuing so few, but it appears that by indicating the approach to be adopted in the defence against gas, the staff hoped that the front line troops would be able to improvise to adopt similar but makeshift devices. Indeed this turned out to be the case, and as Captain E. Byrde of the 2nd Monmouths noted:

> That freezing winter (*of 1914*) the ladies of Pontypool had sent the battalion 800 body belts made out of flannel. The Colonel had them issued to each man with instructions always to carry them and keep them damp so that they could be wound around their heads to cover mouth and nose in the event of a gas attack. Even a safety pin was provided.[1]

At least some effort was being made to combat the threat of the gas but everyone was aware that these were no more that rudimentary, stop-gap, measures. As Sergeant Ernest Shephard, of the 1st Dorsets, commented during the fighting of 1st May on Hill 60, the pads did not fit properly and some men found difficulty in breathing in and out through the pad. The adjustment of the pad on the face was very important; if a man had not paid close attention to this when tying it in place it was not long before he fell victim to the poison. In short it was a lot to do and remember when the enemy were shelling and preparing to attack the trenches. These were issues which had become apparent to the men of the 1st Dorsets the day before, but it is unlikely that this experience would have been known to the men of the 4th Division on the other side of the salient less than twenty-four hours later. It was necessary, at this time, for all the troops involved to make the best arrangements that they could for their defence against gas, and un-fortunately such information as was available was not always passed along to those who really needed it and could make best use of it.

When the gas attack of 2nd May arrived it fell on the 12 and 10 Brigades between Fortuin and Turco Farm. Even then it was not evenly distributed, since the breeze was irregular and caused greater concen-trations of the gas in some areas than others. The 2nd Essex and the 2nd Lancashire Fusiliers were both badly affected whilst the 1st King's Own, in the line between them, suffered much less. The London Rifle Brigade (11 Brigade), on the right beyond Fortuin, also reported the effects of gas, whilst the battalions on the left of the 10 Brigade, to their left, remained largely unaffected. For the Lancashire Fusiliers the effects were devastating. As the gas approached them in the line near Shell Trap Farm there was a frantic hurry amongst the men to prepare themselves in the way that they had been told. In B Company, a little to the east of the farm, the medical officer, Lieutenant W. Tyrrell, ordered the men to use a wetted rag over their noses and mouths to protect themselves. In the confusion that had ensued following the warning of gas much of the available water in the trench, and the tea that had just been prepared, was spilled and Tyrrell immediately urinated on a rag and urged the men nearby to do the same. The natural ammonia in the urine gave added protection against the gas and at least B Company were able to stand to arms as the gas reached them. According to the battalion history, A and D Companies had not been so fortunate since they did not receive Tyrrell's demonstration and suffered accordingly. Tyrrell is reported to have been "more than a hero" on that day and took full part in the defence of the line when the enemy infantry finally appeared.

During the coming minutes another man was to emerge as a hero for the 2nd Lancashire Fusiliers, and his action undoubtedly helped to stem the German infantry assault which was developing by then. Private J. Lynn was one of four machine gunners in the Battalion at the time and as soon as the gas appeared Lynn, anticipating the infantry assault, got his gun working and fired through the encroaching gas cloud. Soon unable to see because of the gas, Lynn got out of the trench with his gun and mounted it on the stump of a tree which he then straddled so that he could move the gun as freely as possible to get the best field of fire. He then poured fire into the cloud as his comrades struggled to keep him supplied with ammunition as the gas cloud passed over them. Soon the gas had thinned sufficiently for Lynn to see his targets and he continued to fire until, with the help of the French artillery firing from west of the Canal and accurate rifle fire from the trenches, the assault gradually died away. Lynn had played a crucial role in the defence of the Lancashire Fusiliers trenches and as a result the line had held. Of course Lynn was one of those who had not been issued with a "respirator"; he had faced the gas totally unprotected and even as the attack died away and Lynn was near to collapse himself, his first thoughts were of his wounded and gassed comrades whom he immediately began to help. Shortly Lynn too collapsed and was carried away to a dressing station, where he died in agony the following day as a result of the gas poisoning he had received in the fighting. For his bravery and self sacrifice in action Lynn was awarded a posthumous Victoria Cross.[2]

Whilst all this was going on it was becoming clear that some Lancashire Fusiliers to the north of Shell Trap Farm had been totally overcome by gas whilst others left the trenches in an effort to get away from its effects. Private G. Ashurst was in the support trenches at the time and his account of the events is quite clear on how it all came about:

> Suddenly there was a noise of thundering feet on the top of our trench and figures began to jump clean over our trench and heads. They were men from our front line, and as this went on someone passed the word along the trench to retire. Whether the order was official or not I don't know but there was a rush to get out of the trench; our officer tried to calm the men but he might as well tried to calm a rough sea. Away we ran across the open, not knowing or caring, so long as it was further away from the horrible gas and bombardment.[3]

This action by some of the men of the Lancashire Fusiliers had caused a small gap in the 12 Brigade front and the 7th Argyll and Sutherland Highlanders were ordered forward to fill it:

> . . . the regiment therefore advanced and reoccupied the trenches, arriving in time to check the enemy's advance before it had developed, in this we were helped by the machine guns which had been left in position in the trench and which were worked by the first officers to arrive. Many of the men were quite useless from the effects of the gasses and so had 25 men afterwards admitted to hospital suffering from the effects.[4]

The gap had been filled in this area and the 5th South Lancashires were brought up in support of those battalions already committed, as were the 4th Hussars and the 5th Lancers of the 3 Cavalry Brigade, who were actually at the time preparing to be evacuated from the salient.

In the centre of the 12 Brigade front things were not as bad. The variable distribution of the gas meant that the 1st King's Own were able to cope; their battalion war diary even called the Germans' infantry assault "half hearted". For all that, the Germans succeeded in getting into a farm (Listening Patrol Farm[5]) on their front, but were soon driven out when a Corporal Cooper led twenty men in a small counter-attack to regain the buildings – unfortunately the British artillery, assuming that the Germans were still in residence, proceeded to shell the farm and Corporal Cooper and his small force were driven back to their own lines.

The vagaries of the gas played another trick on the left of the King's Own when a number of the 2nd Essex were either overcome by the gas or left the trench as a result of its effects:

> The gases were absolutely overpowering; officers and men seemed to lose their senses, most of them getting out of the trenches and reeling towards the rear.[6]

All that remained to man the battalion front was Captain P. Pechell and a dozen men and, but for the presence of mind of the officers in reserve, a critical situation could have developed. Lieutenant N.M.S. Irwin[7] brought up three platoons of A Company (the fourth was already engaged) from some 400 yards behind the front line to the right portion of the trench, while Lieutenant J.V. Atkinson brought up C Company from some 1,500 yards through heavy shellfire and machine-gun fire and was able to reoccupy the centre left of the abandoned trenches. Once again special mention is made in the battalion history of the assistance provided by the French 75s, whose fire had held up the advancing German infantry long enough to allow the Essex reserves to regain the trench. As soon as the danger in this area had been realized, two companies of the 2nd Monmouths were ordered to assist the Essex men. B Company did not receive the order and remained in their trenches near La Brique but C Company, under Captain A.J.H. Bowen, moved forward immediately and they too came under heavy shrapnel fire. They succeeded in gaining the support trench without significant loss and were able to make contact with the Essex to inform them they were ready to help in any way they could should that become necessary. By that time the situation had eased for with the passing of the gas, the Essex were able to beat off any further efforts of the Germans to break through their line.

The story was similar along the line of the 10 Brigade; some battalions suffered quite badly from the effects of the gas whilst others did not. The Battalion war diary for the 1st Royal Warwicks, whilst giving the date for the attack as 3rd May though clearly describing the events of 2nd May, states:

> . . . the gas came on to us, some of our men went back but we formed up as many as possible and made a line in (the) rear. Germans attempted to attack from the Wood[8] which was repulsed with loss.

Other battalions tell of similar events and generally agree that the German infantry assaults were rather ineffective. Nevertheless the shelling and gas were producing casualties all along the 4th Division front. In the 11 Brigade the London Rifle Brigade probably suffered as heavily as anyone and the 4th Yorkshires and the 1st East Lancashires were called upon to assist in holding their trench. One of the LRB wrote about his experiences that day:

> I put on my mask but still got a whiff of it which immediately affected my lungs. My eyes started running and everyone started coughing and it seemed impossible to breathe through the mask. I think some of the boys tore them off but after a few minutes I found I could breathe a little easier and I saw almost everyone was manning their parapet and looking to their front.[9]

The LRB were able to defend their line though not without casualties. Nevertheless, by 8.25 pm they were able to send the following report to Brigade Headquarters:

> Situation quieter. Fear casualties very heavy, will report later. All supports now in trench. Improbable that we can hold length of trench without assistance. Men have had no sleep for seven nights. This, with the incessant shelling, has told on them. Germans are entrenching nearer to us opposite to our centre. No. 3 Company, which is there, hopes that it did good execution on them. Can you send Verey lights?[10]

The LRBs had suffered heavily and by nightfall it was a mixed unit of Londoners, Yorkshiremen and Lancastrians who manned the trenches on the left of the 11 Brigade.

It is interesting to note that the report to Brigade highlights the fact that the Battalion had been in action ever since it had showed up on the scene of the fighting on 25th April. There can be no doubt that the Battalion was tired and depleted, but that did not particularly set it apart from any of its Division or any of those divisions that had been in the line since before the fighting broke out on 22nd April. The war diary of the 1st Royal Warwicks states that fighting of the three days up to and including 2nd May "had somewhat affected the morale of the regiment". All the units were feeling the effects of the continued fighting, most battalions had been engaged more than once and all had had their share of the heavy shelling that had accompanied the fighting up to that date. The losses sustained by some of the units, particularly those, such as in the 10 Brigade, which had been used in the counter-attacks had been so great that they had become shadows of their former selves. It is hardly surprising that by the end of 2nd May some were recognizing problems with morale. However, there was little that could be done for the men. There were almost no reserves and those that were available were not fresh troops – the fresh divisions were needed else-where. Also there were, by that time, moves afoot to withdraw from most of the salient, so that Plumer was more interested in taking troops out of the area than in adding troops to it. There was sense in that approach since a shorter line meant a better chance of relief for all concerned. Unfortunately, on 2nd May, it meant that all those men in the line had to stay put and, what is more, put up a stiff defence should they be required to do so. Until such a time as they were ordered to move it was essential that they gave every appearance of a fully manned and equipped salient. As Plumer had pointed out to Sir John French, the longer the withdrawal was delayed the more difficult it would become, and one of those difficulties was manifesting itself in the battle weariness of the troops that were now required to carry out one of the most difficult manoeuvres for any army. At this stage it was probably just as well that the weight of the Germans' assaults against the 4th Division had not been greater. That they were not is probably reflected in the fact that they believed the line to be more strongly defended than it actually was and that they did not have clear enough objectives, and to that end it is quite clear that, although very tired, the front line units were still putting up sufficient fight to allow Plumer's plan to be completed successfully.

The Official History puts the success of the day, such as it was, down to "deep formation in defence", where supports were close at hand to assist front line troops without delay. To stress the point it goes on to report that the support trenches in the 4th Division area were supplied with signboards which were clearly painted with the words "Counter-attack trenches". This is all very well, but it does paint a rather glossy picture of the actual situation during the day. The units in support had all seen some action already and once they had been called into service there were no more. If there was "deep formation" it was not very deep on the day, though it has to be said that it was deep enough. There is also a belief that the defence of the salient was also assisted by Brigade Headquarters being very close to the fighting and there can be little doubt that, where communications were poor, the speed with which messages could be got to and from Brigade was important. The Brigade Headquarters were, of necessity, very makeshift affairs and the one at La Brique has been described as:

> . . . a five feet deep hole in the ground, with a splinter-proof roof, on the lee side of a house, the walls of the building acting as a shell burster. The hole was divided into two by a sandbag barrier, with an opening through which messages could be handed. In one compartment was the staff, in the other the signallers. There were two entrances, on the Ypres side.[11]

The Second Battle of Ypres had already claimed the lives of two brigadier generals and any number of senior battalion officers, and with places such as La Brique becoming increasingly close to the main firing line it is perhaps fortunate that casualties amongst those directing the battle were not substantially greater.

It was not only in the 4th Division's sector that the defenders were getting a hard time. Elsewhere the Germans had not been able to use their gas and had busied themselves with shelling the line heavily. In the 83 Brigade area (28th Division) for instance, the line was so heavily shelled that many of the soldiers believed it be impossible to get any worse. Of course, this caused casualties as trenches were obliterated and shelters collapsed. Sergeant A. Davies of the 3rd Monmouths wrote to his friends at home giving details of an incident that day:

Our worst time started on May 2nd, when they gave it to us a bit hot. It was on that day that Lce. Corpl. Reg Rumsey and Lce. Corpl. Taylor got buried by a shell bursting on top of their dugout. We managed to get them out after a bit of a struggle, and I think Rumsey acted splendidly. If it had not been for him Taylor would have been dead. After getting his head and arms clear he would not think of anything else but getting Taylor out; in fact he set to at releasing him, and it was rather a good job, for when we got Taylor out he was at his last gasp.[12]

Two soldiers, at least, had had a very lucky escape but the strain of the shelling was having its effect on all troops in the front line and similar incidents and acts of selfless bravery occurred all along the front. The Germans had set about trying to erase the British front line by the best weapon at their disposal, their artillery, and it would probably have served them better to have concentrated on its use, such was its superiority, than to worry about the gas at all. The British had little with which to respond at that time except rifles and machine guns which they used very efficiently when the opportunity arose. However, the Germans may have had better success if their artillery had been used more effectively and in closer conjunction with the infantry tactics of the day. The German artillery was having an effect on the defenders but those who survived the shelling of 2nd May were mistaken in their belief that it could not get any worse; it was not many days before they would see just how bad it could become. It is, perhaps, paradoxical that in an attack designed by the Germans as an experiment on the effectiveness of gas that it was artillery that was becoming the decisive weapon.

On the southern edge of the salient, at Hill 60, the day had been relatively quiet after the ferocity of the fighting the day before. For both sides it was a matter of holding the line and counting the cost. For the 1st Dorsets it was a very sad day as they tried to come to terms with the events of the previous day:

A lot of men are missing, having crawled over back of the trench when gassed and enemy shelled them as they crawled away. We spent a morning looking for these, a few were just living, majority dead.[13]

These words of Sergeant Shephard (1st Dorsets) reflects the sadness and anger that the British soldiers were feeling at the Germans' use of gas, for they knew that they were not able to fight on equal terms in the salient and that was what they wanted. Later that day the Dorsets were relieved by the Devons who had done so much to rescue the situation of the day before. For the moment the Dorsets were to be spared the horror that was the fighting of Hill 60 – but it was not to be long before they would be back in the thick of things in the same trenches.

As suggested by the London Rifle Brigade's report to Brigade, by about 8 pm all was quiet again. The Germans had retired to count the cost of a day's fighting and to contemplate the use of gas on the following day. Bearing in mind the limited success of gas on all but 22nd April, and its complete failure to produce a decisive break on either 1st or 2nd May, there must have been those amongst the enemy command who were beginning to wonder at its effectiveness and usefulness. If the Germans were to make the best use of gas, as they clearly had hoped, then that point had already passed. The element of surprise was no longer with them and without fresh, experienced troops to throw into the assault behind the gas it is difficult to understand what they could possibly be hoping to achieve by its continued use – perhaps it was no more than an experiment in the use of gas in conjunction with advancing infantry. In any event, their lack of success on 2nd May and their willingness to call off the attack in early evening played directly into Plumer's hands. It became so quiet that Plumer was convinced by 9.45 pm that the Germans were not going to make any further moves that day and so he ordered the next phase of the withdrawal to commence immediately. The Official History comments that conditions were favourable for it to commence since sufficient light was provided by both the moon and, sadly, the flames of a burning Ypres which were so intense as to illuminate the countryside for miles around. So the second stage of the withdrawal began, and the reserves that had been available to the three regular divisions were pulled back without any problem, though the two units of cavalry that had been used in support of 12 Brigade were a little late in rejoining the 2 Cavalry Division west of the Canal. All that remained to be completed was the withdrawal of the three divisions left in the apex of the salient to a prepared line along the Frezenberg Ridge though, in fact, the line was far from ready for that eventuality, having no more than limited wire entanglements and trenches that were barely three feet deep. So whilst some problems were being solved, the poor quality of the defences on which the retirement was to take place was to create others which were to become evident in the days to follow. However, the final withdrawal from the apex of the salient still required an element of good fortune simply to achieve this line. Up to the end of 2nd May the Germans suspected nothing as they continued to batter away at the defences – and as long as that was the case then the balance was firmly tipped in the favour of General Plumer.

Notes

1. Dixon, op.cit., p38. Captain Byrde was wounded later in the fighting of Second Ypres, the loss of a leg finished his war.

2. See Appendix II for citation. Private Lynn had already been awarded the DCM. He is commemorated in Grootebeck British Cemetery, Reninghelst.

3. Ashurst, *My Bit. A Lancashire Fusilier at War 1914–1918*, p54.

4. See 7th Argyll and Sutherland War Diary.

5. This farm is thought to be shown as Welch Farm on later maps of the area.

6. See Burrows, op.cit., p126.

7. Lieutenant Irwin finished the war as a Major and had been awarded the DSO and two Bars together with the MC and had been mentioned in despatches no less than five times.

8. The Wood referred to here is likely to be Kitchener's Wood since the Warwicks were at the time in positions near to Shell Trap Farm.

9. See Mitchinson, op.cit., p70.

10. See Maurice, op.cit., p99.

11. See *Official History 1915 Vol. 1*, footnote p292.

12. See Dixon & Dixon, op.cit., p36.

13. Shephard, op.cit., p41.

CHAPTER THIRTEEN

The Battle of Saint Julien
Day 10 – 3rd May 1915

Whilst the withdrawal from the apex of the salient during the night of the 2nd–3rd May had been a success it did mean that the line, now held by three infantry divisions, could expect little support of any kind during the day that must pass before they too could retire. A major feature of this, of course, was that there was almost no artillery support, for although the Royal Artillery had been outgunned for most of the battle, it had always tried to give some infantry cover. This had become increasingly difficult as the battle wore on and it was becoming more than just an ammunition problem. True, the shell shortage was a major problem for the British through most of 1915, to which was added rationing and diversion of resources to other theatres. On top of this was the fact that even if ammunition were plentiful the continued action meant that guns were also becoming a problem. To begin with, some of the larger calibre weapons were of obsolete design and not suited to the fighting of the Western Front, and, furthermore, many of the guns, field guns included, had become so worn as to be on the verge of unre-liability. Barrels had become worn through extended use, increasing the potential for drop-shorts and great inaccuracy, and recoil mechanisms had become worn or broken, rendering guns unusable. The artillery problem was to be an issue far beyond the Second Battle of Ypres, but at least it was an issue that everyone agreed needed addressing and as the year passed things steadily improved for the artillery. However, for the troops holding the salient in the early days of May 1915, it was no use their knowing that things would improve as they were shelled by an enemy that had no shortage of guns – of any calibre – or, apparently, ammunition to use in them. By the dawn of 3rd May, the little artillery cover that was available had all but withdrawn, leaving only some field artillery of 85 and 11 Brigades in the form of some 18-pounder and field howitzer batteries close enough to be of any immediate assistance. The remainder of the artillery had been removed across the Canal where, especially in the case of the worn guns, it was too far away from the apex of the salient to be capable of producing effective cover for the tired infantry. It should be remembered here that portions of the 27th and 28th Divisions had been in the line since before the gas attack and had seen upwards of two weeks of front line duty, during which some of their units had been used to assist in the defence of the northern part of the salient.

Although the Germans could not have known that the larger portion of the artillery had withdrawn from the area, they must have been quite clearly aware of their superiority in artillery, for throughout the battle to that date they had used their artillery with some considerable effectiveness. They began on 3rd May much as they had left off on 2nd, by methodically shelling the British front line and in particular the line in the area of the junction between the 11 Brigade (in the line from Fortuin to Berlin Wood) and the 85 Brigade (positioned from Berlin Wood towards the Roulers railway line). The front line battalions had already endured a day of heavy shelling and the Germans were not going to give them any respite. The account of 1 Rifle Brigade states that their trenches came under fire, from 4.30 am, from a German field gun battery positioned on Gravenstafel Ridge from a range of 1,000 yards. The Rifle Brigade was holding that part of the line, below the Zonnebeke Ridge, to the south and across the Hannebeek stream and to the south-eastern flanks of the Gravenstafel Ridge. To their right, as the line swung into an easterly direction, were the 1st Hampshires followed by the 2nd Buffs in the vicinity of Berlin Wood. To their left was the 1st Somerset Light Infantry and then the London Rifle Brigade, whose left was on the Brigade boundary near Fortuin. It should be remembered here that most of the Gravenstafel Ridge had already been captured by the enemy in earlier fighting and Berlin Wood was just about the last vestige of the ridge still in British hands. Also the line held by the 11 Brigade had been established during the fighting that had resulted in the loss of a large portion of the ridge and it was not as ideally situated as might have been wished. Part of the 1st Rifle Brigade's line, for instance, faced more towards the north-west than anything else, which meant that they could be enfiladed from the German trenches on the Gravenstafel Ridge. To complicate matters further, the line crossed the Haanebeek stream where the ground was inclined to be boggy, such that for seventy-five yards on either side of the stream it was impossible to dig any kind of trench. Whilst it may not have been possible for the Germans to exploit this gap in the defences, it did mean that there were difficulties in communicating with the platoon of A Company of the Rifle Brigade who were manning the north-easterly part of their line, particularly as all movement could readily be observed from the crest of Gravenstafel Ridge. When the shelling started on this section of the line it was not long before the trenches were flattened and all movement became almost impossible. All communications with Brigade were severed in minutes and the shelling was so intense that runners failed to get through. It became necessary for the front line battalions to stay in touch by passing messages from hand to hand along the trench in both directions to allow at least some communication between each battalion and its flanking units.

An hour after the shelling had commenced it became clear that the Germans were beginning to bring men forward along communication trenches, and were massing for an attack. In front of the Rifle Brigade they were digging in as little as 300 yards away in some dead ground in the shallow valley of the Haanebeek. The trenches of the Rifle Brigade were severely damaged by about 8.30 am, but there was no let up in the shelling. One company of the 4th Yorkshires was moved up in support of the Rifle Brigade whilst conditions were deteriorating as the front line trenches were gradually demolished by the German artillery. By late morning A Company, the Rifle Brigade had almost ceased to exist as a result of the gunfire leaving Captain H.G.M. Pleydell-Railston and three men holding about 200 yards of trench south of the Haanebeek. However, it was decided not to reinforce these men unless the enemy actually made a move on the trenches, since it was felt that to send more men forward would simply result in more casualties. Captain Pleydell-Railston, although slightly wounded and at one stage buried by the shellfire, refused to give ground and succeeded in holding his portion of the trench. For his gallantry and determination that day he was awarded the DSO.

To the right of the 1 Rifle Brigade the 1st Hampshires were suffering almost as badly, so much so that the battalion historian points out that the German infantry assault, when it arrived at about 3 pm, was greeted with some relief since, not only did the shelling ease, but the men who had been subjected to about eight hours of shelling were going to be given a chance to fight on more equal terms. As the Germans advanced towards the battered defensive line they found the British soldiers ready for them with rifles and machine guns which was sufficient to halt their advance and to cause heavy casualties amongst the Germans.

However, things were looking bad. There had not been a break in the line but the effects of the German artillery were being felt as casualties mounted and the number of men fit to man the line decreased. Such was the concern that reinforcements were sent up in the form of half the 1st York and Lancasters and half the 5th King's Own, both from the 83 Brigade, to block any gaps that might occur as a result of the infantry assault. Later, further reserves from the 27th Division (2nd King's Shropshire Light Infantry and 2nd Cameron Highlanders, 9th Royal Scots) were sent into the area ready for immediate use. As part of these moves the 3rd Cavalry Division was moved close to Ypres but remained on the west of the Canal, and the 13 Brigade was moved into the vicinity of Brielen for use should the situation deteriorate even further. In the event none of the reserves were required but at 3.30 pm the situation was becoming critical – a German breakthrough on the northern flank which looked to be imminent would have spelled immediate disaster for the 28th Division. The Division would then have needed to have been fighting facing in all directions except south and it would not have been long before they would have been in danger of being cut off. It was also looking increasingly unlikely that General Plumer would be able to make the final withdrawal, though he had issued orders for it at 11.45 am that day. The first German assault was beaten back by the concerted infantry fire but that was not to be the end of it. Once more the Germans shelled the line as their infantry regrouped and then they made another assault on the British, which they concentrated on the positions of the 2nd Buffs in Berlin Wood. The Buffs had suffered heavily during the day and although they had beaten off the enemy once, on the second occasion they were forced to give ground and left Berlin Wood in German hands. With that the last grip of the British on Gravenstafel Ridge was lost. Perhaps this was not important in so far as the intention was to abandon the lines anyway that night but it was still necessary, in the afternoon of 3rd May, to prevent a German break-through if the rest of General Plumer's plan was to be carried out successfully. No sooner had the Germans driven out the Buffs than they turned to their right and attempted to dislodge the 1st Hampshires from their trenches on the flanks of the ridge. The Hampshires held their ground as they met the attack with rifles and machine guns once again, and elsewhere the defenders were able to do the same as the attack gradually came to a halt, although the shelling of the positions continued sporadically for some time.

It had been a severe test for the 11 Brigade, and it must have seemed a very long day as they stood their ground with little artillery support, and took everything that the Germans could throw at them. To be fair, the field artillery remaining in the salient had attempted to respond as soon as the Germans had begun their bombardment. Unfortunately the German counter battery work, with superior numbers of guns, soon swamped the British effort and destroyed a number of the guns that had remained in the salient. Later in the day when the German infantry was massing for an attack in the hollow immediately to the north of Shell Trap Farm, the 39th Battery of XIX Brigade RFA (27th Division), commanded by Major M.J.F. Fitzgerald, opened up with shrapnel in sufficient quantities to cause large numbers of casualties, and succeeded in dispersing the infantry from their assembly point and so lessened the threat from that quarter.

Whilst the shelling and fighting was going on in the north-east corner of the salient, elsewhere, in spite of shelling all along the line, preparations were being made, where they could be, for the withdrawal that was to take place during that evening. In the 84 Brigade, the 1st Monmouths, holding the trenches near Broodseinde, were issued with orders at midday for all company commanders to attend a meeting at Battalion headquarters at 3 pm:

> The meeting was held in the cellar of the Convent in Zonnebeke. Lieut. Col. Robinson informed them that orders had been received for a general retirement from the salient to a position in rear of Frezenberg.[1]

All along the line similar meetings were taking place amongst the officers of the battalions who were not engaged in keeping the Germans out. In the 83 Brigade preparations were not only to include the soldiers who remained in the salient, as one soldier of the 3rd Monmouths recorded:

> I was one of a party that was put to get the civilians out of two farms, the people of the surrounding farms had all fled and left everything behind them. And while we were gathering the people out of the houses we could see the battle raging in front as they were shelling hellish and (we) could see a lot of farmhouses on fire and men and horses and even wounded getting struck down by the shelling.[2]

It is difficult to understand that after months of fighting in the area, some civilians had thought that they could carry on farming whilst all around them there was death and destruction. Admittedly there were few left, though once the military began to get them out it must have signalled to them that this was the final stage of the abandonment of the salient. Unfortunately, the soldier did not describe the reactions of the civilians who were being ejected from their houses and it can only be imagined how they felt since it was the last time that they were to see their homes, for the years of fighting that were to follow obliterated all trace of occupation almost entirely.

Although preparations for the manoeuvre that evening were well underway by mid afternoon, there were tense hours remaining while the fighting continued before the rather isolated divisions could withdraw. If it continued indefinitely then Plumer could not possibly expect to issue the final orders – it would have been impossible to break off in mid-combat to withdraw since this would encourage a full scale German advance which Plumer wanted to delay as long as possible. Besides, there would have been the potential for a full-scale defeat had that been attempted, and Plumer could not have allowed that to happen. As it was his plan was bold and not without difficulty, but if the Germans were unaware of what was going on at least there was a chance of success. Whilst the fighting continued, however, he had no option but to remain in position as long as the Germans were engaging his men. The consequence of that would have been the need to hold the salient for another day with all the problems that would cause, as his front line battalions' casualties mounted as a result of the heavy shelling. Plumer needed to get his tired divisions out as soon as possible but once again the Germans' activity would dictate the final decision. The fighting continued well into the evening, but after their capture of Berlin Wood the Germans made little progress as the 11 and 85 Brigades managed to beat off all the attacks directed at them. By about 9 pm the German infantry called a halt, though shelling continued intermittently throughout the rest of the night. The Germans had suffered heavy casualties as a result of their attack on the British lines, caused by the rifles and machine guns of the British regular divisions. One German account stated:

> Again the attack had come to a standstill, the troops, whose strength had not been kept up, were at the end of their powers. The Companies of the 51st Reserve Division averaged barely 90 men.[3]

The Germans had clearly suffered every bit as badly as some of the British units – at the time a German company should have contained between 180 and 250 men. Whilst they may have had a superiority in artillery, their use of their infantry had been poor as they had hurled men against prepared defences, hoping that some success could be achieved. In that respect, at least, there was little to choose between some of the thinking of the commanders on both sides of the line during the Second Battle of Ypres.

The orders for the final withdrawal from the salient were issued at 11.45 am at the height of the shelling of the forward positions. The first infantry were to move by 9 pm, providing the enemy had stopped their attack, when the first two companies of each front line battalion were removed. In effect this meant that those companies in support were to be moved out of the battle zone first, leaving the front line more or less fully manned to cover their retirement. For the remaining companies there was a tense one and a half hour wait for the next phase of the operation, when half of these would be removed from the front line, halting about halfway between the front line and the new position to await the remaining troops from the front line. The 28th Division was the centre division and therefore it was to be its responsibility to initiate each of the steps involved and to coordinate the movement of the troops taking part. To assist in this an officer from each battalion was assigned to Brigade. In preparation for these manoeuvres, all wounded that could be moved were to be got away as soon as possible; all ammunition, weapons and equipment was to be carried out and anything that could not be carried was to be buried as soon as it was dark so as not to provide anything of any use to the Germans. The 1st Monmouths' records show that they threw several boxes of small arms ammunition and several sacks of bully beef down a well in Zonnebeke brickworks – perhaps this did not constitute the pollution of drinking water which was strictly forbidden under the conventions of warfare at the time! Some of the wounded in the front line were too badly injured to be moved, and these were left in care of the RAMC personnel where possible and so became prisoners of war when the Germans advanced to occupy the trenches the following day. The London Rifle Brigade records, with some pride, that they were able to get all their wounded away, but some battalions were forced to leave as many as fifty men behind – most of these would have been the casualties that had been caused by the shelling during the day. It had been decided that covering parties would not be left behind to engage the German advance on the following day. In the area of the 27th Division, where it was heavily wooded, it was felt that the Germans could have been made to pay dearly for every yard gained. However, to the north in the area of the 28th Division the ground was much more open and it was considered inadvisable to put men at risk in this sector. Therefore, it was decided not to leave covering parties at all once the line had been vacated; it was left empty in readiness for its next occupants.

Eventually the move got under way and although there was some intermittent shelling there were few casualties to hamper the men as they made their way back towards the new line on the Frezenberg Ridge. By approximately 11 pm the only men left in the front line were the parties of about thirty men plus one officer per battalion who had been left to cover the withdrawal. These men were required to man the trenches for another hour during which time it had to appear clear that every trench was fully manned. This was achieved by the small number of men moving up and down their trench and firing randomly from different parts of the line while the officer let off the occasional Very light. The Germans remained convinced, for by midnight these parties began to pull out and were not bothered by the Germans at all. The final stage was completed without casualties, though one man was reported missing, but even he joined his unit during the following morning – he had apparently fallen asleep in the front line trench and had not realized that his comrades had left without him!

In the 11 Brigade there was some relief that they had been able to withstand the attacks of the day and were able to move out that night. Of the 4th Division this brigade had the furthest to move, as their left, and that of the 10 Brigade, tended to rotate about the 12 Brigade with its left fixed on Turco Farm. It was a very tired group of men that marched out of the line that day; for some it was a march to a couple of days' rest, for others it was simply back to the line on Frezenberg Ridge. As they marched, as if to make matters worse, it rained. There were stories of some of the units marching out of the line in step and in the London Rifle Brigade there was even confusion over this though the truth is probably the reaction to the story by a soldier who saw things rather differently:

> Marching in step? What an imagination he must have. We were so bloody weary, I'm not sure we didn't even chuck our arms away. Can you imagine coming out after ten days like that, falling in step? They'd be lucky to get us moving.[4]

The Battalion history simply states that good march discipline was maintained, presumably meaning nothing more than the Battalion stayed together and no one fell out![5]

When the 1st Somerset Light Infantry withdrew it seemed incredible to Captain G.A. Prideaux that they were able to do so without interference from the enemy:

> The Germans were sending up flares all the time and firing their howitzers and field guns at intervals. When we first got to the road we were only about 700 yards away from the German positions and we thought they must hear us, but bar putting two "Little Willies" at us on the road when we were trying to climb over two big trees which had fallen across the road, they never put a shell near us. I have never seen the men march so fast. They marched the same way as they did in the retreat (they were very worn out) with lowered heads and stumbling gait.[6]

The general state of the men as they came out of the line was one of extreme tiredness, tempered with a large amount of relief that they had been able to survive, and there can be no doubt whatsoever that the men who had faced the Germans for the previous days were battle fatigued. The observations made by a member of the 2nd Lancashire Fusiliers as they came out of the line that night are appropriate here:

We must have been pitiable objects, spitting, coughing and dripping wet: our faces blue with cold and the results of the gas; our clothes in a filthy condition; nearly everyone being helped along, and all shambling like old men, but still trying hard to hold our heads up, having faced the worst invention of German warfare and conquered it.[7]

As the night progressed the various units around the great horseshoe front line that was the salient all managed to move without any real problems, but there were some nervous moments, perhaps none more so than for the 1st Monmouths in the 84 Brigade trenches near Broodseinde. Although the withdrawal had commenced without problem there were two incidents recorded in their war diary that indicate how sensitive probably everyone had become as the manoeuvre continued:

> . . . Major Evill was warned by sentries of the N.F's *(Northumberland Fusiliers)* at about 9.30 pm that a strange man, presumably German, had tried to pass over this trench from the British side. He was prevented and disappeared in the darkness. The apprehension was that he might easily have broken through to the German line . . . It is quite certain that if the Germans had suspected this retirement, the Zonnebeke-Ypres road would have been made impassable with shell fire and that there would have been a disastrous loss of life.
>
> About an hour after Lieut. E.S. Phillips had been left with his party of 30 men in trench 18, a German flare was fired over his trench and set an old thatched roof on fire behind his trench, illuminating the trench from behind and giving reason to think that the German suspicions were aroused. He noted the time and had still half an hour to remain as trench garrison. The time, however, passed without further incident.[8]

Whilst these incidents are relatively minor it should be noted that the 1st Monmouths were manning positions across the Zonnebeke road. Along this road would pass much of the 28th Division during the night so that the retirement could be carried out as quickly as possible. If anything had aroused the Germans' suspicions then, as pointed out, they would have shelled this road, and under the circumstances, the effects of that would have been almost as catastrophic as a breakthrough would have been during the day. Once the commitment to the final moves of the withdrawal had been made the worst thing that could have happened would have been for the units involved to have been caught somewhere in the middle of the manoeuvre.

As it turned out these fears were unfounded and General Plumer's plan had worked without a hitch. He had been fortunate insofar as that when the Germans had attacked on 3rd May they had not pressed their attack as hard as they should have. This was at least in part due to the fact that their infantry was also feeling the effects of the fighting, and their casualties were also high. Although Sir John French had been against the withdrawal and had been persuaded to delay it on no fewer than three occasions at the behest of the French, when it was complete he was not sparing in his praise when he came to report it in his official dispatch:

> I am of the opinion that the retirement, carried out deliberately with scarcely any loss, and in face of the enemy in position, reflects the greatest possible credit on Sir Herbert Plumer and those who efficiently carried out his orders.[9]

It had been a great success and with its completion the Battle of Saint Julien officially ended.[10] All that remained was for Plumer's tired divisions to hold the new line, which ran from Hill 60 in front of Hooge, across the Frezenberg Ridge, to Turco Farm by way of Shell Trap Farm. This line had been hastily prepared and poorly constructed and the men coming into it had been in action on and off for almost two weeks. It was going to be a difficult time for all concerned and there was no one who did not believe that the Germans would not follow up on their success of driving the British out of their forward positions in front of Zonnebeke. The next phase of the battle was to demonstrate just how difficult things could get.

Notes

1. See 1st Monmouths War Diary.
2. Dixon & Dixon, op.cit., p36.
3. See *Official History 1915 Vol. 1*, p308.
4. See Mitchinson, op.cit., p72.
5. Maurice, op.cit., p100.
6. See Wyrall, *The History of the Somerset Light Infantry*, p64.
7. See Latter, op.cit., p43.
8. See relevant War Diary and Hughes and Dixon, op.cit., pp 41–42.
9. French, op.cit., p368.
10. It should be noted here that the Battle Nomenclature Committee considered the Battle of Saint Julien to cover the period up to 4th May 1915. The Official History, however, considers that it should more properly cover the period up to 28th April since a new phase of operations, including the withdrawal, commenced thereafter. Whilst this may be correct the terminology of the Battle Nomenclature Committee has been adopted here.

CHAPTER FOURTEEN

The Pause
4th to 7th May 1915

Although the withdrawal of the British from the tip of the salient on the night of the 3rd–4th May was seen as marking the end of the Battle of Saint Julien by the British Battle Nomenclature Committee after the end of the war it is, nevertheless, an arbitrary point within the Second Battle of Ypres. To the front line soldier, who had already endured days of incessant shelling, simply moving to new trenches had not taken him away from the fighting. In the front line they were still in a battle and its intensity during the days covered by the so called Pause should not be underestimated. The days from Tuesday, 4th May to Friday, 7th May are not marked with a "Battle Honour", for the next phase of the Second Battle of Ypres that is officially marked did not begin until 8th May, when the Battle of Frezenberg Ridge is said to have started. The four days preceding 8th May are seen by some as a pause in operations and by others, including the Official Historian, as the opening stages of the Battle of Frezenberg Ridge. It is true that during these four days the German infantry were relatively quiet, but it is equally true that their artillery was not. For those soldiers remaining in the line it would not have seemed to have been anything other than continued action during which the enemy made a number of infantry assaults as if to probe the new line of defences.

The new line ran from Hill 60, on the right, in front of Sanctuary Wood and Hooge towards Shell Trap Farm by way of the Frezenberg Ridge and thence towards Turco Farm where the British and French armies met. The line had been, of necessity, hastily prepared and it was not as deep or as wide as had been hoped for by those men retiring to

199

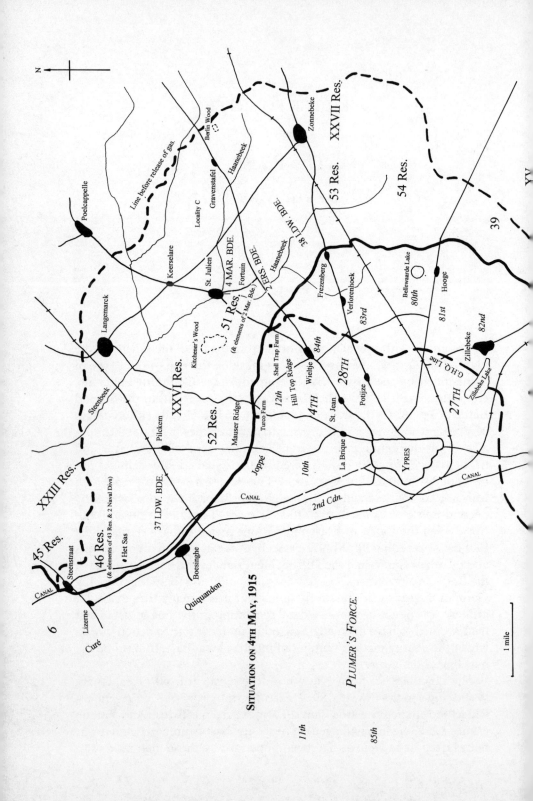

N

Poelcappelle

Line before release of gas

Berlin Wood

Haanebeek

Zonnebeke

XXVII Res.

Gravenstafel

Locality C

53 Res.

54 Res.

39

Keerselare

St. Julien

4 MAR. BDE.

Haanebeek

38 LDW. BDE.

Frezenberg

Verlorenhoek

Bellewaarde Lake

Hooge

Langemarck

Fortuin

2 ERS. BDE.

51 Res.

(& elements of 2 Mar. Bde.)

83rd

80th

81st

82nd

Kitchener's Wood

XXVI Res.

(& elements of 2 Mar. Bde.)

84th

G.H.Q. Line

Zillebeke

Steenbeek

52 Res.

Shell Trap Farm

Wieltje

28TH

Zillebeke Lake

Pilckem

Mauser Ridge

12th Hill Top Ridge

44TH

27TH

Joppé

Turco Farm

St. Jean

Potijze

37 LDW. BDE.

10th

La Brique

YPRES

XXIII Res.

(& elements of 43 Res. & 2 Naval Divs)

CANAL

CANAL

45 Res.

Steenstraat

46 Res.

Het Sas

2nd Cdn.

CANAL

Boesinghe

6

Lizerne

Quiquandon

SITUATION ON 4TH MAY, 1915

Curé

11th

PLUMER'S FORCE.

85th

1 mile

YV

it. To make matters worse it had rained heavily as the retirement proceeded, so that the newly prepared trenches filled up with water, which created new problems for the tired troops manning them, as one member of the 3rd Monmouths noted:

> . . . when we occupied this new line of trenches we found them very badly made and up to our knees in water, and the poor men had no chance of getting any sleep unless they wished to lie down in the water.[1]

Further, the siting of the line left much to be desired for, in some places, particularly in the central portion held by the 28th Division, it was sited on the forward slope of the Frezenberg Ridge. Conventional thinking of the day would have recommended defending the reverse slope, though forward slopes could be defended adequately enough given plenty of artillery support. The position chosen for the line had, to some extent, been forced upon the British commanders, who did not want to give up all the high ground to the enemy by retiring from the Frezenberg Ridge, which would also allow the enemy to bring their guns even closer to Ypres. The lack of suitable artillery meant that the defence of the line was going to be difficult wherever it was sited and there was a feeling that the withdrawal could only go so far, after which it was necessary to be prepared to stand and fight if required. Whilst this may be understandable, it did place the 28th Division in a very difficult position, since all its support needed to crest the low ridge in full view of an enemy with vastly superior artillery.

Nevertheless, by the early morning of 4th May the line had been occupied: the 28th Division in the centre, the 27th Division to its right from north of Bellewaarde Lake to almost Hill 60, and the 4th Division to its left from Shell Trap Farm to Turco Farm. The withdrawal had shortened the line considerably and whilst that did not mean it was going to be easier to defend, it did mean that there was some opportunity to take some of the Brigades out of the line and thereby increase the number of local reserves that were available. In the 28th Division, the 85 Brigade, which had seen heavy fighting to that date, was relieved to the west of the Canal, whilst in the 4th Division the 11 Brigade was moved to the area north-west of Vlamertinge, and the 10 Brigade took up what was essentially a support position behind the French between Turco Farm and the Yser Canal. The Canadians had by this date started on their move to the south, ready for the actions taking place around Aubers Ridge, though on 4th May the 2 Canadian Brigade was still in reserve immediately to the west of the Canal in front of Brielen. It should be remembered at this point that most of the units involved had already seen substantial action during the fighting up to that point and many had suffered substantial casualties. There were not fresh divisions to be had, and therefore those divisions in the line were expected to do the job of holding the line, reinforced and supported as best they could be with those troops that were already to hand. It was not a good situation to be in, but it had been agreed by the Allied commanders that a British offensive at Aubers Ridge, and that of the French in Artois, was of greater importance than the defence of Ypres and, to a large extent therefore, Plumer's Force was to be left to its own devices, and hopefully would succeed in keeping the enemy out of Ypres. It was scarcely the best way to conduct the battle, but since the senior commanders had spoken it was clear that the French were no longer concerned about Ypres and thus Plumer was to put up the best defence he could.

This was not necessarily an entirely bad decision for the defenders of Ypres. Aubers Ridge is about thirty miles from Ypres and an attack there, plus that of the French further to the south in Artois, would certainly have drawn the Germans' attention from their offensive in the salient. This may have been clear to the senior commanders in the area but for the ever diminishing band of defenders it was not going to ease the situation immediately.

On the morning of 4th May the Germans began where they had left off by methodically shelling the old front line. After a couple of hours and the expenditure of much ammunition the Germans realized what had happened during the night and they began to move forward very cautiously. As they did so they brought up their artillery in preparation for further action. General Balk, a German staff officer, was to record his rather romantic view of the events of the early part of the day:

> There was again a scene of mobile warfare, which had not been witnessed for so long, as our leading lines in open order, followed by close supports, broke onto the Flemish landscape, long trains of artillery ammunition columns were brought up at a trot and reserves lay in the green meadows and abandoned British positions. Everywhere in the devastated sector were the mighty results of our weapons to be seen.[2]

It had not taken them long to move to keep up the pressure but they had no precise knowledge of where the British troops actually were – so complete had been the success of the withdrawal – or how strongly the line was likely to be defended. Shortly they came in contact with the British front line as they moved cautiously towards the Frezenberg Ridge. At first it was assumed to be a rearguard, for they met mostly rifle fire and they pressed on hoping to sweep aside this obstacle. It was not long before:

> . . . it became more and more clear that it was not a matter of rearguards at Frezenberg and Westhoek[3] but a forward position of the enemy, behind which stood his main force.[4]

The advance stopped in the face of the British small arms fire and by the afternoon of 4th May the guns which the Germans had been bringing forward began, once again, to shell the forward British positions. It had not taken the Germans long to realize the fact that "the new position could not be taken without a thorough artillery preparation".[5] For the remainder of the 4th May the Germans shelled the line with everything at their disposal:

> They put all the shells you could think of from the "whizz-bang" to the Jack Johnson. We had a lot of men buried in the trench and had to dig another one behind because we could not get the fellows out.[6]

There was little that could be done to respond to this, though the 122nd and 123rd Heavy Batteries were ordered forward to give some support with their old 4.7-inch guns, whose relatively short range required that they move up to Potijze, some 4,000 yards from the new front line. It was a poor response to the bombardment the front line soldiers were receiving. The 3rd Monmouths' (83 Brigade) war diary for the day recorded the effects of the German shelling:

> The new front line which had been hastily and poorly constructed suffered severely from the bombardment. So bad did conditions become that both the 2nd East Yorks and the 5th King's Own were compelled that night to dig a new line just behind the original one. Casualties had been heavy and the wounded were removed with great difficulty, whilst the dead had to be buried where they fell.[7]

By nightfall the shelling had ceased and the Germans contented themselves by digging in at distances of between 200 and 600 yards from the front line.

In the area of the 4th Division it was the 5th South Lancashires which came under the heaviest shellfire as they defended the position around Shell Trap Farm. Here the enemy, recognizing the importance of the ruined farm, made the first of a number of attacks in an attempt to capture it. The enemy worked their way along the trenches so recently abandoned by the British and, in spite of the 5th South Lancs sending out bombing parties, succeeded in moving slowly forward so that by the end of the day they were able to dig in at about 400 yards from their objective. All the fighting had been accompanied by an intense bombardment of the South Lancs trenches, which had increased their difficulty in defending the farm buildings, by now rapidly turning into a pile of rubble.

The dawn of 5th May saw the Germans return to their "preparation" of the ground ready for their infantry, with special attention being paid to the 28th Division front, and it seemed increasingly likely that it would be in that area that the Germans would attempt to break the line. The morning was not very old before the wisdom of siting the trenches on the forward slopes was to be tested to the full. The 2nd East Yorkshires, holding the line immediately south of Frezenberg, were shelled mercilessly and it was not long before their front line trench was so badly damaged as to be almost untenable by the survivors; they called for reinforcements to come forward to assist them to hold what little was left of their position in the face of a particularly determined infantry assault. C Company of the 3rd Monmouths, under Captain O.W.D. Steel, who had been held in reserve in the GHQ line, responded immediately, moving roughly eastwards towards the Ypres-Roulers railway line. As they advanced they came under heavy fire, but worse was to follow. The situation was becoming critical on the East Yorkshires front and so Captain Steel decided to split his company, such that Captain B.M.P. Gorman took half of it by way of the railway cutting to reinforce the right flank of the East Yorks, while he took the other half directly over the crest of the Frezenberg Ridge to reach the left flank more directly. This manoeuvre in broad daylight was recognized to be very dangerous but Captain Steel felt that he had little option, because the East Yorks were suffering so badly from the German fire directed at their trenches and the enemy infantry were rapidly approaching the trenches. Captain Gorman succeeded, under heavy shell and machine-gun fire, in reaching the front line but found that the garrison of the eighty yards of trench he was able to reconnoitre were all dead, victims of the intense shelling, and the line had been almost completely destroyed. As he returned to the railway cutting and his command, he was caught in machine-gun fire and severely wounded. In spite of his wounds he ordered his half company to withdraw to a line just behind the crest of the ridge so as to get as much cover as possible. Captain Steel succeeded in reaching the front line over the crest but not without considerable casualties, and although now supporting the East Yorkshires it was really a question of how long the position could remain tenable. Captain Steel, a doctor by profession, then proceeded to tend the wounded and to bring them under what little cover there was. He was even able to go in search of Captain Gorman whom he found lying in the cutting and was able to make him as comfortable as possible though because of the heavy shellfire there was no chance of evacuating him to the dressing station. Such was the effect of Captain Steel's conduct that day that one of his command, Private A.M. Mitchell, was to write home about the action:

Words utterly fail me to say what a hero Capt. O.W.D. Steel was during that fearful struggle. From every person I meet they tell me the same tale.

Under very heavy shell and maxim fire he went out and fetched in wounded, bandaging them, and if he doesn't deserve a V.C. no man on earth ought to get it. He was a hero in every sense of the word and his men absolutely worship him and I believe would go through hell with him – for such it was that day.[8]

Captain Steel was awarded the MC for his conduct during the Second Battle of Ypres; clearly the higher command had not thought quite as much of his gallant efforts that day as had Private Mitchell. Although the 2nd East Yorkshires had been reinforced, their position was untenable and groups of men dug in behind the front line, filling the gap but not actually occupying the front line. As the day passed, however, small parties did manage to work their way forward to be in front of Frezenberg and near to the positions they had occupied at the start of the day.

In a similar manner, A Company of the 3rd Monmouths, commanded by Captain R.A. Lewis, was called upon to support the 5th King's Own, who were having almost as bad a time of it as the 2nd East Yorkshires. Unfortunately, the results were also similar. Although every effort was made to comply with the order, it was but a limited number of A Company that reached the 5th King's Own trenches. Captain Lewis was one of those to be wounded as the company crested the low ridge and walked into the hail of enemy fire. For the rest of the day the remnants of the company stayed in what little cover they could find and, as one soldier put it:

Talk about hell let loose – it was worse than that . . . and for the whole day we were lying on our faces and hands in the bottom of the trench not daring to move.[9]

The fighting along the front of the 83 Brigade had been dominated by shelling and to a lesser extent the machine guns that accompanied the infantry assaults. Many, if not all, of the casualties sustained by the units engaged on that date were victims of the shrapnel, as the Germans methodically shelled the line, sweeping backwards and forwards across it in an attempt to obliterate all trace of the British occupants. As an example of the effects of the shelling during the day one company of the 2nd East Yorkshires was reduced to no more than twenty effectives. It is hardly surprising that they had asked for support – a full scale infantry assault against the trenches that were so lightly manned could only have resulted in a breakthrough.

At the close of the day C Company, the 3rd Monmouths was withdrawn to its old position in the GHQ line, but A Company went forward to complete the reinforcement of the 5th King's Own and was assisted by D Company. In this sector of the line it had been a bad day which had resulted in substantial casualties as the Germans had used their battering ram techniques. By nightfall things had quietened down and the battered defenders attempted to improve their line and prepare themselves for whatever would come next.

In the vicinity of Shell Trap Farm the story was similar and it was the 5th South Lancs who again took the brunt of the shelling. During the course of the day their trenches were flattened, men were buried alive and there were many casualties. However, they managed to maintain contact with the 1st Welsh on their right and the 1st King's Own on their left. Although they were shelled until approaching midnight they did not give ground and the whole of the line in their sector held. When they were relieved early on 6th May it was a depleted battalion that marched out of its very first battle to support at La Brique where, although they were out of the front line, they were not completely out of danger. Westwards from Shell Trap Farm to the junction with the French army the shelling appears to have been much less and 12 Brigade as a whole were able to maintain their front line without difficulty, though during the hours of darkness some reliefs were made when the 2nd Monmouths moved up to take over the trenches from the 5th South Lancs, one company remaining in support to the 2nd Essex on the left of the 12 Brigade front.

To the south-east of the salient the enemy's tactics were similar as they shelled the lines of the 27th Division throughout the day. For instance, the 2nd Gloucesters, holding a portion of the line near Sanctuary Wood, suffered heavily from the shelling and early in the day lost one of its machine guns to the bombardment. Before the day was out they also lost their dressing station which had been sited in Sanctuary Wood. Later in the day the Division was warned of a German breakthrough in the area of the 5th Division and of Germans cutting the wire in front of one of their own brigades. This latter report seems to have been mistaken, since no meaningful attack developed in this sector. However, the left flank of the 5th Division, against Hill 60, did come under considerable pressure during the course of the day.

At Hill 60 the enemy began the day quite differently. At approximately 8.45 am they released gas with a favourable wind while elsewhere they shelled the line heavily. By 5th May there was some idea of protection against gas and, according to the Official History, some approach towards tactics to combat the use of gas. The front line units were ordered that in the event of a gas attack they were to move to the left and the right out of its way, and to allow the supports to come up through the gas as it dissipated into the rear areas. This appears to be a plausible enough approach and could possibly have worked well enough on a localized scale of a company or, perhaps, a battalion, but the movement of larger units of men, under the threat of gas poisoning, could only have resulted in chaos in the front line trenches and would most likely have resulted in a break in the line. As it turns out this method of defending against gas does not appear to have been tested, for on 5th May the gas tended to drift along the front of 15 Brigade rather than across it which meant that the men in the trenches all became more or less affected. The 2nd Duke of Wellingtons, attached from 13 Brigade, were holding the crest of Hill 60 when the gas was released and Lieutenant C.W.G. Ince recorded:

> We had not received gas masks yet, only a piece of gauze soaked in a preparation prepared by the medical authorities. This solution after a few minutes required renewing, a procedure absolutely impossible, of course, in action. On came the terrible stream of death, and before anything could be done, all those occupying the front line over which it swept were completely overcome, the majority dying at their posts – true heroes.[10]

Immediately there was a gap created where the bulk of the 2nd Duke's had stood, though their supports, some 100 yards behind, appear to have held firm, which probably reflects the manner in which the gas had drifted along the front line rather than penetrating towards the rear areas. However, Brigadier General E. Northey (15 Brigade) ordered forward troops to render assistance, though the first to reach the scene were the 1st Dorsets who had started to move under their own initiative. It is interesting to reflect on this action in the light of the account of one of the 1st Dorsets who took part in the action, for that account is quite scathing about the conduct of the 2nd Duke's. One company of the Dorsets proceeded along the railway line to reinforce the right of the 2nd Duke's line and was followed by the rest of the battalion. According to Sergeant Ernest Shephard (1st Dorsets), as they made their way along the railway they were met by a group of the 2nd Duke's fleeing from the front line and the gas. Upon reaching the support trenches Sergeant Shephard states that they had been abandoned by the 2nd Duke's which is in direct contrast to the account of the events given by the latter battalion. In the opinion of Sergeant Shephard:

> . . . they had no possible excuse for leaving as hardly any gas came over there, and had they hung on there (also the hill) for a few minutes Hill 60 would never have been lost.[11]

Perhaps this is a harsh judgement on the Duke's for of slightly over 500 men who had gone into the line the day before barely 150 were able to answer the roll call following the gas attack on Hill 60. Whatever actually happened, and for whatever reason, the result was as described by Sergeant Shephard, since Hill 60 was indeed lost that day. In the meantime Northey had been able to bring forward the 1st Cheshires and the 6th King's from his reserve but before they could get into action the Germans released more gas against the 1st Bedfords, who had been holding the line to the left of the 2nd Duke's at the start of the day. The result of this was that the right of the Bedfords tended to give way, which increased the size of the gap caused by the departure of the Duke's. There was much confused hand-to-hand fighting as each length of trench was contested bitterly. The Dorsets were in danger of being cut off at this stage as the Germans attempted to work through the gap between them and the Bedfords and to move around to their rear. Fortunately the 1st Cheshires, supported by a company of the 6th King's, arrived and in the fierce fighting that followed the Germans were prevented from exploiting their early successes. Gradually, although the fighting continued, the situation began to ease and Sergeant Shephard recorded:

> We could now pay attention to our wounded and men dying from gas poisoning . . . Most pitiable scenes, several men died in my own arms as I was helping them.[12]

The ordeal was not yet over for those fighting for the hill because the German artillery was, by early afternoon, shelling the whole area vigorously. To make matters worse, when the British artillery made a limited response it was to shell the trenches that had already been regained by the infantry, which caused yet more casualties amongst the hard pressed defenders. There was no way to stop the British artillery since the telephone wires had been cut and all the front line soldier could do was to endure the shelling from friend and foe alike. However, gradually throughout the afternoon the mixed force of Cheshires, King's, Bedfords, Dorsets and Duke's pushed back the enemy to a point where the Dorsets had first entered the fighting at about 9 am that morning. Nevertheless, at 7 pm the crest of Hill 60 remained in the hands of the enemy and everyone knew it was going to be very difficult to drive them off it.

At 9 pm 13 Brigade (Brigadier General Wanless O'Gowan) arrived on the scene with three of its battalions (1st Royal West Kents, 2nd KOSB and the 2nd KOYLI), with orders from the 5th Division to counter-attack on the left to recapture the hill. The 2nd KOSB were ordered to attack the hill itself with two companies, holding two in support for consolidation purposes, while the 1st Royal West Kents were ordered to attack on the left to capture the trenches to the north of the hill. The attack was planned for 10 pm and consequently at 9.40 pm a short bombardment of the hill began "which warned without cowing the enemy"[13] in their trenches on the crest of the hill. To add to all the other problems these two battalions already had, they were to be attacking over battle scarred ground littered with the debris and corpses of the best part of a month of solid fighting and they were doing it in darkness. Nevertheless, at the appointed time both battalions set off. The 2nd KOSB battalion history describes the attack:

> C's attack was crushed instantaneously by heavy fire. D reached their objective, but were exposed to enfilade fire from the Caterpillar, and were also bombed from close range. Both companies had to retire and occupy the trenches from which they started.[14]

The attack of the 2nd KOSB was witnessed by Lieutenant A. Greg of the 1st Cheshires from his position in Trench 40 and his graphic account of the action best describes the conditions on the hill that night:

> At the allotted time they climbed over the parapet. The order was to go half right. They were met with a storm of rifle and machine gun fire from the hill. Our artillery had not yet stopped and soon theirs started. The poor Scots were simply blown back with lead. They started again and went half left. Their wounded were pouring into my trenches. The sounds were terrible, men shrieking, the fierce cackle of machine gun fire and the cruel shriek of the shrapnel. This was battle. When the next volley of star lights went up there were noticeably more bodies in no man's land. Wounded and belated Jocks were still returning, some helping other wounded back or bringing back the body of some comrade. The shattered remains of a fine regiment all found their way back to my already overcrowded trench and its continuation to the right.[15]

The 2nd KOSB suffered over 130 casualties; they had achieved nothing. The 1st Royal West Kents were met with a hail of shellfire and made no progress and they too were forced to retire to the trenches they had started from. The Germans were still firmly in control of the crest of Hill 60. The 2nd KOSB historian (Captain Stair Gillon) raises the point concerning Hill 60 which had certainly bothered some of the senior officers, when he states that to hold Hill 60 and the small salient which it formed without capturing the rest of the high ground was "doomed" to failure. It had been thought that it would be necessary to capture the Caterpillar on the other side of the railway cutting when Hill 60 was captured, but the limited objective set and achieved on 17th April had, ultimately, to be yielded once again to the Germans in whose hands it looked like remaining for the time being. The Official History considers that the hill might have been held had it not been for the Germans' use of gas. This is an optimistic view of the situation, bearing in mind the Germans' overwhelming superiority in firepower which would have, in all probability, made the hill untenable for the

British – the use of gas speeded up the inevitable and, paradoxically, may actually have served to limit the casualties both sides suffered in the awful fighting for the hill. Perhaps the most moving description of the events on the hill on 5th May comes from the record kept by Lieutenant Ince, 2nd Duke's:

> The Battalion suffered over 300 casualties that morning, large numbers dying as a result of the barbarous gas. The writer will never forget the sight of men writhing in agony and slowly dying from the asphyxiating effects of chlorine, nor of the feeling of helplessness at being unable to do anything for them.[16]

There was one further attempt to regain the hill on 7th May, which is described later.

The 5th May had been a very trying day all along the front as the defenders had endured severe shelling in their new line. The line had held, but that was more because the Germans had not made any determined effort to attack, than for any other reason. The shelling was having the desired effect for the Germans in so far as it was causing casualties and making parts of the line untenable, as well as destroying other parts of it completely. To finish the day the British had to accept the fact that Hill 60 had been wrested from their grasp and that the bloodshed on that scrap of land had been to no avail. It had been a bad day and there would have been many, officers and men alike, who would have been wondering just how much worse it could get.

On the morning of 6th May the Germans began in much the same manner as they had on the days immediately prior to it. The salient had shrunk to little more than a large artillery target and the Germans, their guns now well registered, shelled the lines around the salient without any real interference from the British artillery. The war diary of the 3rd Monmouths records quite simply, "Bombardment of trenches but not so severely", but nonetheless the shelling continued throughout the day. To an officer of the 1st Welsh, on the left of the 28th Division's line, it seemed as if the Germans targeted a section of the line, approximately a battalion wide, shelled it for about two hours and then moved on to the next section. This might have been the case for it was the Germans' intention to shell all portions of the line sufficiently so that it may be prepared for the infantry assault they were planning. The officer of the 1st Welsh was to remark, somewhat unhappily:

> As it was dawn about 3 am and not dark till 9 pm , the days seemed, and were, hideously long, without anything to relieve the monotony. After dark all the wounded going back had to run the gauntlet of the road for several hundred yards, through intermittent shelling and pretty continuous machine gun fire. We felt we were simply canon fodder.[17]

This officer is speaking for all the men that were subjected to the intense bombardment of the British lines about Ypres in early May 1915. All around the salient the conditions were very similar. In some areas it became apparent to some soldiers that German sniping had increased during 6th May, and it was suggested that this was a direct result of the Germans completing their task of digging themselves in to their new line. There was no real let up in the shelling throughout the day, towards the end of which preparations were being made for a counter-attack to recover Hill 60 from the Germans. It is difficult to understand the logic behind this attack. An immediate counter-attack using two battalions on the night of 5th May had failed with high casualties. Now, a day later, by which time the Germans had certainly consolidated their gain there was to be a further attack, again at night over the same battle scarred ground, by one battalion, the 2nd King's Own Yorkshire Light Infantry. It must be imagined that this battalion, which had been in reserve for the attack the night before, must have viewed the prospect with some apprehension in the light of the results achieved in the previous counter attack.

The 1st Cheshires held some of the trenches immediately in front of Hill 60, namely: Trench 38, immediately against the railway line; Trench 39, extending in a sweeping curve northwards in front of the hill itself; and part of Trench 40, carrying the line around the base of the hill. The Germans had occupied the remainder of Trench 40 and both they and the Cheshires had erected a block within the trench. To consolidate their gains during their attack, the Germans had dug a trench across the mouth of the salient formed in their lines by the trenches they had occupied and were, therefore, about 100 yards distant at a maximum and in possession of the hill. The plan for the attack, which was to commence at 2.30 am on 7th May was for the block in Trench 40 to be exploded from the Cheshires' side to give the signal for the 2nd KOYLI to attack from Trench 41 straight to the new German line and into the salient beyond. There is no record that any artillery preparation or support was to be used in this attack and bearing in mind the efforts the Germans had used to remove the British from the hill, it would seem to have been a simplistic plan which had not been clearly thought through and was doomed to failure. At the appointed time the 2nd KOYLI sent two companies (A and B) into the attack, even though the planned explosion at the block in Trench 40 had not taken place, and they met with a withering machine-gun fire and rifle fire. Although very reduced in numbers these two companies succeeded in capturing the new German trench and in going into the salient beyond towards the crest of the hill. Later during 7th May Captain C.E.D. King, who had been in charge of B Company, was able to report that he and a party of eight had managed to reach a point about twenty-five yards from the enemy, where they were pinned down throughout the daylight hours. Upon his report it was quite clearly realized that only a small number of men had survived to cross the enemy's first trench and although supported by the remaining two companies, and some of the Cheshires who had succeeded in detonating the explosion at the block in Trench 40 and had advanced some forty yards, the attack had been a complete failure. The gallantry of the men carrying out the attack cannot be doubted but the poorly conceived attack had cost the 2nd KOYLI eleven officers and 177 other ranks killed, wounded and missing. At the end of the day they were withdrawn and the hill stayed in German hands. Mercifully, no further attempt was made to wrest it from the Germans during this period of the war – the hill stayed in German hands until June 1917 when it fell as part of the operations of Messines Ridge. The fighting for Hill 60 during April and May, 1915 had cost the 5th Division 100 officers and over 3,000 other ranks as casualties. The capture of the hill had been cheap, there can be no doubt about that, but holding it had proved to be far too expensive.

Early on 6th May General Smith-Dorrien, whose command had been severely reduced by the formation of Plumer's Force, wrote to the Commander-in-Chief for clarification of the situation, and pointed out that the lack of trust that French had demonstrated in his action had seriously weakened the chain of command. Therefore, he suggested it would be appropriate for him to serve elsewhere. It was, in effect, his resignation, and Sir John French accepted readily. That evening Smith-Dorrien received orders to hand over his command to Lieutenant General Plumer and to return to England. He was not given the courtesy of an explanation of any kind. With immediate effect Lieutenant General Sir Herbert Plumer took over command of the Second Army and Lieutenant General Sir Edmund Allenby took over the command of V Corps from Plumer. Although Plumer's Force had been reducing in number as various units were returned to their commanders, it did not cease to exist until 6 am on the morning of 7th May, by which time Plumer was in his new role as Army commander. Thus ended one of the saddest episodes in the whole battle. At the height of the fighting, two senior officers of the Army had a difference of opinion on the continuing conduct of the battle and at least one of them allowed personal grievances to get in the way of coming to the correct decision. Unfortunately, it was to lead to the dismissal of one of the more capable commanders when Smith-Dorrien was ordered back to England.[18] He never served in France again and the only loser in that was the British Army. He was later given command of the East African forces but a bout of pneumonia prevented him from taking up the appointment. This was seen by some as evidence of the breakdown of his health which had been cited by French as part of his reasons for his dismissal. This may suggest that Smith-Dorrien would never have held a senior post in France for long. Although French's point on his pessimism[19] was overstated as a reason to dismiss him it is seen by some as indicative that he was unsuited to the stresses of Command in a European war. French's attitude towards Smith-Dorrien was unfortunate, but the Commander-in-Chief's star was not long in the ascendancy and before the end of a bloody and unsuccessful year he, too, had been replaced by General Sir Douglas Haig – and Great War military historians never tire of arguing about that particular soldier's approach to the war.

During the night of 6th and 7th May there had been some relief of the battalions and companies around the line. The 1st Welsh, which had endured days of shelling, were relieved by the 2nd Northumberland Fusiliers, but their Battalion history says that they were somewhat envious of the incoming Fusiliers since everyone felt that there was going to be an infantry assault soon. Then they would have been able to use their rifles to get a little bit of their own back for the suffering of the previous few days. For much of the Second Battle of Ypres it was the lot of the infantryman to endure heavy shelling without having any way of striking a blow for himself, so it is perhaps not an empty wish that was expressed by the Welsh as they left their trenches that night. The shelling did not abate during the day and during the following night elements of the German 2 Marine Brigade launched an attack against the area of Shell Trap Farm, including the lines of the 2nd Northumberland Fusiliers (84 Brigade) and the 2nd Monmouths (12 Brigade). It was a determined assault which lasted into the early hours of the morning of 8th May and could, possibly, be seen as the start of the next phase of the battle when the Germans started all-out infantry assaults against the ground their artillery had been preparing in the preceding days. In the Fusiliers' trenches there was heavy fighting as they beat off the attack, though they suffered only three fatalities as they inflicted more substantial losses on the advancing enemy. In the Shell Trap Farm area the 2nd Monmouths had a bit more of a problem. This was partly because the attack caught them in the middle of a company relief. The outgoing company immediately turned around to render assistance as the farm came under heavy fire. A shell landed amongst the garrison of the ruined buildings and the two officers and all the NCOs were put out of the fight. At that point Drummer D. White took charge of the situation and swam across the few yards of the moat surrounding the farm to get information and orders. He was told to go back and hold the position with such men that were still able to fight and this he did, surviving shot and shell until he was back in position and fighting the Germans again. For his conduct during the action Drummer White was awarded the DCM. Supporting the garrison of the Farm was C Company, 2nd Monmouths commanded by Captain A.J.H. Bowen, who led his men into the thick of the fighting.[20] Sergeant C. Love recorded the scene on his arrival in the trenches:

> The first thing that caught my eye was our commanding officer, with his jacket off firing like hell from a "buckshee" rifle to let Jerry know there were still a few of us left to fill the gap they had made shelling during the day. The work of our commanding officer was an inspiration and encouragement to us. It gave us the bit of devil needed at the time.[21]

The fighting died away and the farm was secured but the fighting of the evening caused a number of casualties in the battalion; Captain I.E.M. Watkins was amongst those killed.

With this attack on the positions near Shell Trap Farm the so called Pause in the German operations is considered to have ended. In view of the intense artillery bombardment that had taken place during the four days concerned, and the heavy fighting that had occurred in the Hill 60 area, it is difficult to understand why this period should be considered a pause at all. To the front line soldier there would have been no recognition of a pause in the fighting, particularly since he was suffering such heavy shelling, often in exposed and poorly constructed defences – dugouts in 1915 were seldom more than splinter proof and provided next to no protection from the style of shelling that the Germans had been able to bring to bear on the line. It is therefore appropriate to consider these four days as part of the Battle of Frezenberg Ridge, since they are separated, quite clearly, from the Battle of Saint Julien by the withdrawal to the new line of defences. Whichever nomenclature is adopted, it is fair to say that the four days had been ones of stress and tension when the defenders realized they were in the middle of a big battle, and waited somewhat hopelessly for the next all-out German attack, which all but the most optimistic believed must follow all the heavy shelling.

Notes

1. Dixon & Dixon, op.cit., p38.
2. Quoted in *Official History 1915 Vol. 1*, p308.
3. The position of the British 83rd and 80th Brigades respectively.
4. Quoted in *Official History 1915 Vol. 1*, p308.
5. ibid.
6. Dixon & Dixon, op.cit., p41.
7. 3rd Mons. War Diary (WO95/2274).
8. Dixon & Dixon, op.cit., p43.

9. ibid., p45.

10. See Bruce, *History of the Duke of Wellington's Regiment*, p139.

11. Shephard, op.cit., p42.

12. ibid., p43. Shepard was later commissioned and was killed on the Somme in 1916.

13. See Gillon, *The K.O.S.B. in the Great War*, p66.

14. ibid., p66.

15. See Crookenden, *The History of the Cheshire Regiment in the Great War*, p45.

16. Quoted in Bruce, op.cit., p140.

17. See Marden, *The History of the Welch Regiment, Vol. 2*, p347.

18. See Haythornthwaite, op.cit., p346.

19. See Holmes, op.cit., p284.

20. Bowen was to be awarded the first of two DSOs for his part in this action.

21. Dixon, op.cit., p40.

CHAPTER FIFTEEN

The Battle of Frezenberg Ridge
Day 1 – 8th May 1915

Although the Germans had been preparing the ground around the salient for a concerted infantry attack, it was not until 8th May that they considered that they had brought sufficient men and equipment forward for the task of the repeated assault on the British positions. By that time they had three army corps in the line around the salient. Their XV Corps occupied the line from Zillebeke to Bellewaarde Lake and was facing, more or less exactly, the 27th Division of the British Army. North of this the Germans had the XXVII Reserve Corps in the line from roughly Bellewaarde Lake to Frezenberg, where they opposed the 83 Brigade (28th Division). Finally, there was the XXVI Reserve Corps, positioned from Frezenberg to beyond Shell Trap Farm, which was the line held by the 12 Brigade (4th Division). To the three army corps he had in the line the enemy was able to add the 37th and 38th *Landwehr* Brigades and the 2 Reserve Ersatz Brigade and the 4 Marine Brigade, dispersed between the XXVI and XXVII Reserve Corps. Thus it can be seen that there was a considerable numerical superiority in the Germans' favour though, since they were not able to reinforce at will, most of their units had also seen substantial fighting and were under strength. Nevertheless, the Germans were able to put at least six divisions in the sector from approximately Hill 60 to Turco Farm, opposing no more than three British divisions. It was from this point of strength and their superiority in artillery that the Germans hoped to be able to erase the salient from their military maps, and no doubt encouraged by the British withdrawal of 4th May they firmly believed that they could do just that.

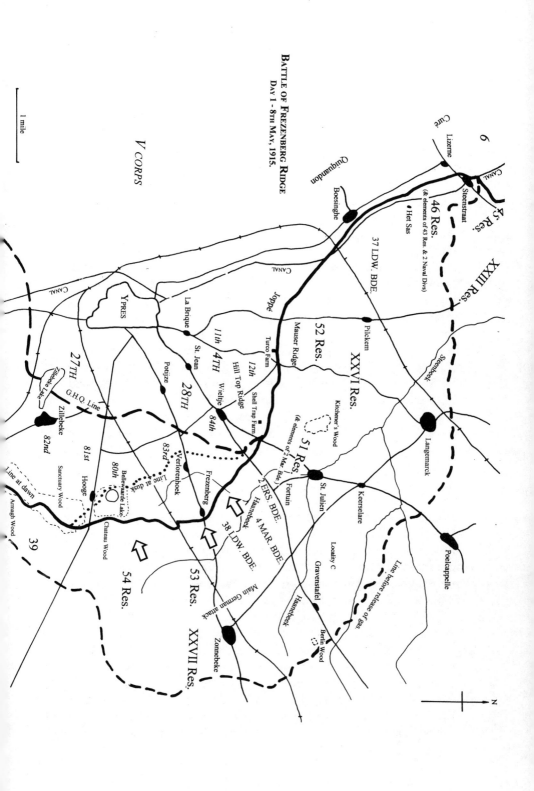

BATTLE OF FREZENBERG RIDGE
DAY 1 - 8TH MAY, 1915.

1 mile

V CORPS

6

Curé

Lizerne

45 Res.

CANAL

Steenstraat

46 Res.
(& elements of 43 Res. & 2 Naval Divs)

Het Sas

XXIII Res.

Quiquandon

Boesinghe

37 LDW. BDE.

CANAL

Joppé

Steebeek

Pilckem

52 Res.

XXVI Res.

Langemarck

CANAL

YPRES

La Brique

Mauser Ridge

Turco Farm

Kitchener's Wood

11th

St. Jean

12th

Shell Trap Farm

Hill Top Ridge

Poelcappelle

4TH

Wieltje

84th

51 Res.
(& elements of 2 Mar Bde.)

Fortuin

St. Julien

Keerselare

Line before release of gas

Zillebeke Lake

G.H.Q. Line

27TH

28TH

83rd

Verlorenhoek

Frezenberg

Line at dusk

2 ERS. BDE.

Hanebeek

4 MAR. BDE.

Locality C

Gravenstafel

82nd

81st

Potijze

Zillebeke

Hooge

80th

Bellewaarde Lake

38 LDW. BDE.

Hanebeek

Berlin Wood

Sanctuary Wood

Chateau Wood

Main German attack

53 Res.

Line at dawn

39

54 Res.

Zonnebeke

XXVII Res.

Armagh Wood

N

The British line was not of the best for defensive purposes. In the southern sector (the right) it was partially shielded from observation and sheltered from fire by Armagh Wood, Sanctuary Wood and Château Wood, but on the left of the 27th Division, held by the Princess Patricia's Canadian Light Infantry, the line was more exposed. Immediately to the left of this the line, manned by the 28th Division, was on the reverse slope of the Frezenberg Ridge as far as the Ypres-Roulers railway line. Beyond this point the trenches had been prepared on the forward slope of the ridge almost as far as Shell Trap Farm, which was itself set back below the crest of the ridge. From here the line was occupied by the 12 Brigade of the 4th Division and was sheltered on the reverse slope of Mauser Ridge. It should be remembered that this line had been hastily constructed and was often shallow, no more than three feet deep in places, narrow and often without traverses. Of course, the depth of the trench was controlled by the water table and sometimes the trenches tended to fill with water. The line chosen was certainly not the best line to defend but, at the time, it was considered to be the best option available. Behind this line, at distances of up to 3,000 yards, was the so-called General Headquarters Line (GHQ line) which ran from Zillebeke, in front of Wieltje and towards Shell Trap Farm. On 8th May this line was manned by the local reserves of the divisions in the front line. In between Wieltje and the Ypres-Langemarck road the 4th Division had established a divisional back-line supporting the 12 Brigade. Behind this line of defences, and still under construction by the Royal Engineers, was a line which was given the name of the "Canal Line". This line was being constructed immediately east of the canal under the ramparts of Ypres and was clearly seen as the last line of defence for the town itself, if ever that were to be needed. To the west of the Yser Canal the zone of defence was extended as far as Brandhoek, some four miles west of Ypres, by a series of strong points. A number of lines of defence were also proposed, but by 8th May these were at the planning stage and throughout the next few days the importance of the choice of the line on the Frezenberg Ridge was to be the issue of the greatest importance, as the Germans sought to push home the advantage they had in artillery and manpower.

The choice of the line had to some extent been forced upon the British commanders, since they would not have wanted to concede all the high ground in their withdrawal. The choice of the forward slopes in part of the 83 and 84 Brigade sectors was not an easy one, since it was clear that it was overlooked by the enemy from the higher ground to the east, and was therefore exposed to anything that the Germans wished to throw at it. The defence of a forward slope would normally require good artillery support, which was lacking, since to reinforce it with both men and equipment required cresting the hill first. The danger of this manoeuvre was clearly demonstrated by the losses of the 3rd Monmouths on 5th May which were discussed in the previous chapter. The defence of a reverse slope likewise was improved by good artillery cover, but required the crest of the slope to be held, if only for observation purposes. Either way, the British needed to hold the crest of the hill for as long as they could and, under the circumstances, the forward slope defensive line seemed to be as good as anything else. If the artillery had been available in greater numbers this would have proved to be the best solution to the defence of Ypres. However, in spite of all the shelling that had preceded 8th May, no one had any real idea of how powerful the German artillery could be. For the British part the artillery had problems in the available ammunition and the guns to fire it. For instance, the heavy guns available for the defence of Ypres comprised six 60-pounder batteries and twelve 4.7-inch guns, which were augmented later by five batteries of 5-inch howitzers from the 50th Division. The 4.7-inch guns were of an old type and had seen more action than they should have. Of the twelve of these guns available, eight were pushed to the east of the Canal since their range of about 4,000 yards was considered to be inadequate to assist the front line soldiers from west of the canal. Similarly, when the 5-inch guns arrived on the scene they were immediately attached to the 28th Division east of the canal. The Germans faced these old guns, which lacked ammunition, with an array of guns of all calibres and plentiful ammunition with a superiority that has been estimated to have been as much as 8 to 1. The salient had become an artillery target for the Germans, but just how big a target was to be demonstrated by the German artillery during the opening exchanges of the Battle of Frezenberg Ridge. Nevertheless the British artillery did all it could and found sufficient ammunition to offer some resistance to the German onslaught. In its own way this was very important for the morale of the average British soldier who believed, without question, in the ability of the Royal Artillery to out-shoot its German counterpart. For his part General Plumer stressed, in an order circulated on 8th May, the importance of the line he had chosen and that it should be held with all tenacity. Of course Plumer did not want anything to happen in front of Ypres that could jeopardize the operations on Aubers Ridge that were due to start on 9th May. He did not want a situation to arise where he would have to call for reinforcements that would otherwise be used in that attack, and that meant that at the time the defence of the salient was taking on an important strategic role.

The fighting of 8th May was dominated by the main German thrust against the 83 Brigade astride the Ypres-Zonnebeke road. Since the consequences of the fighting in this area impacted upon the adjacent units throughout a large portion of the day, this part of the fighting in the central area is dealt with first, which then sets the scene for a discussion of the fighting on both the right and left flanks.

The 83 Brigade was manned by units which had been in the front line since the battle had started on 22nd April. All of its battalions had been involved in some kind of action and all were in need of relief. On the right of this portion of the line, alongside the 27th Division, was B Company of the 3rd Monmouths, under the command of Captain K.F.D. Gattie.[1] To their left was the 1st KOYLI, commanded at the start of the day by Major C.R.I. Brooke, separating them from the main body of the 3rd Monmouths commanded by Lieutenant Colonel H.W.Worsley Gough. To their left, and up to the Brigade boundary on the banks of the Haanebeek, were the 2nd King's Own, commanded at the beginning of the battle by Lieutenant Colonel A.R.S. Martin. Beyond these units, to the left was the 84 Brigade and on the right the 80 Brigade; both would figure in the fighting of 8th May.

As dawn broke it was greeted by the thunder of the Germans' guns starting the bombardment which was to be a feature of the day's fighting. By 5.30 am the bombardment was very heavy, shells crashing into the British positions all along the line, but in particular on the easily observed forward slope of the Frezenberg Ridge. By 7 am the bombardment had reached an intensity the like of which no one had ever witnessed before and soon any semblance of a trench line had almost disappeared. Men were killed by the shelling or simply buried alive as the trenches disappeared – the casualties were made all the greater because the trenches had been hastily prepared and were largely without traverses. The shelling of the previous days had been bad and caused a thinning of the ranks and now that job was nearing completion as the Germans used everything at their disposal in the attempt to clear the way towards Ypres. The fury of the shelling continued until 8.30 am when it was followed by a determined infantry attack. The accounts of some of the 3rd Monmouths in the centre of the 83 Brigade give a clear picture of the events of the day. In the words of Private W.H. Badham:

> They started bombarding at the same time in the morning and... afterwards we could hear a long blast of a whistle, and the attack started. We were only a handful of men, and they came on in thousands, but we kept them at bay.[2]

Private A.L. Devereux carried this story forward in a letter he wrote to his family a day or two after the battle:

> Hundreds of them were put out of action with shells and it left very few men to man the trenches. After, the Huns shelled all the country for a

couple of miles . . . stopping any reinforcements from being brought up and thousands of the rabble charged our trenches in their favourite massed formation. The few boys that were left in our trenches showed then the kind of stuff Britain can turn out and thousands of the Germans were put out of action.[3]

It was much as Private Devereux described, the Germans isolated the front line by shelling the rear areas, preventing any supports being brought up or wounded getting away. For all that, the first assault on the battered British soldiers was completely unsuccessful and prompted the historian of the German Reserve Regiment No. 242 to comment:

The effect of the heavy artillery was devastating, one shell crater ran into another . . . only a few desperate survivors defended themselves obstinately.[4]

All across the 83 Brigade front the story was the same, as small groups of men defended the line that had disintegrated from a makeshift trench to no more than a series of shell holes. However, the defence was sufficient as rifles and machine guns worked as quickly as they could to beat off the Germans. By 9 am the Germans realized that their attack was making no progress, and they fell back so that the artillery could return to its task on the front line trenches. By 9.10 am the bombardment of the exposed slopes of the Frezenberg Ridge was as intense as at any time that morning. There was nothing that the British soldier could do except try to find what little cover he could; one soldier wrote:

. . . it was awful slaughter, it was hellish to see our chaps killed and buried and hear them shouting in agony.[5]

The renewed shelling was endured for about another half an hour before a second infantry assault fell on the unfortunate defenders of the line. By this stage the line was very thinly manned, the three battalions of the 83 Brigade having suffered many casualties in the four hours or so of more or less incessant shelling of the morning of 8th May. Nevertheless, the enemy attack was beaten off yet again. It must have been a surprise to the Germans that after all they had thrown at the line in the way of artillery there were still sufficient defenders, in a very poor line, to beat off an infantry assault of considerably superior numbers. Unfortunately, for many soldiers this lesson was not learned well, and the tactics for an infantry assault remained more or less unchanged, by both sides, for over a year. It was not until many lives had been lost that it was realized that the artillery needed to be used differently to achieve the success that was required of the infantry. In a number of accounts, both in battalion histories and personal accounts, there is mention of the use of gas in the early stages in the fighting of 8th May. The Official History and most of the regimental histories make no reference to gas as a weapon used on this day for the Germans were relying on their superior weight of artillery. Gas had been used elsewhere on a limited scale and it may have been used locally during the attack on Frezenberg Ridge. However, elsewhere during the month of fighting, particularly at Hill 60, it had been noticed that the Germans' high explosive shells had been giving off some particularly irritant fumes subsequent to exploding and, bearing in mind that even the German field guns were firing high explosives that morning, it would seem to be highly likely that some, if not all, the reports of gas, actually refer to that effect.

By the time that the second German assault had been beaten back there were very few men left in the forward line, and it was becoming clear that if the Germans persisted then they would succeed in breaking the line. At 10 am orders were received from Brigade by the front line units that they were to withdraw to their support line some 400 yards to the rear. This was being carried out as the Germans commenced a third infantry assault on the line and amidst the confused movements the Germans began to make progress that was to become very dangerous to the line as a whole. Lieutenant Colonel H. Worsley Gough of the 3rd Monmouths called for a company of the 2nd King's Own to occupy his support line while he organized a counter-attack in the hope of at least stalling the Germans briefly. The 2nd King's Own complied providing B Company, under Captain T.B. Forwood for the work. Meanwhile, Lieutenant Colonel Worsley Gough ordered Sergeant B. Jenkins and RSM T.W. Hatton to gather together as many men as possible as they came back from the front line and to turn them around for the counter attack he had planned. There was little time to plan anything; he was simply putting his unit back together as best he could on the battlefield to throw it back at the Germans, who were by that time making progress up the forward slope of the Frezenberg Ridge. It is questionable whether or not Lieutenant Colonel Worsley Gough expected any real success from this small-scale counter-attack, since there was no real weight behind it. He can only have thought to use his men to convince the Germans that there was still something in their way. The small band was led forward by Worsley Gough himself and he succeeded in reaching the western edge of the village of Frezenberg before it was halted by the German fire. He then ordered his men back to supports as quickly as possible, having achieved very little except perhaps a slight pause in the Germans' progress on a very narrow front. Of course, it had not been without casualties and RSM Hatton was seriously wounded and taken prisoner.[6] For all that it is likely that the effect of this minor counter-attack would have been to encourage those men in the forward positions who had been ordered to retire. To the left of the 3rd Monmouths, the 2nd King's Own had been overwhelmed and Lieutenant Colonel Martin had been killed. The surviving members of the Battalion, then under Major H.K. Clough, then moved so as to occupy the supports. To many men in the front line that morning the strength of the German assault had made the withdrawal to the reverse slope of the ridge almost inevitable. This was pointed out by Private Badham of the 3rd Monmouths:

> . . . but I knew we would have to give way before long. The fellows on our left and right were retiring and we had orders to do the same, but we did not go until we put some more shots into them. It was in the retirement that we lost a lot of men. They were bayoneting our wounded that we had to leave behind.[7]

There is no evidence for the treatment of the wounded that day except in the letters home, and it would appear that in some cases the Germans were very brutal, whilst in others the wounded were treated with all the consideration possible. Not one battalion wanted to leave any wounded behind but as they retired up the hill they were completely exposed to all the fury of the Germans. Once over the crest of the ridge those men who made it into supports at once took up position in the fire trenches to fight again along with those men who had been waiting there since dawn.

As soon as there were signs of a breakthrough, Brigadier General R.C. Boyle ordered his reserve, the 2nd East Yorkshire, forward at once to cover the area immediately behind the line that the 2nd King's Own and the 1st KOYLI had taken up. At about the same time Major General Bulfin ordered forward the 85 Brigade who were at the time in Vlamertinge in divisional reserve. Both these actions serve to indicate the severity of the situation as the generals reacted to provide all the help they could muster for the three badly mauled battalions of the 83 Brigade. Shortly after these orders had been issued, Major C.R.I. Brooke of the 1st KOYLI arrived, wounded, in the 83 Brigade Headquarters with the very grave news that his Battalion was coming away from the line after his left flank had been exposed by the withdrawal in the centre of the brigade sector. This was not entirely true for two companies of the 1st KOYLI, under Captain H. Mallinson, and B Company of the 3rd Monmouths (Captain K.F.D. Gattie), were still in the line on the right of the brigade sector and neither officer had any intention of letting his men withdraw without a real fight. It should not be a surprise that the picture was unclear. Communications had been almost completely disrupted as soon as the shelling had severed all telephone links, so that information on the disposition of any unit was gathered on the ground by officers using runners who sometimes did not make it through the fighting to report the conditions. Clearly, Major Brooke had made an assessment of conditions he could see and, whilst it was only partially true, it was nevertheless very worrying for the senior commanders who relied on such reports to make their assessments of the battle. To make matters worse there was also a report that the left flank of the 80 Brigade was also retiring. This was completely untrue as we shall see later, but in the confusion of the battle there was no way that any of the senior commanders could be absolutely sure. To Brigadier General Boyle it seemed foolhardy to be sending his reserves forward when there were reports of the brigade to his right retiring. Boyle, therefore, issued an order that was to make matters even worse, when he ordered the 2nd East Yorkshires not to advance beyond the GHQ line behind which the 3rd Monmouths and the 2nd King's Own could retire if that was seen to be necessary. In this order, well meaning but based on incorrect information, can be seen one of the major problems of the First World War battlefield. The Brigadier General had made a decision and issued orders which had, in fact, served to confuse the situation still further. Instead of providing support for the 3rd Monmouths and the 2nd King's Own he had given them the option to retire, but by halting the support he had made that choice inevitable, though unfortunately for these battalions not all of the men got to hear the order to withdraw. As the Germans came over the crest of the ridge they were met by rapid rifle fire and concentrated machine-gun fire wherever possible and the Germans suffered heavily. However, they persisted with the attack closing on the defenders continually. As Private Devereux put it:

> After they had finished with our fire trench they came on, thinking they had us beaten completely, but there was a company of men in the support trenches and when Mr. Fritz came over the ridge he found another trench about 500 yards away. The boys in support had had more sleep than those in the fire trench and had not been subjected to such severe shelling, and they soon showed Fritz what a rifle, when handled properly, could do.[8]

Private Devereux had put the morning's fighting in a nutshell: whilst the Germans had been able to attack with all manner of artillery, the defence of the salient relied completely on the infantryman and his rifle. However, the infantryman can do only so much and when they did not receive the orders to withdraw, many groups of men fought on until ammunition ran out or they were surrounded. Even when the order was received it was sometimes difficult to comply simply because the units were in such close contact with the Germans. Private R. Jones of A Company the 3rd Monmouths wrote:

A good many of our men were lying killed and wounded in the trenches to the left and right of where I was. I was shot in the face by a rifle bullet about 11 o'clock when the word was passed up "All for yourselves". We then commenced to retire and four of us – Capt. Baker, his orderly, the telephonist and myself – were all together in that part of the trench and immediately retired down the communication trench and got out on the open ground at the back. I took shelter in a shell hole made by a Jack Johnson shell and on looking out I saw Capt. Baker lying on the ground a few yards away. He had been shot, I think, in the hip or lower part of the body and was quite unable to rise. I went to his assistance and dragged him about seven yards nearer the shell hole when he told me to look after myself . . . When I left Capt. Baker the Germans were only about 600 yards away and were coming on swiftly all the time.[9]

Captain R.L. Baker[10] died on the battlefield that day as did many others of his company, in which all the officers were put out of action. That evening only thirteen survivors of A Company were present at roll call. D Company of the battalion fared little better when only sixteen men answered the roll that night.[11] The causes for these losses are not straightforward, for whatever happened it has to be remembered that the defenders of the 83 Brigade were outnumbered and the effect of the artillery was simply overpowering. That the situation was worsened by some ambiguity in the orders issued by Brigade should not be denied and there was absolutely no chance to check the meaning of the orders. The front line units were under far too much pressure for that. Added to these factors was a keen sense of duty in all ranks which perhaps led men to fight on in impossible circumstances. For all that, as soon as it became clear to Brigadier General Boyle that his order had been mis-interpreted, he once more ordered the 2nd East Yorkshire forward, this time supported by the 5th King's Own (Lieutenant Colonel, Lord Cavendish) to reoccupy the lost trenches. Although they had a combined strength of only 550 these two battalions complied at once and succeeded in reaching a point about half way between the GHQ line and the old front line. They suffered heavy casualties in this manoeuvre to move forward about 1,000 yards but it appears that their action dissuaded the Germans from continuing their advance, for they made no further effort in that area to take advantage of their earlier success.

Whilst all this was going on in the centre and left of the 83 Brigade the fortunes on the right were somewhat different. In spite of the belief of Major Brooke, two companies of his 1st KOYLI were still holding their position in the front line. Also, to their right, was Captain Gattie's B Company of the 3rd Monmouths. He and his company were, in theory, answerable to Major Brooke, but in the latter's absence Gattie took responsibility for his men and decided that they would not retire. Captain Mallinson, commanding the two companies of the KOYLI still in the line, made the same decision. This area had suffered the same amount of shelling as any other part of the line, but the units there had made good use of natural cover to establish their defensive position and, although suffering heavy losses, both units were able to hold on throughout the rest of the day. The half of the 1st KOYLI remaining were exposed on their left but managed to form some kind of flank so as to be able to hold their line, as the Germans concentrated their efforts on working around the left flank (84 Brigade) of the breach they had created. Throughout the day communications with adjacent units all but ceased. B Company 3rd Monmouths made contact with the Patricia's of 80 Brigade three times during the course of the day, but each time enemy pressure severed the contact. This became such a problem that 80 Brigade believed that 83 Brigade had completely disappeared and, in the absence of any other information, began to form a flank for themselves. In fact these two remaining units of 83 Brigade hung on with all the tenacity that had been asked of them by General Plumer. The 3rd Monmouth's battalion history states that B Company had held the line until they were the most forward of all British troops in the salient on that day. Inevitably their position became untenable, though according to some accounts this was as much because of the fire coming from the British line that was established in their rear, as it was because of German pressure. At nightfall these two units withdrew to the trenches of the support line, where they were to remain for the night. It had probably come as something of a surprise to all concerned that these units had not been wiped out, although they had suffered heavy casualties.

On the right the line of 80 Brigade was shelled heavily from first light and although it was at least in part protected by the woodland and the reverse slope of the Bellewaarde Ridge, the two battalions on the left of the brigade, that is against the 83 Brigade, were far more exposed and accordingly they suffered heavily from shrapnel and high-explosive shells during the opening hours of the battle. On the extreme left was the Princess Patricia's Canadian Light Infantry (Major A.H. Gault) and on their right was the 4th KRRC (Major H.J. Majendie). Considerable responsibility for maintaining the line was to rest on these two units, as 83 Brigade was forced to retire from the front of the Frezenberg Ridge and the Germans attempted to widen the gap they had created to the left and the right. In this area the pattern of the battle was exactly the same as elsewhere. The heavy shelling continued until about 8.30 am when it slackened to allow for the infantry to attack. Once again it was reported, this time by the Patricia's, that the shelling had been

226

accompanied by the use of gas shells which fell on their line, making it steadily more difficult to defend. Major Gault of the Patricia's was wounded early in the day by shellfire but carried on until a second and more serious thigh wound put him out of action, when the command devolved to Captain A. Adamson. The defence of the line here as elsewhere was mainly achieved by rapid rifle fire and where possible machine-gun fire as the soldiers manned the trenches as best they could to beat off the German infantrymen. Lines of communication between the forward area and Brigade were destroyed early in the day by heavy artillery fire and runners were used in an attempt to keep some communication open as the battle developed. Before 9 am 4 Rifle Brigade, then in reserve, had sent up runners to ascertain the situation in the 4th KRRC sector and the latter called upon the reserve battalion to send up one company to assist in the defence of the line. Similarly in the Patricia's line the shelling had caused a large number of casualties and the commanding officer called up all the Patricia's he could to fill the gaps that were becoming obvious. These included pioneers, orderlies and officers' servants, so that by about 9 am every available Patricia was in the line fighting to hold off the German infantry attacks. The fighting in this area was every bit as fierce as elsewhere on the morning of 8th May and often relied on individual acts of gallantry. Machine gunners were obvious targets for the artillery and the Patricia's guns were buried repeatedly. One gun commanded by Corporal C. Dover, was buried no fewer than three times, but each time he dug it out and recommenced firing. Eventually it was put out of action by the enemy shelling and Dover was seriously wounded – he was to be killed by a sniper later in the day. It was a similar story for the guns of Corporal H. McKenzie[12] and Corporal B. Stevens and both men did everything they could in an attempt to keep their guns firing. Both men were awarded the DCM for their determined bravery that day. It became a day of grim endurance for the Patricia's as they fought, mainly with rifles, against overwhelming odds. At about 9.30 am Captain Adamson was wounded in the shoulder by shrapnel but still kept working to give all the aid he could to the defence of the line.[13] One of the battalion wrote:

I recall seeing Captain Adamson with an arm hanging down, getting ammunition from the dead or dying and handing it to us. The front line had gone, so we moved up the support trench to enter the front line further on, but this could not be accomplished. Our rifles got so hot we had to change rifles to keep firing.[14]

It was about this time that things started to become critical along the Frezenberg Ridge. The German infantry attack at about 10 am had gradually forced back the centre of 83 Brigade and, of course, this was having a serious effect on the left flank of the Patricia's. Lieutenant H.W. Niven was sent to attempt to make contact with the 1st KOYLI and B Company of the 3rd Monmouths, but whilst this was achieved it was a contact that was very difficult to maintain under the continued shelling and persistant infantry action and before the end of the day it was to prove to be impossible.

In the 4th KRRC trenches the situation was much the same, as the line gradually disappeared under the weight of shelling. At about 10.30 am they received support from two half companies (A and D) of 4 Rifle Brigade which helped to ease the situation. At about the same time 4 Rifle Brigade, sent up all its machine guns to give support to the Patricia's, since their guns had all been put out of action by that time, and they were able to help by bringing fire to bear on the Germans who were by that time starting to occupy the 83 Brigade forward line.

In the Patricia's sector the battle wavered back and forth between the front line and the support line as each yard of the ground was fought over. The Patricia's had taken their camp colour (the Ric-A-Dam-Doo) into the line with them and at one stage RSM A.G. Fraser, half crazed as a result of a head wound, stood on the parapet of their trenches waving the colour to encourage the Patricia's whilst simultaneously shouting abuse at the oncoming Germans. RSM Fraser died later that day as a result of the wound he had received early in the day. There was no lack of spirit in the Patricia's as they fought hard throughout a long morning, but eventually they were forced to give a little ground and the Germans began to occupy some of their old forward positions by about 1.30 pm.

> The Germans had already, with usual industry, gotten the trench into some sort of shape again, with the parapet shifted over to the other side and facing Bellewaarde Wood. And everywhere along its length I noticed the bodies of our dead built into it to replace sandbags while others lay on the parados at the rear. It was not nice. The faces of men we had known and called comrade looked at us now in ghastly disarray from odd sections of both walls. Already they were taking on a brick like shape from the weight of the filled bags on top of them.[15]

By 2 pm Lieutenant Niven, now acting battalion commander for the wounded Adamson, reported to Brigade that he would not consider withdrawing his battered and depleted command because they had so many wounded to bring out and he would not leave them behind. He also stated that if stretcher bearers could be supplied he would withdraw at dusk. That was still a along way off, but the determination of the Patricia's to hold the line cannot be doubted. In mid-afternoon contact with 83 Brigade was lost for the third time and as far as the

Patricia's could ascertain 83 Brigade had disappeared completely. This worrying development, although not accurate, meant that the left flank of the Patricia's, and indeed the Brigade, was hanging in the air. Immediately this news was received by the 27th Division Headquarters, Major General Snow ordered the 80 Brigade front to be extended north-west towards the railway line whilst he ordered the 2nd King's Shropshire Light Infantry into position to form a flank. This movement took the line behind the Bellewaarde Ridge, but unbeknown to Snow the remnants of the 1st KOYLI and the 3rd Monmouths were still fighting on the forward slope of the ridge, almost completely abandoned and without support. Nevertheless, the 2nd KSLI (Lieutenant Colonel R.J. Bridgeford) moved into the line and formed a flank facing approximately towards the north. This manoeuvre was supported by the 1st Argyll and Sutherland Highlanders (Lieutenant Colonel H.B. Kirk) and half of the 9th Battalion of the same regiment, commanded by Lieutenant Colonel J. Clark. The line now had a sharp re-entrant north of Bellewaarde Lake as the 2nd KSLI made efforts to link with the line being defended by the remains of 83 Brigade, who were by that time fighting from the support trenches. In the meantime the Germans had done all they could to work through the gaps in the line and had occupied some of the high ground (known as Hill 50) at the junction of the Patricia's and the 4th KRRC. There are numerous reports from this time of men being more or less surrounded and fired upon from all sides. Fortunately, with the arrival of reinforcements, this German infiltration tended to die away and, since there had been no attack south of the Menin Road, Snow was able to report that his Divisional line had held. At 11.30 pm the Patricia's were relieved by the 3rd KRRC, though there were precious few of them to relieve as the Battalion marched out of the line with four officers and 150 men. The remains of the Patricia's, most of whom had minor wounds, left the battlefield under the command of Lieutenant Niven who about eight months before had joined the regiment as a private. It had been a magnificent defence by the Patricia's and one which prompted Major General Snow to comment in his report to V Corps:

> The PPCLI were relieved that night, but only a remnant of the Regiment was left. No regiment could have fought with greater determination or endurance. Many would have failed where they succeeded.[16]

It was a fair assessment of the day's fighting on the left flank of 80 Brigade, but the Patricia's were not the only battalion to suffer heavy losses, for the 4th KRRC had suffered over 300 casualties during the day. It had been a stern test for all concerned, but at the end of the day the line still held and very little ground had been yielded to the enemy in spite of his superiority in artillery that had caused so many problems throughout the day.[17]

The day began on the northern flank of the salient as it had elsewhere with dawn bringing the blistering bombardment to the lines of 84 Brigade (28th Division). The 1st Suffolks, still commanded by Lieutenant Colonel W.B. Wallace, were on the right of the Brigade and their regimental history gives a good idea of just how bad things were at the time:

> The din was terrific. The enemy were sending over projectiles of every calibre and description. High explosive shells crashed in all directions scattering bricks and timber like chaff before the wind. Huge guns and howitzers roared incessantly, shaking the earth, and the crackle of machine guns and musketry, mingling with the boom of mortars and bombs, made a noise that sounded like an army of riveters at work during some titanic thunder storm.[18]

Added to all this there was the new spectre of poison gas which, according to their history, was released against the 1st Suffolks and which caused sufficient problem for some men to leave the trenches.

To the left of the Suffolks were the 2nd Cheshires (Major A.B. Stone), the 1st Monmouths (Lieutenant Colonel C.L. Robinson) and, near Shell Trap Farm, the 2nd Northumberland Fusiliers (Lieutenant Colonel S.H. Enderby). Beyond this Brigade was 12 Brigade of the 4th Division, elements of which had already seen heavy fighting.

The events of the day were similar to those described for the centre (83 Brigade) and the right (80 Brigade) sectors of the front. That is, there was very heavy shellfire early in the morning followed up by infantry assaults. The 84 Brigade line was, like the 83 Brigade line, also on the forward slope of the Frezenberg Ridge but unlike the line in the 83 Brigade sector, it was not as readily enfiladed as a direct result of it being on the flank rather than the apex of the salient. It was, however, every bit as exposed to observation and the Germans shelled the line heavily with the same devastating effects, as the trenches were steadily and systematically destroyed. The early infantry attacks in the area were beaten off, but following the collapse of the front line in the 83 Brigade area, it soon became apparent to the battalions on the left that their positions were in jeopardy. The Germans began moving northwards against their flank at the same time as they attacked the brigade area frontally, in the hope that the combined action would allow them to roll up the line. For the battalions in the front line it meant that they were soon coming under fire from both their front and their right flank. At about 11.15 am Brigadier General Bols ordered the 12th London

(Rangers) forward to support the 1st Monmouths. The Rangers were an under-strength unit which had seen much action on the preceding days, but the 200 or so men that remained went forward without hesitation to attempt to carry out their orders. The Official History records that as soon as they reached the gaps in the GHQ line wire they came under heavy fire of all kinds and were overwhelmed, but some struggled on and managed to reach the 1st Monmouths' positions. This would seem to be at variance with the accounts of the Monmouths themselves and indeed that of the Northumberland Fusiliers. The 1st Monmouths' war diary for the day records the event as follows:

> Supports were seen to be advancing under terrific shellfire. The advance of these supports (afterwards found to be the 12th London Regt.) was most gallant, but only a few men survived to reach within 300 yards of the trenches and these were forced to retire in twos and threes as best they could later in the day.

Although the attempt to reinforce the 1st Monmouths had almost completely failed there was one point in favour of the attempt. The 12th London's machine gun had been brought forward, and although its crew were all casualties the gun was operated to good effect by Lieutenant C.W. Hepburn of the 1st Monmouths, until he too was wounded and unable to maintain the fire on the advancing Germans.

The repeated frontal infantry attacks, the heavy shelling and the enemy beginning to work from the right flank were all having a serious effect on the line. At 1 pm the front line, where the 2nd Cheshires had stood, was broken and the Germans began to work left and right to widen it. The 1st Suffolks refused to move and fought on throughout the rest of the day in isolated pockets of resistance whilst the Germans tried to work their way around them. In the early afternoon the Cheshires tried to leave their front line by moving through the 1st Monmouths' trenches, but were stopped by Captain H.T. Edwards who refused to get his men out of the way to allow the retirement and he continued to fight the Germans from his position. Captain Edwards also stationed Sergeant W. Garbutt,[19] with fixed bayonet, at the entry to a communication trench with instructions to stop anyone trying to leave the trench for the rear. Captain O. Williams, 1st Monmouths, later wrote to his parents with some details of the day:

> It was impossible to get our men, where I was, more to the right owing to the congestion of the wounded in the narrow trench, and the men of another regiment retiring. I called on a few to follow me over the traverse, and we dived over it to the right. Then I saw a white flag up and I shouted to them that I would shoot if it was not put down and I fired my revolver in the air. The officer shouted that they had orders to surrender, then I

231

saw other white flags on the right flank at right angles to me and the Germans on my right were no more than a hundred yards away.[20]

It is impossible to say how accurate this account is or whether any surrender actually occurred that day, but there can be no doubt that as the Germans punched a hole in 84 Brigade some prisoners were taken, and the white flags seen by Captain Williams may have indicated small groups of men who had run out of ammunition and for whom there was little point in fighting on. However, it is safe to say that there was definitely no large-scale surrender of any of the battalions in the line on that day.

As the afternoon wore on the Germans began to get around the rear of the 1st Monmouths and the 2nd Northumberland Fusiliers and gradually parties of both units became surrounded and overwhelmed. Captain Edwards, D Company 1st Monmouths, was determined to stand his ground, and as reported by Captain Williams:

> When he was called upon to surrender he said "Surrender be damned", and was seen by our men firing at the enemy, He was then shot and – the men reported – killed.[21]

A similar story is told of Captain A.C. Hart of the 2nd Northumberland Fusiliers who lost his life in circumstances so close to those described above it could almost have been the same incident. The sacrifice of these officers, and others like them, may seem to be a little unnecessary but most officers saw their duty very clearly that day and led their men by example even to their own deaths. The effect of such leadership on the men is unknown but both officers mentioned above had earned the respect of their men long before this battle started and their actions, probably calculated to set the right example, would have lifted any flagging spirits at a very critical period of the battle.

Gradually the line was becoming very difficult to defend as the Germans had brushed aside the Cheshires and a large part of the 1st Suffolks and continued to do the same to the 1st Monmouths and the 2nd Northumberland Fusiliers. It soon became clear to Lieutenant Colonel Robinson that his battalion, now on the right of the brigade, would not be able to hold their position indefinitely and that he would need to try and form a flank if they were to stand any chance at all. At 5 pm Robinson informed Lieutenant Colonel Enderby of the 2nd Northumberland Fusiliers that he was going to do just that. Enderby agreed as to the necessity but asked Robinson to occupy some high ground when he made the manoeuvre so as better to protect the flank of the Fusiliers. It was agreed and shortly afterwards Robinson began to move his battalion into communication trenches to form an *en echelon* defensive flank. The history is taken up by Captain M.C. Llewellin, 1st Monmouths:

> The whole right flank had given way. A, B and part of C Companies still held on but were being surrounded so Robinson told me he was going to withdraw, and was making his way back through the shallow communication trench when he was shot through the neck. I bandaged him but he was dead before I had finished. I got what was left of the 1st and 2nd Platoons of A Company on the road and told them to retire and reform when out of fire. I then attended to some of the wounded and waited for Major Evill to come up with the other platoons of A Company. I saw Evill crawling up a hedgerow under heavy fire and was just about to make a move to get to him when I was hit for the sixth time by a rifle bullet which went through me just above my heart and knocked me out . . .[22]

Even the retirement to form a defensive flank was no simple matter for, as in 83 Brigade, the battalions had to crest the low Frezenberg Ridge and were clearly in the Germans' field of fire. Many more men succumbed to the infantry fire at this stage, and perhaps it was not as orderly as might have been hoped for in all cases. Private W. Watts, who was only seventeen at the time, wrote in a letter home:

> We retired, we had to throw away our rifles and equipment and had to crawl through trenches, piled up with dead, and streams in the same condition.[23]

The 1st Monmouths were almost wiped out but the remnants made their way back to the 4th Division support line, where those who still had their rifles joined the 2nd Royal Irish Regiment. They opened rapid fire on the Germans, pushing forward to make the best of the advantage they had gained as the 84 Brigade line had collapsed.

The withdrawal of the 1st Monmouths had increased the difficulty for the 2nd Northumberland Fusiliers and at 6.15 pm it was clear to Lieutenant Colonel Enderby that he could not maintain his position for very much longer. Therefore he went forward to let all his front line know that he was planning a withdrawal at dusk, which was still an hour or so away. At about 7 pm, while Enderby was still issuing orders to his men, the enemy began shelling the line furiously once again, then, following a signal flare, the shelling stopped as suddenly as it had begun, and the Germans started to move in force to occupy the trenches recently vacated by the 1st Monmouths. Three companies of the Fusiliers in the front line were rushed by the enemy and there was much confused fighting during which both Enderby and his adjutant, Captain R. Auld were captured, though they were not together at the time. Auld had gone forward to deliver a message to another part of the line and was with a stretcher bearer when they were surrounded. The stretcher bearer was immediately bayoneted and Auld would have received the same treatment had it not been for the intervention of a German sergeant who recognized his rank and thought he might be able to provide further information. During this confused fighting much was left to the initiative of the ordinary soldier, many of whom showed great bravery as the 2nd Northumberland Fusiliers refused to give ground. The fighting continued until well after darkness when the Germans, perhaps influenced by the two counter-attacks made by the British a little further south, (described below), had to satisfy themselves by digging some 300 yards) in front of the British positions.

To the left of 84 Brigade, 12 Brigade had also been attacked, but their successful defence of their line on the night of 7th and 8th May had allowed them to establish themselves quite firmly in the area from Turco Farm to Shell Trap Farm, and all efforts made by the Germans in front of them were readily beaten off and the line was maintained. Although there was no breakthrough the troops in this area still had a hard day of fighting and, of course, casualties occurred. C Company the 2nd Monmouths had been in the thick of things since the night of 7th May and the company commander, Captain A.J.H. Bowen was among the casualties reported on 8th May, as Sergeant C. Love was to explain:

> He was cut about the head and face, and he was covered in blood and dirt of which he was not aware. He was badly wounded in the back. He was holding his shirt away from his skin as it was sticking and causing added pain. I really thought he was "going on". I suggested to him that it would be better to get his wounds dressed as he was bleeding badly, but he had no intention of leaving the line because we were so short of officers. He was sick and becoming weaker, and the commanding officer gave him instructions to go that evening.[24]

Bowen survived his wounds and was awarded the DSO for his gallantry during the day. Later in the war he commanded the Battalion and won a second DSO before being killed in front of Sailly-Saillisel in 1917.

It had been a difficult day of fighting for 84 Brigade. Four battalions had been almost completely destroyed and, whilst there may have been some criticism levelled at the time at certain battalions, it is fair to say that all had fought gallantly against overwhelming odds. The 1st Suffolks were only twenty-nine men strong at the end of the fighting; the 2nd Cheshires had lost thirteen officers and 382 other ranks; the 1st Monmouths had lost twenty-one officers and 439 other ranks whilst, after their gallant attempt to provide support, the Rangers were only fifty-three strong and were commanded by Sergeant W.J. Hornall. The

2nd Northumberland Fusiliers, who were still in the line at nightfall had lost 482 men and fourteen officers. The 84 Brigade's six battalions had been reduced to 1,200 men and these were reorganized into two composite units during 9th May. In spite of the losses and the individual acts of gallantry all along its line, by nightfall there was a gap in the line which extended from the 1st KOYLI in the south to the 2nd Northumberland Fusiliers in the Shell Trap Farm area – a distance of approximately two miles. Throughout the day, however, there had been moves to attempt to fill this gap and minimize the German advance into the British lines.

As soon as it was clear that there had been a break in the 83 Brigade front, Major General Bulfin began organizing a counter-attack by which he hoped to regain the lost ground. He ordered the 3rd Middlesex, commanded by Major G.H. Neale, and by that time only 500 strong, to begin moving to Potijze in preparation for the attack. The 1st York and Lancaster of the 83 Brigade were also placed at the disposal of the 85 Brigade (Brigadier General A.J. Chapman). This Battalion had already seen action during the Second Battle of Ypres and although the Battalion, commanded by Lieutenant Colonel T.E.B. Isherwood, was reported as being 950 strong, many of the men were drafts that had arrived since 1st May and were new both to the Western Front and to battle. It was, however, numerically the strongest battalion at his disposal on the afternoon of 8th May and it was ordered forward to take part in the counter-attack. The 3rd Middlesex were positioned south of the Ypres-Roulers railway in the vicinity of Railway Wood in readiness for the attack, whilst the 1st York and Lancaster were between the railway and the Ypres-Zonnebeke road. By 2.40 pm, or about four hours after the initial German breakthrough, the two-battalion attack had commenced; by 3 pm the 2nd East Surreys (Lieutenant Colonel C.C.G. Ashton) had arrived on the scene and were pushed into the attack astride the Ypres-Zonnebeke road on the left of the York and Lancaster. Simultaneously, the remains of the 2nd East Yorkshires and the 5th King's Own, who had already seen action that day, were ordered to add weight to the left between these two battalions. At 5 pm the 3rd Royal Fusiliers (Major A.V. Johnson) became available and were added to the attack immediately adjacent to the railway line. By that time a total of six battalions, or parts of battalions, were taking part in the counter attack. The Germans, of course, held the higher ground and, according to the Official History, also had air supremacy, giving their artillery the best possible chance to aid in any defence of the ground they had so recently won. As soon as the troops of the counter-attack began to move forward from the vicinity of the GHQ line they came under heavy shrapnel fire and casualties mounted rapidly. The

3rd Middlesex managed to make contact with the left flank of the 80 Brigade but made little progress beyond this, and the report by the officer commanding A Company makes this clear:

> The trenches we hold contain A Company with about one and a half platoons up the line. Two companies KSLI in touch on either side of railway. York and Lancs in touch on left of line. The shellfire too great to advance yet. C Company are partly in trench and partly lining the railway. The casualties are heavy.[25]

The fortunes of the York and Lancaster were no better for although they struggled hard to make headway their casualties mounted. Nevertheless, according to their Battalion history, a small number of men did make it to the enemy trenches where they were immediately killed by the Germans. Every effort was made by the battalions involved to close with the enemy but although the attack was pressed until 8 pm, in the end it had to be admitted that the casualties that had occurred were far too heavy to carry on. Therefore, a line was established which ran from west of Verlorenhoek and thence roughly east of south to connect with 80 Brigade near the railway line. The battalions involved had all suffered heavily, but none more so than the 1st York and Lancaster, which by the time the attack had been broken off had been reduced to ninety-three men commanded by a sergeant – all the officers had become casualties and Lieutenant Colonel Isherwood had been killed. Similarly the 5th King's Own who had been in action twice during the day had been reduced to a trench strength of ninety-one. If the attack had not been called off it would soon have stopped simply because there would have been insufficient men left alive to have continued it. It had not been a success, but it had been pressed with sufficient determination to bring to a halt the Germans' action against the left flank of the 80 Brigade. It was, at least, something to show for all the effort and bloodshed of the late afternoon and evening of 8th May.

Whilst this attack was progressing, Brigadier General Bols (84 Brigade) was also making attempts to strengthen the position in his area. He had used a portion of his reserve when he sent the Rangers to the assistance of the 1st Monmouths, but that had not been successful since it had reduced the Rangers to a handful of men. Bols ordered the 1st Welsh, by that time about 200 strong, into the GHQ line ready for a last ditch defence if necessary, and later in the day their machine guns were able to offer some assistance as the 2nd East Surreys made their move along the Ypres-Zonnebeke road. Bols also approached the 4th Division for assistance to stabilize his front line. Major General H.F.M. Wilson had his reserves in the vicinity of Vlamertinge to the east of the Yser Canal, which was too far away to offer immediate assistance to Bols and his battered brigade. At 3 pm Wilson therefore ordered some of the local reserve, in the form of a half battalion of the 5th South Lancs (12 Brigade) and A and C Companies of the 1st Royal Irish Fusiliers (10 Brigade), to the vicinity of Wieltje, though the order received by the latter battalion seems to have been a little vague:

> Send two companies at once to occupy Wieltje and vicinity and, if possible, get into touch with any troops on the right south of Wieltje and report situation.[26]

It would appear that by the time this order was issued the situation was so fluid and the shelling so intense that there was little idea of the actual conditions on the battlefield, which had been a feature of the fighting on more than one occasion during the Second Battle of Ypres. Shortly after this manoeuvre was underway it became clear that there had been a break in the 84 Brigade front, and the 1st Warwicks and the 2nd Royal Dublin Fusiliers, together with the remaining companies of the 1st Royal Irish Fusiliers, were placed at the disposal of General Bols. The help was needed for Bols realized that a gap had developed between the 2nd Northumberland Fusiliers, still holding the line near Shell Trap Farm, and the GHQ line making the flank and the rear of the 4th Division very vulnerable. Bols decided to use these two and a half battalions to push diagonally into this gap and thus catch the enemy in the flank. Not for the first time during the battle, however, the German artillery were to play a very important role in this plan. The rear areas were all being very heavily shelled and in particular the roads were receiving considerable attention, making all troop movements on them nearly impossible. Consequently the 1st Royal Warwicks (Lieutenant Colonel A.J. Poole) and the 2nd Royal Dublin Fusiliers (Lieutenant Colonel A. Loveband) who had been positioned immediately west of the canal, had to move into position across country in artillery formation. This made for slow progress and these battalions did not reach the GHQ line until 7.30 pm, or about four hours after their initial instruction to move. By that time it was far too late, and becoming too dark in any case, to begin the attack in any meaningful manner. However, it was decided that they should move forward a short distance in extended order after which they would dig in and attempt to gain touch with those units already in the forward positions. It was not a true counter-attack, but the appearance of these troops on the field late in the day had an unexpected effect on the Germans, as they withdrew from Hill 33, east of Wieltje, and retired as far as Frezenberg. The Germans had, in turn, been forced to abandon the ground they had won earlier in the day, as the German account of the events runs:

A great counter attack that was only stopped at Frezenberg threw the *Fourth Army* on the defensive and compelled the *XXVI Reserve Corps* and also the *XXVII Reserve Corps* to abandon the position captured. Only the *XV Corps* held its ground.[27]

It is interesting to note that the German account considered the advance by two and a half under-strength battalions as a "great counter-attack". It was no such thing, of course, but clearly the Germans believed it was sufficiently great to withdraw to Frezenberg though the British forces did not move much beyond Verlorenhoek. It did have the effect of easing the situation across that part of the front and it has led to speculation as to what could have happened had the British generals been able to field a completely fresh brigade which was well supported by artillery. It is obviously idle speculation, since neither were available, but nevertheless the German withdrawal was welcomed by the British command, and after all the fighting that had occurred on 8th May they no doubt felt satisfied that they had not been forced to give up any more ground than they had.

At about this time, just as the 7th Argyll and Sutherland Highlanders and the 1st East Lancashires were arriving on the scene, there was a report that Wieltje had fallen. These battalions were ordered to turn out the enemy at the point of the bayonet, while the staff called for a counter-attack to retake all the trenches that had been lost in the 27th and 28th Division areas. This would have been a very tall order even if abundant fresh troops had been available but, as has been described already, there were no fresh troops available, just battered and weakened battalions who were just about managing to hold the reduced line. The staff cannot have had any idea of the actual state of the men they were calling on to make such a great effort. The order brought about an unusual situation for the British army, for the battalion commanders, in many cases captains and lieutenants at this stage of the battle, protested strongly to their superiors on the grounds that it was too dark to attack unprepared positions and the men asked to do it were too few, too scattered and too mixed up for there to be any real hope of success. Just after midnight the orders were cancelled. If they had not been and an attack had gone through, then many of the tired units would have, in all probability, ceased to exist. At that point the orders were to prepare a line across the gap and ensure it was held. That effectively brought the fighting of 8th May to a close.

There can be no way that 8th May can be looked upon as a successful day for the British Army. Two of its brigades had been all but wiped out and casualties for the day had been very heavy. It had been forced to yield ground about a mile deep at its deepest but had still managed

238

to maintain a line. The Official History sees the ground that had been given up as ground that would have been impossible to hold for any length of time and in that context it may be seen as an intermediate line in the overall plan of the withdrawal. Whilst this may be the truth of the situation, it is fair to say that Plumer would have preferred it to have been held. If, indeed, he had expected to lose it so quickly it is unlikely that it would have been chosen for the line of defence, for its loss cost many lives that day and one thing that the army in front of Ypres needed above all else was men. After the losses of April and early May all the units involved had suffered substantial casualties and some, like the 12th London, the 1st Monmouths and the 1st York and Lancaster, for instance, had all but ceased to exist following the fighting of 8th May. If any good can be said to have come out of the fighting, it was the way in which the battalions in the front line stuck to their task as they were gradually surrounded and overwhelmed. A German communiqué for 8th May details 800 prisoners of war taken that day which, bearing in mind the numbers of men involved in the fighting, is a small number. The Official History points out also that no fewer than eleven battalion commanders fell during the day and all units involved lost a large proportion of their officers. Some have suggested that this was a consequence of the fact that many of the units were filled with untried replacements and, whilst not lacking in courage or the will to fight, they needed much personal leadership from the officers. What the Official History neglects to mention is that many of the men who became casualties were led by young officers who had no more experience of warfare than themselves. At this stage of the Great War the British army was still learning its trade and the price paid for this was the loss of many men in the heavy fighting throughout 1915, as Britain mobilized and trained its eager young men. Apparently the German commanders recognized the efforts and the sacrifice made in front of Ypres on 8th May. Lieutenant Colonel Enderby of the 2nd Northumberland Fusiliers, captured during the evening, was later entertained by a German general. Of course, Enderby was unhappy about his capture and the almost complete destruction of his battalion and he expressed as much to the German who replied:

> Maybe so. But you may reflect but had it not been for the resistance of that battalion I would not now be here. I should have been in Ypres tonight.[28]

Whilst the German may have been happy to overstate the case to his prisoner there can be no doubt that the sentiment expressed can be amply justified, since all along the heavily shelled front line the infantryman had mostly stood his ground and fought against tremendous odds. Casualties had been high but the line held. At the close of the 8th May the line ran through Verlorenhoek northwards before swinging west to join the 12 Brigade at Shell Trap Farm, whilst to the south contact had been regained with the 80 Brigade near Bellewaarde Wood. Time had been bought to allow the defenders to prepare themselves for the next phase of the battle – sadly for many of the units that were now so weakened there was little chance of them playing any part in any major action for some time to come.

Notes

1. Captain Kenneth Francis Drake Gattie was awarded the MC for his part in this action. By the end of the war he had also been awarded the DSO and had been mentioned in despatches five times. He then took a regular commission in the 2nd South Wales Borderers.
2. Dixon & Dixon, op.cit., p49.
3. ibid.
4. *Official History 1915 Vol. 1*, footnote p314.
5. Dixon & Dixon, op.cit., p50.
6. RSM Hatton was one of the first prisoners to be exchanged – he survived the war by only a few days and died of the effects of his wounds in December, 1918 and is buried in the town cemetery in Cwm, Monmouthshire.
7. Dixon & Dixon, op.cit., p51.
8. ibid., p54.
9. ibid.
10. Captain Baker is buried in Poelcappelle British Cemetery, near Ypres.
11. The 3rd Monmouths were able to raise four officers and 130 men, including those on HQ duty, at the end of the fighting. Stragglers reported over the next few days and the strength rose to about 250 in total. The battalion never recovered from the losses of Second Ypres and was eventually disbanded in August 1916.
12. Corporal H McKenzie was later commissioned and was to win the VC. He was killed in action in 1917.
13. Adamson's wound put him out of action for some months but he returned to the battalion later in the year. He finished the war as Lieutenant Colonel commanding the Patricia's.
14. Quoted in Newman, *With the Patricia's in Flanders. 1914–1918*, p54.
15. ibid., p57.
16. ibid., p59.
17. The Patricia's thought of this defence to be amongst their finest achievements of the war. The regimental memorial is sited at Westhoek on the battlefield they had defended so gallantly on 8th May, 1915.
18. Quoted in Murphy, *The History of the Suffolk Regiment 1914–1927*, p76.
19. Both Edwards and Garbutt were killed later in the action.

20. Quoted in Hughes & Dixon, op.cit., p53.
21. ibid., p54. Captain Edwards is burried in New Irish Farm Cemetery.
22. ibid., p55.
23. ibid., p56.
24. Dixon, op.cit., p40.
25. Wyrall, op.cit., p114.
26. War Diary of the 1st Royal Irish Fusiliers.
27. Quoted in *Official History 1915 Vol. 1*, p336.
28. Quoted in Sandilands, *The Fifth in the Great War*, p99.

CHAPTER SIXTEEN

The Battle of Frezenberg Ridge
Days 2 to 5 – 9th to 12th May 1915

It is surprising, perhaps, that after their successes against the 28th Division on 8th May, the Germans did not follow up with a further attack on 9th May in the same area. The fact that they did not may reveal much about how they saw the battle developing. To begin with, the defence offered by the 28th Division had been quite robust, bearing in mind that it was mostly limited to rifle fire, and as such it is to be expected that the German casualties in the XXVII Reserve Corps, in particular, were quite high and there was a need for this Corps to pause to allow reorganization and to bring up any available reinforcements. Secondly, the Germans had seen the counter-attack, or rather the advance, of the 10 Brigade as a "great counter-attack". This suggests that they were indeed weakened themselves and also that they had absolutely no idea of the condition of the British forces facing them. If this was indeed the case, as seems likely, then the lack of action on that particular part of the front may be better understood. Had the Germans pursued their offensive against the 28th Division then it could have resulted in a greater success than clearly even they anticipated, and in all probability far greater success than resulted from the course of action they chose to take from 9th May. Of course, it should be remembered that 9th May also saw the commencement of the British offensive on Aubers Ridge, and the French in Artois, and this would certainly have had a bearing on the Germans' attitude in front of Ypres. The Germans attacking Ypres had suffered large numbers of casualties during the fighting and with actions occurring elsewhere there could have been little hope for sufficient reinforcements or relief of those units that had been attempting to force a breakthrough at Ypres since the release of gas on 22nd April. Though the Germans were feeling the effects of the fighting they were still numerically superior to the British and, as must have been totally clear to them, their artillery was in control of the battlefield. Therefore, although the emphasis for 9th May and the following days shifted somewhat, the Germans were not about to give up the fight in their effort to flatten the Ypres salient and capture ground from the Allies.

The tactic chosen by the Germans on 9th May was to attack the 27th Division, which had already seen some heavy fighting on its left flank alongside the 28th Division. At 5.30 am the Germans commenced shelling the front line in the area from Zwarteleen to the Ypres-Roulers railway, which covered all of the 27th Division front. A large portion of their effort was directed on that part of 80 Brigade then straddling the Menin Road and 81 Brigade then holding the forward edge of Sanctuary Wood. From this approach it would appear that the Germans were using a straightforward battering-ram technique, whereby they hoped to force the British line back on that defended by the 28th Division west of Verlorenhoek in the centre of the salient. It lacked any subtlety, but since they had far superior firepower the approach is at least understandable. Further, by attacking about the Menin Road they were able to use their XV Corps which up to that date had missed much of the heavy fighting and contained the freshest troops that they had at their disposal.

On the left of the British line involved in the day's fighting was 80 Brigade with the 2nd KSLI on the left occupying the line from the junction with the 28th Division to approximately Bellewaarde Lake, where the line was continued successively towards the Menin Road by the 4th Rifle Brigade and the 4th KRRC to the boundary of 81 Brigade, adjacent to the road itself. To the south of the road the line was occupied by the 2nd Cameron Highlanders and the 2nd Gloucesters around the front edge of Sanctuary Wood. It was on these units that the bulk of the responsibility for the fighting on 9th May was to rest. By that date the capability of the German artillery was clear to everyone in the salient and the intensity of the shelling of the 27th Division can hardly have been a surprise. In places the Germans continued their shelling for nine hours, giving the line the same kind of treatment that had been meted out to the 28th Division the day before. Guns of all kinds were trained on this limited area, and soon the forward lines became untenable as trenches disappeared in an inferno of high-explosive shells; as they disappeared so did many of the defenders, who were buried alive or forced to leave trenches that were being pounded away to nothing.

In the 2nd Gloucesters' sector in Sanctuary Wood, Major F.C. Nisbet of B Company gave an order before the start of the bombardment to reduce the numbers of men occupying an advanced trench held by two platoons, commanded by Lieutenant E.D.O. Aplin and Sergeant Coopey, by half. This helped to reduce their casualties, but the Gloucesters' front line trench was also to come under very heavy fire during the bombardment which commenced at 6.30 am. The initial fire did so much damage that Aplin and his half platoon that had remained in the advanced trench were completely cut off and, shortly afterwards a similar fate was to befall Sergeant Coopey and his garrison. Major Nisbet realized what was happening and immediately reduced the strength of the front line trench also in the attempt to limit the effects of the shelling, and to keep as many men as possible fit for the infantry assault that everyone knew must follow the intense shelling.

According to the Gloucesters' War Diary for the day, the enemy made his first move against their position at 7.15 am whilst the heavy shelling continued all along the line. In these initial moves the Germans succeeded in making some progress, as described above, when they captured a number of outlying trenches. The Gloucesters fought back and one of their machine guns was particularly effective. Nevertheless, the Germans continued to make progress and began digging themselves in. Their casualties were estimated at the time as being 350, so the ground had not been gained cheaply. This fighting continued for about two hours when Lieutenant Colonel G.S. Tulloh decided the time had arrived to make some kind of counter-attack to regain the ground that had been lost. To that end he ordered two bombing parties to begin working their way forward through the two communication trenches to their old positions. This was not a success, its failure blamed on the quality of the bombs then at their disposal. Tulloh then decided to send in an attack directly against the Germans who had, by that time, managed to turn the trench, at least partly, to their favour. He ordered a total of five platoons into action, and by 3 pm all were in position ready for the counter-attack to commence. Whilst this was a small-scale local affair Tulloh managed to organize artillery support in the form of 96th Battery RFA and 61st Field Howitzer Battery RFA, and no doubt he felt he had done all he could to ensure the success of his operation. At 3.45 pm, after the signal of a half a minute rapid rifle fire, the assigned parties moved into the attack, which the War Diary describes:

This attack was met with a terrific fire from the enemy who had a M.G. in the corner of (the) wood and 2 more near Stirling Castle. The ground, owing to fallen trees, shell holes and wire, was entirely difficult to advance over and being met by the terrific fire the attack got up to 15 to 20 yards of the enemy where a firing line was established. If supports could have been got up at once the attack would have pushed into (the) enemy's trenches, but the condition of the ground made the bringing up of

244

support a very long proceeding, and before support could arrive the attacking party was practically wiped out . . .

It had been a costly venture for the Gloucesters[1] and by the time it had finished they had lost their commanding officer, killed in action, together with thirty-nine men and over 100 wounded and missing. Major Nisbet then assumed command of the Battalion and the Gloucesters satisfied themselves with holding their original front line trench, considering all additional effort to regain the ground lost as pointless. It is quite interesting to note that apart from the sharp fighting in the Gloucesters' sector, 81 Brigade was considered to have escaped rather lightly. Indeed the 2nd Cameron Highlanders' history of the day does not even note that there was heavy fighting to its right but notes that 80 Brigade on its left suffered most severely, and it is to this action that the story now turns.

In 80 Brigade's sector there would appear to be no general agreement as to the intensity of the fighting on 9th May. The history of the 4th KRRC suggests that the bombardment, whilst heavy, "was not nearly as intense as yesterday" (8th May). The 4th Rifle Brigade history, however, remarks upon the intensity of the bombardment and points out that the trench line soon disappeared. Oddly enough the history of the 3rd KRRC, which had relieved the Patricia's on the extreme left of the Brigade on the night of 8th May, states that "9th May passed quietly enough". At this stage of the battle it would appear that adjacent units did not seem to have been aware of the problems each other were having and, compared to the fighting in the Gloucesters' front, all would seem to have had a relatively quiet day. Even the bombardment seems to have commenced at markedly different times in this part of the line. It is safe to say that the Germans began shelling 80 Brigade very early, sometime between 6 and 8 am, and that it lasted until about 2 pm, when there was a pause. Half an hour later the bombardment recommenced, but it then moved systematically along the line, gradually increasing in intensity until about 4 pm when it reached a peak, at which it was maintained for approximately twenty minutes before the Germans rose to attack the front line. This was recorded in the 2nd KSLI Regimental History as follows:

Soon after four o'clock the shelling developed into an absolute furnace of fire. For about twenty minutes the rain of shells continued. Shells of every description, from "Jack Johnsons" to 9-pounders fell in and about our trenches. Suddenly it ceased. It was obvious that an infantry attack was coming, and an order to clean rifles was passed along.[2]

The history states that the Germans rose from trenches about 250 yards in front of the 2nd KSLI and came forward almost shoulder to shoulder and in three waves. There was almost a sigh of relief in the British trenches as the front line soldier welcomed the chance to fight back after enduring the murderous shellfire for most of the day. Soon rifle fire crackled along the front line, the German waves were broken up, and they withdrew leaving many dead and wounded on the battlefield. At least those units facing this infantry assault agree that it was a fairly weak affair and lacked any real determination so that it was readily beaten off at all points. A number of histories record that some of the Germans coming at them were wearing British uniforms, and in some cases kilts, which it is presumed were taken from the dead left on the battlefield as the British had withdrawn during the days immediately preceding. Whilst this has not been substantiated it is an oft-repeated story of this battle. As darkness fell on the front line, soldiers began working in the attempt to repair their badly battered trenches and every effort was made to ensure that rations, water and ammunition were taken to the forward troops.

The Germans had achieved very little by the end of the day. There had been some minor adjustments of the line in the area to the north of Bellewaarde Lake as units established contact with the new line in the centre of the salient, and the Germans had gained a small amount of ground in front of Sanctuary Wood as the Gloucesters had withdrawn from their advanced position to defend the main front line trench. Otherwise, it had not been a particularly successful day for the Germans as more of their infantrymen had fallen in yet more abortive attacks. The heavy shelling had once again demonstrated, however, just how fragile the British front line was. Nevertheless, it was fortunate for the 28th Division that the Germans had directed their efforts away from their front for it had enabled that tired and badly mauled Division to be reinforced. The 1st Cavalry Division was brought forward to support it, and its 1st and 2nd Cavalry Brigades were sent to occupy the GHQ line whilst the 4th Dragoon Guards were sent into the 85 Brigade line to reinforce that Brigade subsequent to its abortive counter-attack of 8th May. The 9 Cavalry Brigade was ordered to the left of the area where they commenced preparing a trench between the GHQ line and the 4th Division back line, thereby completing a second line of defence in the event of another German breakthrough. In view of the fact that, in spite of some effort, the Germans had not made any substantial progress around the salient, 9th May should probably be seen as one of the easier days of the battle for the British forces defending Ypres.

The dawn of 10th May was greeted, as so many dawns during the battle, by the commencement of yet another German bombardment. This time its focus was the area either side of the Menin Road or roughly the junction between 80 and 81 Brigades. The shelling continued throughout the morning and at 10.30 am its intensity was increased by the addition of fire from a number of howitzer batteries. The front line battalions had no doubt that this was preparation for another infantry assault upon their lines. At about 1.30 pm, in the vicinity of the Menin road, the Germans commenced their attack under the cover of a small amount of gas. The 2nd Camerons held the line across the Menin road where part of its D Company, dug in just north of the road, was forced to give ground. The remainder of the Battalion hung on despite their flank being partly opened and the Germans making repeated attacks upon them in the effort to drive them back along the road. They were ably assisted in this when Lieutenant Colonel D.A. Callendar of the 1st Royal Scots, positioned to their right, ordered Captain L.S. Farquharson to take B Company to assist the defence along the north of the road:

> He found that the unit on the left of the 1st Royal Scots had been literally blown from its trenches, and the Germans were on the point of occupying them when the Lowlanders appeared on the scene. Captain Farquharson with admirable decision ordered his men to charge, and the enemy flinching before the gleaming bayonets of the Royal Scots fled in disorder and confusion.[3]

The Royal Scots' company then occupied the line, up to and including part of the 4th KRRC line, until they were replaced later in the day by B Company, the 1st Argyll and Sutherland Highlanders, who had come up in support, and prevented any further German moves in that direction.

In 80 Brigade the 4th KRRC came under heavy fire also, and with their trenches blasted away they were forced to retire to their supports. These trenches were little more than waist deep but they offered better protection because they were not under direct observation by the enemy. However, by occupying these trenches they had been in part responsible for the gap that formed between them and the Camerons and which was filled by the advance of Captain Farquharson and his Royal Scots. Lieutenant Colonel Campbell of the 2nd Camerons had been placed in charge of other troops in the area and had called upon the 1st Argylls to come to his assistance when the problems on the left flank became apparent. This unit moved at once to reinforce the line near Hooge:

> Their advance across an area of a mile in depth, swept by shell fire, was magnificently carried out. Casualties were few, due to the excellent formation of each company. No time was lost and discipline was perfect, it was an inspiring sight.[4]

The 9th Argylls also moved forward at this time to support the Camerons. The Germans continued to make infantry attacks throughout the afternoon of 10th May but, as on previous occasions, they met with rapid rifle fire from the British trenches and made very little headway.

By about 6 pm the German infantry attack had all but ceased and Major General Snow began to consider the possibility of a counter-attack to restore the line either side of the Menin Road. It soon became clear to Snow that this would not be possible because of the shell beaten ground and the number of fallen trees which combined to make the ground almost impassable, and that before any consideration of the fire the Germans could bring to bear had been made. In view of this Snow decided it would be fruitless to attempt such a venture and it was decided to construct a new line immediately behind the abandoned one which could be defended the next day if necessary. To this end the 1st and 2nd Wessex Field Companies RE (both 27th Division) were sent forward to begin work. However, the conditions that had prevented Snow making his counter-attack also prevented the sappers from preparing the line – the ground conditions were that bad. Therefore, the decision was made that the second line, running behind Bellewaarde Lake, would be defended and that line was manned immediately by the 4th KRRC and 4 Rifle Brigade. To continue the line south of the Menin Road it was necessary for communication trenches parallel to the road to be occupied to complete the link with the 2nd Camerons south of the road and still holding part of Sanctuary Wood.

The angle formed in the line by this arrangement was to become the scene of heavy fighting during 11th May – clearly the Germans had identified it as a point of weakness and saw an attack upon it as being their best chance of success. They began by shelling the whole of the 27th Division front line from about 7.30 am and in the process continued to create considerable damage to the front line trenches which were already in a poor state after days of shellfire. The shelling continued for about three and a half hours before the Germans launched their infantry at the sharp angle in the British line in the vicinity of the Menin Road. Once again the Germans discharged gas to assist their attack but it was in such small quantities that those units involved, the 2nd Camerons and the 1st Argylls, reported that it had little effect. In fact there was a sudden change in the direction of the wind which blew the gas back on the German infantry causing two battalions to be caught in full view of the British machine guns, which were put to immediate use in helping to break up the attack. The first attack was beaten back but continued pressure throughout the after-noon resulted in the Camerons leaving their forward trenches as they were pushed backwards into Sanctuary Wood, where they made a stand amongst the shattered trees and tumbled debris. Two officers, Captain

R.H. M'Call and Lieutenant J.R.H. Anderson then took it upon themselves to rally the troops in the wood to lead a counter-attack which was successful, in so far as it regained a portion of the ground lost; however, Anderson was killed and M'Call, who had arrived only the night before with a draft, was wounded. The latter was awarded the MC for his part in the action. During the confused fighting of the morning and early afternoon one of the Camerons' machine guns, commanded by Lance Corporal G. Garden, became surrounded by a party of nine Germans. All of Garden's gun team had already been put out of action and he did not want to see the gun captured. He immediately picked up an axe and attacked the Germans, and in a brief hand-to-hand struggle he killed two, after which the rest ran away from the axe wielding Cameron Highlander. For his part in saving the machine gun, Garden was awarded the DCM. Unfortunately for the Camerons their commanding officer, Lieutenant Colonel Campbell, was wounded during the morning and his command then fell on Lieutenant Colonel H.B. Kirk of the 1st Argyll and Sutherland Highlanders.

The net effect of the fighting in the area was that the Germans were able to gain a high point on the bend of the Menin Road which allowed them to enfilade the trenches of the 27th Division further south in front of Sanctuary Wood. The history of the 1st Argylls commented on the day:

> All ranks had shown great endurance during the day's fighting, the majority fighting without rations or water. Casualties had not been very severe, but there was a shortage of officers, A and B Companies having only one each. Rifle shooting had not been up to standard, but the spirit shown by all ranks had been wonderful.[5]

By the end of the day the Germans still had the small hill to their credit and it was with a view to regaining this that additional troops were brought back into the area. At 7.45 pm the 2nd Gloucesters, who had been taken out of the line after the fighting of 9th May, had been ordered back to support 81 Brigade. As darkness fell the larger part of the responsibility for recapturing the ground during the night fell upon this Battalion. By 11 pm it had been discovered that the enemy was bringing up reinforcements onto the hill, so an immediate counter attack was decided upon and two companies of the 1st Leinsters were attached to the Gloucesters for the purpose. Two attempts to recapture the hill were unsuccessful and it was not until 4 am on 12th May that B Company of the Gloucesters, under Captain J. Fane, was able to drive the Germans off it. The stay was short-lived for by 4.45 am the Gloucesters had been forced from the position again. Fane attacked with the remains of his company later in the morning and briefly held the hill again, but his company had by this time suffered sufficiently heavy casualties for them not to be able to hold the position. Although efforts were made to retake the hill well into the morning the losses incurred by the battalion eventually dissuaded them from any further attacks and the small hill was left in the hands of the Germans.

Beyond the fighting for this small vantage point on the bend of the Menin road a little to the east of Hooge, there was no further fighting during 12th May. The Germans contented themselves with shelling the salient throughout the rest of the day and their infantry appear to have been resting from its efforts to that date. This allowed the British some respite in which to reorganize their line and to bring up reserves and reliefs. The 27th Division had almost no reserves since the combined unit which had been made of the Patricia's and the 4th KRRC, recently relieved from front line duty, was so battle-worn as to be of very little real use in the event of a crisis arising. To help ease the situation for Major General Snow, 150 (York and Durham) Brigade, then at Vlamertinge, was placed at his disposal and he immediately ordered the 5th Durham Light Infantry forward so that it could reinforce the Camerons, the Argylls and the two battalions of the Royal Scots then holding the front line in the 81 Brigade front. The IV (Durham) Howitzer Brigade and an additional 60-pounder battery were also placed under Snow's command.

During the night of 12th and 13th May the opportunity was taken to relieve the 28th Division. Of all the units that had been involved in the fighting 28th Division had suffered the greatest hardship and casualties. Its battalions had been in the thick of things more or less since the beginning of the battle some three weeks earlier. All had seen some heavy fighting and most had suffered considerable casualties. It was replaced by the 1st and 3rd Cavalry Divisions which, under the command of Major General de Lisle, became known as the Cavalry Force. This Force took over the line from the trenches of the 2nd KSLI, on the left of the 27th Division, up to the junction with the 4th Division in the vicinity of Shell Trap Farm. The 28th Division went into Army Reserve. In the course of the fighting in front of Ypres between 22nd April and 12th May the Division had suffered over 15,000 casualties and, even with the replacements it had received, it was still under strength at a little over 8,000 all ranks. For all the effort that they had made and all the suffering they had withstood there seems to have been little understanding from the cavalry, as one staff officer of the 1st Cavalry Division was to remark about the 28th Division staff "... things not right here; everyone looks tired".[6] It can be hardly surprising that everyone looked tired since they had been under the continual stress of battle for over three weeks. The Division had

250

conducted itself well under the circumstances and there can be little reason for anyone to be critical of it.

During the day news also was received via air reconnaissance that the Germans were sending reinforcements to the Arras front, and not to Ypres, since they were needed to defend against the French attack in the area. This was encouraging news for the British commanders, for at least it meant that it was unlikely that the German offensive in front of Ypres could become any stronger. However, to offset that news there was a growing ammunition crisis. Artillery ammunition had been short for most of the battle and the diversion of supplies to the Gallipoli campaign simply made matters worse. It was now time for the infantry to recognize a problem too, for there was a shortage of machine guns in the army in France and there were no guns in stock to replace those destroyed in battle. Thus, the army fought on in France and Flanders short of at least forty-two machine guns. Further it had been calculated that by the end of the second week in May the stock of small arms ammunition had also been reduced to no more than ninety-three rounds per rifle[7] or, to put it another way, less than ten minutes use in the hands of an experienced front line soldier. This situation of supply shortages did not end there for, even if there had been sufficient ammunition, the supply of rifles was becoming so short that there were few to send to France. It was even suggested that drafts being sent to France should leave England without rifles! As for other items such as hand grenades and trench mortars, they too were in alarmingly short supply. For those men engaged in the heavy fighting in front of Ypres it would have come as small consolation to know that it was the same throughout the British Army.

Notes

1. The Gloucesters' Regimental Memorial can be found at Clapham Junction on the Menin Road near Gheluvelt. Major Nisbet was later awarded the DSO.
2. Wood, *The History of the King's Shropshire Light Infantry in the Great War. 1914–1918*, p81.
3. Ewing, *The Royal Scots 1914–1919*, p100.
4. Anderson, *History of the Argyll and Sutherland Highlanders*, p37.
5. ibid., p38.
6. Home, *The Diary of a World War I Cavalry Officer*, p67.
7. *Official History 1915 Vol. 1*, p331.

CHAPTER SEVENTEEN

The Battle of Frezenberg Ridge
Day 6 – 13th May 1915

If the German accounts are to be believed, 13th May was to herald the beginning of a great attack which was to carry them to victory in front of Ypres. The fact that it did not occur is put down to a shortage of ammunition by the same accounts. It may well be that the Germans themselves felt that they had insufficient ammunition for complete success, and bearing in mind the vast quantity of ammunition they had expended up to 13th May to achieve a limited and qualified success this standpoint could be justified if not entirely understood. To the British in the salient it must have seemed that the Germans had a limitless supply of ammunition of all kinds, for since the battle had started the defenders had suffered the prolonged effects of heavy shelling by guns of all calibres from the field gun upwards. Whether or not the shortage of ammunition alluded to by the Germans was actual or perceived, for the front line British soldier 13th May began as had many days previous to it – with heavy shelling. The Germans commenced shelling at 4 am and the line from a little south of Bellewaarde Lake to Turco Farm was subjected to an intense bombardment. Facing this bombardment were, on the right 80 Brigade, to their left the Cavalry Force comprising the 3rd Cavalry Division adjacent to 80 Brigade and the 1st Cavalry Division to its left. The cavalry occupied the line from Bellewaarde Lake to the vicinity of Wieltje with a total of four brigades in the front line (6 and 7 Brigades of the 3rd Cavalry Division; 1 and 2 Brigades of the 1st Cavalry Division) with two brigades (8 and 9 Brigades) held in reserve. Each brigade contained about 800 – 900 men and fifty officers, which made a cavalry brigade roughly equivalent to an up to strength infantry

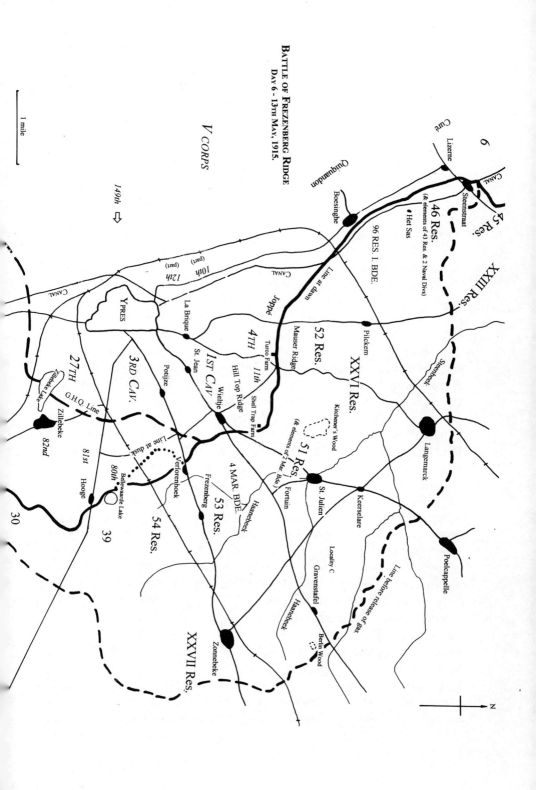

BATTLE OF FREZENBERG RIDGE
Day 6 - 13th May, 1915.

1 mile

V CORPS

149th ⇨

6

Cure

Lizerne

CANAL

Steenstraat

45 Res.

46 Res.
(& elements of 43 Res. & 2 Naval Divs)

● Het Sas

Quiquandon

Boesinghe

96 RES. I. BDE.

Line at dam

CANAL

Pilckem

52 Res.

XXVI Res.

XXIII Res.

Steenbeek

10th (part)

12th (part)

CANAL

Jeppé

Mauser Ridge

Turco Farm

4TH

11th

Shell Trap Farm

Hill Top Ridge

Kitchener's Wood

51 Res.
(& elements of 2 Mar Bde)

Fortuin

St. Julien

Langemarck

Poelcappelle

Keerselare

Line before release of gas

YPRES

La Brique

St. Jean

1ST CAV.

Wieltje

Potijze

3RD CAV.

G.H.Q. Line

27TH

Zillebeke Lake.

82nd

Zillebeke

81st

Hooge

80th

Line at dusk.

Verlorenhoek

Bellewaarde Lake

39

54 Res.

Frezenberg

53 Res.

4 MAR. BDE.

Haanebeek

Zonnebeke

XXVII Res.

Locality C

Gravenstafel

Haanebeek

Berlin Wood

30

N

battalion. To the left of the cavalry and manning the line around Shell Trap Farm as far as Turco Farm was the 4th Division, with its 11 Brigade holding the forward line whilst 12 Brigade was in reserve. Adjacent to the cavalry were the 5th London (London Rifle Brigade) and to their left were the 1st East Lancashires with their left against Shell Trap Farm, which was occupied by 1 Rifle Brigade on the dawn of 13th May. Beyond these were the 1st Hampshires and the 1st Somerset Light Infantry who linked with elements of General Joppé's 152nd Division at Turco Farm. The cavalry were relatively fresh troops, though they had been involved elsewhere since the battles for Ypres had begun. On the other hand the infantry had all been involved in heavy fighting and had suffered substantial casualties up to that date and there can be little doubt that they were in need of relief as soon as possible. It is fair to say that neither the 4th Division nor the 27th Division had suffered as badly as the 28th Division but they were, nevertheless, battle weary units and all the battalions were under strength to a greater or lesser degree. So it was with tired and under strength units that the British were forced to face a German army that was, by its own measure, short of ammunition.

The stages of the day's fighting followed a very similar pattern to those of preceding days in so far as the German preparation was followed by infantry attack against stubborn, if at times inadequate, defence. The intense bombardment which commenced at 4 am was recorded by V Corps as being the heaviest so far endured by the men in their hastily prepared defences. If the Germans were short of ammunition it was not apparent to anyone else in the Ypres area that morning. The Official History states that the heaviest shrapnel shelling was directed at 80 Brigade and the Cavalry Force; that is, approximately between Hooge and the Ypres-Saint Julien road. To make matters worse for the defenders the weather was bad; it rained all day, which aided the shelling in turning the zone into a quagmire before the morning was over. After about four hours of preparatory shelling the Germans made an advance which carried them into the trenches of 7 Cavalry Brigade. These trenches had been lightly held because of their unfavourable position on a long and gentle forward slope. Gradually the Germans gained a foothold and by bombing in both directions succeeded in driving back the defenders from the cavalry brigade. The Leicestershire Yeomanry, holding the right of the sector with two squadrons, were steadily forced from their trenches and to their right, and into the sector of the line held by 6 Cavalry Brigade, whilst the 2nd Life Guards and the 1st Life Guards successively to their left were forced from their trenches with considerable loss of life. A contemporary account puts the casualties at over 500 for 7 Cavalry Brigade alone. Fortunately, one squadron of the Leicestershire Yeomanry was manning support trenches some 300 yards behind the firing line and were able to bring sufficient fire to bear, in spite of their rifles jamming in the muddy conditions, to prevent the Germans exploiting their early success in the sector.

Further to the left, near Wieltje, 2 Cavalry Brigade also suffered as the early morning shelling took its toll on both the men and the defences. The trenches of the 18th Hussars against the Wieltje-Gravenstafel road, and those of the 5th Dragoon Guards (1 Cavalry Brigade) to their right soon disappeared; the remnants of the Hussars were forced to man shell holes to maintain any sort of line. It was not long before they were forced to withdraw leaving a gap in the defences about the road. To their left, in the 4th Division sector, things were little better. The London Rifle Brigade had relieved the 2nd Royal Dublin Fusiliers and had found the trenches to be very poor: wide, shallow and badly knocked about by the German shelling. In fact the trench had in part disappeared completely leaving a gap of about ten yards which could not be manned to the left of the Wieltje-Saint Julien road. This meant that 8 Platoon on the extreme right, and across the road, was isolated from the main body of the battalion. Bearing in mind that the 18th Hussars had also retired, this platoon was in a very difficult position to defend the right flank of the entire 4th Division. For all that, the London Rifle Brigade, and the other units of 11 Brigade, had received orders that they were to hold the line at all costs. This was all very well but, with communications with their own Brigade becoming increasingly difficult and with the adjacent cavalry almost non-existent, that was going to be a tall order to follow. During the morning the London Rifle Brigade called two companies from reserve to reinforce the forward trenches, and although it was necessary to cross over the low ridge they managed to complete the reinforcement with few casualties. The regimental history puts this down to good discipline and the adoption of the artillery formation as the sections moved forward. The 1st East Lancashires, to their left, were less fortunate and lost heavily as they attempted a similar manoeuvre. At about midday the following message was received from 2 Cavalry Brigade:

> The left regiment of the 2nd Cavalry Brigade had been very much cut up by shell fire, and its trenches practically destroyed. The remnants of the regiment retired. There is thus a gap of about 300 yards between my next regiment and your right. It is impossible to hold this gap thoroughly as we cannot dig trenches owing to machine gun fire. Two squadrons are doing their best to occupy the gap by holding the shell holes. I have asked them to try and get in touch with your right. Will you let me know how the right of your battalion is situated.[1]

Clearly, under the circumstances, it was going to be difficult to form a defensive line let alone hold it. When the 18th Hussars were eventually

255

forced out of their trenches Captain Husey of the London Rifle Brigade went out in the open under terrific shellfire in an attempt to get them back into some kind of line. One of the Londoners noted:

> . . . but a man further over to my right told me afterwards that he had seen Captain Husey scrambling between the shell bursts waving his revolver at the bewildered cavalrymen. Of course we couldn't hear what he was saying but it was probably something polite like "Get back into those trenches or else."[2]

Captain Husey was wounded in his efforts to close the gap that had, by that time, left the flank of the entire division exposed. Within this gap of about 300 yards there was one small party of the London Rifle Brigade under the command of Sergeant D.W. Belcher. Belcher's command was no more than two lance corporals and six riflemen but according to the contemporary accounts Belcher had quickly realized the situation and resolved to hold his ground. From his position between the Wieltje-Saint Julien and the Wieltje-Gravenstafel roads, Belcher and his small group maintained such a volume of fire that they convinced the Germans that the post was rather more strongly held than it actually was. Throughout the rest of the day, by collecting rifles and ammunition from the dead and wounded this party held the ground and for his part in commanding the gallant little force throughout the defence Sergeant Belcher was awarded the Victoria Cross, the first soldier in the ranks of the Territorial Force to win such a great honour.[3] Whilst Belcher is justifiably remembered, the other men who took part are seldom referred to, but their part is no less worthy of mention for they acted every bit as gallantly under the direction of this excellent NCO. The other men who were present in this part of the action on Frezenberg Ridge were: Lance Corporals H.J.C. Rowe and J.H. Wheatley, who was wounded, and Riflemen H.G. Buck (wounded), C.M. Evans, G.M. Freeman (killed), H. Parker, H.W. Rowe and R.S. Weeks (wounded). Lance Corporal Rowe and Rifleman Buck were also honoured by the award of the Military Medal. There can be little doubt that the action of this small group had done much to dissuade the enemy from exploiting a gap that was seriously jeopardizing the right flank of the 4th Division and the left flank of the 1st Cavalry Division.

To the left, in the area of Shell Trap Farm, another crisis was developing. The trenches were held by 1 Rifle Brigade and, like the rest of the line that morning, they had been heavily shelled since the early hours. The shellfire directed at Shell Trap Farm was particularly intense and at its peak it was recorded that 100 shells a minute were falling on the farm and its immediate vicinity. A little before 7 am the German infantry assaulted this portion of the line but they were easily repulsed, except at Shell Trap Farm, where it appears that the garrison had been wiped out. By 7.05 am the Germans had gained a foothold in the ruins of the building. Once the Germans had succeeded in making progress against the farm, things became very difficult for A Company of the 1st East Lancashires to the right. The Germans were able to launch an attack against their positions using bombers supported by fire from those in the farm buildings. Two platoons of the 1st East Lancashires that were nearest the farm buildings were all but destroyed as their position took vicious fire from the Germans, who were now in close contact with them. The platoon, under Major E.F. Rutter, was slightly further to the right but was able to hold out only slightly longer as it too was being shelled and sniped. Eventually all officers became casualties and all that remained were two unwounded privates. They had held out long enough, however, for B Company to come up and reinforce the remnants of A Company and thereby hold the line until help in the form of the 2nd Essex could arrive.

Shell Trap Farm, which had already been the site of much fighting, was seen to be important all through the battle, first as a dressing station for the Canadians, and then as the front line closed upon it, as an observation post for all the area to the north. Therefore, it was not going to be given up easily. To this end Lieutenant Colonel L.O.W. Jones of the 2nd Essex, attached from 12 Brigade, acted upon his own initiative and ordered his battalion forward to retake the farm. Lieutenant J.V. Atkinson took C Company forward and discovering the farm occupied, as had been correctly anticipated by Jones, he attacked the farm at once. His command came under fire immediately and there were a number of casualties. However, with the assistance of covering fire from a machine gun manned by Sergeant J. Couzens, the Essex recaptured Shell Trap Farm by 8 am. Twenty minutes later the battalion received a Brigade order which stated:

> Retake at once the front line from Shell Trap Farm to the Fortuin-Wieltje road a frontage of 1,000 yards.[4]

This order was necessitated by the fact that the units to the right of the farm had all suffered severely from the German shelling. The 1st East Lancashires and, as described above, the London Rifle Brigade, had been forced back in their supports as the German fire gradually, but surely, levelled their front line trenches. To their right, 2 Cavalry Brigade had suffered many casualties and a gap had been opened in that area which had been at least partly filled by the local commander ordering forward the 11th Hussars, at the same time as the 2nd Essex had made their first move towards Shell Trap Farm. Although there had

257

not been a complete breakthrough, the front line had been vacated as the 11 Brigade commanding officer had stated in his order, and since the Essex were already moving to rectify the situation the decision to use them in the attempt to re-establish the forward line could not have been difficult to make. One company of the Essex (C Company) had already been employed in recapturing Shell Trap Farm and the other three companies were deployed immediately to comply with the recently received order from Brigade. A Company was to retake the trenches between the Wieltje-Saint Julien and Wieltje-Gravenstafel roads, whilst B Company was to extend the line from the former road towards Shell Trap Farm. D Company was to move forward behind B Company, moving gradually to the left as the latter company moved forward, thereby side-slipping into the gap between B and C Companies and at the same time receiving cover from both. It was a fairly complicated arrangement to be made in the heat of battle but within ten minutes of the order being received the Essex were moving into the forward area. The Essex men soon reached the low ridge behind the vacated front line, and were subjected to very heavy machine-gun and shellfire. The regimental history states that the battalion did not falter and doubled across the ridge only to find the front line trench almost completely useless. There were casualties, particularly in B Company where a large number of inexperienced men of a recently received draft fell as they bunched together in easy targets for the German gunners. They also lost the company commander, Captain P. Pechell, wounded by a shell fragment, and CSM F.H. Cumbers killed, as these men tried to sort out the newcomers. Nevertheless the Essex reached their objective and it is recorded that they were cheered on their way as the London Rifle Brigade (5th London) stood up in their trenches to give them all the encouragement they could. A and B Companies were in contact and B Company's left was in touch with the forward position of the 1st East Lancashires who still held the low ridge to the left of Shell Trap Farm. Therefore, D Company immediately dug-in in support of the latter battalion. In approximately two hours the Essex had swept forward to regain the line and began clearing the enemy. It had been a very worthy effort which had cost the battalion a total of 180 casualties.

To the left the morning had taken a similar course for the battalions between Shell Trap Farm and Turco Farm. The right of 1 Rifle Brigade was, as described, forced out of Shell Trap Farm and their left had also received severe punishment as a gap was opened between them and the 1st Hampshires, who immediately extended their front to keep touch with the neighbouring battalion. An officer of the Hampshires wrote:

It *was* a shelling, at one time the whole of the line of trench disappeared

258

in a yellow cloud of smoke and the earth was absolutely shaking.[5]

In this area the width of no man's land was about 300 yards, which according to the Hampshires' account was too wide for the enemy to cross in the face of the heavy and accurate fire they, and the Somersets to their left, were able to bring to bear – a few of the enemy managed to get as far as the wire but died there as the attack faded away. D Company of the 1st Hampshires had been holding a forward trench with a garrison of about forty men. The intense fire had reduced this garrison to five and it was forced to withdraw down a communication trench to the relative safety of the main front line. Drummer Eldridge created a block across the communication trench and defended it by throwing all the bombs he could get his hands on. In so doing he was wounded but before he withdrew he had managed to hold up the Germans' progress for half an hour. He later returned to the evacuated trench, as the German attack faded, and tended to the wounded he found there. He was awarded a DCM for his bravery. The Germans made two further attacks during the morning but, almost to the disappointment of the defenders in the area, they fell back with heavy casualties. The Germans then resorted to further shelling of the line, but it remained intact and no further effort was made to break the line on the extreme left of the British front line.

During the afternoon the enemy continued shelling, but on the left the situation had been controlled by the 4th Division so that there was only one point of potential danger remaining, where 7 Cavalry Brigade had stood. The situation in this area was far from clear to the commander of the Cavalry Force (Major General de Lisle) since, as elsewhere, communications with his front had been lost early in the day. Added to this there was a pall of smoke, a result of the heavy shelling, hanging across the line, so that the extent of the gap was completely unknown. The commander was even unaware that the gap that had been forced in the line had been at least partly blocked by one squadron of the Leicestershire Yeomanry. Likewise he was unaware of what had become of the North Somerset Yeomanry or the Queen's Bays who were, in fact, holding on to positions to the right and left of the gap respectively.

With all these things to consider and with little hope of the situation improving without some kind of action, Brigadier General Bulkeley-Johnson was ordered to deploy his 8 Cavalry Brigade to block the gap. At 10 am Brigadier General Briggs ordered Bulkeley-Johnson to make a counter-attack to regain lost trenches. The planning was begun immediately and artillery support was ordered for noon. In the event this did not commence until 2 pm and it lasted for half an hour before the attack commenced. The 8 Cavalry Brigade, supported by the 9th

259

(under Brigadier General Greenly) and the survivors of the Leicestershire Yeomanry moved forward into the shellfire. For such a rapidly prepared and executed plan it met with some success, in so far as the Cavalry managed to regain the line in places though they were caught in heavy shrapnel fire as they reached the low ridges. One senior cavalry officer wrote of the action:

> The counter attack was ordered for 2.30 pm and was brilliantly carried out by Bulkeley-Johnson's 8th Cavalry Brigade being helped by one squadron of the Royals from Campbell's 6th Brigade. They reached the old line and got into the old trenches but were shelled out of them once again – only 200 out of 700 coming back again.[6]

The Germans made any chance of holding the old line impossible by the weight of fire that they were able to bring to bear on it. Although there were some local successes and some of the Germans were chased beyond the old line there could be only one outcome. The line had all but disappeared and the shrapnel and machine-gun fire meant that no one could survive for long there. Consequently the attackers withdrew about 1,000 yards to the reverse slope of the low ridge they had so recently crossed and prepared a new line of defence which consisted mostly of linked up shell holes. This line ran from Railway Wood on the right to the flank of 1 Cavalry Brigade on the left. It had been a costly day for the cavalry, in which two brigades had almost ceased to exist and a number of regiments had suffered very heavily. The success of the day lay in the fact that the gap had been plugged by those units at hand, and both the Cavalry Force and the 4th Division had relied heavily on the prompt actions of the local commanders before things had become too bad to recover. It is true that there had been some loss of ground but it was relatively small and in the case of 7 Cavalry Brigade's front the Germans did not even occupy the ground. In the cavalry sector 151 (Durham Light Infantry) Brigade was brought forward in the late afternoon to occupy the GHQ line behind the threatened portion of the line and that was the way the situation remained for the rest of the day.

There was one more flurry of activity before the day finished and once again it took place around Shell Trap Farm. At dusk Lieutenant Colonel G.H. Lawrence, of the 1st East Lancashires, was ordered to take charge of the situation in his area, including the farm which he was ordered to garrison with a party from his battalion. The 1st East Lancashires had been holding the line to the right of the farm which had itself been in the hands of C Company of the 2nd Essex since about 8.30 am. It is not clear from the regimental and official histories of the units involved what had happened at Shell Trap Farm during the day.

The 2nd Essex account states simply that its company (C Company) was relieved by the reserve company of the 1st East Lancashires, though it implies quite strongly that at the time of the relief the Germans had gained another foothold in the farm buildings.[7] According to the 1st East Lancs' account Captain G.D. Leake took two platoons of B Company to attack the farm and although it was pressed vigorously enough it was unsuccessful. Leake was killed and the two platoon commanders (Lieutenants G.H.T. Wade and S. Casson) were wounded. Lieutenant H.A. Lane with a platoon of D Company, then made another unsuccessful effort in which the officer was killed. Finally, two platoons of D Company, under the command of the adjutant (Lieutenant R.W. Palmer) succeeded in driving the enemy out of the farm, whereupon Lieutenant Colonel Lawrence sent back C Company of the 2nd Essex, and two companies of the 5th South Lancashires were brought up as reserve. With these actions the fighting of 13th May gradually died away and as it did so the Battle of Frezenberg Ridge also came to a close.

The Battle of Frezenberg Ridge is considered to have ended by midnight on 13th May, 1915. It was followed by a lengthy pause in the Germans operations against Ypres which are described in the following chapter. For the Germans it had been a qualified success, since they had been able to remove the bulk of V Corps from the Frezenberg Ridge and in so doing had been able to gain a slice of the salient which was about a mile deep at its deepest. On the other hand, they had not been able to break the British line sufficiently to capture the town of Ypres, though they had significantly reduced the salient, and had expended a large effort in both men and equipment to do just that. Their extensive use of artillery "preparation" both before and during the battle was to set the standard for many more battles that would be fought on the Western Front over the next three and a half years. Whilst their weight of firepower was far superior to the British at Ypres and can only have been horrific to those who faced it, it can hardly have been said to have been a great success during the Battle of Frezenberg Ridge. In spite of all the shelling and preparation the British infantry continued to hold the ground. The infantry was battered and tired and was present in ever decreasing numbers but often fighting from the flimsiest of cover they refused to be budged, particularly after the losses of the 8th May. That demonstrated clearly for all concerned the difficulty of holding the forward slope in the face of an enemy which was vastly superior in artillery. Nevertheless, once this had been vacated the Germans had little enough success in removing them again even with the superiority in firepower.

For the British, Frezenberg Ridge was almost a disaster. That they were not soundly defeated as the portion of the line collapsed on 8th May had as much to do with the Germans as anything else. For all that, the British forces fought hard and well throughout the battle to give as good an account of themselves as they could. This was particularly marked on 8th May by the defence of the 28th Division and parts of 80 Brigade, which fought until there was almost nothing left with which to fight. The effort of the 28th Division can be seen quite clearly in the official casualty figures for the six days of the battle. During the battle V Corps sustained 9,391 casualties, of which 3,889 were from the 28th Division, which was withdrawn before the end of the battle. It had been a stern test for all the British units concerned, and before the battle was over, a number of the battalions had been so reduced in numbers that they had ceased to be effective fighting units – witness, for instance, the fact that the 1st and 3rd Battalions of the Monmouthshire Regiment were combined after the fighting of 8th May and even then were barely stronger than one peacetime company. There were many similar instances and this, of course, caused other problems of organization as new drafts were hastily added to depleted units and rushed back into the line. In some cases the new drafts were so inexperienced that they were little more than targets for the German machine guns and artillery. It was unfortunate that the British army was very stretched during this period with commitments being made elsewhere, including, for instance, Gallipoli. The commitments that the Germans had elsewhere meant that they could not call on all the reserves they would have liked, particularly at the crucial stages of the battle when breakthrough was at least a possibility. Their planning for the experiment with gas had not been as thorough as it should have been and that fact allowed an under-strength and ill supplied British force to hold on to the salient. Whether or not that was a great advantage to the British is open to much discussion. A fresh British brigade on 8th May could have turned the battle; similarly, a fresh German division at the same time could have had a devastating effect on the British line. Neither was available and the battle ground on to its somewhat inconclusive end on 13th May. Whilst it had called for great endurance and sacrifice by the men in the forward trenches, like so much of the Great War all of the fighting had resulted in very little except great loss of life. On the evening of the 13th May the line held by the 4th Division, the Cavalry Force and the 27th Division was little changed and although there had been some loss of ground, the Germans had ultimately failed in their effort to shell the British defenders into oblivion.

Notes

1. Maurice, op.cit., p106.
2. Mitchinson, op.cit., p76.
3. See Appendix II for citation.
4. Quoted in Burrows, op.cit., p129.
5. Quoted in Atkinson, *The Royal Hampshire Regiment*, p64.
6. Home, op.cit., p68.
7. See Burrows, op.cit., p130.

CHAPTER EIGHTEEN

The Battle of Bellewaarde Ridge
24th – 25th May 1915

In the ten days since the fighting for the Frezenberg Ridge had subsided it must have seemed to some as if the battle that had raged for over three weeks had finally ended. During those days the tired divisions of V Corps which had withstood the onslaught of the first two weeks of May were given some chance to rest and to strengthen the defences of the line, such as they were. There was, throughout the salient, a feeling of tension, since the defenders of Ypres had been severely tested and weakened by the fighting and there were those who wondered if it would be possible to withstand another German assault should they choose to make it – and choose to make it they did on 24th May, 1915.

On this day the main part of the salient was still held by the same divisions of V Corps that had seen such ferocious fighting from the start of the battle. On the right flank, near Hill 60, was 83 Brigade (28th Division) with 1 Cavalry Brigade (1st Cavalry Division) to its left as far as the Menin Road. Beyond the Menin Road as far as Bellewaarde Lake the line was held by 2 Cavalry Brigade. From Bellewaarde Lake to the Zonnebeke Road was 85 Brigade (28th Division) with attached units from 151 Brigade (50th Division). It was this mixture of units which held the central portion of the salient, from approximately the Menin Road to the Zonnebeke Road, and on whom a great responsibility for the security of the line would be placed during the fighting of 24th May. To the left of 85 Brigade were 10 and 12 Brigades of the 4th Division occupying the line between the Zonnebeke Road and the junction with the French 152nd Division at Turco Farm. This was the line that had been established following the fighting on the Frezenberg Ridge, and

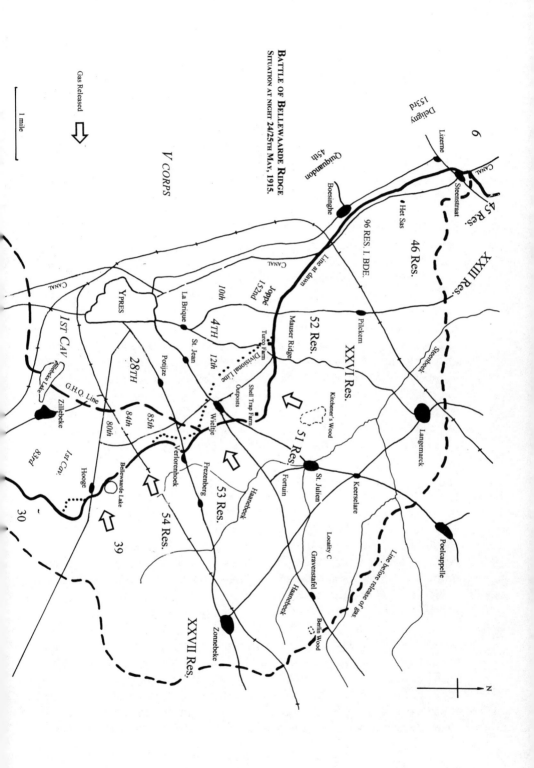

BATTLE OF BELLEWAARDE RIDGE
SITUATION AT NIGHT 24/25TH MAY, 1915.

Gas Released

1 mile

V CORPS

6
Deligny 153rd
Lizerne
Steenstraat
45 Res.
XXIII Res.
Quiquandon 45th
Boesinghe
96 RES. I. BDE.
Het Sas
46 Res.
CANAL
Line at dawn
Pilckem
Steenbeek
CANAL
La Brique
10th
153rd
52 Res.
XXVI Res.
YPRES
4TH
Mauser Ridge
Langemarck
St. Jean
12th
Turco Farm
Divisional Line
Kitchener's Wood
1ST CAV.
28TH
Potijze
Outposts
Shell Trap Farm
51 Res.
CANAL
Keerselare
G.H.Q. Line
84th
Wieltje
St. Julien
Poelcappelle
Zillebeke
85th
80th
Fortuin
Locality C
Verlorenhoek
Haanebeek
Gravenstafel
Line before release of gas
Ist Cav.
83rd
Hooge
Bellewaarde Lake
Frezenberg
53 Res.
Haanebeek
Berlin Wood
30
39
54 Res.
Zonnebeke
XXVII Res.

N

any significant alteration to this line could have jeopardized the whole defence of Ypres, since by that time the only fallback position available to the defenders were the ramparts of the town itself. Thus while the units manning the line were, for the most part, weakened by the earlier fighting, there was a determination to hold on to all they possibly could. As each day of relative quiet passed it seemed more and more likely that they could consolidate the position, as the defences were improved and drafts arrived to fill partially the severely depleted ranks.

According to the German records of the time they were opposing the British part of the line with a total of five divisions: the 39th Division, 53rd Reserve and 54th Reserve Divisions in the centre, and the 51st Reserve Division on the north-east of Ypres (German right flank), while the 30th Division was south of the Menin Road (German left flank). This meant that at the outset of the Battle of Bellewaarde Ridge the Germans were numerically superior in so far as they were able to put five divisions in the front line as opposed to six brigades on the British side of the line. It should be remembered, however, that these German divisions had also been weakened by the earlier fighting and were also under strength after three weeks of persistent attacking. To add weight to the German effort, and perhaps most crucially, there was the large superiority in artillery of all calibres and, furthermore, the ammunition to allow the guns to fire to their capacity. This had been a feature throughout the battle as the Germans had pounded the ground before each infantry attack. The shell shortage that had affected the British artillery effort ever since its arrival in France was not to be a hindrance for the Germans in the closing phase of the 1915 Battle of Ypres. Ten days of respite may have given the defenders of the salient a chance to reorganize, but it also gave the Germans an opportunity to bring up more supplies to further their attack. Fortunately for the British, however, the German army was unable to bring up any fresh divisions since all the available divisions had been committed to the front line either elsewhere on the Western Front or against the Russians on the Eastern Front. Nevertheless, the German command felt that they had sufficient superiority in front of Ypres to push home another attack without jeopardizing their commitments elsewhere – and they still had the new terror weapon of gas at their disposal. Thus the scene was set for the final German move of the Second Battle of Ypres and early on the morning of 24th May they made it.

The late spring days had lengthened and by the end of May the nights were short and dawn was early, about 2.30 am on the 24th, so that by 2.15 am all front line troops were at "Stand to" as part of their normal routine. Therefore, when the Germans launched their attack at 2.45 am it can have come as little surprise to the men in the front line. It was a clear spring day with a light north-easterly breeze. This breeze had been

266

noted by officers and men alike and, since the first gas attack in April, the gas drill in place was ready to alert the front line trenches at the immediate sign of gas. The first indication that something was about to happen was when the Germans put up one red flare, immediately followed by two more and then three more in quick succession, in front of the Wieltje sector of the salient. The German artillery immediately opened up and began to shell the British line with all calibres at their disposal. The artillery barrage was joined by the rattle of machine-gun and rifle fire from the enemy trenches. Accompanying this, and which clearly heralded the beginning of an attack, was the release of a cloud of gas across almost the whole of the British front from near the Menin Road to Turco Farm. It was the biggest release of gas so far seen in the war, stretching almost five miles and rising to a height of forty feet above the ground. In places the front lines were so close that the gas could be heard hissing from the cylinders as the defenders hurried to put on their improvised protection. During the next few hours the gas was to have a considerable impact on the conduct of the battle as it developed into a fierce struggle for possession of Bellewaarde Ridge. This is partly because of the light breeze that drove the gas slowly over the lines, taking as much as forty-five minutes to clear parts of the front line and hanging over the battlefield as a whole for much longer.

The battle for Bellewaarde Ridge is perhaps best understood by considering the action in the three parts of the front separately: the right flank up to approximately Bellewaarde Lake, the central section between Bellewaarde Lake and the Zonnebeke Road, and the left flank from the Zonnebeke Road to Turco Farm. In each sector the battle developed differently with different consequences and as such each sector will be dealt with in turn to complete the picture of a day of heavy fighting across the salient. During the day there was considerable confusion as weakened units fought themselves to a standstill to prevent the Germans from attaining their ultimate goal – the straightening of the line in front of Ypres.

In the line to the south of the Bellewaarde Lake and across the road towards Hill 60 was the 1st Cavalry Division, with 1 and 2 Cavalry Brigades holding the line. The 1 Cavalry Brigade was on the right, holding half of Sanctuary Wood with the 5th Dragoon Guards, the Queen's Bays and the 11th Hussars. To their left, and straddling the Menin Road, was 2 Cavalry Brigade, with the 9th Lancers and 18th Hussars holding the line, with support from the 4th Green Howards and the 5th Durham Light Infantry which had been attached from 150 Brigade for that purpose. The gas cloud moved slowly across the front line in this area and as it did so it lingered long enough to obscure good view of the enemy whom everyone expected to be following up closely behind. Consequently rapid rifle and machine-gun fire was opened up through the gas cloud to hinder the unseen attackers as much as possible. Fortunately for 1 Cavalry Brigade the gas drifted to their north and they remained largely unaffected by it and were able to man their defences throughout the day. To the north, however, the situation was different, as the gas enabled the Germans to penetrate the junction of 2 Cavalry Brigade and 85 Brigade in the centre section of the front. In this area the gas had a severe effect on the defenders and gradually the pressure of the German attack told. The situation was described in Lieutenant Colonel (later Brigadier General) A.S. Home's diary:

> At about 5.00 am we began to get news . . . As far as we could make out then, only a bit of the line at Bellewaarde Lake had given. Soon Mullens was brought back in a state of collapse and Bertie Paget his Brigade Major shortly afterwards, he was very bad. Nicholson was also bad – the matter was serious as the 2nd Cav. Bde. were without commander or staff. We then heard Greenly (9th Cav. Bde.) had moved his two regiments forward (15th and 19th Hussars) to support his front line and was bringing on the 4th Dragoon Guards that were temporarily attached to him.[1]

The 2 Cavalry Brigade had lost its commander, Brigadier General R.L. Mullens, and his staff to the effects of gas whereupon Brigadier General W.H. Greenly (9 Cavalry Brigade) was directed to take charge of the situation. By about 10 am resistance began to waver as troops of the German 39th Division began to pour through the gap to the north of Bellewaarde Lake and overran the 18th Hussars' position. Fortunately Greenly had already ordered his Brigade from reserve to assist in the defence and the 15th and 19th Hussars were sent into the hard pressed front line. The 9th Lancers and the attached infantry were able to form a defensive line facing north about Hooge. The Germans seemed reluctant to pursue the issue here, beyond occupying the trenches they had captured. At this stage Greenly also ordered the 4th Dragoon Guards forward to the GHQ line to act as support but, because of the confusion and the breakdown in telephone communications, it was found to be occupied by some 400 men attached to the 2 Cavalry Brigade. In this manoeuvre the 4th Dragoon Guards had a number of casualties as a result of the intense shelling of the entire area throughout this part of the day. Support for the hard-pressed cavalry was also sent from 85 Brigade who dispatched one company of the 2nd Buffs, and 83 Brigade sent two companies of the 1st Yorks and Lancasters. Lieutenant Colonel Home continued:

> News was scarce, all wires being cut, but from our position the whole country up to Hooge could be seen and I saw no retirement from south of the road. This meant that our fellows were hanging on and was very

comforting indeed. By mid day the 1st Cav. Div. was all out and nothing more could be done. The infantry was organizing a counter attack north of the Menin road.[2]

The situation by midday was easing to some extent and although there was still of lot of fighting to be undertaken the initial breakthrough of the Germans, aided by gas, had been halted and a little time had been bought to begin bringing up the reserves that were available into the line and to allow the planning of a counter-attack to recover the ground lost earlier in the day.

To the north of the cavalry, as far as the Zonnebeke road to the west of Verlorenhoek, was 85 Brigade, holding the line with the 3rd Royal Fusiliers and the 7th Durham Light Infantry (attached from 151 Brigade) south of the Ypres-Roulers railway, and half the 8th Middlesex, the 2nd East Surrey and the 9th Durham Light infantry (attached from 151 Brigade) north of the railway. Here the line was on the reverse slope of the Bellewaarde Ridge and the trenches were in a very poor condition, since the rain of early May had turned them into muddy channels with crumbling walls undercut by water, which could do little to protect the defenders from the sustained shelling that the Germans opened up early on the morning of 24th May. As if that were not enough to cope with, there was the gas to deal with as well. Here, as in other parts of the line, good gas drill, and the rudimentary respirators that had only recently been issued, were no doubt responsible for reducing the effects of the gas, but nevertheless hundreds of men were to succumb to its effects before the day was out.

The Germans' attack against the 8th Middlesex and the 2nd East Surrey is regarded by the Official History as being particularly fierce and in a matter of two hours or so the line held by the Middlesex and one company of the East Surreys was completely overrun, creating a gap three companies wide, which the Germans then began to exploit both towards the north and towards the south. The 8th Middlesex War Diary for the day is in conflict with the account in the Official History, since it states that there was "momentary panic during which several men left the trenches" but there is no mention of a breakthrough in its line. However, the War Diary then goes on to state that the gap was created south of the railway line, where the 3rd Royal Fusiliers trenches were occupied, allowing the enemy to enfilade the 8th Middlesex trenches. A break in the line, or even a withdrawal, is not indicated or suggested at all in the Middlesex account for the day. Further, the diary goes on to say that the men who left the trenches reached the GHQ line and continued to the rear, gathering men from that line as they went. This conflicts with the 28th Division account, which states that there were very few stragglers

269

and none from its battalions.[3] These differing accounts serve to indicate the level of confusion on the battlefield subsequent to the Germans' release of gas in the area, such that even on the compilation of the Official History a decade later a clear picture of the events could not be established. Be that as it may there does appear to have been a break in the line about the railway line which allowed the Germans to attempt to work along the front line in both directions. They were unsuccessful in their attempt to move north, being halted by the remains of the 8th Middlesex and the 2nd East Surreys, but it was their success to the south that ultimately brought pressure to bear on the 1st Cavalry Division in the vicinity of the Bellewaarde Lake and the Menin Road.

To the south of the railway the 3rd Royal Fusiliers tried to prevent German progress by sending half a company to cover its northern flank. In this they were unsuccessful for together, with the two companies of the 7th Durham Light Infantry, they were forced to abandon their trenches. Most of the garrison had, by this time, been killed or wounded or were suffering from the effects of gas, and all the officers of both units were out of action. During the day the 3rd Royal Fusiliers sustained 552 casualties and as the battalion War Diary states:

> By 8 am our fire trenches were occupied by the Germans – all the officers being wounded and the majority of the men gassed or wounded (a large number of men had only the small old fashioned respirator, which proved of little use). The commanding officer (Major Johnson) was hit and finally with but 150 men left out of 880 with the assistance of 200 Buffs who were ordered up in support – the third line of trenches some 600yds in rear of the original fire trench was held until the end of the day.[4]

Three companies of the 2nd Buffs had been sent up by Brigadier General C.E. Pereira as soon as he was aware of the situation in the Royal Fusiliers trenches. The first two companies suffered heavy casualties as they tried to reinforce the front line. Consequently the remains of the Royal Fusiliers, the 7th Durham Light Infantry and the Buffs were rallied in the third line in Railway Wood, or rather what was left of it after a month of heavy fighting. During this fighting the 2nd Buffs suffered almost 400 casualties. The conditions during the day were graphically described by Second Lieutenant R.M. Haythornthwaite in a letter to his parents which he wrote during a lull in the fighting:

> At 2.30 am this morning the Germans started a terrific bombardment, using their vile gas. Our lads were splendid and stuck it. About 5.30 am we got a message to reinforce the firing line with my Company, "B". Unfortunately there was very bad communication and our 1st Platoon did not reinforce. I went out to try and find out what was happening, and worked my way up to the front line, about 1,000 yards ahead, and found

out what was happening and then returned to our trenches. "B" Company immediately pushed forward, as the line wanted reinforcing, but I stayed back to report to Headquarters. After doing that I started with one other fellow to work my way up. The shrapnel was terrific, but our luck was in and we reached a ruined house just behind the firing line, and found there a good many wounded, poor beggars. I got a stretcher party together and we pulled in several badly wounded fellows in a field, but unfortunately they sniped at us, the brutes! Two of our poor chaps were hit. Since then we have done what we can to make them comfortable, but it is awfully hard for them. We can do little for them till dark, and even then it isn't safe. The shelling is something terrific, one burst on this house knocking bits over our wounded, and gave a few more nasty cuts. All we can do is keep boiling water – it is not safe to drink otherwise – and give them sips of tea and Bovril, of which we have luckily got a certain amount. Unfortunately it is very hot and their thirst must be terrific. I know mine is. It is just that fiendish gas. I have had nothing to eat since 7 pm last night, it is now 4 pm. Only a few sips of different things, and this gas keeps up a horrible choking feeling, which prevents one working as hard as one wants to. What will happen to us I don't know. I think we are advancing now, and in that case all ought to be all right.[5]

Second Lieutenant Haythornthwaite was wounded in the advance, and died in the cottage where he had tended the wounded after he had been taken there by Private J. White of the 3rd Royal Fusiliers. According to the account given by Private White, in the confusion of the advance (see below) Haythornthwaite was attempting to take a party of soldiers from another unit forward when he was hit – he was twenty-one years old and was just one of the many casualties that day.

When it was realized that the front line had been lost, Brigadier General Pereira's first reaction was to organize a counter-attack to regain it. Unfortunately he had almost nothing at his disposal to complete the job except two weakened companies of the 8th Middlesex and those men of the 2nd Buffs that had not already moved forward, probably amounting to one platoon as mentioned in Second Lieutenant Haythornthwaite's letter. It was woefully inadequate for the purpose but Pereira began his organizing and only stopped when Major General Bulfin of the 28th Division notified him that 84 Brigade and 80 Brigade (attached to 28th Division) were being sent up for that purpose. Since the enemy had entered the Fusiliers' trenches by 8 am and the two brigades being brought forward had some distance to travel, it was necessary for 85 Brigade to hold on in and around Railway Wood until this counter-attack could be developed. Fortunately, every further effort made against 85 Brigade was repulsed, though throughout the day losses mounted making reinforcements of greater importance than counter-attack.

To the north of the Zonnebeke Road the line was held by elements of 10 and 12 Brigades of the 4th Division. The right of the 1st Royal Irish Fusiliers was on the Zonnebeke Road and the left of the 2nd Royal Dublin Fusiliers was on Shell Trap Farm, with a half battalion of the 7th Argyll and Sutherland Highlanders between them. To the left of Shell Trap Farm the 2nd Royal Irish Regiment, 1st King's Own and the 2nd Essex held the line as far as Turco Farm, where the right of the French 152nd Division was found. The Divisional support line was approximately 1,000 yards behind the front line, to the west of the road joining Wieltje with Turco Farm. Here, as in the rest of the line, the German attack was not really a surprise, since the men were all at "Stand to". Captain T.J. Leahy of the 2nd Royal Dublin Fusiliers wrote:

> Colonel Loveband, Major Magan[6], second in command, Russell, RAMC and I, acting as adjutant, had just finished dinner in our headquarters dug-out at 2.30 am. Previous to this the Colonel and Magan had been round the front line trenches and spent considerable time in Shell Trap Farm. Something suggested "gas" to the Colonel during his round of the trenches as he personally warned all company officers to be prepared and Russell had inspected all the Vermorel sprayers[7] and warned each company about damping their respirators. There were ten sprayers in working order that night – one with each machine gun and the remainder distributed along the trenches.[8]

Lieutenant Colonel Loveband's feeling that a gas attack was imminent was soon justified, for shortly after they had finished their dinner they were to see the first of the "red lights" signalling the start of the attack. Leahy remarked that the noise of the discharging gas could be heard in the Dublins' trenches accompanied by the start of the barrage from the German guns. As elsewhere in the line, the gas moved slowly over 10 and 12 Brigades and generally speaking the lack of any real surprise and good gas drill served to minimize its immediate effects, allowing the trenches to be fully manned as orders were shouted to get all available men to the fire-step and ready for the infantry attack they all knew must be following close on the discharge of the gas. A number of the battalion histories of the units concerned record that initially some men began to leave the trenches as the gas reached them, but overall discipline was maintained so that there were few stragglers. The officers were able, in many cases, to gather men together to reorganize them for the defence that looked to be necessary.

It was not long before the German infantry appeared and the fighting began. A strong German effort fell on the area around Shell Trap Farm and by about 4 am the Royal Dublin Fusiliers there were feeling the effects of the German pressure and began to give ground. Lieutenant

Colonel Loveband requested the 9th Argylls to move forward from a retrenchment some hundreds of yards behind and they proceeded to cover the gap that was developing between the Dublins' right and the 7th Argylls. Later in the morning this manoeuvre was supported by the 1st Royal Warwicks from Brigade reserve as they moved via Cross Road Farm to regain some of the front line, which was then held for the rest of the day with the help of further reinforcement by two companies of the 2nd Seaforth Highlanders.

On the extreme right of this portion of the line the 1st Royal Irish Fusiliers were also able to beat off the attack directed at their trenches without too great an effort, but early in the day their right company (B Company, Captain G. Bull) came under enfilade fire from a group of buildings supposedly held by the 2nd East Surreys on the Zonnebeke Road. It was clear to Captain Bull that something was amiss here and he dispatched Lieutenant W.H. Liesching and twelve men to sort it out. The garrison of the buildings had been gassed and were no longer able to defend their position but Liesching and his men were able to bring effective fire to bear on the enemy and in so doing stabilized the situation. Further, when the 7th Argylls to their left came under pressure as a result of the problems around Shell Trap Farm, Captain E.H. Fforde, of A Company, held in local reserve, was able to dispatch two platoons of the 1st Royal Irish Fusiliers to their assistance. These platoons, sent up at about 3.15 am, remained with the 7th Argylls throughout the rest of the day and, it is reported, "suffered somewhat severely". The situation in front of the 1st Royal Irish Fusiliers was, compared with the rest of the Brigade area, relatively under control, as can be seen from the fact that not only was Fforde able to offer assistance elsewhere but, when called upon to move forward to support the front line trenches, his men were not actually required to man them. It is interesting to note the recommendations for reward for service that day appended to the report on the action compiled by Lieutenant A.R. Burrowes. In particular, Burrowes singles out Private J. Kirkham, the telephone operator, who continued to deliver messages by hand when all the lines were cut by the German shelling, in spite of being wounded. The problems associated with communications seem to have been a feature of the day and it is remarked upon in other battalion accounts. Of course, part of the purpose and effect of the initial German barrage was to cut many of the telephone lines so that communications were immediately difficult and would become worse as the day wore on. In many cases commanders had to rely on the good fortune of orderlies and runners crossing gas filled country swept by artillery and machine-gun fire. Under these conditions it is remarkable that any defence was maintained, though it is clear that a large portion of the responsibility for its success lay with the battalion officers who took full responsibility for directing the defence in their immediate area – often at some considerable cost to themselves and their men.

By about 4 am the conditions around Shell Trap Farm and the area to its immediate right was deteriorating rapidly. It became clear to Lieutenant Colonel Loveband of the 2nd Royal Dublin Fusiliers that the enemy was occupying the trenches of the 2nd Royal Irish Regiment to his left. He sent a message to the 1st King's Own warning them of this fact, as the enemy appeared to be bombing along the trenches towards the position of that battalion, who were on the left of the 2nd Royal Irish Regiment. He received a reply to the effect that the 1st King's Own would deal with the enemy in those trenches if the Dublins would handle those in Shell Trap Farm. For their part the 2nd Royal Irish Regiment had suffered heavily from the initial gas attack and as a result of the Germans getting into Shell Trap Farm from where their trenches were enfiladed. Lieutenant Colonel C.J. Griffin of the 2nd Lancashire Fusiliers recognized the difficulties and immediately sent A Company, commanded by Captain J. Collis-Browne, to assist the 2nd Royal Irish Regiment. Unfortunately the fire coming from the direction of Shell Trap Farm tended to push the would-be saviours towards the left and they ended up occupying the trenches immediately to the right of the 1st King's Own. Even though some of the Lancashires reached the trench, out of the 120 men that had set out in support, only thirty reached the front line, and their commanding officer had been wounded in the stomach. However, the 1st King's Own had lived up to their response to Lieutenant Colonel Loveband and stopped the further progress of the Germans in their direction. This was largely thanks to the efforts of Captain A.B. Woodgate, Lieutenant R.C. Leach and a bombing party who succeeded in turning the tables on the Germans, and managed to recapture about fifty yards of the Royal Irish trenches. The citation for the DSO that Captain Woodgate won that day gives the following details:

> For conspicuous gallantry on the 24 May, 1915, when, after the Germans had captured the trenches held by the battalion on his right, he, with another officer and three men, held up the enemy from working along the trench. Although the enemy was in force and with an unlimited supply of hand-grenades he not only held them up but succeeded under heavy shell fire, in capturing two traverses and a German flag which had been used to mark their position[9].

It had been a hard morning for the 2nd Royal Irish Regiment for, when they were finally able to reorganize, the battalion was placed under the command of Lieutenant McKay, the sole surviving uninjured officer remaining.

The loss of these trenches and Shell Trap Farm was a serious blow to the defence of the northern part of the salient. It was considered necessary that everything should be done to recover them as soon as possible. Brigadier General C.P.A. Hull (10 Brigade) ordered the 1st Royal Warwicks to make a counter-attack to achieve just that. Simultaneously, Brigadier General F.G. Anley (12 Brigade) ordered the 2nd Lancashire Fusiliers to do the same and thus a joint counter-attack was arranged. It met with little success, although the battalions involved made every effort to get forward. The enemy had quickly turned the captured trenches to their advantage, and the 2nd Royal Dublin Fusiliers' history remarks:

> It was marvellous how quickly they converted the parapet and everything was done without confusion and with proper method.[10]

German efficiency held up the counter-attack and both commanders realized that they would not make great progress without artillery support, since it was realized that the whole of the Royal Irish trenches had been occupied by the enemy.

The situation on the 2nd Royal Dublin Fusiliers' front was almost as bad:

> Meanwhile "heavies" were being dumped into our trenches and there was a severe enfilade machine gun fire opened on us from the Royal Irish trenches to the left of the farm. Getting messages down to Battalion Headquarters was a difficulty and it was impossible to get an orderly back to the divisional support line without his being badly hit – every orderly who came to and went from us was hit, yet every time there was a message to go there was a volunteer to take it.[11]

At about this time Lieutenant Colonel Loveband was shot through the heart and died without a word, though "he tried to say something". It would appear that his death was a result of the confusion on the battlefield;[12] whilst Loveband and his officers were organizing the defence of their line they were fired on from behind, presumably by some of the various troops that were by that time moving forward. Captain D.B. Burt-Marshall, attached from the Seaforths, had just arrived at battalion headquarters and was also wounded, shot in the shoulder, but ran off to stop the firing. It was an unfortunate incident and one which depleted the command of the Royal Dublin Fusiliers still further. All across the battalion front the news was bad as men began to attempt to withdraw. Where possible the remaining officers tried to rally the men and organize a defence but with the continued German pressure and dwindling numbers this became increasingly difficult. Captain Basil MacLear sent a message to say that very many of the men were becoming surrounded and that reinforcements were essential. Shortly afterwards he led a bombing party to clear a trench of Germans and was killed. Second Lieutenant R.J. Kempston, now in charge of B Company, sent a message, "For God's sake send some help, we are nearly done",[13] and then died fighting with his company that could not be reinforced. By noon all organized defence in the area of Shell Trap Farm had ceased and the Germans occupied a gap running from south of the farm to the 1st King's Own position in the north, a distance of about 1,200 yards. Captain Leahy, who survived the day uninjured, wrote of the fighting:

> From about 2.30 pm there was no fighting in our trenches; everyone held on to them to the last; there was no surrender, no quarter was given or accepted; they all died fighting at their post.[14]

When the 2nd Royal Dublin Fusiliers were withdrawn at 9 pm that night all they could muster was one officer (Captain Leahy) and twenty-one other ranks – all that remained of the seventeen officers and 651 other ranks who had stood to arms about half an hour before the attack began on the morning of 24th May, 1915.

Thus by midday the situation was such that there were two large holes in the defensive positions in front of Ypres. On the north 12 Brigade, in the form of the 2nd Essex and the 1st King's Own, held on and were ably assisted by the French 75 mm field guns firing from the west of the Yser Canal. It was fortunate that the enemy in this area had decided, for whatever reason, not to exploit the gap northwards and surround the remains of 12 Brigade. South of this brigade there was then a gap to beyond Shell Trap Farm, but the right of 10 Brigade and the left of 85 Brigade held firm in the centre of the salient, forming a solid block between the Wieltje-Saint Julien road and the Ypres-Roulers railway. There was then another breach in the defences south of the railway line as far as the Menin Road where units of 85 Brigade and 2 Cavalry Brigade had suffered heavily during the morning. Their flank south of the Menin Road had been held by 1 Cavalry Brigade extending, with 83 Brigade, in a continual unbroken line to the southern edge of Sanctuary Wood. South of this the line had not been attacked during 24th May.

On the left flank it was clear that there were some desperate decisions to be made during the course of the afternoon. Brigadier General Anley (12 Brigade) was given command of all the 4th Division troops east of the Yser Canal, but he acted in close liaison with Brigadier General Hull (10 Brigade) in an attempt to regain the lost ground. It soon became clear to these experienced soldiers that this would require far more effort than a local counter-attack and as such would require far greater resources than either of them had at their disposal. Further, any attack that was organized to recapture the trenches would now have to contend with enfilade fire coming from the captured ground at the eastern end of Hill Top Ridge in the vicinity of Shell Trap Farm. Therefore, Anley decided that at least for the moment they would have to remain on the defensive and if necessary be prepared to occupy the divisional support line. Brigadier General Hull concurred with this decision and his brigade was placed in readiness for a withdrawal should it become necessary. Since the divisional line was some 1,000 yards behind the original front line it would mean giving up a roughly triangular piece of ground to the Germans, which would effectively smooth out the corner that had developed around Shell Trap Farm. However, because of the stern defence put up by units in this portion of the line there was at least a temporary lull in the fighting, giving the impression of stability in the line, while the Germans had possibly suffered sufficient casualties from accurate rifle fire for them to consider their options before pressing home the advantage they had gained in the morning.

On the southern flank of the salient the battalions either side of the gap created around Bellewaarde Lake were desperately defending the line, whilst trying to turn a flank to meet the pressure being brought to bear by the Germans who had now reached as far as Railway Wood and had established outposts as far west as Witte Poort Farm. Early in the day these battalions had been ordered not to make a counter-attack with their weakened units, but to wait for the arrival of 84 and 80 Brigades, who were in reserve to the west of Ypres and who would be brought forward for that purpose. The 2nd Cheshires of 84 Brigade had already been sent forward early in the morning to occupy the GHQ line and at 9.45 am the 2nd Northumberland Fusiliers were joined by the 1st Welsh in preparation for the brigade to move to attempt to restore the front line. At this point it is necessary to comment upon the condition of the battalions that were being called upon to carry out this task. 84 Brigade had been repeatedly involved in action throughout the month of fighting and all the battalions had suffered casualties. The 1st Welsh was considered to be a strong battalion, numbering as it did about 600, though it was actually only able to put about 450 into the line for the attack that day. Unfortunately, even in this strong battalion, most of the men were replacements and were inexperienced and, furthermore, most of the company officers were little better equipped. In the 2nd Northumberland Fusiliers the situation was similar. The lack of experienced officers was so marked in this battalion that Captain C. Wreford-Browne, hearing of his battalion's plight whilst in hospital, arranged his discharge and returned to the front to take command of the battalion on 22nd May. To make matters worse, on 24th May 84 Brigade was ordered forward before it had been able to feed the men – the Germans were pressing and there was no time to spare. The historian of the 2nd Northumberland Fusiliers sums up the situation as they moved:

> In short it had fallen to the weak battalions of the 84th Brigade, led for the most part by young officers whose gallantry could not compensate their inexperience, to undertake on empty stomachs a task which might be deemed to represent a severe test for fresh and seasoned troops under experienced leaders.[15]

In fact 84 Brigade numbered little more than 2,000 men, or less than half of its establishment had the battalions involved been up to strength. At noon the brigade was underway, with all battalions making preparations for the attack. The plan was straightforward. The brigade was to attack, if possible in conjunction with 80 Brigade, in the area between the railway line and the Menin Road and to drive the Germans out of Hooge and the area around Bellewaarde Lake. To achieve this, two battalions, each on a one-company front and arranged in three waves, were to attack towards Railway Wood and Witte Poort Farm. The 2nd Cheshires were on the left and attacking with their left tight against the railway line, whilst the 2nd Northumberland Fusiliers were to attack with their right against the Menin Road. The third battalion involved in the attack was the 1st Suffolks, and their job was to attempt a flanking manoeuvre to attack in an almost south-westerly direction to drive the Germans out of Y Wood. The 1st Welsh was to act as a support to the main thrust against Witte Poort Farm. The fifth battalion, a composite battalion of the 1st and 3rd Monmouthshire Regiment, about 300 strong, was directed to GHQ line as reserve. By this stage it had become clear that it would be necessary for 84 Brigade to attack without the assistance of 80 Brigade and to make matters worse, there was inadequate intelligence as to the precise positions of the enemy they would be attacking.

By early afternoon the 2nd Northumberland Fusiliers were assembling in the railway cutting immediately to the south of Hellfire Corner. It was not inappropriately named, for the Germans began to shell almost immediately and the battalion suffered a number of casualties whilst there. At a little after 2.30 pm the battalions began to move out of this cutting and to negotiate the gaps in the wire of the GHQ line before finally forming up in their positions as described above. The 2nd Northumberland Fusiliers suffered more casualties in this manoeuvre, presumably as groups of inexperienced men bunched together to crowd through the gaps. The 1st Welsh fared a little better though they had lost their commanding officer, Lieutenant Colonel T.O. Marden, seriously wounded in the cutting as they prepared for the attack. His place was taken by Major R.T. Toke. This officer succeeded in getting the battalion through the GHQ line wire in short rushes and thereby the battalion did not suffer any casualties at that stage of the preparation.

It was 5 pm before all was in place for the attack to be launched. Barely had the battalions moved from their assembly positions when they came under heavy and accurate machine-gun and rifle fire from Railway Wood, Witte Poort Farm and the Germans who were now consolidating their gains in front of Bellewaarde Lake and Hooge. The North-umberland Fusiliers' historian bemoans the fact that the battalion had no idea that Witte Poort Farm would need to be captured or what sort of strength the enemy were in. As far as that battalion was concerned, Witte Poort Farm was merely the direction in which they were required to attack, and there was a measure of surprise when it was discovered they would be required to fight for its possession. Once again the attack had been hastily prepared and once again this haste was to be paid for with the lives of both officers and men. The attack made some progress, but at tremendous cost. The 2nd Northumberland Fusiliers managed to carry Witte Poort Farm and even advanced a little further, to the line of Cambridge Road. By that time it was the remnant of a battalion that tried to dig in, having lost a number of officers, including their commanding officer, Captain Wreford-Browne. Here with darkness falling the attack ran out of momentum and the Northumberland Fusiliers, exhausted as they now were, could do little more than to stay put. To their left the 2nd Cheshires had succeeded in getting forward through Railway Farm but had failed to make any greater progress than the Fusiliers. The 1st Welsh followed along in support of the Fusiliers and suffered much the same fate. The southern portion of the attack also made no progress as the 1st Suffolks came under heavy fire from the direction of Y Wood and were halted before they reached their objec-tive, a little to the north of the Menin Road. Each of these battalions had acted more or less in isolation and now, admittedly after making small advances, were not in touch with each other. The Welsh made efforts by moving to left and right to make contact with the Northumberland Fusiliers on their left and the Suffolks on their right. In reality there was little that could be done until darkness fell and a new attack could be organized, hopefully with the aid of 80 Brigade, which was just coming on to the scene.

Whilst all this was going on 80 Brigade (Brigadier General W.E.B. Smith) was on the move. It had been in Corps reserve and was billeted in the general area of Busseboom, a little to the south-east of Poperinge. At 6.30 am it had been ordered to form up at Brandhoek, on the main Ypres-Poperinge road, ready for a move to the front to support the division already engaged. At 1 pm it was placed at the disposal of the 28th Division and Major General Bulfin immediately directed it to

Kruistraat, south of Ypres, in readiness to move into the line to accompany 84 Brigade in its counter-attack. As was often the case during the fighting for Ypres in 1915 there was considerable delay in getting orders to the right place and in moving men and equipment into position, and it was 4.30 pm before the Brigade received orders to move forward, by which time 84 Brigade was already deployed for the attack discussed above. Consequently 80 Brigade could not assist 84 Brigade as its battalions made their brave but more or less futile attempt to regain the ground lost early in the morning. It was not until 7.30 pm that the 80 Brigade finally reached the GHQ line where it was to wait still further while contact was made with the cavalry, supposed to be on its right, and 84 Brigade. Eventually Brigadier Generals Smith and Bols were able to meet and a joint night attack was agreed. The War Diary of 84 Brigade details the arrangements:

> Two battalions of the 80th Brigade were to attack between Bellewaarde and Eclusette[16], while the 84th Brigade pushed on on their former line, backed by two battalions of the 80th Brigade. The 84th Brigade was by this time somewhat muddled – the inexperienced company commanders had been unable to keep touch or direction, NCOs were insufficient to control untrained troops. The men had had no food since the early morning and were completely exhausted. The G.O.C. saw the O.C. Welsh and Suffolk and a representative of the Cheshire. The Northumberland Fusiliers appeared to have been so heavily punished in the first attack that as a battalion they were a negligible quantity. The Monmouth, sent for at 11.30 pm did not arrive until 2.30 am – too late to use (it was getting light at 2.30 am).[17]

This entry implies the confusion and general state of affairs without saying as much directly. There is a feeling in the account that the attack proposed was ill-advised, with its reference to exhausted troops and depleted ranks, but nevertheless the attack was continued. The 80 Brigade was deployed with 4 Rifle Brigade against the Menin Road and the 3rd King's Royal Rifle Corps on their left. The 4th KRRC were next on the left but were initially in support of the 1st Welsh of 84 Brigade. The 2nd King's Shropshire Light Infantry were on the left, again behind the remains of 84 Brigade, against the railway line. The Princess Patricia's Canadian Light Infantry were held in reserve.

The attack commenced at 12.30 am on 25th May. In the light from an almost full moon the remains of 84 Brigade and 80 Brigade moved forward and at first they drew no fire, though everyone knew they must be clearly visible to the German defenders. The Germans knew they were coming and held their fire until it was difficult to miss. The 1st Welsh pushed forward, with the Suffolks on their right, and were soon fighting through Railway Wood and on to the hill behind it. In this rush

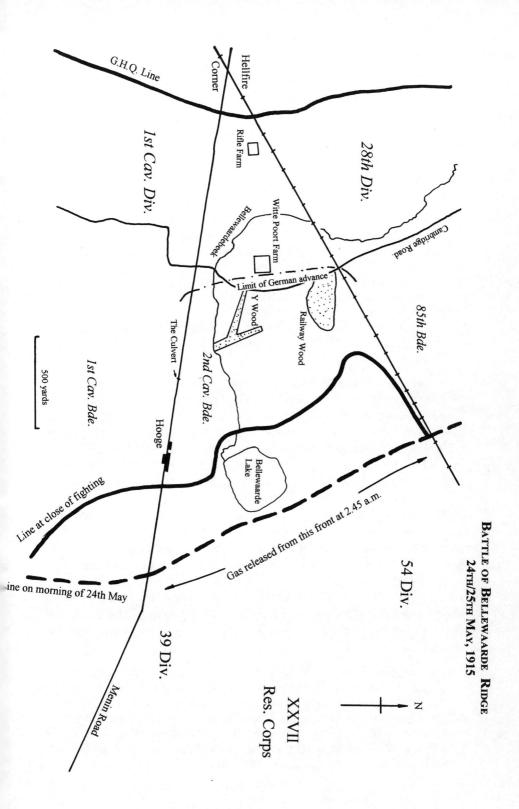

BATTLE OF BELLEWAARDE RIDGE
24TH/25TH MAY, 1915

XXVII
Res. Corps

39 Div.

54 Div.

N

Menin Road

Line on morning of 24th May

Gas released from this front at 2.45 a.m.

Line at close of fighting

Hooge

1st Cav. Bde.

500 yards

2nd Cav. Bde.

The Culvert

Bellewaarde
Lake

Y Wood

Railway Wood

Limit of German advance

Witte Poort Farm

Bellewaardebeek

85th Bde.

Cambridge Road

28th Div.

Rifle Farm

1st Cav. Div.

G.H.Q. Line

Hellfire
Corner

they were met with heavy fire and they sustained heavy casualties but succeeded in driving "the Germans back at the point of the bayonet". When a platoon of the 2nd Shropshires attempted to reinforce them it was entirely wiped out by machine-gun fire, leaving the Welsh with little more than a handful of men to defend the ground gained in the rush. The Shropshires, too, had met with some success and Y Company had succeeded in getting into the enemy trenches in the initial rush but had suffered heavy casualties. The 1st Suffolks' historian continues the story:

> The attack was to be launched on a front of about 400 yards. Two compa-
> nies were put into the firing line on the extreme right, the other two, under
> Lieut. Venning, being in support. Again the order was given to charge,
> and the battalion led by Major Maycock[18] began to advance, but imme-
> diately came under a withering fire as on the previous occasion. Men fell
> in heaps everywhere, and within minutes the advance was definitely held
> up. The attack as a whole failed, but 2nd Lieut. T. Pickard and C.S.M.
> Pye, with a corporal and half a dozen men, managed to dig themselves in
> on a sunken road, where they were joined by men from other units until
> their number rose to nearly a hundred.[19]

The sunken road spoken of here is thought to be the road running immediately to the east of Witte Poort Farm, which was known as Cambridge
Road. This was more or less the line that had been gained by 84 Brigade
in the initial attack on the afternoon of 24th May. Little had been gained
by the counter-attacks but there had been many casualties. This story is
echoed in the account of the 2nd Northumberland Fusiliers, who had
suffered so heavily in the first attack that they were not included in the
formations quoted in the Official History for the second attack. In fact,
they took part in that attack, but by then they were only three officers
and a handful of men strong and were commanded by Lieutenant
E.H. Salier. When the order to advance reached Salier he took his piti-
fully small command forward. As soon as they broke cover from the
hedge on the side of the sunken road they came under heavy fire,
Lieutenant Salier was wounded and Second Lieutenant M.V. O'Dowd
was killed leaving Second Lieutenant C.R. Freeman in charge of the
rapidly shrinking 2nd Northumberland Fusiliers; he related the events
that followed:

> It was beginning to get light enough to see around and apart from the one
> sergeant in the shell hole with me, there was, as far as I could see about
> half a dozen of us in shell holes with the Germans in holes or a trench not
> very far from us. On the right and left of us we had no flank troops at all.
> I saw the men on either side of me shot and I had a few rounds duel with
> a tin helmet in front of me. I never knew more of the outcome of this than
> that my opponent stopped plugging the parapet on my shell hole.[20]

Freeman realized he was in a hopeless position and he ordered those men close to him to withdraw. During this withdrawal back across Cambridge Road he was shot through the shoulder, but continued in his attempt to find out what was happening on his flanks, and managed to get a message to Brigadier General Bols giving his situation report before he collapsed as a result of his wounds. During the two attacks of the 2nd Northumberland Fusiliers all thirteen officers that had marched up during the morning had become casualties, together with 350 other ranks. They had been a weakened unit before but by the end of the second attack they were almost non-existent. Eventually the attack of the two brigades died away and the survivors dug-in where they were or made their way back to their lines. The Welsh Regiment History comments:

> The wounded had been got away in the dark, and shortly after dawn, realising that they were isolated, and that the attack by the 80th Brigade had not been successful, the survivors of the battalion crawled on hands and knees back to the shelter, if such it could be called, of the sunken road, to the west of the Wood. It had been a gallant attack, but in vain.[21]

At the end of the fighting in the early morning of 25th May, the 1st Welsh occupied the line they had gained in the first counter-attack on the previous afternoon. The 1st Welsh had gone into that attack as the strongest battalion of the brigade with some 450 men engaged; by the end of the second counter-attack they had lost seventeen officers and 389 other ranks – they too had all but ceased to exist.

The same, or similar, stories could be told of all the units engaged that night. The end of the fighting in the early hours of 25th May found the 4th KRRC in trenches some 500 yards or so to the west of Hooge, which was approximately the line that had been established in the earlier attack. The counter-attacks had achieved little, but the gap between 2 Cavalry Brigade and 85 Brigade had been filled, albeit with the depleted ranks of 80 and 84 Brigades.

It is interesting to note that even some soldiers close to the fighting had very little appreciation of the effects of the counter-attacks on the infantry carrying them out. Lieutenant Colonel Home closes his diary account of the events of the day as follows:

> The situation to my mind is thoroughly unsatisfactory – the troops up here are tired out. We want fresh troops to give the others a rest. The Infantry attack has no sting in it.[22]

Bearing in mind how quickly the casualties in the infantry had mounted in the two brigades engaged, it is hardly surprising that it had no "sting"!

As if to mitigate the losses of the night the Official History records a "small successful night operation". This operation occurred when Brigadier General Greenly ordered Major G.E. Bayley, 1st York and Lancaster, to send one company out of Zouave Wood to clear the houses on the Menin Road, which were all that were left of Hooge. From a tactical point of view the removal of the enemy from such advanced positions was useful and placed the Germans holding Y Wood in a vulnerable position but, set against the major losses of the night, it was of rather limited importance.

On the left flank of the salient there had been a measure of hope and confusion following Brigadier General Anley's decision to assume a defensive position subsequent to the loss of the trenches about Shell Trap Farm. It was quite clear to Anley that he was going to require substantial reinforcement if he was going to stand any chance of regaining the lost ground; it was just as clear to him that these reinforcements were going to be difficult to find, bearing in mind the calls that were being made on the reserves elsewhere. There had been a little hope during the afternoon, for shortly before 5 pm V Corps had informed Anley that three battalions of the French 152nd Division were to be placed at his disposal to reinforce a counter-attack which he was ordered to make after dark. Anley lost no time in getting things moving but about two and a half hours later, with the planning for the attack well advanced, Captain W.C. Garsia (GSO 3 4th Division) brought the news that the three French battalions were not to be used for anything other than support for a counter-attack. This severely limited the manner in which the attack could be launched, for it still left Anley with the weakened, tired units to spearhead his attack. It was not a satisfactory situation. Within minutes of the news arriving Lieutenant Colonel A.A. Montgomery (GSO 1 4th Division) turned up at 12 Brigade Headquarters to finalize the details of the counter-attack, unaware of the conditions that the French had placed on the use of their battalions.

It was clear to all concerned that a major decision needed to be made and made very quickly. If the attack was to go ahead the units involved would need to be got into position and the artillery support arranged. If a withdrawal was to be ordered then that would need to be done almost immediately to allow it to be carried out in the few hours of darkness that could be expected. There was no time to spare and delay would cause problems whichever choice was made. It was not possible to make contact with Major General Henry Wilson at Divisional Headquarters, since all the telephone wires had been destroyed. To send a message by hand would cause unwanted delay. There was no need for approval for the counter-attack since that had already been given, though with the understanding of French participation. It was necessary, however, for the officers to consider the forces available to carry out Wilson's order to counter-attack; these were limited and weakened forces comprising about two companies of the 2nd Lancashire Fusiliers and two battalions that could be brought from 11 Brigade. These were not considered to be enough to bring results and at 8 pm Lieutenant Colonel Montgomery gave the order for the withdrawal of the 7th Argylls (10 Brigade) and the 1st King's Own and 2nd Essex (12 Brigade) to the Divisional Line and the French Switch, which were situated behind and parallel to the road joining Wieltje to Turco Farm. This meant giving up a triangular piece of ground 1,000 yards deep at its deepest point. The 2nd Monmouths were employed in digging a line from the trenches of the 1st Royal Irish Fusiliers, which they had held all day, to Wieltje Farm to join the new front line. Outposts to this new line were established at Cross Roads Farm and in front of Wieltje village. The French, after some persuasion, adjusted their line in the area of Turco Farm to conform to the new defensive position.

When Major General Wilson was informed of the decision he immediately confirmed it and the 4th Division was withdrawn successfully during the night without any further hindrance from the enemy. As is pointed out by the Official History, the decision to withdraw was a sound one which could only have been strengthened when the news of the lack of success of the attacks by 80 and 84 Brigades reached the commanders on the left flank. Whilst it had been necessary to surrender ground to the enemy it was a relatively small piece and it had not significantly jeopardized the defence of the salient. It had not been a good day for the defenders. The infantry had fought through a long day with little artillery support, though the guns of the 27th Division were fought throughout the day in spite of the diminishing stocks of shells. At the end of the day the British troops were still in front of Ypres and still keeping the Germans at bay.

That night (the night of the 24th–25th May) the German Fourth Army received orders "that no more major operations should be undertaken". With that order the fighting that had defined the Battle of Bellewaarde Ridge, and the Second Battle of Ypres, died away. It would appear that the Germans attackers were by that stage every bit as tired as the British defenders. The Battle of Bellewaarde Ridge had seen the last effort of the Germans to capture Ypres – and it had failed. It is possible that had the Germans been aware of the state of the defenders at that time they might have continued to fight. The British artillery was, by the end of the fighting, so short of supplies that there were virtually no shrapnel shells left in the whole of the BEF. Added to this there was only a limited supply of high explosives, for example only 272 rounds of 18-pounder HE left in the BEF. It was fortunate that the enemy did not know how bad things were. The infantry were so tired and worn out that all units that had been involved needed to rest and most had suffered such severe losses that large drafts were now essential to bring them back to fighting strength. The Germans were unaware of all these things when they called a stop to their offensive; if they had been able to field a couple of fresh divisions it is quite clear that the outcome would likely have been markedly different.

Notes

1. Home, op.cit., p69.
2. ibid., pp69–70.
3. *Official History 1915 Vol. 1*, p343.
4. War Diary 3rd Battalion the Royal Fusiliers.
5. See de Ruvigny, *Roll of Honour: Part 1*, p179. Second Lieutenant Rycharde Mead Haythornthwaite is commemorated on the Menin Gate.
6. Major A.T. Magan 3rd battalion attached 2nd battalion.
7. A device originally intended for agricultural use for spraying of insecticide was adapted to spray the necessary chemicals to disperse low lying gas.
8. See Wylly, op.cit., pp44–45.
9. Creagh & Humphries, *The Distinguished Service Order 1886–1923*.
10. Wylly, op.cit., p48.
11. ibid.
12. Lieutenant Colonel Arthur Loveband CMG is commemorated on the Menin Gate.
13. Wylly, op.cit., p49. Second Lieutenant Robert James Kempston is commemorated on the Menin Gate.
14. ibid., p50.
15. Sandilands, op.cit., p101.
16. "Eclusette"; believed to be "The Culvert" under the Menin Road, opposite Wing House.
17. Quoted in Sandilands, op.cit., p103.
18. Major F.W.O. Maycock DSO was killed in action 25.5.15 and is buried in Tyne Cot Cemetery.
19. See Murphy, op.cit., p79.
20. Quoted in Sandilands, op.cit., p103.
21. Marden, op.cit., p351.
22. Home, op.cit., p70.

CHAPTER NINETEEN

The Second Battle of Ypres
A Summary

As the fighting on Bellewaarde Ridge faded away in the early hours of 25th May the fighting that was later to become known as the Second Battle of Ypres was finally closed. It had been an indecisive battle for all of those concerned. The Germans, for their part, had expended much effort but had failed to capture Ypres. The British and their Allies, on the other hand, had made great sacrifice to hold on to the shrinking ground that was almost all that remained of "gallant little Belgium". It was not a satisfactory conclusion for either side since one had suffered lost ground whilst the other had objectives which had not been achieved. In some aspects the fighting for Ypres in the spring of 1915 has been seen by some as encapsulating all the aspects that were to come to characterize the Great War as a whole. It is possible to point to the massive increase in use and importance of artillery to support this idea while the technological and scientific advances that became apparent during Second Ypres – perhaps most noticeably the use of poisonous gas and the rapid reaction of the Allies to find a countermeasure to it might also be given as examples for this theory. Perhaps the one thing that was present in Second Ypres which did come to symbolize war for an entire generation across Europe, but especially the British, was the fortitude and largely unquestioning self-sacrifice of the soldiers who faced each other over the gas-drenched salient during the month of fighting and above all the great gallantry shown at all stages of the battle. It is difficult to generalize on the German soldiers conduct in a history that has relied largely upon the Allied accounts, but in many of the British and Canadian accounts there is a feeling that there is a grudging respect for the German infantryman who always seems to have stuck to his task no matter what was asked of him, though perhaps this was not always apparent in soldiers' letters home. The German soldiers' spirit is seen in the dogged and determined fighting to gain Gravenstafel Ridge or in the massed attacks made on Frezenberg Ridge. In that respect at least the German soldier should not be thought of as too different to any of his enemies – after all he too was fighting for a great cause in what, in 1915, was still widely held to be "just" war and it was, at that stage, a cause in which he could believe.

Whilst Second Ypres may be seen as demonstrating both the courage and callousness of war there are a number of issues arising from the conduct of the battle that were to have a wider consequence on the overall conduct of the war and repercussions that were to be felt in the coming years of war on the Western Front. These issues can be summarized in four questions listed below, though not necessarily in any order of importance:

- Why was no notice taken by the Allies of the warnings of an impending gas attack?

- Why were the Germans apparently so unprepared for its success?

- Why didn't the Germans have reserves ready to exploit any successes?

- Why did the British expend so much effort in many fruitless counter-attacks?

The answers to these questions are fundamental to an understanding of the battle and its outcome. Unfortunately, as with many issues affecting the Great War, the answers are neither simple nor straightforward since they involve various strands of military and, to a lesser extent political reasoning that came together at the time to produce the Second Battle of Ypres and its far-reaching effects. To some extent the answers are subjective and rely on features that may not have been readily apparent during the battle itself, particularly to the commanders of the opposing armies. But as a way of summarizing the overall battle these issues will now be dealt with briefly.

The use of poisonous gas as an offensive weapon had been outlawed by the major world powers by the signing of the Hague Congress of 1907. This may have had a bearing on the way military commanders were thinking in 1915. However, it is more likely that senior commanders could not see any easy or effective method for the delivery of gas and, therefore, discounted it as a possibility in warfare. This mentality meant that warnings of a gas attack were not only disbelieved but also that they were unbelievable. The reliability of the sources that were giving the warnings in March and April 1915 must also be considered in this discussion of raising the alarm for gas on the battlefield. True, there were sources behind enemy lines that implied that some kind of respirator was being prepared by the German military machine. Taken in isolation this information was probably difficult to interpret for the Allied commanders who were starting from the standpoint that poisonous gas could not be used. What possible use could respirators be on the battlefield? When August Jager deserted to the French on 14th April, just days before poisonous gas was to be used, it may have been difficult for his captors to believe the story he carried with him. He was after all, a deserter, he had simply walked over to the French and given himself up. He had seen enough fighting and wanted out and was, possibly, already near nervous exhaustion to have reached this position. What reliability could anyone place on such a man's story? For all his questionable qualities as an informant, Jager did carry a pad designed to cover his nose and mouth which he explained was a kind of respirator. Was that sufficient proof of a poisonous gas attack? Could he have been sent to give himself up to confuse the defenders? Questions such as these appear to have been raised by his interrogators of the 11th French Division, and after all the questions had been asked it appears that the French divisional commander was sufficiently convinced by the story to pass on the information to his superiors. At this stage the rumour of gas was dismissed as nonsense – once again the commanders were starting from the point of view that it could not be done. Nevertheless, the French passed on the information to the British who thought much the same as their ally and dismissed the issue, believing it to be no more than a rumour set to cause disquiet in the trenches. The dismissal of the report[1] of the use of poisonous gas may be seen, with hindsight, as a grave error of judgement but perhaps there is an alternative view. Those concerned with the decision-making in 1915 were essentially career soldiers who may, or may not, have seen action during the South African War or other colonial wars. It is fair to say that the senior commanders had gained much experience from such conflicts as the Boer War. The Boer War had a significant impact on the thinking of many officers – not least Sir John French who had had a particularly good war.[2] It might also be true to point out that the Staff College had spent time analysing the American Civil War, which is seen as the first modern, technological war. However, whilst there may have been a wealth of experience and theoretical expertise it must be considered that there were very few of the senior officers who had truly grasped the full implication of the large-scale technological warfare in which imperial powers were capable of throwing great effort into the pursuance of war. Gas warfare must be seen against this background;

the signing of the Hague Congress, and the perhaps simplistic belief that it could not be done, militated against the acceptance of the possibility that it might be done. The question of "should it be done?" is unlikely to have entered their thoughts. It may not be the way to wage war – and to soldiers just beginning to get used to the idea of the machine gun as a weapon of war that was no small issue – but there was no evidence to suggest that gas could be delivered effectively. If there had been then it is likely that the signatories to the Hague Congress would have been somewhat fewer. If any one of the Allied commanders had believed in the possibility of gas warfare then and only then would the warnings of a gas attack been heeded. It would, however, have required a commander of some considerable seniority to enable measures to be put in place to deal with the threat. With all these issues having a bearing on the question of notice of gas warnings being taken seriously, it is hardly surprising that all the warnings went unheeded, and that many men had to die to make those in power sit up and demand answers to the questions of how it could be delivered effectively and what would be effective protection against it. It did not take long for both questions to be answered in some depth and within six months gas was used by the British, by which time it was considered to be an acceptable and at least potentially, effective weapon of war.

The effectiveness of gas was reviewed during the Second World War since it was not used. This may reflect some of the thinking of the men experienced in the Great War since many of the commanders of the Second World War had experienced the effects of gas – Hitler himself had suffered from gas poisoning – and it had left a lasting impression upon them. The Second World War was a different kind of warfare in so far as it tended to be more mobile and gas was likely to be less effective. Nevertheless soldiers and civilians, of both sides, were prepared for its use. Whilst gas as a weapon might have limited uses it has been used, for instance in the Iran – Iraq war of the 1980s. The development of new types of gas, particularly the nerve agents, has made the use of gas an increasing possibility in warfare and it is considered to be a major issue by all major military powers in the early years of the twenty-first century.

A further point which should be considered is that of the action that would have been available to the commanders had the warning of an impending attack been heeded. According to the information supplied by Jager the gas was ready for use, needing only a favourable wind for its release. Therefore, the attack could have taken place even whilst the French interrogated the deserter. Paradoxically, the fact that an attack did not occur tended to negate the warning for some of those involved. In this case the credibility of Jager's story is less of an issue than what could have been done. Even had he been believed there was little or no indication of the gas that was to be used. The pad that Jager carried may have supported the fact that gas was to be used, but without the solution in which it was to be soaked there was no real clue of the type of gas that the deserter was talking about. So the information given freely by Jager, though potentially useful, was incomplete. Even if the Allies had acted immediately and had known the type of poisonous gas that was to be used in an attack that could take place at any time, there was little chance of producing any protection for the thousands of men holding the line in the salient. So what alternatives were there that could have saved the lives of many of the defenders and played a significant role in the defence of the salient in April and May? Warnings of a new type of attack would probably have helped but since no one, not even Jager, had any idea of what a gas attack would look like, what were the warnings to be? It may have been possible to reduce the numbers of men manning the front line, as indeed happened later in the war, leaving a garrison to raise the alarm. Of course, thinly manning the line may have been playing directly into the enemy's hands and this would naturally raise the suspicions of the commanders of the various divisions and corps around the line. Also, since the effects of gas were completely unknown, how thinly was the line to be manned and where were the main forces to be stationed? Whilst this argument may not justify the senior commanders' actions since their reasoning has not been recorded, it does indicate that there could have been reasons for the lack of action by the Allied commanders in the field. To raise an alarm of some unknown terror would not have assisted the morale of the front line units and it may be that the commanders sought justification by leaving well alone.

Why were the Germans so unprepared for the success of the very first gas attack? This question may have much to do with the similar kind of mentality amongst their military hierarchy as in both the French and the British camps. That is to say that not only was it considered that the use of poisonous gas was not the way to wage war but also that it could not be effectively delivered. This latter point is especially true when it is considered that the Germans were in the wrong position to make the best use of the prevailing wind on the Western Front; that is, the winds mostly blew towards them – a serious consideration when proposing the use of cloud gas. It appears that General von Diemeling, the German commander responsible for the release of gas, expressed distaste and reluctance at the first use of poisonous gas as a weapon of war. This may have had a bearing on the manner in which his preparations were made and on the expectation of its success. The first use of gas at Ypres was essentially an experiment and one in which even the Germans would appear to have had no real faith. Further, like the Allies, they had no real idea how the gas attack would develop or what its effects would be upon the battlefield. The success of the gas in that first attack may also require some qualification. In the first instance the attack was not able to begin when the Germans would have liked, since it depended on the wind direction. Consequently the attack commenced late in the afternoon of a spring day with darkness not too far off. Whilst fighting need not have stopped on the Western Front with nightfall, it did mean that all communications, movement and supply of the attacking force and so on became more difficult, as did the already hazardous command of the battle. The difficulties experienced by the British commanders during that first night after the release of gas were, to some extent, felt by the Germans, though they were feeling them from a position of strength. Further, the Germans had been fortunate to release much of the gas against two relatively low quality French divisions. There had only recently been a change in the line which had seen the French 11th (Regular) Division replaced by the 45th (Colonial) Division so that in the line they now had a Colonial and a Territorial division side by side. The Germans were likely to have been unaware of this and were, in all probability, expecting the much stiffer opposition that would have been offered by a regular division even though they had no clear idea of the effects of gas on soldiers or their ability to fight. To some extent this argument can be sustained, since when the gas was released against the Canadians, who were all volunteers, there was no full-scale route and the Germans gained ground only after very heavy fighting. Thus, the effects of gas upon the French divisions were likely to have been totally unexpected and would have caused a measure of confusion amongst the German Staff as they rushed troops forward to fill the gap they had caused by their use of poisonous gas. The Germans called a halt to their advance at Mauser Ridge – no small gain by the standards of the day – to allow for consolidation and reorganization of their attack; with the rapidity of the advance and darkness having fallen across the battlefield this was not a bad idea. It was during this pause that the Germans lost the initiative once and for all for, during the month of fighting that was to follow, they were never in a better position to eradicate the salient completely which had been their primary objective and excuse for the experiment with the gas. However, to consider the situation from their standpoint, they had troops moving forward at an unexpected speed and effectively they began to outstrip the supplies, guns and so on for the battle that they had apparently envisaged. Even had the great success been expected it would have been difficult for a 1915 army to respond in a way that would have continued the momentum through the first evening of the attack. A pause became necessary, and with darkness falling, that pause became extended. It may be wondered what would have happened had the Germans been able to attack in the early morning of 22nd April.

Another feature which is likely to have affected the manner in which the Germans pushed forward was that they, too, were short of reserves. Even before the attack commenced it had been made clear to the commanders that they fought with what they had – there were no extra divisions to be put into the line because of the German army commitments in both Russia and France. In fact a number of divisions had been moved from the Western Front to the Eastern Front and Second Ypres is seen by some as a cover for this movement. Since this was the case, the commanders in Flanders adopted an approach that was designed to conserve their resources. To have committed all they had available from the start would have left them vulnerable. Paradoxically, had they committed everything at their disposal on the opening day, the battle could only have ended quickly and there would have been less need for the commanders to conserve their manpower. Thus the Germans were constrained by their thinking and their perceived lack of resources, which undoubtedly had a significant effect on their conduct of the battle during the days following their initial successes. Of course, for a German commander to commit all resources would have been unthinkable – indeed it would have been for any of the commanders. The prize of a quick victory in which all objectives are gained might be great incentive but the defeat that could result from rash moves and poor judgement was not to be countenanced. Although they had a chance of victory the features discussed above conspired against this chance and then the defenders saw to it that the Germans could not have everything their own way as the battle dragged on for another month to an inconclusive close.

During the war on the Western Front the Germans made only four offensives; their opening invasion of France and Belgium; the Second Battle of Ypres; Verdun and the Spring Offensive of 1918. The Second Battle of Ypres was essentially small-scale compared to the others. The fact that after the initial successes of 1914 the Germans remained essentially on the defensive on the Western Front may also give some indication of their thinking when they were on the offensive. It appears that the German strategy on the Western Front was based mostly on the concept of "what we have we hold". Thus, any offensive was seen in the light of strengthening that position and not necessarily by over extending and weakening the strength they believed they held. Second Ypres was an experiment for them but without clear objectives beyond the general idea of removing the salient. On the face of it, at least, the Germans do not appear to have thought very far beyond the release of gas; there was no real strategy for them to exploit any advantages that could have resulted as they pounded away day after day long after they had allowed the initiative to slip away from them. To some extent this kind of thinking can be traced in their other major offensives and, perhaps, it was eventually to cost them the war.

The casualties of the Second Battle of Ypres are often cited to show that the attacking side (the Germans) did not necessarily always lose more than the defenders (the French and the British). The Germans sustained just over half the casualties of the British alone (about 35,000 as opposed to roughly 60,000).[3] Some of the variation may be explained away by the differences in recording casualties in the two armies. In the German army if a soldier were able to return to duty following treatment at an aid post he would not be recorded as a casualty. In the British army under similar circumstances, the soldier would be recorded as a casualty. This undoubtedly has some effect on the overall figures, but there is an overriding fact affecting casualty figures which is sometimes overlooked: that in defence the British and Canadians, and to a much lesser extent the French, spent a considerable effort on attacking prepared German positions. This is not a unique feature of the Second Battle of Ypres, the Germans were particularly aggressive in the counter-attack, for instance during the Somme fighting of 1916 and to some extent suffered accordingly. During the Second Battle of Ypres this is particularly true of the British during the Battle of Gravenstafel Ridge and the Battle of Saint Julien. It is only necessary to think of the losses sustained by the 10th and 16th Canadians or 10 Brigade in the first few days of the fighting to realize the effects these attacks had. Add to these the attack of the 4th Canadians and the Lahore Division and it is hardly surprising that casualty rates were very high. Over and over again men were sent into attack, with little imagination in the planning, with little support or reserve and often very little artillery cover. Following the losses of the 22nd–23rd April it should have been readily clear to the British commanders that such attacks were costly and pointless. Worse than that, in all probability, it was recognized by the divisional commanders, but they followed their orders since there was no other course of action. The root cause of this problem is, of course, Sir John French's desire to fulfill his orders and to be seen to be cooperating with General Ferdinand Foch. From the very outset the French believed that they could counter-attack and regain all the ground lost during the gas attack on the first day of the battle. They did not have, however, a clear picture of how they could achieve this. Nevertheless, each time they asked for support from Sir John French he ordered more attacks to be prepared and carried out, with losses mounting daily in an army that could not afford them. Each time the French asked for support they made little or no move themselves and many British,

294

Canadian and Indian lives were lost in the attacks that were doomed to failure without the French as flank support. Why did Sir John French persist? That is more difficult to answer directly since there are several strands to the problem. Firstly, as mentioned above, he needed to be seen to be giving every assistance to the French as he had been ordered to by the British Government. Secondly, he was, in all probability, swayed by the French leader who has been considered to have been a better soldier and commander.[4] Thirdly, he needed to be seen to be in total control by certain elements of his own command. This spilled over during the battle when Smith-Dorrien was dismissed for suggesting that a withdrawal to a shorter and more readily defensible line was the best approach to adopt. The way this was viewed by French was that a withdrawal was not maintaining support for the French, it was suggesting that he was not in total control of the troops in front of Ypres and hence the situation that had developed there since the release of gas. He was telling the French he could put troops in the field to mount counter-attacks, while there was a subordinate (Smith-Dorrien) who was suggesting that not only could this not be done but that the line should be shortened by withdrawal closer to Ypres. The attitude adopted by French also suggests great insecurity in the man since he was not so stupid that he could not understand the sense in the advice he was offered by Smith-Dorrien. However, he was stupid enough to ignore it. It is suggested by a biographer of Sir John French that he was not a great general and that his intellect was not up to the command he had been given. That this has some truth is no better displayed than in his dealing with Smith-Dorrien. It may be that Smith-Dorrien would not have lasted long in France but the fact remains that he was dismissed by French for reasons which were considered rather "thin"[5] but in all likelihood more because he saw his own position undermined by the suggestions of withdrawal. There had been a lack of trust between the two men for some time and this is more important than the argument over the withdrawal though when that suggestion was made its motives were also mistrusted.[6] If the situation is not seen in this light then it is difficult to understand French's action at all since a short time later he accepted similar advice from Plumer and a withdrawal ensued. Sir John French's attitudes to his allies and to his staff were incompatible and he strove unsuccessfully to reconcile both. He could not satisfy the wishes of the French without losses which were advised against by his own commanders and which he should have realized he could ill afford. The military know-how and political guile of Foch held sway, at least to begin with when successive counter-attacks brought heavy casualties. Sir John French's conduct during this battle was summed up by Liddell Hart in his assessment of the battle:

To throw good money after bad is foolish. But to throw away men's lives where there is no reasonable chance of advantage, is criminal. In the heat of battle mistakes in the command are inevitable and amply excusable. But the real indictment of leadership arise when attacks that are inherently vain are ordered merely because if they could succeed they would be useful. For such "manslaughter", whether it springs from ignorance, a false conception of war or want of moral courage, commanders should be held accountable to the nation.[7]

Whether or not the term "manslaughter" is justified is irrelevant. During the Second Battle of Ypres Sir John French was being played by the French commander and to a lesser extent by his own government. His reaction to this was confusing to those around him as he swung from bouts of pessimism and optimism while he tried to control a situation that was not entirely of his making. He was not astute enough to deal with Joffre or Foch and it is, perhaps, to his credit that he was able to maintain as much control as he did. He was not suited to the command as a junior partner to the French and reacted to the last order rather than taking a longer term view. He did not fully understand the warfare in which he was involved but at least he was not alone there. The political situation seems to have been beyond his grasp. Unfortunately, he did not have the strength of character to face either his own government or the French with the situation that was developing in front of Ypres until it was almost too late, because he saw his own position threatened. Nevertheless, when the war ended he was made Earl French of Ypres by a government who sought to recognize his part in the defence of that Flemish town.

Whilst this may be the truth of the matter, it appears that French had some appreciation of the sacrifice of his divisions and whether by his own insistence or recommendations from his staff he toured the various units as they were relieved and, with minor changes to detail, delivered the following address:

I came over to say a few words to you and to tell you how much I, as Commander-in-Chief of the army, appreciate the splendid work that you have all done during the recent fighting. You have fought the Second Battle of Ypres, which will rank among the most desperate and hardest fights of the war. You may have thought, because you were not attacking the enemy, that you were not helping to shorten the war. On the contrary, by your splendid endurance and bravery, you have done a great deal to shorten it. In this, the Second Battle of Ypres, the Germans tried by every means in their power to get possession of that unfortunate town. They concentrated large forces of troops and artillery, and, further than that, they had recourse to that mean and dastardly practice, hitherto unheard

296

of in civilized warfare, namely the use of asphyxiating gases. You have performed the most difficult, arduous and terrific task of withstanding a stupendous bombardment by heavy artillery, probably the fiercest artillery fire ever directed against troops and warded off the enemy's attacks with magnificent bravery. By your steadiness and devotion both the German plans were frustrated. The enemy was unable to get possession of Ypres – if he had done this he would probably have succeeded in preventing neutral powers from intervening – and was also unable to distract us from delivering our attack in conjunction with the French in the Arras-Armentières district. Had you failed to repulse his attacks and made it necessary for more troops to be sent to your assistance our operations in the south might not have been able to take place, and would certainly have not been as successful as they have been. Your Colours have many famous names emblazoned on them, but none will be more famous or more well deserved than that of the Second Battle of Ypres. I want you one and all to understand how thoroughly I realize and appreciate what you have done. I wish to thank you, each officer, non-commissioned officer and man, for the services you have rendered by doing your duty so magnificently, and I am sure your country will thank you too.

This speech, undoubtedly designed to boost the flagging spirits of those who had been fortunate to survive is full of the glory of war. French is at pains to point out the importance of holding the enemy at Ypres to allow the attack to develop further south. These attacks were designed to bring pressure on the Germans and the fact that they diverted attention from Ypres should be considered of major strategic importance. The speech seems to have been important to the units concerned, since it is repeated in many of the regimental histories compiled in some cases many years after the war and French had done his best to ensure that all felt part of a major war effort in their defence of Ypres. Whilst the men who had survived could feel justifiably proud and satisfied with what had been achieved, they had been let down by the commanders, but they would not have been aware of that at the time. To act as a counterweight to the grandeur of French's speech the content of the following letter should be considered as indicative of the effects of the Second Battle of Ypres on the troops concerned. The letter, published on 21st May 1915, was written by Captain O.W.D. Steel, then commanding C Company, 3rd Monmouths, who had suffered so badly during the fighting on Frezenberg Ridge. It runs:

I would be obliged if you would insert this short note in the next edition of your newspaper.
It is almost impossible to write to the relatives of every man of my company who have suffered, partly because the losses have been so severe, and partly because it is difficult to trace all cases, but if anyone

would care to write to me, I will endeavour to supply all available information.

May I express my deepest sympathy with all those who have suffered.[8]

This was the human effect of the war and of the Second Battle of Ypres and it was something that was to be felt well into the summer of 1915 as casualty lists continued to be published. Second Ypres had been a costly and grim battle for all those involved.

Notes

1. See Appendix VI.
2. See Holmes, op.cit., for an account of French during the Boer War.
3. See note in Appendix VII.
4. See Haythornthwaite, op.cit., p326.
5. See Holmes, op.cit., p284.
6. The lack of trust that had existed between French and Kitchener since 1914 did not seem to have influenced Kitchener enough to remove French. French admits to this lack of trust in his book, *1914*, published at the end of the war (see page 333).
7. Liddell Hart, *History of the First World War*, p192.
8. Published in the *South Wales Argus* on 21st May 1915, which was the same day that the 3rd Monmouths heard French's speech quoted here.

OFFICER CASUALTIES: HILL 60 AND SECOND BATTLE OF YPRES

The following is a list of the officer casualties for the fighting around the town of Ypres between 17th April, 1915 (the date the mines at Hill 60 were exploded) and 31st May, 1915. These dates are chosen to encompass the fighting of Second Battle of Ypres and includes those officers who died of wounds after the end of the Battle of Bellewaarde Ridge which ended on 25th May, 1915. The details are given in alphabetical order with details of the battalion in which the officer was serving at the time of his death. The main source for information for this list is, of course, *Officers Died in the Great War* but this has been supplemented by *The Bond of Sacrifice*, Marquis de Ruvigny's *Roll of Honour, The Cross of Sacrifice* and *Officers of the Canadian Expeditionary Force Who Died Overseas 1914-1918*. Further details have been gleaned from the Commonwealth War Graves Commission burial registers and reference to the Order of Battle has been necessary to identify those units that were involved in various parts of the Battles for Ypres 1915. Where possible the battalion in which the officer was serving when killed is given, but in some cases this has not been recorded and the officer's burial or memorial is taken as an indication that he was killed during the fighting for Ypres, 1915.

ABERCROMBIE, Robert Henry Chester. 2nd Lieut. kia. 3.5.15. 8th Middlesex.†‡

ACTON, Reginald. 2nd Lieut. dow. 9.5.15. 5th South Lancs.

ADAMS, John Gould. Capt. kia. 5.5.15. 1st Leinster.† ‡

ADAMSON, Robert William. 2nd Lieut. kia. 26.5.15. 7th DLI.

ADCOCK, St. John. Major. kia.

9.5.15. 3rd Leinster att. 1st King's Own.†

AGER, George Samuel. Lieut. kia. 22.4.15. 16th Battn. Canadian Inf.

ALLARDICE, Colin McDiarmid. Lieut. 26.4.15. 14th Sikhs att. 47th Sikhs.†

ALLEN, Reginald Arthur Sinclair.

Capt. dow. 30.4.14. 5th Battn.
Canadian Inf.

ALT, George Earl. Capt. kia. 18.4.15.
3rd KOYLI att. 2nd Battn.

ANDERSON, Abdy Fellowes. Capt.
kia. 23.4.15. 3rd Cameronians att.
2nd KOSB.‡

ANDERSON, Alexander Campbell.
Capt. kia. 20.4.15. RAVC.

ANDERSON, Andrew Douglas
McArthur. Lieut. kia. 8.5.15. 9th
Argyll & Sutherland.†

ANDERSON, James Richard Haig.
kia. 11.5.15. 2nd Cameron
Highlanders.†

ANDERSON, Mervyn Kebble. 2nd
Lieut. dow. 11.5.15. 2nd R. Irish.
Reg.‡

ANDREWS, Charles Raymond.
Capt. kia. 24.5.15. 2nd Cheshires.

ANSON, Henry Percival Richmond.
Capt. kia. 25.5.15. 1st Middlesex
att. 8th Battn.

APLIN, Elphinstone D'Oyly. Lieut.
dow. 13.5.15. 2nd Gloucesters.† ‡

ARBUTHNOT, Ashley Herbert.
Capt. dow. 15.5.15. 12th
London.†

ARBUTHNOT, Kenneth Wyndham.
Major. kia. 25.4.15. 2nd
Seaforths.†‡

ARNOLD, Karl Ferdinand Franck
William. Capt. kia. 23.4.15. 1st
Suffolk. ‡

ASFORTH, Isaac John. 2nd Lieut.
dow. 27.4.15. 15th Lancers.

ATKINSON, William Henry Jepson
St. Leger. Capt. kia. 12.5.15. 1st
Royal Dragoons.

ATTREE, Francis William Wakeford
Town. Capt. kia. 10.5.15. 1st
Suffolk.†

AVELING, Lancelot Neville. Lieut.
dow. 29.4.15. 2nd Connaught
Rangers.† ‡

BADCOCK, Stanley Edgar. Major.
kia. 26.4.15. 6th DLI.†

BAILEY, Cecil Arthur. Lieut. kia.
5.5.15. 4th W. Yorks att. 2nd
Duke of Wellington's.

BAINBRIDGE, Thomas Lindsay.
Lieut. kia. 29.4.15. 5th
N'humberland Fus.† ‡

BAINES, Frederick Athelstan
Fanshawe. 2nd Lieut. kia.
25.5.15. 4th KRRC.†

BAKER, Reginald Lawrence. Capt.
kia. 8.5.15. 3rd Monmouths.†

BALL, Albert Ransome. Lieut. kia.
29.4.15. 10th Canadians. ‡

BAMFORD, Edwin Scott. Capt.
dow. 24.4.15. 1st York and
Lancs.† ‡

BANKES, Edward Nugent. Capt. kia.
26.4.15. 3rd R. Dublin F. att. 2nd
Battn.† ‡

BANKS, Percy d'Aguilar. kia.
26.4.15. Corps of Guides att. 57th
Wilde's Rifles.† ‡

BARBER, Geoffrey Carew. Capt. kia.
25.4.15. 5th Yorkshire Reg.†

BARGH, George. 2nd Lieut. kia.
10.5.15. King's att. 1st Suffolk.

BARR, John Young. Lieut. kia.
26.4.15. 7th Argyll & Sutherland

BARRELL, Philip James. 2nd. Lieut.
kia. 1.5.15. 2nd Essex.†

BASTEDO, Alfred Carbut. Lieut.
kia. 23.4.15. 1st Battn. Canadian
Inf.

BATES, Stanes Geoffrey. Capt. kia.
13.5.15. 7th Hussars att. as Adj.
North Somerset Yeo. ‡

BATES, Stanley Knight. Lieut. kia.
9.5.15. 5th King's Own.† ‡

BATES, William George Henry.
Capt. kia. 26.4.15. 1st Leinster. ‡

BAVIN, Nigel Benjamin. Lieut. kia.
23.5.15. 2nd Essex. ‡

BEACALL, Hugh. Lieut. dow.
14.5.15. 2nd KSLI.

BECKHAM, Arthur Thomas
Grafton. Capt. kia. 26.4.15. 32nd
Pioneers att. 34th Pioneers.

BELCHIER, Frank Elliot. MC. Capt.
kia. 20.5.15. 1st East Lancs.† ‡

BELL, (Alfred) Ray Lancaster. 2nd
Lieut. kia. 21.5.15. 5th att. 2nd R.
Dublin Fusiliers. ‡

BELL, Andrew Leslie. Lieut. kia.

22.4.15. 10th Battn. Canadian Inf.

BENHAM, John Russel. 2nd Lieut. dow. 4.5.15. Royal Artillery.† ‡

BENNETT, George W. Major. kia. 23.4.15. New Irish Farm 2nd Battn.

BENINGFIELD, John Philip. 2nd Lieut. dow. 27.4.15. Royal Artillery.

BERRY, William Herbert Stuart. Lieut. kia. 24.5.15. 4th R. Innis. Fus. att. 2nd R. Irish Reg.

BERTIE, Ninian Mark Kerr. 2nd Lieut. kia. 8.5.15. 4th KRRC. ‡

BIDDLE-COPE, Anthony Cyprian Prosper. 2nd Lieut. kia. 25.4.15. 2nd KSLI. ‡

BINGHAM, Frank Miller. Capt. kia. 22.5.15. 5th King's Own. ‡

BIRCHALL, Arthur Percival Dearman. Lieut. Col. kia. 24.4.15. R. Fus. att. 4th Canadians.‡

BIRRELL, George Henry Gordon. 2nd Lieut. kia. 12.5.15. 9th Argyll & Sutherland.† ‡

BIRRELL-ANTHONY, Henry Anthony. 2nd Lieut. kia. 8.5.15. 1st Monmouths.

BLACK, Francis Henry. Lieut. (T/Capt.) kia. 25.4.15. 4th R. Warwick. att. 1st Battn.†

BLACKABY, Arthur. 2nd Lieut. kia. 17.5.15. Cheshires.

BLACKETT, Charles Robert. 2nd Lieut. kia. 25.4.15. 2nd KSLI.

BLAIR, Sidney Barclay. 2nd Lieut. kia. 16.5.15. 3rd R. Warwick. att. 1st Battn.†

BLAND, Charles Ernest William. Capt. DSO. kia. 23.4.15. 2nd KOSB.† ‡*+

BLATCHLY, Walter John Atherton. 2nd Lieut. kia. 12.5.15. 1st Leinster.

BLOFIELD, Frank D'arcy. 2nd Lieut. kia. 13.5.15. 2nd Life Guards. (Blofeld?)† ‡

BOLES, Hastings Fortescue. 2nd Lieut. kia. 24.5.15. 17th Lancers att. RFC. (?) ‡

BOLITHO, William Torquill Macleod. Lieut. kia. 24.5.15. 19th Hussars.

BOLSTER, Herbert G. Major. kia. 24.4.15. 2nd Battn. Canadian Inf.

BOND, Frederick Hamilton Bligh. 2nd Lieut. dow. 13.5.15. Royal Artillery.†

BOND, Thomas Morgan. Pte. kia. 2.5.15. 5th London (London Rifle Bde.) gazetted 2nd Lieut. 11th Irish Rifles. ‡

BONHAM-CARTER, Guy. Capt. dow. 15.5.15. 19th Hussars att. Oxford Yeo.† ‡

BONNAR, James Crawford. Lieut. kia. 22.5.15. 9th Argyll & Sutherland.

BOONE, William Ernest. 2nd Lieut. kia. 20.4.15. 1st KOYLI.

BOOSEY, Rupert George. 2nd Lieut. kia. 22.5.15. 4th Dragoon Guards.

BOURKE, Bertram Walter. Capt. kia. 9.5.15. 2nd R. Dublin F. ‡

BOURNS, Charles. Lieut. kia. 25.5.15. 6th Rifle Brigade att. 4th Battn.

BOWDEN, Edward Ratcliffe. Lieut. dow. 29.4.15. 6th N'humberland Fus.‡

BOWLBY, Geoffrey Vaux Salvin. Capt. kia. 13.5.15. Royal Horse Guards.‡

BOYD, William Noel Lawson. 2nd Lieut. kia. 23.4.15. 2nd Seaforths.

BOYLE, Russell Lambert. Lieut Col. dow. 25.4.15. 10th Battn. Canadian Inf.

BRADLEY, Philip Warden. Lieut. kia. 23.4.15. 1st R. West Kent.

BRADLEY, Shephin (Stephen). Lieut. kia. 25.5.15. 1st Suffolk Reg.†

BRAMLEY, Harold. 2nd Lieut. kia. 13.5.15. Leicester. Yeo. gazetted to 2/5th KOYLI. ‡

BRANT, Cameron Donald. Lieut.

kia. 24.4.15. 4th Battn. Canadian Inf.

BRASS, James Robson. Lieut. dow. 26-27.4.15. 8th DLI.

BRENAN, Byron Edward. 2nd Lieut. kia. 18.4.15. 3rd Gloucesters att. 2nd Battn.

BRISCOE, Frederick John. Lieut. kia. 11.5.15. 3rd York and Lancs att. 1st Battn.†

BROADHURST, Gerald Henry. Lieut. died 8.5.15. Royal Artillery.†

BROCK, Edgar Nathaniel Loftus. Capt. kia. 21.5.15. 5th Worcesters att. 3rd Battn.

BROCKLEHURST, Edward Henry. Capt. kia. 5.5.15. 6th King's.† ‡*

BRODHURST, Bernard Maynard Lucas. Major. kia. 27.4.15. 1/4th Gurkha Rifles.†

BRODIGAN, Francis John. Capt. kia. 9.5.15. 1st Gloucesters att. 2nd Battn.

BROMLEY, Herbert Assheton. Lieut. kia. 24.4.15. 7th Battn. Canadian Inf. ‡

BROOKE, George Townshend. Capt. kia. 6.5.15. Royal Engineers.

BROOKS, Thomas Edward. Lieut. kia. 13.5.15. Leicestershire Yeomanry.

BROTHERHOOD, Wilfred Cashel. Lieut. kia. 24.4.15. 14th Battn. Canadian Inf.

BROWN, Archibald Gibson. Capt. kia. 22.5.15. 9th Argyll & Sutherland.

BROWN, Eric (Frederick) William. 2nd Lieut. kia. 3.5.15. 5th South Lancs.

BROWN, George Sydney Robert Johnston. 2nd Lieut. dow. 3rd R. Scots Fus. att. 1st Battn.

BROWN, James Cartmell Dennison. 2nd Lieut. dow. 28.4.15. 5th DLI. ‡

BROWN, James Macpherson Gordon. Lieut. kia. 6.5.15. 2nd KOSB.†

BROWN, Oscar. Lieut. kia. 24.4.15. 7th Lancers att. 4th Dragoon Guards.† ‡

BROWNE, Charles Nichols Foster. 2nd Lieut. kia. 13.5.15. 1st Royal Dragoons.

BRYANT, Henry Grenville. Capt. DSO. dow. 1.5.15. 2nd KSLI.†+

BURNESS, Alfred Richard. Lieut. dow. 25.4.15. 2nd Seaforths.

BURT, Arthur George. Lieut. Col. kia. 23.4.15. 1st York and Lancs.

BUTCHER, Charles Geoffrey. Lieut. killed. 2.5.15. 1st Dorset.

BUTTANSHAW, Edward Henry Underwood. Lieut. kia. 27.4.14. 2nd Buffs.

CADENHEAD, George. 2nd Lieut. kia. 10.5.15. 3rd Cameron Highlanders att. 2nd Battn.†

CAIRD, John (James) Roberts. Capt. kia. 23.4.15. 2nd KOSB. ‡

CALLARD, Stanley Edwin. 2nd Lieut. kia. 23.4.15. 2nd East Yorks.

CALLINAN, Thomas William. 2nd Lieut. kia. 25.4.15. 8th DLI.

CAMERON, Arthur Ian Douglas. 2nd Lieut. dow. 25.4.15. 2nd Seaforths.† ‡

CAMPBELL, Kenneth James. 2nd Lieut. kia. 12.5.15. 9th Argyll & Sutherland.† ‡

CAMPBELL, Robert Charles Cowburn. Capt. dow. 19.5.15. 2nd KOSB. ‡

CANTON, Herbert Westrup. Lieut.(T/Capt.) kia. 13.5.15. 1st East Lancs. ‡

CARDEN, Derrick Alfred. Lieut. Col. dow. 25.5.15. 2nd Seaforths att. 7th Argyll & Sutherland.

CARDEN, John Rutter. Major. dow. 30.4.15. 15th Sikhs.‡

CAREW, Cyril Joseph Theodore. 2nd Lieut. dow. 29.4.15. 2nd East Yorks.

CARR, Edgar Joseph Austin. Lieut. dow. 18.5.15. 5th King's Own.

CARTER, William Arthur Rowe.

Capt. kia. 23.4.15. 5th King's Own.‡

CHALCRAFT, George Arthur. Lieut. dow. 7.5.15. 4th W.Yorks att. 2nd Duke of Wellington's.

CHALMERS, Ralph. Capt. kia. 10.5.15. 2nd Suffolk.

CHAMIER, Cyril Kinnaird. Lieut. kia. 23.4.15. 1st York and Lancs.

CHAPLIN, Humphrey Marmaduke. Lieut. kia. 11.5.15. 3rd Cheshires att. 1st Battn. ‡

CHAPMAN, Arthur Thomas. Capt. kia. 26.4.15. 3rd E. Surrey att. 1st Hampshire.† ‡

CHAPMAN, George Martin. Lieut. kia. 13.5.15. R.A.M.C. att. 2nd Dragoon Guards† ‡

CHAYTOR, Alban Kingsford. 2nd Lieut. dow. 26.5.15. 6th Worcesters att. 3rd Battn. ‡

CHILD, Gerald Julius. Lieut. kia. 18.4.15. 2nd KOYLI.

CHRISTIE, James Hugh. Capt. (T/Major). kia. 24.5.15. 2nd R.Irish Reg.†

CHRISTOPHER, Leonard de Lona. Capt. kia. 26.4.15. 40th Pathans. ‡

CHRYSTAL, George Gordon. Lieut. kia. 25.5.15. 9th Argyll & Sutherland.

CHURCH, Frederick James. 2nd Lieut. DCM. kia. 10.5.15. 2nd R. Dublin F.

CHUBB, Francis John MacLardie. 2nd Lieut. kia. 18.4.15. 3rd KOYLI att. 2nd Battn.

CLARK, James. Lieut. Col. CB. kia. 10.5.15. 9th Argyll & Sutherland.†

CLARKE, Montagu Christian Cuthbert. Lieut. kia. 10.5.15. 1st Argyll & Sutherland.† ‡

COATES, Alan David. Lieut. kia. 27-28.4.15. 4th London.

COCHRANE, Donald James. Capt. kia. 8.5.15. Royal Artillery.

COCKBURN, John. 2nd Lieut. kia. 25.4.15. 1st R. Warwick.‡

COLES, Edgar Ralph. Capt. kia. 12.5.15. 3rd Dragoon Guards.

COLOMB, Mervyn William. 2nd Lieut. dow. 11.5.15. 4th London.

COLSTON, Harold Kelway. Major. kia. 23.4.15. 1st York and Lancs.†

COMPTON, Lord Spencer Douglas. Lieut. kia. 13.5.15. Royal Horse Guards.

CONNER, Richard. Major. dow. 7.9.15. (wounded 9.5.15.) 2nd Glosters. ‡

CONSIDINE, Christopher Daniel. 2nd Lieut. kia. 24.5.15. 2nd R. Dublin F.†

CONYERS, Charles. Major (T/Lieut. Col.) dow. 12.5.15. 1st R. Irish Fus. att. 1st Leinsters.

COOK, James Robert. Capt. kia. 26.4.15. 21st Punjabis att. 47th Sikhs.†

COOKE, Charles Ernest. 2nd Lieut. kia. 25.5.15. 3rd R. Irish Fus. att. 1st Battn.†

COPELAND, William Alan. 2nd Lieut. kia. 25.4.15. 1st Royal Scots.†

CORBALLY, Lewis (Louis) William. Capt. dow. 6.5.15. Royal Artillery.† ‡

CORBETT, Charles Harold. Major. kia. 13.5.15. 18th Hussars.†

COTTRELL, George Frederick. 2nd Lieut. kia. 11.5.15. Royal Garrison Artillery.‡

COUPLAND, Henry. Lieut. dow. 24.4.15. 5th King's Own.† ‡

COURT, William Hubert Roylance. Capt. kia. 24.5.15. 9th Lancers. ‡

COWIE, Hugh Norman Ramsay. Major. CMG. DSO. dow. 20.5.15. 1st Dorset.+

COX, Douglas Weld. 2nd Lieut. dow. 17.5.15. 3rd Suffolk. att. 1st Battn.

CRAMSIE, Arthur Butler. Lieut. kia. 8.5.15. 2nd N'humberland Fus. att. 5th Battn.

CRASTON, John. 2nd Lieut. dow. 19.4.15. 3rd R. West Kent att. 1st Battn.

CRAWFORD, Edward. Lieut. dow. 27.5.15. 3rd R. Inniskilling Fus. att. 2nd R. Irish Reg.‡

CRAWFORD, Richard Culpin (Gilpin). Lieut. dow. 9.5.15. Bailleul Com. PPCLI. ‡

CREE, Arthur Thomas Crawford. Lieut. kia. 12.5.15. 7th DLI.

CRIPPEN, George Oliver. Lieut. kia. 14.5.15. 5th South Lancs.

CROFT, John Arthur Christopher. 2nd Lieut. kia. 18.4.15. 4th R. Warwicks att. 2nd Duke of Wellington's.

CROFT-SMITH, Edwin Spencer. 2nd Lieut. kia. 8.5.15. 1st KRRC att. 4th Battn.

CROUCHER, Frederick William. 2nd Lieut. kia. 27.4.15 1st R. West Kent.

CROWLEY, Cedric Hugh. Lieut. kia. 25.4.15. 4th R. Warwicks. att. 1st Battn.†

CRUICKSHANK, Arthur Henry Prinsep. Capt. dow. 28.4.15. 32nd Pioneers att. 34th Pioneers.†

CUFFEY, Maurice O'Connor. Lieut. kia. 20.5.15. 2nd R. Dublin F.†

CULLING, Evelyn Claude. Capt. kia. 24.4.15. 2nd Battn. Canadian Inf.

CULME-SEYMOUR, George. Capt. kia. 7.5.15. KRRC. att. 9th London.

CUMMINS, Herbert Waller. Lieut. kia. 24-25.5.15. 4th Yorkshire Reg.†

CURWEN, Wilfred John Hutton. Capt. kia. 9.5.15. 6th R. Fus. att. 3rd Battn.†

CUTHBERT, Gordon, Capt. kia. 27.4.15. 8th Middlesex.†*

DALMAHOY, John Francis Cecil. kia. 26.4.15. 40th Pathans.† ‡

DALRYMPLE, Ian Douglas. Capt. MC. kia. 5.5.15. 2nd HLI att. 2nd KOSB.

DANIELS, Albert Murdock. Capt. kia. 24.4.15. 15th Battn. Canadian Inf.

DARWIN, Erasmus. 2nd Lieut. kia. 25.4.15. 4th Yorkshire Reg. ‡

DAUBNEY, Giles Robert. 2nd Lieut. kia. 23.4.15. 1st R. West Kent.

DAVIS, Henry William Warren. Lieut. kia. 18.4.15. 1st Welsh.

DAVIS, John Charles Reginald. Lieut. kia. 13.5.15. 2nd Essex.

DAVIS, Wilfred Allen. 2nd Lieut. kia. 21.4.15. 4th E. Surrey att. 1st Battn.

DAVSON, Thomas Gordon. Lieut. kia. 13.5.15. Royal Horse Guards.

DAWSON, Walter Henry Mountiford Westropp. 2nd Lieut. kia. 24.5.15. 2nd Cheshires.

DAY, Calvin Wellington. Lieut. kia. 23.4.15. 2nd Battn. Canadian Inf.

DE PENTHENEY-O'KELLY, Henry Arundel. Capt. dow. 19.5.15. 18th Hussars.

DE TUYLL, Maurice Arthur. Capt. kia. 13.5.15. 10th Hussars. ‡

DEACON, Edmund. Lieut. Col. kia. 13.5.15. Essex Yeomanry.

DELEPINE, Helenus George Sheridan. 2nd Lieut. kia. 17.4.15. 1st DCLI.

DELMEGE, James O'Grady. 2nd Lieut. died (dow.) 27.5.15. 4th Dragoon Guards.‡

DENNY, Leon Serena. Capt. kia. 13.5.15. 5th Dragoon Guards.

DENNISON, Harry Stuart. Lieut. kia. 8.5.15. PPCLI.

DERING, Rupert Cholmeley Yea. Capt. dow. 19.4.15. 2nd KOSB.

DICKENSON, Laurence Aubrey Fiennes Wingfield. 2nd Lieut. kia. 10.5.15. 4th Bedfords att. 2nd R. Irish Rifles. ‡

DICKINSON, George Bairnsfather. Lieut. kia. 3.5.15. 3rd East Lancs.att. 1st Battn.

DILLON, William Pearson. Major died. No.2. General Hospital. 4.5.15. le Treport.

DIMSDALE, Edward Charles. Capt. kia. 8.5.15. Rifle Brigade att. 1st Monmouths.

DIXON-NUTTALL, Frederick John.

Lieut. kia. 21.5.15. Royal
Engineers.

DODWELL, Oscar Wilfred. 2nd
Lieut. kia. 10.5.15. 1st York and
Lancs.

DOTHIE, Elvery Ashton. 2nd Lieut.
killed. 9.5.15. East Lancs.

DOX(S)EE, William John. Lieut. kia.
26.4.15. 2nd Battn. Canadian Inf.

DRUMMOND, Guy Melfort. Lieut.
kia. 22.4.15. Tyne Cot Cem. 13th
Battn. Canadian Inf.

DUFTY, Thomas Ernest. Lieut. kia.
19.5.15. 5th Yorkshire Reg. †

DUMSDAY, Cyril Robert. Capt. kia.
27.4.15. 8th Middlesex.

DUNNINGTON-JEFFERSON,
Wilfred Mervyn. 2nd Lieut. kia.
22-29.4.15. 7th R. Fus. att. 3rd
Battn.† ‡

DURRANT, William Blencowe Wells.
2nd Lieut. kia. 8-11.5.15. 6th
Rifle Bde. att. 4th Battn.‡

DUVAL, George Louis Josiah, MD.
Major. dow. 26.8.15. (wounded
25.4.15.) Canadian Army Medical
Corps.‡

EAST, Hubert James. Capt. kia.
10.5.15. 1st York and Lancs. †

EDGELL, Richard Fayrer Arnold.
Lieut. kia. 5.5.15. 2nd KOSB.

EDWARDS, Arthur Noel. Capt.
dow. 24.5.15. 9th Lancers.

EDWARDS, Harold Thorne. Capt.
kia. 8.5.15. 1st Monmouths.† ‡

EDWARDS, Norman Allan. Lieut.
kia. 8.5.15. PPCLI.

EDWARDS, Percy Howarth. Lieut.
kia. 24.5.15. 5th N'humberland
Fus.

EGERTON, Charles Caledon. Lieut.
kia. 18.4.15. 2nd (?) Duke of
Wellington's.

EGERTON, George Algernon. Major
dow. 13.5.15. 19th Hussars.

ELLIS, Thomas Martin. Capt. kia.
18.4.15. 2nd Duke of
Wellington's att. W. Yorkshires.

ENGLISH, Robert Ernest. Capt. kia.

13.5.15. North Somerset
Yeomanry.†

ERSKINE, Walter Augustus. Capt.
kia. 24.5.15. Royal Garrison
Artillery.

ETLINGER, Henry. Capt. dow.
27.4.15. 9th Bhopal Infantry.†

EVANS-FREKE, Hon. Percy
Charles. Lieut. Col. kia. 13.5.15.
Leicestershire Yeomanry.†

EYKYN, Gilbert Davidson Pitt. Capt.
kia. 25.4.15. Royal Scots. (poss
att. 4th Yorkshire Reg.)† ‡

FAIRBAIRN, Andrew Herbert. 2nd
Lieut. dow. 5.6.15. (wounded
24.5.15.) 3rd R. Irish Reg. att.
2nd Battn.

FALCONER, William Keay. Lieut.
kia. 26.4.15. 7th Argyll &
Sutherland.† ‡

FARDELL, Hubert George Henry.
Lieut. kia. 23.4.15. 3rd E. Surrey
att. 2nd Battn.† ‡

FARMER, Henry Charles MacLean.
2nd Lieut. kia. 10.5.15. 6th
KRRC att. 4th Battn. ‡

FARQUHARSON, Lewis Shaw.
Capt. kia. 12.5.15. 1st Royal
Scots. ‡

FARRELL, Bede. Capt. kia. 24.4.15.
4th East Yorks.

FAUSSET, Charles Reginald. 2nd
Lieut. kia. 3.5.15. 3rd R. Irish
Reg. att. 1st Battn.

FAWCETT, Robert Heath. 2nd
Lieut. kia. 26.4.15. 4th
Bedforshire att. 1st Battn.‡

FAZAKERLY-WESTBY, Gilbert
Basil Joscelyn. Capt. kia. 21.4.15.
9th London. ‡

FEATHERSTONE, Cecil Frederick.
Lieut. kia. 25.4.15. 3rd E. Surrey
att. 2nd Battn .† ‡

FETHERSTONHAUGH-
FRAMPTON, Philip Tregonwell.
Lieut. kia. 3.5.15. R. Warwick.
att. 2nd East Kent.

FEILDEN, Granville John Henry.
2nd Lieut. kia. 25.4.15. 2nd
Seaforths.† ‡

FERGUSON, Duncan Macintyre Grant. Lieut. dow. 14.5.15. 2nd KOSB.†

FERGUSSON, James Scott Elliott Gillon. Lieut. kia. 27.4.15. 5th Middlesex att. 3rd Battn.

FIDLER, Frederick. Capt. kia. 26.4.15. 1st Hampshire.†

FITZPATRICK, Wilfred. Lieut. kia. 24.4.15. 5th Battn. Canadian Inf. ‡

FLEMING, Hamilton Maxwell. Capt. kia. 24.4.15. 16th Battn. Canadian Inf.

FLEMMING, Herbert Otto. Capt. dow. 7.5.15. 9th London (Queen Victoria's Rifles).

FORD, A. 2nd Lieut. kia. 9.5.15. 3rd R. Fus.

FORSTER, Herbert Cyril. Capt. kia. 25.5.15. R. Fus.

FORWOOD, Thomas Brittain. Capt. kia. 8.5.15. 2nd King's Own.

FOUCAR, James Lewis. Major. kia. 8.5.15. 12th London.†

FOWLER, Alan Arthur. Capt. kia. 28.4.15. 2nd Cameron Highlanders.†*

FOX, George. 2nd Lieut. dow. 24.5.15. Royal Artillery.†

FRANKLIN, Francis. 2nd Lieut. kia. 3.5.15. 3rd R. Fus.

FRASER, Alexander Evan. Lieut. kia. 2.5.15. 2nd Monmouths.

FRENCH, Charles Stockley. Lieut. kia. 25.4.15. 2nd R. Dublin F.

FRIEDBERGER, William Sigismund. Capt. kia. 24.5.15. 3rd R. Fus. att. 5th Battn.

GAMBLIN, John Louis. 2nd Lieut. kia. 8.5.15. Royal Artillery.

GARDNER, Robert. 2nd Lieut. kia. 5.5.15. 5th King's Own.

GARDNER, Robert Oswald. Capt. kia. 8.5.15. 3rd Monmouths.

GARTON, Arthur Richmond. Lieut. kia. 26.4.15. 6th N'humberland Fus.

GASELEE, Alec Mansel. 2nd Lieut. kia. 24.5.15. 15th Hussars.

GEDDES, Augustus David. Lieut. Col. kia. 27.4.15. 2nd Buffs.† ‡#

GEDDES, John. Capt. kia. 24.4.15. MG 16th Battn. Canadian Inf.†

GIBB, Richard. 2nd Lieut. kia. 11.5.15. 1st Argyll & Sutherland.†

GIBSON, Robert. Lieut. kia. 5.5.15. 2nd KOSB.‡

GILLILAND, Valentine Knox. Capt. kia. 8.5.15. 2nd Royal Irish Rifles.

GLASS, James Fraser. 2nd Lieut. dow. 26.4.15. 2nd Seaforths.

GLEDSTANES, Sheldon Arthur. Capt. dow. 9.5.15. 1st Bedfordshire.†

GLOSSOP, Ernest Edward. 2nd Lieut. dow. 4.5.15. 1st Somerset LI. † ‡

GLOVER, John Donald. Capt. kia. 23.4.15. 4th Battn. Canadian Inf.

GODDEN, Henry William. Lieut. kia. 9.5.15. RAMC att. 2nd R. Irish Reg.

GOODBODY, Henry Edgar. Capt. kia. 12.5.15. 4th Leinster att. 1st Battn.‡

GODDING, Herbert Robert Witham. Lieut. kia. 13.5.15. 5th London.

GORDON, Geoffrey. Lieut. kia. 30.4.15. 12th Lancers.

GORDON, Walter Leslie Lockhart. Capt. kia. 23.4.15. 2nd Battn. Canadian Inf.

GOSLING, Douglas Edward. Lieut. kia. 20.5.15. Royal Engineers.

GOWANS, William. Major. dow. 2.5.15. 1st att. 2nd KOYLI.

GRADY, Walter Henry. 2nd Lieut. killed 22.4.15. 6th R. Fus. att. 3rd Battn.†

GRAHAM, Cyril. Lieut. kia. 27.5.15. 5th Border Reg. ‡

GRANT, Duncan. 2nd Lieut. kia. 10.5.15. 7th Cameron Highlanders att. 2nd Battn. ‡

GREENLAND, Charles Stirling Walter. Lieut. kia. 9.5.15. 2nd Gloucester.†

GREENWOOD, John Francis Bernal. Lieut. kia. 2.5.15. 1st King's Own.† ‡

GRENFELL, Francis Octavius. Capt.
VC. kia. 24.5.15. 9th Lancers.†‡

GRENFELL, Hon. Julian Henry
Francis. Capt. DSO. dow.
26.5.15. 1st Royal Dragoons.† ‡+

GRESSON, John Edward. 2nd Lieut.
kia. 24.5.15. 3rd Cheshires att.
2nd Battn.†#

GRIFFITH, John Gwynne. Major.
kia. 24.5.15. 32nd Lancers att.
HQ 9th Cavalry Brigade.†‡#

GROSE-HODGE, Dorrien Edward.
2nd Lieut. kia. 24.4.15. 3rd
Suffolk att. 1st Battn.‡*

GROVES, Francis Neville. Lieut. kia.
8.5.15. 3rd Monmouths. ‡

GUDGEON, Sidney. 2nd Lieut. kia.
14.5.15. 3rd Manchesters att. 2nd
Battn.†

GUISE, Henry George Christopher.
kia. 6.5.15. 5th Gloucesters att.
2nd Battn.†

GUNN, Arthur. 2nd Lieut. kia.
5.5.15. 2nd Duke of Wellington's
(West Riding) Reg.†

GUNTER, Francis. James. Lieut. kia.
24.5.15. 11th Hussars.†

HAGUE, Owen Carsley Frederick.
Lieut. dow. 2.5.15. Hazebrouck.
2nd CFA. ‡

HAINES, Alec Crichton Cooper.
Lieut. dow. 8.5.15. 2nd R. Dublin
F. † ‡

HALL, John Ramsay Fitz-Gibbon.
2nd Lieut. kia. 24.5.15. 2nd R.
Dublin F.

HAMILTON-DALRYMPLE, John
Raphael. Lieut. dow. 23.4.15. 2nd
KOSB.

HAMMOND, Douglas William. 2nd
Lieut. kia. 24.5.15. 2nd Buffs.†

HARE, John Maxwell. 2nd Lieut. kia.
24.5.15. 6th DLI.

HAROLD-BARRY, J. Capt. kia.
24.5.15. 3rd att. 2nd. R. Dublin
F.

HARRISON, Leonard John. Lieut.
kia. 24.5.15. Indian Army att. 2nd
Lancashire Fusiliers. ‡

HART, Arthur Charles. Capt. kia.
7.5.15. 2nd N'humberland Fus.

HART-MCHARG, William
Frederick Richard. dow. 27.4.15.
7th Battn. Canadian Inf.

HARVEY, Leslie. 2nd Lieut. kia.
25.4.15. 8th Middlesex.† ‡

HASLER, Julian. Brig. Gen. (11th
Brigade) kia. 26.4.15. 2nd Buffs. ‡

HASWELL, Fredrick. 2nd Lieut.
dow. 23.4.15. 3rd East Yorks att.
2nd Battn. †

HAWKINS, Oliver Luther. 2nd Lieut.
dow. 26.4.15. 3rd East Yorks att.
2nd Battn.†

HAYES-NEWINGTON, Charles
Wetherall. Capt. kia. 11.5.15. 2nd
Cheshires.†

HAYTHORNTHWAITE, Rycharde
Mead. 2nd Lieut. kia. 24.5.15.
2nd Buffs.‡

HAZARD, Douglas George. Lieut.
kia. 23.5.15. 3rd KSLI att. 2nd
Battn.†

HELLYER, Sidney Hannaford. 2nd
Lieut. kia. 8.5.15. 4th East
Yorks.‡

HELMER, Alexis Hannum. Lieut.
kia. 2.5.15. 2nd CFA.

HERRON, Cyril Douglas. 2nd Lieut.
kia. 13.5.15. 2nd Dragoon
Guards.

HEWITT, Hon. Archibald Rodney.
Capt. DSO. kia. 25.4.15. 2nd E.
Surrey.†+

HICKS, Frederick Richard. Lieut.
Col. dow. 12.6.15. (wounded
8.5.15.)1st Hampshires.‡

HILL, Maurice Cridland. Lieut. kia.
24.5.15. 5th N'humberland Fus.†

HINGSTON, Frank (Frederick)
Leonard. Capt. kia. 26.4.15. 1st
DCLI.† ‡

HITCHINS, Henry William Ernest.
Lieut. Col. kia. 28.4.15. 1st
Manchesters.† ‡

HOBBS, Herbert Edward. 2nd Lieut.
kia. 25.5.15. 2nd N'humberland
Fus.†

HOBSON, Alwyne Chadwick. Lieut.
kia. 13.5.15. 2nd Life Guards.

HODGES, Henry Burden. 2nd Lieut. kia. 18.4.15. 2nd KOYLI. ‡

HOLMES, Carleton Colquhoun. Lieut. kia. 24.4.14. 7th Battn. Canadian Inf.

HOPKINS, Eric Arthur. 2nd Lieut. kia. 5.5.15. 3rd Bedforshire att. 1st Battn.

HORNBY, Geoffrey Phipps. 2nd Lieut. kia. 10.5.15. 3rd att. 1st Suffolk Reg.

HOSKINS, Ronald. Lieut. kia. 22.4.15. 10th Battn. Canadian Inf.

HOSTE, Sir William Graham (Bart). 2nd Lieut. 9.5.15. Rifle Brigade.

HOWARD, Hon. Robert Henry Palmer. 2nd Lieut. kia. 9.5.15. 4th E. Surrey att. 2nd Battn.

HUBBERT, Francis Stanley William. 2nd Lieut. kia. 23.5.15. 2nd East Yorks.†

HUGHES, Henry Kent. Capt. kia. 9.5.15. 1st KOYLI.†

HULTON, Alan Edward Grey. Lieut. dow. 6.5.15. RASC.†

HULTON-HARROP, Hugh De Lacy. Lieut. kia. 12.5.15. 1st Life Guards.

HUNT, Ronald Francis. 2nd Lieut. kia. 25.4.15. 3rd R. Warwicks att. 1st Batt.

HUNTER, Charles Gawain Raleigh. Lieut. kia. 24.4.15. 2nd KOYLI.†

HUNTER, George Edward. Capt. kia. 26.4.15. 6th N'humberland Fus.†

HUNTER, Howard Tomlin. Capt. kia. 27.4.15. 6th N'humberland Fus.†

HUTCHINSON, Edgar Francis. 2nd Lieut. dow. 24.5.15. 4th Yorkshire Reg.†

HUTH, Austin Henry. Capt. kia. 20.4.15. 4th E. Surrey att. 1st Battn. ‡

HUTTON, Frederick Robert Hughes. Lieut. kia. 12.5.15. 9th Argyll & Sutherland.†

HYAMS, Alec Hallenstein. Lieut. kia. 3.5.15. 9th R. Fus. att. 3rd Battn.

I'ANSON, Leonard Percy. Lieut. kia. 25.4.15. 4th Yorkshire Reg.†

IRWIN, Dewitt Oscar. Hon. Capt. kia. 28.4.15. 10th Battn. Canadian Inf. (& YMCA)

IRWIN, Herbert Quintus. Capt. kia. 26.4.15. Connaught Rangers.

ISHERWOOD, Francis Edmund Bradshaw. Lieut. Col. MID kia. 8.5.15. 2nd York and Lancs att. 1st Battn.

JACKSON, Alan James. 2nd Lieut. kia. 27.4.15. 3rd Middlesex.

JACKSON, John. Lieut. killed 22.5.15. 9th Argyll & Sutherland.

JACKSON, Wilfred George. Lieut. kia. 27.4.15. 1st Buffs att. 2nd Battn.

JAMESON, George Willis. Capt. kia. 23.4.15. 16th Battn. Canadian Inf.

JARVIS, William Drummer Powell. Lieut. kia. 23.4 15. 3rd Battn. Canadian Inf.

JEFFORD, William Arthur. 2nd Lieut. kia. 8.5.15. 12th London.

JESSOP, Napier Arnott. Lieut. kia. 29.4.15. 7th Battn. Canadian Inf.‡

JOB, Bernard Graig Keble. 2nd Lieut. kia. 20.4.15. 3rd R. West Kent att. 1st Battn.? ‡

JOHNSON, Luther Vincent Burgoyne. Capt. kia. 26.4.15. 8th DLI.† ‡

JOHNSON, Richard Digby. Major. kia. 24.5.15. 3rd R. Dublin F. att. 2nd Battn.‡

JOHNSTON, Geoffrey Stewart. Lieut. kia. 14.5.15. Essex Yeomanry.†

JOLLIE, Francis Ormonde Holden. Capt. kia. 25.4.15. 2nd E. Surrey.

JOSLIN, Francis John. Major. kia. 18.4.15. 1st Royal West Kent.‡

JOWITT, Arthur. Lieut. kia. 25.4.15. 1st R. Warwicks.†

JUDD, Frederick George Kerridge. 2nd Lieut. kia. 24.5.15. 2nd Dublin F.†

JUDGE, Charles Harland. 2nd Lieut. dow. 17.5.15. 4th East Yorks.†

JUNG, Henry Adolph. 2nd Lieut. died. 9.5.15. 3rd N'humberland Fus. att. 1st Battn.

KAHN, Edgar. 2nd Lieut. kia. 5.5.15. 1st Leinster.†

KELLIE, Esmond Lawrence. 2nd Lieut. kia. 19.4.15. 1st Bedfords.‡

KELLY, Edward Thomas. Major. kia. 24.4.15. 4th Battn. Canadian Inf.

KELLY, Percy Ewart. 2nd Lieut. kia. 27.4.15. 8th Middlesex.

KELLY, Terence O'Neil William. 2nd Lieut. dow. 2.5.15. 4th Gordon Highlanders.

KEMPSTON, Robert James. Lieut. kia. 24.5.15. 2nd R. Dublin F.

KENT, Alan Williamson. 2nd Lieut. dow. 27.4.15. 7th N'humberland Fus.

KENWORTHY, Donald. Lieut. kia. 17.5.15. 1st Somerset LI.

KENWORTHY, John Gibson. Lieut. kia. 24.5.15. 16th Battn. Canadian Inf.

KEVILL-DAVIES, William Albert Somerset Herbert. Lieut. dow. 15.5.15. 9th Lancers.†

KIMMINS, Albert Edward. Major. kia. 24.4.15. 1st Battn. Canadian Inf.

KING, Alexander Duncan Campbell. 2nd Lieut. kia. 24.5.15. 18th Hussars.‡

KING, Andrew Buchanan. Major. dow. 28.5.15. 7th Argyll & Sutherland.†

KING, Lucas Henry St. Aubyn. Lieut. kia. 8.5.15. 4th KRRC.

KING, Robert Anderson (Andrew) Ferguson Smyly. 2nd Lieut. dow. 23.5.15. 2nd R. Dublin F.

KING-MASON, Charles George Dalegarth. Lieut. kia. 24.4.15. 5th Battn. Canadian Inf.

KIRK, Gerald. 2nd Lieut. dow. 24.4.15. 5th King's Own.‡

KIRKPATRICK, Alexander Douglas. Lieut. kia. 23.4.15. 3rd Battn. Canadian Inf.‡

KIRSH, (Kirch) Charles Sidney. 2nd Lieut. kia. 19.4.15. 1st Bedfords.

KLOTZ, Hubert Norman. Lieut. kia. 23.4.15. 2nd Battn. Canadian Inf.

KNIGHT, Frederick Thornton. 2nd Lieut. kia. 13.5.15. 1st East Lancs.

KYLE, David Logan. 2nd Lieut. kia. 19.5.15. Royal Engineers.

KYNOCK, Colin Smith. 2nd Lieut. kia. 26.4.15. 6th DLI.‡

LAING, Charles William. 2nd Lieut. kia. 24.4.15. 2nd Buffs.

LAMBERT, George. 2nd Lieut. kia. 22.4.15. 3rd R. Fus.

LAMBERT, Henry McLaren. Capt. kia. 13.5.15. 1st Royal Dragoons.†

LAMBERT, Kenneth. Capt. kia. 9.5.15. 2nd KOYLI. (1st?)

LANCASTER, James. Capt. kia. 8.5.15. 3rd Monmouths.†

LANCASTER, John Cecil. Major. kia. 1st R. Warwicks.

LANE, Hector Allan. Lieut. kia. 13.5.15. 1st East Lancs.†

LANE, Percy E. Lieut. kia. 10.5.15. PPCLI.

LANGMUIR, Gavin Ince. Lieut. kia. 22.4.15. 15th Battn. Canadian Inf.

LARGE, Ernest Lynton. Capt. dow. 21.5.15. 5th London.†

LARGE, Philip Martin. Major. kia. 27.4.15. 3rd Middlesex.

LATTA, Robert Peter. Lieut. kia. 29.4.15. 7th Battn. Canadian Inf.

LAWRENCE, Frank Helier. 2nd Lieut. kia. 9.5.15. 3rd Gloucesters att. 2nd Battn.

LAWS, Bernard Courtney. Lieut. dow. 25.5.15. 3rd York and Lancs. att. 1st Battn.†

LAWSON, Frederick Henry. Capt. kia. 24.5.15. 5th N'humberland Fus.‡

LEACH, Francis James. Capt. dow. 26.4.15. 2nd KSLI. †

LEAKE, George Dalton. Capt. kia. 13.5.15. 1st East Lancs.†

LEATHER, Edward Wilberforce. Capt. kia. 18.4.15. 3rd Yorkshire reg. att. 2nd KOYLI.‡

LECKIE, John Harvey. Lieut. kia. 13.5.15. 1st Royal Dragoons.

LEES, Gerald Oscar. Capt. kia. 25.4.15. MG 13th Battn. Canadian Inf.

LEES, Thomas Prior. Major. kia. 21.4.15. 9th London.‡

LE MESURIER, Frederick Neil. Capt. kia. 25.4.15. 2nd R. Dublin F.†

LEGARD, Geoffrey Philip. Lieut. kia. 8.5.15. 2nd N'humberland Fus.

LEGGE, Hugo Molesworth. Lieut. kia. 5.5.15. R. Fus.†

LIEBERT, Bernard Robert. Major. kia. 13.5.15. Leicestershire Yeomanry.

LINDSAY, Arthur Lodge. Lieut. dow. 22.4.15. 16th Battn. Canadian Inf.

LINES, Sidney Martin. 2nd Lieut. kia. 13.5.15. 5th London.

LINTOTT, Richard. 2nd Lieut. kia. 3.5.15. 5th London.†

LITTLE, Andrew. 2nd Lieut. kia. 25.4.15. 9th DLI.† ‡

LIVINGSTONE, Harold Gordon. 2nd Lieut. kia. 1.5.15. Royal Artillery.

LLEWELLYN-JONES, Vivian Bruford. Lieut. kia. 4.5.15. 2nd Suffolk Att. 1st Welsh.† ‡

LLOYD, Lewis John Bevenall. Lieut. kia. 25.4.15. 9th KSLI att. 2nd Battn. ‡

LLOYD, Robert Arthur. 2nd Lieut. kia. 27.4.15. 4th King's.†

LOCKHART, Thomas Downey. Lieut. kia. 23.4.15. 1st Battn. Canadian Inf.

LOUSADA, Bertie Charles. Capt. kia. 9.5.15. 1st York and Lancs. #

LOVEBAND, Arthur. Lieut. Col. CMG. kia. 25.5.15. 2nd R. Dublin Fus.

LUCIE-SMITH, Evan. Lieut. kia. 25.4.15. 1st R. Warwick.

LUCKETT, John Spokes. Lieut. dow. 24.5.15. 2nd R. Irish Reg.

LUMSDEN, Bertie Noel. Capt. kia. 23.4.15. 2nd Seaforths.

LUMSDEN, David Aitken. Capt. kia. 1.5.15. 4th King's.†

LUNAN, George Harold. Lieut. kia. 13.5.15. RAMC.

LUNNON, George John. 2nd Lieut. kia. 27.4.15. 2nd DCLI.†

LYDDON, Frederick Cyril. 2nd Lieut. dow. 26.4.15. 4th King's.(att. from Indian Army)†

LYNCH, John. 2nd Lieut. kia. 3.5.15. Royal Artillery.

LYNCH, Francis William. 2nd Lieut. kia. 27.4.15. 4th Connaught Rangers att. 1st Battn.

LYON, Walter Scot Stewart. Lieut. kia. 8.5.15. 9th Royal Scots.

LYNDEN-BELL, Donald Percival, Lieut. kia. 25.4.15. 1st R. Irish. Fus.

MACDONALD, Mado Daniel. Lieut. kia. 23.4.15. 3rd Battn. Canadian Inf.

MACDONNELL, Herbert Creagh. Capt. dow. 24.5.15. R. Irish Reg. & RFC.†

MACDUFF, Alexander. Capt. kia. 24.4.15. 2nd Cameron Highlanders.‡

MACEY, Clifford James. 2nd Lieut. kia. 25.5.15. 1st Dorset. †

MACFADYEN, Neil Douglas. 2nd Lieut. kia. 6.5.15. 3rd Cameron Highlanders att. 2nd Battn.

MACINTOSH, Robert Rae. Lieut. kia. 24.4.15. 7th Cameron Highlanders att. 2nd Battn.‡

MACIVER, Andrew Tucker Squarey. Capt. kia. Royal Engineers.†

MACKENZIE, John. Major. VC. kia. 17.5.15. 1st Bedfords.

MACKIE, George Neville. Capt. kia. 26.4.15. 54th Sikhs att. 57th Wilde's Rifles.

MACKINTOSH, James Lawton. 2nd Lieut. kia. 4.5.15. 1st HLI. ‡

MACLACHLAN, Kenneth Douglas MacKenzie. Capt. dow. 27.4.15. 2nd Seaforths.

MACLAGLAN (MacLagan), Gilchrist Stanley. Lieut. kia. 25.4.15. 1st R. Warwicks.†

MACLEAR, Basil. Capt. kia. 24.5.15. 2nd R. Dublin F.†

MACMAHON, John Aquila. Lieut. dow. 12.5.15. (wounded 27.4.15) RAMC att. 1st Somerset LI.

MALET, Hugh Arthur Grenville. Lieut. kia. 18.4.15. 2nd KOSB. ‡

MANGER, John Kenneth. 2nd Lieut. kia. 8.5.15. 2nd N'humberland Fus.

MARION, Donald. 2nd Lieut. kia. 9.5.15. 2nd Seaforths.

MARSHALL, William. Lieut. kia. 27.4.15. 8th DLI.

MARTIN, Aylmer Richard Sancton. Lieut. Col. kia. 9.5.15. 2nd King's Own.‡

MARTIN, Charles Herbert George. Lieut. kia. 2.5.15. 3rd Monmouths.†‡

MARTIN, Herbert. 2nd Lieut. dow. 26.5.15. Royal Artillery.

MARTIN, William Francis. Major. kia. 13.5.15. Leicestershire Yeomanry.

MATHER, Edward Noel. 2nd Lieut. kia. 26.4.15. 6th N'humberland Fus.

MATTHEWS, Harold Carey. Major. kia. 25.4.15. 4th Yorkshire Reg. ‡

MAURICE, Sterling. 2nd Lieut. dow. 11.5.15. Royal Engineers.†

MAYCOCK, Frederick William Orby. Major DSO. kia. 25.5.15. 1st Suffolks.

MAYNARD, John Wilmot. 2nd Lieut. kia. 24.4.15. 3rd KRRC. † ‡

MCCOLL, Douglas Chambers. Lieut. kia. 22.4.15. 10th Battn. Canadian Inf.

MCCULLOCH, Robert Arthur Douglas. 2nd Lieut. kia. 3.5.15. Lancs. Fus.†

MCDIARMID, Kenneth. Capt. kia. 18.4.15. 3rd KOSB. att. 2nd Battn.‡

MCGREGOR, Archibald Robert. Capt. kia. 24.4.15. 15th Battn. Canadian Inf.

MCGREGOR, John Herrick. Hon. Capt. kia. 24.4.15. 16th Battn. Canadian Inf.

MCGREGOR, Ronald Malcolm. 2nd Lieut. kia. 24.5.15. 2nd Cheshires.†

MCGUIRE, Harry Boulton. Lieut. dow. 24.4.15. 4th Battn. Canadian Inf.

MCKENZIE, Wallace Alexander. Lieut. kia. 25.4.15. 8th Battn. Canadian Inf.

MCKIEVER, Victor Comley. 2nd Lieut. dow. 18.5.15. 3rd Manchesters att. 2nd Battn.

MCLAREN, Joseph. Major. kia. 23.4.15. 10th Battn. Canadian Inf.

MCLERNON, Robert William. 2nd Lieut. kia. 8.5.15. Royal Artillery.†

MCLOUGHLIN, James Patrick. Lieut. dow. 24.5.15. 4th R. Dub. Fus. att. 2nd R. Irish Reg.

MEDLAND, Frederick Ross. Lieut. kia. 24.5.15. 3rd Battn. Canadian Inf.

MEEK, John. Lieut. kia. 24-26.5.15. 7th DLI.

MERRIMAN, Gordon Holland. Capt. kia. 12.5.15. Royal Artillery. †

MERRITT, Cecil Mack. Capt. 23.4.15. 16th Battn. Canadian Inf. ‡

MIDDLETON, William Archie Arbuthnot. Capt. kia. 25.4.15. 2nd Seaforths.

MILBANK, Robert Charles Alfred Paslo Edmund. Capt. dow. 10.5.15. 2nd Duke of Wellington's (West Riding) Reg.

MILLAR, Arthur James. Lieut. kia. 25.4.15. 3rd R. Irish Fus. att. 1st Battn.† ‡

MILLER, Henry Thornton. Lieut. kia. 6.5.15. 3rd East Yorks. att. 2nd Duke of Wellington's.†

MILNER, John Lewis. 2nd Lieut. kia. 9.5.15. Royal Artillery. ‡

MITCHELL-INNES, Gilbert Robert. Lieut. dow. 13.5.15. 19th Hussars.†

MITFORD, Hon. Clement Bertram Ogilvy. Major. kia. 13.5.15. 10th Hussars.

MOIR, Archibald Gifford. Lieut. kia. 26.4.15. 7th Argyll & Sutherland.† ‡

MOLINEUX, George King. Lieut. kia. 5.5.15. 2nd N'humberland Fus. ‡

MONKHOUSE, Joseph Thompson. Capt. kia. 27.4.15. 6th DLI.

MORAN, Gerald Charles. Lieut. dow. 26.5.15. 2nd R. Dublin Fus.

MORIARTY, Redmond George Sylverius. Lieut. Col. kia. 24.5.15. 2nd R. Irish Reg.

MORTIMER, Edmund. Lieut. kia. 26.4.15. 6th N'humberland Fus.

MORTON, Daniel. 2nd Lieut. MID. kia. 10.5.15. 4th KRRC.

MORRIS, Henry Gage. 2nd Lieut. killed. 23.4.15. 2nd DCLI.† ‡

MUCHALL, George William Stuart. 2nd Lieut. kia. 10.5.15. 2nd King's Own. ‡

MUNTZ, Herbert Gerard. Capt. dow. 30.4.15. 3rd Battn. Canadian Inf.

MURCHLAND, Charles. Lieut. kia. 26.5.15. Royal Artillery.†

MURPHY, James Nevill Herbert. 2nd Lieut. kia. 10.5.15. 5th R. Dublin F. att. 2nd Batt. †

MYTTON, Percy. Lieut. kia. 2.5.15. 8th Middlesex.

NANCARROW, John Vivian. Capt. kia. 25.4.15. 4th Yorkshire Reg.† ‡

NASH, Fountain O'Key Colbourne. Major. kia. 27.4.15. 5th N'humberland Fus.

NASMYTH, James Thomas

Hutchinson. Lieut. kia. 22.4.15. 10th Battn. Canadian Inf.‡

NEELY, Hugh Bertam. 2nd Lieut. kia. 25.4.15. 5th Suffolk att. 1st Battn.

NEVILLE, Thomas Villiers Tuthill Thacker. Capt. kia. 13.5.15. 3rd Dragoon Guards.†

NEWINGTON, John. Lieut. kia. 22.5.15. 3rd E. Surrey. att. 1st Battn. & Cheshires.†

NEWLAND, Norman Chester. 2nd Lieut. dow. German hands. 31.5.15 1st Monmouths.

NICHOLSON, Hugh Hathorn, 2nd Lieut. kia. 24.5.15. 3rd Cheshires att. 2nd Battn. †

NICHOLSON, Leonard Sampson. 2nd Lieut. kia. 2.5.15. 12th London. ‡

NICOLAI, Ronald Claud. (Renato Claudio). Lieut. kia. 25.4.15. 1st R. Warwicks.

NOBLE, William Black. Lieut. kia. 26.4.15. 6th N'humberland Fus.

NORSWORTHY, Edward Cuthbert. Major. kia. 22.4.15. 13th Battn. Canadian Inf.‡

NORTON, Tom Edgar. 2nd Lieut. kia. 20.4.15. 4th E. Surrey att. 1st Battn.

NOSWORTHY, Philip Chorlton. 2nd Lieut. kia. 11.5.15. 2nd Cheshires.

NUGENT, Hon. William Andrew. Capt. dow. 29.5.15. 15th Hussars.

O'CALLAGHAN, Gerard Arthur. Capt. dow. 24.5.15. R. Irish Reg.†

O'DOWD, Maurice Vernon. 2nd Lieut. kia. 25.5.15. 3rd N'humberland Fus. att. 2nd Battn.

OLDHAM, Joseph Haslope. 2nd Lieut. kia. 18.4.15. DCLI att. 2nd KOYLI. ‡

ONIONS, Wilfred. 2nd Lieut. dow. 25.4.15. 3rd Monmouths.

ORDE-POWLETT, William Percy. 2nd Lieut. kia. 17.5.15. 4th Yorkshire Reg.†

OSBORN, Gordon Chadwick. 2nd Lieut. kia. 18.4.15. RE.

OTTLEY, Algernon Glendower. Capt. dow. 22.5.15. 2nd East Yorks.

OWEN, Rowland Hely. Lieut. kia. 18.4.15. 3rd Duke of Wellington's att. 2nd Battn.

PALMER, William Lucius. 2nd Lieut. kia. 8.5.15. 3rd Monmouths.

PALMES, Guy Nicholas. Lieut. kia. 9.5.15. 2nd KOYLI. ‡

PARGITER, Reginald Amhurst. 2nd Lieut. kia. 10.5.15. 3rd Suffolk att. 1st Battn.

PARKER, John Ernest. Capt. kia. 8.5.15. 12th London.

PATERSON, Leslie Arnott. 2nd Lieut. dow. 16.5.15. 3rd Essex att. R. Berks.†

PATERSON, Walter Herbert. Lieut. Col. (Major) kia. 20.4.15. 1st E. Surrey.

PAYNE, John Oswald. Lieut. kia. 25.4.15. 4th R. Warwick. att. 1st Battn.†

PAYTON, Charles Mervin. Lieut. kia. 18.4.15. 3rd R. West Kent att. 1st Battn. ‡

PEAKE, Colin. Lieut. killed 13.5.15. Leicestershire Yeomanry.† ‡

PEARCE, John Francis Bryce. 2nd Lieut. Capt. kia. 29.4.15. 3rd KRRC.

PEARSON, Robert William. Capt. killed 15.5.15. 9th DLI. att. 5th Battn.†

PECKER, Henry Cyril. 2nd Lieut. kia. 20.4.15. 3rd Royal Scots att. 1st Battn. ‡

PEEL, Charles William Maberly. 2nd Lieut. kia. 24.4.15. 3rd R. Dublin F. att. 2nd Battn.

PENROSE, Edward John McNiel. Capt. MID. kia. 25.4.15. 1st R. Irish Fus.

PERKINS, Aneas Charles. Major. dow. 28.4.15. 40th Pathans.†

PERN, Montague. Lieut. kia. 9.5.15. RAMC att. 4th R. Fus.

PERRY, Benjamin Lewis. Capt. kia. 26.4.15. 1st Monmouths.†*

PHILLIPS, Hon. Colwyn Erasmus Arnold. Capt. kia. 13.5.15. Royal Horse Guards.

PHILLIPS, Edward Stone. Lieut. kia. 8.5.15. 1st Monmouths.

PHILLIPS, John Noel. Capt. MID. dow. 18.4.15. 1st Lincolns.

PHILLIPS, Leslie. Capt. kia. 25.5.15. 1st Welsh.

PIERSON, Roy. Lieut. kia. 30.4.15. 2nd Essex.

PIGGOTT, Gerald Wellesley. 2nd Lieut. dow. 14.5.15. Royal Artillery.† ‡

PILTER, Charles. Lieut. dow. 30.5.15. 18th Hussars.

PINHEY, Hammet Eardley. 2nd Lieut. kia. 19.4.15. 3rd DCLI att. 2nd Battn.

PLAYFAIR, Hon. Lyon George Henry Lyon. Capt. kia. 20.4.15. RFA. ‡

POCOCK, Beril Edmund. 2nd Lieut. kia. 13.5.15. 5th London.

POLAND, Henry Arthur. 2nd Lieut. kia. 18.4.15. 3rd R. West Kent att. 1st Battn.

POOLE, Hugh Edward Algernon. 2nd Lieut. dow. 2.6.15. (wounded 24.5.15.) 11th Hussars.‡

PORTEOUS, Dick MacDonald. Capt. DSO. kia. 10.5.15. 1st Argyll & Sutherland.‡+

POTT, Frank. Capt. kia. 24.4.15. MG. 10th Battn. Canadian Inf.

POTTINGER, Charles Evan Roderick. Lieut. dow. 11.5.15. Royal Engineers.†

POUND, John Russel. Capt. dow. 27.4.15. 3rd KSLI att. 2nd Battn.†

POWER, George Henry Fosbrooke. Lieut. dow. 9.5.15. 6th Middlesex.

PRETTY, Donald Sherrington. 2nd Lieut. dow. 11.5.15. 4th Suffolk.†

PRICE, Harold Strachan. 2nd Lieut. kia. 24.5.15. R. Fus. †

PRICE, Henry Bertram. Lieut. kia. 3.5.15. 5th London.

PRICHARD, Frederick Giles. Lieut. dow. 9.8.15. (wounded 3.5.15.) 2nd E. Yorkshire.‡

PRICHARD, Rowland George. Lieut. kia. 24.4.15. 1st Suffolk.† ‡*

PRYOR, Robert Selwyn. 2nd Lieut. kia. 1.5.15. 1st King's Own. ‡

PULLEN, Guy Harper. 2nd Lieut. kia. 13.5.15. Royal Horse Guards.† ‡

RAIT-KERR, Sylvester Cecil. Capt. kia. 13.5.15. Royal Artillery.‡

RAMSAY, Alexander. Lieut. dow. 28.4.15. 5th R. Fusiliers att. 1st R. Warwicks. ‡

RAWLINSON, Curwen Vaughan. 2nd Lieut. kia. 21.5.15. 3rd Dorset att. 1st Battn.† ‡

RAWLINSON, Leonard Hugh. Lieut. kia. 10.5.15. 2nd King's Own.#

RAYNER, George Biddulph. 2nd Lieut. kia. 12.5.15. 3rd Essex att. 2nd Gloucesters.

REED, Charles Sydney. Lieut. kia. 8.5.15. 3rd Monmouths.

REED, Henry William Terrent. 2nd Lieut. kia. 2.5.15. 2nd Monmouths.#

REED, Robert. 2nd Lieut. kia. 24.5.15. 1st Devons.†

REID, Edward Harington. Capt. kia. 30.4.15. 2nd Suffolks.

REID, Geoffrey Percy Nevile. Lieut. kia. 14.5.15. Essex Yeomanry.

RENNICK, Frank. Lieut. Col. dow. 26.4.15. 40th Pathans.

RENWICK, Thomas Buchanan. Lieut. kia. 29.4.15. 6th Rifle Brigade att. 3rd Middlesex.

REYNOLDS, John Edward. Lieut. kia. 23.4.15. 8th Battn. Canadian Inf.

RHODES, Arthur. Lieut. kia. 25.5.15. 7th DLI.

RHODES-MOORHOUSE, William

Barnard. Lieut. VC. kia. 26.4.15. No.2 Squad. RFC.‡*

RICHARDSON, Basil Hutton. 2nd Lieut. died 31.5.15. 8th DLI.†

RICHMOND, Cuthbert Laurence. 2nd Lieut. killed 24.5.15. 5th N'humberland Fus.

RIDELL, James Foster. Brig. Gen. C.O. 149th Infantry Brigade. kia. 26.4.15. † ‡

RIORDAN, Hubert de Burgh. Capt. kia. 10.5.15. 2nd E. Surrey.

RISHWORTH, James. Lieut. killed. 3.5.15. 4th East Yorks.

ROBERTS, George Bradley. 2nd Lieut. dow. 7.5.15. 1st Manchesters.‡

ROBERTS, John Henry Charles. 2nd Lieut. dow. 2.5.15. 1st Dorset.

ROBERTS, Thomas. 2nd Lieut. kia. 25.5.15. 3rd Cheshires att. 2nd Battn.

ROBERTSON, Hugh Grant. Capt. killed. 26.4.15. Connaught Rangers.

ROBINS, George Upton. Capt. dow. 7.5.15. 3rd East Yorks att. 2nd Battn.

ROBINSON, Arthur Hine. 2nd Lieut. 26.4.15. 1st Manchesters.

ROBINSON, Charles Lawson. Lieut. Col. kia. 8.5.15. 1st Monmouths.

RODDICK, Andrew. Major. kia. 14.5.15. Essex Yeomanry.†*

RONALD, James McBain. Capt. kia. 23.4.15. 2nd Buffs.‡

ROSS, George H. Capt. kia. 24.4.15. MG 16th Battn. Canadian Inf.

ROTTMAN, Richard Charles. Lieut. kia. 24.4.15. 3rd E. Surrey att. 2nd Battn.†

ROUTH, John Cyril. Capt. kia. 6.5.15. 1st Cheshires.†

ROWAN-ROBINSON, William James. Major. kia. 12.5.15. 2nd KSLI. *

RUMSEY, Charles Gordon. Lieut. kia. 25.5.15. 3rd SWB att. 1st Welsh.

RUSHBROOKE, Bartle Davers.

Capt. kia. 25.5.15. 3rd Suffolk att. 2nd Battn.

RUSTON, Arthur Cecil. Major. kia. 2.5.15. 8th Middlesex.

RUTTER, Eustace Frederick. Major. MID kia. 13.5.15. 1st East Lancs.

RYERSON, George Crowther. Capt. kia. 23.4.15. 3rd Battn. Canadian Inf.

ST. GEORGE, Guy Staniforth Wemyss. Lieut. dow. 28.4.15. 1/1st Gurkha Rifles.†‡

SADLER, William Edward. 2nd Lieut. kia. 8.5.15. 2nd South Lancs.† ‡

SALVESEN, Edward Maxwell. 2nd Lieut. kia. 25.4.15. 4th R. Dublin F. att. 2nd Battn. ‡

SANDEMAN, David Richard. Major. kia. 24.4.15. 5th Battn. Canadian Inf.

SANDEMAN, George Amelius Crawshay. Capt. kia. 26.4.15. 3rd Hampshire. att. 1st Battn.

SANDEMAN, Sydney Robert. Lieut. kia. 22.4.15. Royal Garrison Artillery.

SASSE, Frederick Hugh. Capt. dow. 8.5.15. 1st East Yorks. att. 2nd Battn.†

SAUNDERS, Charles Robert Edgar. Capt. dow. 28.4.15. 4th London.†

SAUNDERS, Edwin Walter. Lieut. kia. 5.5.15. 1st Cambridge.

SAXELBYE, Frank Norman. Lieut. dow. 11.5.15. 4th East Yorks.

SCHREIBER, William Eric Brymer. Lieut. dow. 4.5.15. CASC.

SCOTT, Arthur de Courcy. Lieut. Col. kia. 6.5.15. 1st Cheshires.†

SCOTT, Norman Sawyers. 2nd Lieut. kia. 23.4.15. 2nd KOSB.

SCOTT, Templar Henry. Capt. kia. 26.4.15. 87th Punjabis att. 47th Sikhs.

SCOTT, Thomas Rennie. Capt. kia. 9.5.15. 1st King's Own.

SCUDAMORE, George Prince Mountford. 2nd Lieut. kia. 9.5.15. 2nd King's Own.†

SEALY, Charles Noel Frederic Prince. 2nd Lieut. kia. 24.5.15. 7th R. Fus. att. 3rd Battn.†

SELLERS, John Harrison. 2nd Lieut. kia. 24.5.15. 3rd N'humberland Fus. att. 2nd Battn.

SHANN, Kenneth. 2nd Lieut. kia. 8.5.15. 3rd N'humberland Fus. att. 2nd Battn.†

SHANNON, George Strangman. MC. MID. kia. 5.5.15. 1st Dorset Reg.

SHARPE, Charles Lancelot Arden. 2nd Lieut. kia. 26.4.15. 3rd Middlesex Reg.

SHAW, George Herbert. Lieut. Col. VD. kia. 24.4.15. 4th East Yorks.†

SHAW, William Easterby. Lieut. dow. 18.5.15. 2nd KSLI.

SHEARMAN, Eustace Robert Ambrose. Lieut. Col. kia.13.5.15. 10th Hussars.

SHENNAN, Douglas Francis Fairfax. Lieut. kia. 8.5.15. 4th KRRC.

SHERRIFF, John George. Lieut. kia. 26.4.15. 7th Argyll & Sutherland.†

SHINE, Hugh Patrick. 2nd Lieut. kia. 25.5.15. 1st R. Irish Fus.†

SIM, Bueth Vernon. Capt. dow. 7.5.15. 4th Middlesex.†

SIMPSON, Anthony Bean Tracey. 2nd Lieut. kia. 6.5.15. 2nd Duke of Wellington's (West Riding) Reg.

SIMPSON, John Parker Norfolk. 2nd Lieut. dow. 27.5.15. 5th R. Fus. att. 3rd Battn.

SINGLETON, Mark Rodney. Lieut. kia. 7.5.15. 2nd KOYLI.

SMITH, Charles Theodore. 2nd Lieut. dow. 22.5.15. 3rd Dragoon Guards.†

SMITH, Sydney Ferrar. 2nd Lieut. kia. 7.5.15. 2nd Cheshires.

SNAPE, Frank William. 2nd Lieut. kia. 25.05.15. 2nd KOYLI.†

SORBY, Charles Malin Clifton. 2nd Lieut. kia. 8.5.15. 3rd Monmouths.†

SPARROW, Francis. 2nd Lieut. kia. 25.4.15. 2nd R. Dublin F.

SPENCER, Hugh Maitland. Capt. kia. 25.4.15. 2nd Seaforths.†

STAIRS, George William. Lieut. kia. 24.4.15. MG 14th Battn. Canadian Inf.

STANNARD, William Lanagan. Capt. kia. 4.5.15. 5th South Lancs.†

STANTIAL, Frank Evered. 2nd Lieut. dow. 4.5.15. 3rd Suffolk att. 1st Battn.

STANTON, Claude Wilfred. Capt. kia. 8.5.15. 1st Monmouths.

STEACHIE, Richard. Capt. kia. 22.4.15. 14th Battn. Canadian Inf.

STEAD, Charles Henry. 2nd Lieut. kia. 27.4.15. 8th Middlesex.†

STEDMAN, Philip Bertram Kirk. Lieut. dow. 19.8.16 (wounded 27.4.15.) 4th London.

STEELE, George Frederick. Lieut. Col. CMG. dow. 22.5.15. 1st Royal Dragoons.

STEELE, Robert Kingsley. 2nd Lieut. kia. 24.5.15. 5th N'humberland Fus.

STEIN, Colin Hunter. 2nd Lieut. kia. 24.5.15. 7th Argyll & Sutherland.†

STEPHENSON, Ernest William Rokeby. Lieut. Col. kia. 27.4 15. 3rd Middlesex.†

STERLING, Robert William. Lieut. kia. 24.4.15. 3rd R. Scots Fus. att. 1st Battn. ‡

STEVENSON, George Arthur. 2nd Lieut. dow. 9.5.15. 3rd East Yorks att. 2nd Battn.

STEWARD, Charles. 2nd Lieut. kia. 25.5.15. 3rd KSLI att. 2nd Battn.

STEWART, Gerald Charles. Capt. kia. 13.5.15. 10th Hussars.

STEWART, Herbert. Lieut. kia. 23.4.15. 3rd DLI. att. 2nd DCLI.

STEWART, James Alexander Logan. Lieut. kia. 13.5.15. 1st Rifle Brigade.‡

STEWART, William Victor. 2nd Lieut. kia. 8.5.15. 1st Monmouths.† ‡

STIRLING, Robert Archibald. Lieut. kia. 24.4.15. 2nd Battn. Canadian Inf.

STIRLING-COOKSON, Samuel Baillie. Capt. kia. 17.5.15. 1st R. Scots. Fus.

STOCKDALE, Arthur William Sinclair. kia. 24.5.15. 7th DLI.

STOCKER, Thomas Fuller. 2nd Lieut. kia. 19.5.15. Royal Engineers.†

STOLLERY, John Cecil. 2nd Lieut. kia. 24.5.15. 5th Royal Fus. att. 1st Warwicks.

STONE, Arthur Brabazon. Major. kia. 10.5.15. 2nd Cheshires.

SUMMERHAYS, Dudley Leycester. 2nd Lieut. kia. 21.4.15. 9th London.

SUTTIE, William Campbell. 2nd Lieut. kia. 24.5.15. 7th Argyll & Sutherland.†

SWABEY, Alan Maurice Eustace. 2nd Lieut. kia. 20.4.15. 3rd SLI att. 1st KOYLI.

SWINTON, Ernest. 2nd Lieut. MID. dow. 28.5.15. Royal Artillery.

SWIRE, Alexander Glen. 2nd Lieut. killed 14.5.15. Essex Yeomanry.†

TALBOT, Edward Charles. Capt. dow. 29.4.15. 47th Sikhs. ‡

TARRANT, Herbert Sutton. Capt. kia. 27.4.15. 1st HLI. †

TATHAM, Basil Owen. Capt. kia. 23.4.15. 3rd East Yorks att. 2nd Battn.

TAYLOR, Edward. 2nd Lieut. kia. 13.5.15. 18th Hussars.

TAYLOR, Ernest George. 2nd Lieut. kia. 2.5.15. 2nd King's Own.

TAYLOR, Ernie Rumbold. Capt. kia. 18.4.15. 2nd Duke of Wellington's att. E. Yorkshire.

TAYLOR, Geoffrey Barron. Lieut. kia. 24.4.14. 15th Battn. Canadian Inf.

TAYLOR, William Aloysius. Capt. dow. 11.5.15. 5th South Lancs.

TELFER, Somerville Goodman. 2nd Lieut. kia. 8.5.15. 12th London.

TENAILLE, Daniel Jean. Major. kia. 24.4.15. 5th Battn. Canadian Inf.

THACKERAY, Frederick Renell. Lieut. MC. kia. 18.4.15. 2nd Duke of Wellington's.

THEILMAN, Carl Erik. Major. kia. 24.4.15. 4th East Yorks.

THOMAS, Daniel Gwyn. 2nd Lieut. kia. 25.5.15. 3rd R. Dublin Fus. att. 2nd Battn.

THOMSON, Samuel Pestel Donald. Lieut. killed 13.5.15. Leicestershire Yeomanry.

TIGAR, Harold Walter. Lieut. kia. 9.5.15. 3rd Middlesex.

TILLYER, Richard Bateson Blunt. Lieut. kia. 25.4.15. 1st R. Warwick.

TIMMIS, Richard Sutton. 2nd Lieut. dow. 10.5.15. 3rd KRRC. †

TODD, Alexander Findlater. Capt. dow. 21.4.15. 3rd Norfolk att. 1st Battn.

TOPHAM, Henry Augrave Cecil. 2nd Lieut. dow. 25.5.15. 1st Welsh. † ‡

TORKINGTON, Charles Coke. Capt. kia. 25.5.15. 1st Welsh.

TOWNSEND, Hugh Vere. 2nd Lieut. kia. 6.5.15. 3rd Monmouths.

TOWNSEND, Sidney John. 2nd Lieut. kia. 13.5.15. 2nd Life Guards.

TRENCHARD, Frederick Alfred. Lieut. kia. 24.5.15. Royal Artillery.†

TREVELYAN, Wilfred. 2nd Lieut. kia. 4.5.15. 5th Rifle Brigade att. 4th Battn. ‡

TREVOR, Frederick Pelham. 2nd Lieut. kia. 8.5.15. 3rd DCLI. att. 2nd Battn.

TROTTER, Kenneth Stuart. 2nd Lieut. kia. 26.4.15. 6th Rifle Brigade att. 1st Battn.†

TUFF, Cecil Thomas. Capt. kia. 18.4.15. 3rd R. West Kent. att. 1st Battn.

TUKE, Arthur Harold Seymour. 2nd Lieut. dow. 7.5.15. 3rd

N'humberland Fus. att. 2nd Battn.

TULLIS, Robert Ramsey. Capt. dow. 25.5.15. 7th Argyll & Sutherland.†

TULLOH, George Swinton. Lieut. Col. kia. 10.5.15. 2nd Gloucesters.

TURNER, Alan Fletcher. Lieut. kia. 13.5.15. Leicestershire Yeomanry.

TURTON, Zouch Austin. Lieut. kia. 23.4.15. Norfolk Reg. att. 2nd E. Yorks.†

TWINING, Cecil Francis Harvey. Capt. kia. 3.5.15. 3rd Hampshire. att. 1st Battn.†*

TYLER, John Collet. 2nd Lieut. kia. 18.4.15. RA. ‡*

TYNDALL, William Ernest Marriott. Major. dow. 1.8.16. (wounded 19.5.15.) 2nd Duke of Wellington's.

UNWIN, Lancelot Urquhart. Capt. kia. 27.4.15. Hampshire Reg.†

VANSITTART, Arthur Bexley. 2nd Lieut. dow. 12.5.15. 11th Hussars.

VAUGHAN, John Montgomery. 2nd Lieut. dow. 25.5.15. 3rd R. Fus. †

VERSCHOYLE, Francis Stuart. 2nd Lieut. kia. 25.4.15. Royal Anglesey Royal Engineers.†

VIVIAN, Charles Augustus. Lieut. Col. kia. 27.4.15. 15th Sikhs.† ‡*

WADE, Graham Hardie. Capt. kia. 26.4.15. 7th Argyll & Sutherland.†

WALFORD, George Henry. Major. kia. 19.4.15. Brigade Major 84th Brigade. 1st Suffolk Reg.†

WALFORD, Leonard Nithsdale. Lieut. kia. 8.5.15. 12th London.

WALFORD, Oliver Robson. 2nd Lieut. kia. 26.4.15. 1st Hampshire.

WALKER, Basil Scarisbrickle. 2nd Lieut. kia. 9.5.15. 5th Cheshires.

WALKER, Edmund Basil. 2nd Lieut.

MID. kia. 18.4.15. 1st R. West
Kent.‡

WALKER, Henry John Innes. Capt.
kia. 25.4.15. 1st R. Warwicks.

WALLACE, Henry Atholl Charles.
Capt. kia. 22.4.15. 10th Battn.
Canadian Inf.‡

WALLACE, John Roger. 2nd Lieut.
kia. R. Scots. Fus.† ‡

WALLACE, Robert. Capt. died
6.5.15. 2nd East Yorks.

WALLIKER, Lester Charles. 2nd
Lieut. dow. 15.5.15. 2nd E.
Surrey.†

WALTERS, Henry James. Lieut. kia.
5.5.15. 2nd Monmouths.

WARD, Charles Francis. Capt. kia.
15.5.15. Royal Artillery.†

WATKINS, Illtyd Edwin Maitland.
kia. 5.5.15. 2nd Monmouths.† ‡

WATSON, Francis. Lieut. kia. 9.5.15.
3rd E. Surrey att. 2nd Battn.

WATSON, Geoffrey Launcelot. Capt.
kia. 20.4.15. 3rd E. Surrey att. 1st
Battn.

WAWN, Frederick Middlemont.
Capt. kia. 25.5.15. 7th DLI.

WEATHERHEAD, George Ernest.
Capt. kia. 8.5.15. 2nd King's
Own.

WEBB, John Boyer. Lieut. kia.
21.4.15. 4th North Staffs att. 1st
Bedfords.‡

WELLS, Leslie Howard Elliott. 2nd
Lieut. died. 4.5.15. 3rd Lancs.
Fus. att. 2nd Battn.†

WENDOVER, Albert Edward
Charles Robert (Viscount). Lieut.
dow. 19.5.15. Royal Horse
Guards.†‡

WEST, Walter Montague. Lieut. dow.
5.5.15. 1st Cambridge.†

WESTBY, Edmund Henry Herbert.
Capt. kia. 25.5.15. 1st Welsh.†

WESTMACOTT, Spencer
Ruscombe. Lieut. kia. 8.5.15. 2nd
Leinster att. 1st Battn.‡

WHARTON, Guy Fitzgerald. Lieut.
dow. 9.5.15. DLI. att. 1st
KOYLI.†

WHITAKER, Charles Frederick.

Lieut. kia. 5.5.15. 2nd Duke of
Wellington's (West Riding) Reg.

WHITE, James Pringle. 2nd Lieut.
kia. 26.5.15. 10th King's.

WHITE, Roger Wingate. Major. kia.
18.5.15. Royal Artillery. †

WHITE, William. 2nd Lieut. kia.
25.4.15. 4th R. Dublin F. att. 2nd
Battn.

WHITEHEAD, Lionel Ward. Capt.
kia. 22.4.15. 13th Battn.
Canadian Inf.

WHITEHOUSE, Alfred Ernest. 2nd
Lieut. kia. 8.5.15. 12th London.

WHITFIELD, Frederick
Ashburnham Hooker. 2nd Lieut.
kia. 23.4.15. 3rd Middlesex.†

WHYTE, John. Lieut. dow. 26.4.15.
7th Argyll & Sutherland.

WICKHAM, Montagu Hill Clephane
De Crisoforo De Bouillon. Capt.
MID. dow. 9.5.15. Connaught
Rangers att. 2nd Royal Irish Reg.

WILKINSON, Clement Arthur.
Major. kia. 2.5.15. 2nd KSLI. †

WILLIAMS, Edward Styant. Major.
kia. 8.5.15. 1st Monmouths.†

WILLIAMS, Robin A.W. Lieut. kia.
18.4.15. 2nd KOYLI.

WILLIAMS, William John. Lieut.
dow. 12.5.15. 2nd Monmouths.

WILLIAMSON, George Massey.
Lieut. kia. 23.4.15. 14th Battn.
Canadian Inf.

WILLS, Percy. 2nd Lieut. dow.
19.4.15. 1st DCLI.

WILSON, Cyril Frederick. Lieut. kia.
13.5.15. 5th Dragoon Guards.†

WILSON, Herbert Stanley. Capt.
dow. 13.5.15. Royal Garrison
Artillery.

WILSON, Thomas Wilson. Lieut. kia.
5.5.15. 6th King's.†

WINFIELD, Frank. 2nd Lieut. dow.
31.5.15. 5th N'humberland Fus.

WINGATE, Thomas Paterson. Capt.
kia. 18.4.15. 1st KOSB. att. 2nd
Battn.‡

WINGFIELD, Cecil John Talbot
Rees. Capt. dow. 29.4.15. 4th
KRRC.†

WINTON, Harry George Denys. Lieut. kia. 3.5.15. 2nd Suffolk Reg. †

WOOD, Collingwood Lindsay. Capt. kia. 24.5.15. 18th Hussars.†

WOOD, William. 2nd Lieut. kia. 8.5.15. 4th Rifle Brigade.

WOODMASS, Kenrick Talbot. Capt. kia. 23.4.15. 2nd East Yorks.†

WOOKEY, Guy Richard Penny. Lieut. dow. 10.5.15. 3rd East Yorks. (att. 2nd Battn.?)

WORTON, John Paton. Lieut. kia. 8.5.15. 3rd Monmouths.

WREFORD-BROWN, Claude Wreford. Capt. DSO. kia. 25.5.15. 2nd Northumberland Fusiliers. ‡+

WRINCH, Stanley. 2nd Lieut. kia. 8.5.15. 3rd Suffolk att. 1st Battn.

WYLEY, Francis John. Capt. dow. 23.4.15. 2nd KOYLI.

WYLIE, William Stanley. Lieut. dow. 10.5.15. 3rd York and Lancs. att. 1st Battn.

WYLLIE, Hugh Tweed Walford. Capt. kia. 24.5.15. 4th Dragoon Guards.

WYNTER, Philip Cecil. Capt. dow. 20.4.15. 1st E. Surrey.‡

WYNYARD, Damer. Capt. MID. kia. 20.4.15. 1st E. Surrey.

YARROW, Eric Fernandez. 2nd Lieut. kia. 8.5.15. 7th Argyll & Sutherland.† ‡

YATES Francis William. Capt. dow. 25.4.15. 2nd KOYLI.

YOUNG, Henry Harman. 2nd Lieut. kia. 24.5.15. 3rd R. Fus.

YOUNG, Mervyn Cyril Nicholas Radford. 2nd Lieut. dow. 25.5.15. 2nd R. Dublin. F.

YOUNG, Norman Mitchell. Lieut. kia. 25.4.15. Royal Scots.† ‡

---

†   Further details can be found in *Bond of Sacrifice.*

‡   Further details can be found in *De Ruvigny's Roll of Honour.*

★   Further details can be found in *British Roll of Honour*

+   Further details can be found in *The Distinguished Service Order 1886-1923*

Further details can be found in *Leaving All That Was Dear. Cheltenham and the Great War*

APPENDIX II

VICTORIA CROSS WINNERS
AND CITATIONS

Lieutenant George Rowland Patrick Roupell. 1st Battalion The East Surrey Regiment.

For most conspicuous gallantry and devotion to duty on the 20th April, 1915, when he was commanding a company of his battalion on Hill 60, which was subjected to a most severe bombardment throughout the day. Though wounded in several places, he remained at his post and led his company in repelling a strong German assault. During a lull in the bombardment he had his wounds hurriedly dressed, and then insisted on returning to his trench, which was again being subjected to a severe bombardment. Towards evening, his company being dangerously weakened, he went back to his battalion head-quarters, represented the situation to his commanding officer, and brought up reinforcements, passing backwards and forwards over ground swept by heavy fire. With these reinforcements he held his position throughout the night, and until his battalion was relieved next morning.

Lieutenant Benjamin Handley Geary. 4th Battalion (attached 1st Battalion) The East Surrey Regiment.

For most conspicuous bravery and determination on Hill 60, near Ypres, on 20 and 21 April, 1915, when he held the left crater with his platoon, some men of the Bedfordshire Regiment and a few reinforcements which came up in the evening and night. The crater was first exposed to a very heavy artillery fire which broke down the defences, and afterwards, during the night, to repeated bomb attacks, which filled it with dead and wounded. Each attack was, however, repulsed, mainly owing to the splendid personal gallantry of Second Lieutenant Geary. At one time he used a rifle with great effect, at another threw hand grenades, and exposed himself with entire disregard to danger in order to see by the light of the flares where the enemy were coming on. In the intervals between the attacks he spent his whole time arranging for the ammunition supply and for reinforcements. He was severely wounded just before daylight on the 21 April.

Lieutenant Geoffrey Harold Woolley. 9th (County of London) Battalion the London Regiment.
For most conspicuous bravery on Hill 60 during the night of the 20-21 April, 1915. Although the only officer on the hill at the time, and with very few men, he successfully resisted all attacks on his trench, and continued throwing bombs and encouraging his men till relieved. His trench during all this time was being heavily shelled and bombed and was subjected to heavy machine gun fire by the enemy.

10523 Private Edward Dwyer. 1st Battalion The East Surrey Regiment.
For most conspicuous bravery and devotion to duty at Hill 60, on the 20th of April, 1915. When his trench was heavily attacked by German grenade throwers, he climbed on to the parapet, and although subjected to a hail of bombs at close quarters, succeeded in dispersing the enemy by the effective use of his hand-grenades. Private Dwyer displayed great gallantry earlier in the day in leaving his trench, under heavy shell-fire, to bandage his wounded comrades.

24066 Lance Corporal Frederick Fisher. 13th Battalion Canadian Infantry.
On the 23rd April, 1915, in the neighbourhood of St. Julien, he went forward with the machine gun of which he was in charge, under heavy fire, and most gallantly assisted in covering the retreat of a battery, losing four of his gun team. Later, after obtaining four more men, he went forward again to the firing line, and was himself killed while bringing his machine gun into action under heavy fire, in order to cover the advance of supports.

1539 Sergeant Major Frederick William Hall. 8th Battalion Canadian Infantry.
On the 24th April, 1915, in the neighbourhood of Ypres, when a wounded man who was lying some fifteen yards from the trench called for help, Company Sergt. Major Hall endeavoured to reach him in the face of heavy enfilade fire which was being poured in by the enemy. The first attempt failed, and a non-commissioned officer and a private soldier, who were attempting to give assistance, were both wounded. Company Sergt. Major Hall then made a second most gallant attempt, and was in the act of lifting up the wounded man to bring him in when he fell mortally wounded in the head.

Captain Edward Donald Bellew. 7th Battalion Canadian Infantry.
For most conspicuous bravery and devotion to duty near Keerselaere on the 24th April, 1915, during the German attack on the Ypres salient. The enemy attack broke in full force against the front and right flank of the battalion, the latter being exposed owing to a gap in the line. The advance was temporarily stayed by Capt. Bellew, who had sited the guns on the left of the right company. Reinforcements were sent forward but were surrounded and destroyed. With the enemy in strength less than 100 yards from him, with no further assistance

in sight, and with his rear threatened, Capt. Bellew and Sergt. Peerless, each operating a gun, decided to stay where they were and fight it out. Sergt. Peerless was killed and Capt. Bellew was wounded and fell. Nevertheless, he got up and maintained his fire till ammunition failed and the enemy rushed the position. Capt. Bellew then seized a rifle, smashed his machine gun, and, fighting to the last, was taken prisoner.

Captain Francis Alexander Caron Scrimger. Medical Officer 14th Battalion Canadian Infantry.
On the afternoon of the 25 April, 1915, in the neighbourhood of Ypres, when in charge of an advanced dressing station in some farm buildings, which were being heavily shelled by the enemy, he directed under heavy fire the removal of the wounded, and he himself carried a severely wounded officer out of a stable in search of a place of greater safety. When he was unable alone to carry this officer farther, he remained with him under fire until help could be obtained. During the very heavy fighting between the 22 and 25 April, Capt. Scrimger displayed continuously day and night the greatest devotion to his duty among the wounded at the front.

Mir Dast, I.O.M. Subadur Bahadur. 55th Coke's Rifles (Frontier Force) attached 57th Wilde's Rifles (Frontier Force).
For most conspicuous bravery and great ability at Ypres on 26th April, 1915, when he led his platoon with great gallantry during the attack, and afterwards collected various parties of the regiment (when no British officers were left) and kept them under his command until the retirement was ordered. Jemadar Mir Dast subsequently on this day displayed remarkable courage in helping to carry eight British and Indian officers to safety, while exposed to very heavy fire.

A/Corporal Issy Smith. 1st Battalion The Manchester Regiment.
For most conspicuous bravery on the 26th April, 1915, near Ypres, when he left his company on his own initiative and went well forward towards the enemy's position to assist a severely wounded man, whom he carried a distance of 250 yards into safety, whilst exposed the whole time to heavy machine-gun and rifle fire. Subsequently Corpl. Smith displayed great gallantry, when the casualties were very heavy, in voluntarily assisting to bring in many more wounded men throughout the day, and attending to them with the greatest devotion to duty, regardless of personal risk.

1272 Pte. John Lynn. 2nd Battalion The Lancashire Fusiliers.
For most conspicuous bravery near Ypres on the 2nd May, 1915. When the Germans were advancing behind their wave of asphyxiating gas, Pte. Lynn, although almost overcome by the deadly fumes, handled his machine gun with very great effect against the enemy, and when he could not see them, he moved his gun higher upon the parapet, which enabled him to bring even more effective fire to bear, and eventually checked any further advance. The great courage displayed by this soldier had a fine effect on his comrades in the very trying circumstances. He died the following day from the effects of gas poisoning.

7602 Private Edward Warner. 1st Battalion The Bedfordshire Regiment.
For most conspicuous bravery near Hill 60 on the 1st May, 1915. After Trench No. 46 had been vacated by our troops, consequent on a gas attack, Private Warner entered it single-handed, in order to prevent the enemy taking possession. Reinforcements were sent to Private Warner, but could not reach him owing to the gas. He then came back and brought up more men, by which time he was completely exhausted, but the trench was held until the enemy's attack ceased. This very gallant soldier died shortly afterwards from the effects of gas poisoning.

9539 Lance Sergeant Douglas Walter Belcher. 1/5th (City of London) Battalion The London Regiment (London Rifle Brigade).
On the early morning of the 13th May, 1915, when in charge of a portion of advanced breastwork south of the Wieltje-St. Julien Road, during a very fierce and continuous bombardment by the enemy, which frequently blew in the breastwork, L. Sergt. Belcher, with a mere handful of men, elected to remain and endeavour to hold his position after the troops near him had been withdrawn. By his skill and great gallantry he maintained his position during the day, opening rapid fire on the enemy, who were only 150 to 200 yards distant, whenever he saw them collecting for an attack. There is little doubt that the bold front shown by L. Sergt. Belcher prevented the enemy breaking through on the Wieltje Road and averted an attack on the flank of one of our divisions.

British Order of Battle:
Hill 60 and the Battles of Ypres 1915

3rd DIVISION: Major General J.A.L. Haldane

7 Brigade: Brigadier General C.R. Ballard

3/Worcestershire	1/Wiltshire	Hon. Art. Coy. (TF)
2/S. Lancashire	2/R. Irish Rifles	4/S. Lancashire (TF)

8 Brigade: Brigadier General A.R. Hoskins

2/R. Scots	4/Middlesex	4/Gordons (TF)
2/Suffolk	1/Gordons	

9 Brigade: Brigadier General. W. Douglas Smith

1/N'humberland Fus.	1/Lincolnshire	10/King's (TF)
4/Royal Fus.	1/R. Scots Fus.	

R.F.A.Brigades

XXIII.(107, 108, 109 Btys).	XLII. (29, 41, 45 Btys).
XL. (6, 23, 49 Btys).	XXX. (How.) (128, 129 Btys).

R.G.A.: 5/Mountain Battery.

Field Coys. R.E.: 56 & 1/Cheshire (TF)

Mtd. Troops: C Sqdn. N. Irish Horse   Cyclist Coy.

4th DIVISION: Major General H.F.M. Wilson

10 Brigade: Brigadier General. C.P.A. Hull

1/R. Warwickshire	1/R. Irish Fus.	7/Argyll & Suth.(TF)
2/Seaforths	2/R. Dublin Fus.	

11 Brigade: Brigadier General J. Hasler.

1/Somerset LI	1/Hampshire	London Rif. Brig.(TF)
1/E Lancashire	1/Rifle Brigade	

12 Brigade: Brigadier General F.G. Anley

1/King's Own	2/Lancashire Fus.	5/S. Lancashire (TF)
2/Royal Irish	2/Essex	2/Monmouthshire (TF)

R.F.A.Brigades.

XIV. (68, 88 Btys.)	XXXII. (27, 134, 135 Btys.)
XXIX. (125, 126,1 27 Btys.)	

R.G.A.: 2/Mountain Battery

Field Coys. R.E.: 9 & 1/W.Lancashire (TF)

Mtd. Troops: A Sqdn. Northants Yeo.   Cyclist Coy.

5th DIVISION: Major General T.L.N. Morland

13 Brigade: Brigadier General R. Wanless O'Gowan

2/KOSB	1/R. West Kent	9/London (TF)
2/D.Wellington's	2/KOYLI	

14 Brigade: Brigadier General G.H. Thesiger

1/Devonshire	1/DCLI	5/Cheshire (TF)
1/E.Surrey	2/Manchester	

15 Brigade: Brigadier General E. Northey

1/Norfolk	1/Cheshire.	6th King's (TF)
1/Bedfordshire	1/Dorsetshire	

R.F.A.Brigades

XV. (52, 80 Btys.)	XXVIII. (122, 123,1 24 Btys.)
XXVII. (119, 120, 121 Btys.)	XXX. (How.) (130 Bty.)

Field Coys. R.E.: 59, 2/Home Counties (TF) & 1/N. Midland (TF)

Mtd. Troops: C Sqdn. Northants Yeo.   Cyclist Coy.

27th DIVISION: Major General T.D'O. Snow

80 Brigade: Brigadier General W.E.B. Smith
2/KSLI	4/KRRC	PPCLI
3/KRRC	4/Rifle Brigade	

81 Brigade: Brigadier General H.L. Croker
1/R. Scots	2/Camerons	9/R. Scots (TF)
2/Gloucestershire	1/Argyll & Suth.	9/Argyll & Suth (TF)

82 Brigade: Brigadier General J.R. Longley
1/Royal Irish	2/R.Irish Fus.	1/Cambridgeshire (TF)
2/DCLI	1/Leinster	

R.F.A. Brigades.

I. (11, 98, 132, 133 Btys.)   XX.(67, 99, 148, 364 Btys.)
XIX. (39, 59, 96, 131 Btys.) (All four gun Batteries)
VII. (How.) (61st. Bty.)

Field Coys.R.E.: 17, 1/Wessex (TF) & 2/Wessex (TF)

Mtd.Troops: A Sqdn. Surrey Yeo.   Cyclist Coy.

28th DIVISION: Major General E.S. Bulfin

83 Brigade: Brigadier General R.C. Boyle
2/King's Own	1/KOYLI	5/King's Own (TF)
2/E. Yorkshire	1/York & Lancaster	3/Monmouthshire (TF)

84 Brigade: Brigadier General L.J. Bols
2/N'humberland Fus.	2/Cheshire	12/London (TF)
1/Suffolk	1/Welch	1/Monmouthshire (TF)

85 Brigade: Brigadier General A.J. Chapman
2/Buffs	2/E. Surrey	8/Middlesex (TF)
3/Royal Fus.	3/Middlesex	

R.F.A. Brigades

III. (18, 22, 62, 365 Btys)   CXLVI. (75, 149, 366, 367 Btys).

XXXI .(69, 100, 103, 118 Btys.) (All four gun batteries)

VII. (How.) (37 & 65 Btys.)

Field Coys. R.E.: 38, 1/Northumbrian (TF)

Mtd. Troops: B Sqdn. Surrey Yeo.   Cyclist Coy

50th (1/NORTHUMBRIAN) DIVISION (TF): Major General Sir W.F.L. Lindsay

149 Brigade (1/Northumbrian): Brigadier General J.F. Riddell
4/Northumberland Fus.   6/Northumberland Fus.
5/Northumberland Fus.   7/Northumberland Fus.

150 Brigade (1/York & Durham): Brigadier General J.E. Bush
4/E. Yorkshire   5/Green Howards
4/Green Howards   5/Durham LI

151 Brigade (1/Durham L.I.): Brigadier General H. Martin
6/Durham LI   8/Durham LI
7/Durham LI   9/Durham LI

R.F.A. Brigades
I. Northumbrian   II. Northumbrian (All 15-pdr Brigades)
III. Northumbrian   IV. Northumbrian (5-in Hows)

Field Coy. R.E.: 2/Northumbrian

Mtd. Troops: A Sqdn. Yorks. Hussars. Cyclist Coy.

1st CANADIAN DIVISION: Lieutenant General E.A.H. Alderson

1 Canadian Brigade: Brigadier General M.S. Mercer
1st Bn.(Western Ontario Regt.)   3rd Bn.(Toronto Regt.)
2nd Bn.(Western Ontario Regt.)   4th Bn.

2 Canadian Brigade: Brigadier General A.W. Currie
5th Bn.(Western Cavalry)   8th Bn.(Winnipeg Rifles)
7th Bn.(1st Brit. Columbia Regt.)   10th Bn.(10th Canadians)

3 Canadian Brigade: Brigadier General R.E.W. Turner, VC
13th Bn.(R. Highlanders of Canada) 15th Bn.(48th Highlanders)
14th Bn.(R. Montreal Regt.)   16th Bn.(Canadian Scottish)

Canadian F.A. Brigades

I. (1, 2, 3, 4 Btys)   II. (5, 6, 7, 8 Btys)
II. (9, 10, 11, 12 Btys) (All 4 gun batteries)

R.F.A.Brigade: CXVIII. (How.) 458 & 459 Btys.

Canadian Field Coys: 1, 2, 3.

Mtd. Troops: Service Sqdn. 19th Alberta Dragoons. Cyclist Coy.

LAHORE DIVISION: Major General H.D'U. Keary

Ferozepore Brigade: Brigadier General R.G. Egerton
    Connaught Rangers   57th Wilde's Rifles   4/London (TF)
    9th Bhopal Inf.   129th Baluchis

Jullundur Brigade: Brigadier General E.P. Strickland
    1/Manchester   47th Sikhs   4/Suffolks (TF)
    40th Pathans   59th Scinde Rifles

Sirhind Brigade: Brigadier General W.G. Walker, VC
    1/Highland LI   1/1st Gurkhas   4/King's (SR)
    15th Sikhs   1/4th Gurkhas

R.F.A. Brigades
    V. (64, 73, 81 Btys.)   XVIII. (59, 93, 94 Btys.)
    XI. (83, 84, 85 Btys.)   XLIII. (How.) 40 & 57 Btys.

Engineers: 20 & 21 Coys. 3rd Sappers & Miners

Pioneers: 34th Sikh Pioneers

Mtd. Troops: 15th Lancers

1st CAVALRY DIVISION: Major General H. de B. de Lisle

1 Cavalry Brigade: Brigadier General C.J. Briggs
    Queen's Bays   5/Dragoon Guards   11/Hussars

2 Cavalry Brigade: Brigadier General R.L. Mullens
    4/Dragoon Guards   9/Lancers   18 Hussars

9 Cavalry Brigade: Brigadier General W.H. Greenly
    15/Hussars   19/Hussars

R.H.A. Brigade: VII. (H.I & Warwickshire (T.F.) Btys.)

Field Sqdn. R.E.: No.1.

2nd CAVALRY DIVISION:
Major General C.T.McM. Kavanagh

3 Cavalry Brigade: Brigadier General J. Vaughan
    4/Hussars   5/Lancers   16/Lancers

4 Cavalry Brigade: Brigadier General Hon. C.E. Bingham
    6/Dragoon Guards   3/Hussars   Oxfordshire Hussars (Yeo.)

5 Cavalry Brigade: Brigadier General Sir P.W. Chetwode
    R. Scots Greys.   12/Lancers.   20/Hussars.

R.H.A. Brigade: III. (D, E, J Btys.)   *Field Sqdn. R.E.:* No.2

3rd CAVALRY DIVISION: Major General Hon J.H.G. Byng

6 Cavalry Brigade: Brigadier General D. Campbell
   3/Dragoon Guards   1/Royal Dragoons   N. Somerset Yeo.

7 Cavalry Brigade: Brigadier General A.A. Kennedy
   1/Life Guards   2/Life Guards   Leicester Yeo.

8 Cavalry Brigade: Brigadier General C.B. Bulkeley-Johnson
   R/Horse Guards   10/Hussars   Essex Yeo.

R.H.A. Brigade: XV. (C, K, G Btys.)   *Field Sqdn. R.E.:* No. 3.

French Order of Battle
(April 1915)
(Détachement D'Armée De Belgique)

18th Division: General Lefèvre (Justinien)
   35 Brigade: 32nd and 66th Infantry Regiments
   36 Brigade;:77th and 135th Infantry Regiments
   One Squadron. 3 groups of artillery (75-mm)

45th Division: General Quiquandon
   90 Brigade: 2nd *bis Zouaves de marche*;
   1st *Tirailleurs de marche*; 1st & 2nd *Battalions D'Afrique*
   91 Brigade: 7th *Zouaves de marche*; 3rd *bis Zouaves de marche*.
   One Squadron. 3 groups of artillery (75-mm)

152nd Division: General Joppé
   304 Brigade: 268th and 290th Infantry Regiments
   4 Moroccan Brigade: 1st Moroccan Infantry;
   8th *Tirailleurs de marche*.
   Two Squadrons. 2 groups of artillery (75-mm)

152rd Division: General Deligny
   306 Brigade: 418th Infantry Regiment
   2nd and 4th Battlions *Chasseurs à pied*.
   3 Moroccan Brigade: 1st *mixte Zouaves et Tirailleurs*
   9th *Zouaves de marche*
   Two Squadrons. 2 groups of artillery of 90-mm and
   1 group (2 batteries) of 95-mm

87th Territorial Division: General Roy
   173 Brigade: 73rd and 74th Territorial Regiments
   174 Brigade: 76th, 79th and 80th Territorial Regiments
   186 Brigade: 100th and 102nd Territorial Regiments
   Two Squadrons. 2 groups of artillery (90-mm)

German Order of Battle:
Hill 60 and the Battles of Ypres 1915.

(part of Fourth Army)

Commander: General Duke Albrecht von Württemberg.

Chief of Staff: Major-General Ilse.

XV Corps: (General von Deimling)
30th Division
60 Brigade: 99th and 143rd Regiments
85 Brigade: 105th and 136th Regiments

39th Division
61 Brigade: 126th and 132nd Regiments
82 Brigade: 171st and 172nd Regiments

XXII Reserve Corps (part) (General von Falkenhayn)
43rd Reserve Division
85 Reserve Brigade: 210th and 202nd Reserve Regiments
86 Reserve Brigade: 203rd and 204th Reserve Regiments
15th Reserve *Jäger* Battalion

44th Reserve Division
207th Reserve Regiment (of 88 Reserve Brigade) only

XXIII Reserve Corps (General von Rathen)
45th Reserve Division
89 Reserve Brigade: 209th and 212th Reserve Regiments
90 Reserve Brigade: 210th and 211th Reserve Regiments
17th Reserve *Jäger* Battalion

46th Reserve Division
91 Reserve Brigade: 213th and 214th Reserve Regiments
92 Reserve Brigade: 215th and 216th Reserve Regiments
18th Reserve Battalion

XXVI Reserve Corps (General von Hügel)
51st Reserve Division
101 Reserve Brigade: 233rd and 234th Reserve Regiments
102 Reserve Brigade: 235th and 236th Reserve Regiments
23rd Reserve *Jäger* Battalion

52nd Reserve Division
103 Reserve Brigade: 237th and 238th Reserve Regiments
104 Reserve Brigade: 239th and 240th Reserve Regiments
24th Reserve *Jäger* Battalion

XXVII Reserve Corps (General von Carlowitz)
53rd Reserve Division (Saxon)
105 Reserve Brigade: 241st and 242nd Reserve Regiments
106 Reserve Brigade: 243rd and 244th Reserve Regiments

25th Reserve *Jäger* Battalion

54th Reserve Division (Württemberg)
107 Reserve Brigade: 245th and 246th Reserve Regiments
108 Reserve Brigade: 247th and 248th Reserve Regiments
28th Reserve *Jäger* Battalion

37 Landwehr Brigade: (attached to XXVI Reserve Corps)
73rd and 74th *Landwehr* Regiments

38 Landwehr Brigade: (attached to the XXVII Reserve Corps)
77th and 78th *Landwehr* Regiments

2 Reserve *Ersatz* Brigade: (Attached to the XXVI Reserve Corps)
3rd and 4th Reserve *Ersatz* Regiments

2 Marine Brigade
2nd Marine Regiment only

4 Marine Brigade
4th and 5th *Matrosen* Regiments

Note: Only the infantry units are given in the German Order of Battle shown here.

APPENDIX IV

SECOND ARMY CORRESPONDENCE

The following Operation Orders and letters are those that relate to the main events of the Second Battle of Ypres.

Second Army   O.A.M. 950

Evidently not much reliance can be placed on the two French Divisions on your left. We do not know where the division ordered from Arras is at the present, but it ought to be in action by noon somewhere N.E. of Poperinghe. We are enquiring.

It is of course of the first importance that our left should not be turned, and your dispositions should be such as to safeguard the left. The Chief is not fully aware of your dispositions or of the details of the situation, but he considers all of the cavalry should be used north of the line Ypres – Poperinghe, supported by the two brigades from the 4th Division. This will enable you to use the Northumbrians E. of the Canal. The Chief thinks that vigorous action E. of the Canal will be the best means of checking the enemy's advance from the line Lizerne – Boesinghe.

The Lahore Division is being ordered to proceed in the direction of Poperinghe. Further information regarding it will be sent to you later.

9.30 a.m.   W.R. ROBERTSON
24.4.15.   Lieut. General C.G.S.

Priority
To Second Army
O.A. 959. 24th April
    Every effort must be made at once to restore and hold line about St. Julien or situation of 28th Division will be jeopardised. Am sending General Staff officer to explain Chief's views. Acknowledge.

F. Maurice
Br. General, G.S.

From G.H.Q.
    4.15 p.m.

OPERATION ORDER NO. 10
by
LIEUT. GENERAL E.A.H. ALDERSON, C.B.
Commanding Canadian Division

24th April 1915

1. By orders of the Corps commander a strong counter-attack will be made early to-morrow morning in a general direction of St. Julien with the object of driving the enemy back as far north as possible and thus securing the left flank of the 28th Division.
2. Br. General Hull commanding the 10th Brigade will be in charge of this counter-attack.
3. The following troops will be placed at the disposal of Br. General Hull for this purpose, viz.:

    10th Infantry Brigade,   York & Durham Brigade
    K.O.Y.L.I. and Queen Victoria's Rifles of the 13th Brigade.
    1st Suffolks and 12th London Regiment of the 28th Division, 4th
        Canadian Battalion and one battalion of the 27th Division.

4. The O's C. these units will report for instruction at 9 p.m. to-night to General Hull, whose Hqrs. will be at the road junction in I1c and d up to midnight.
5. The Northumberland Brigade and the Durham Light Infantry Brigade of the Northumbrian Division, forming the Corps reserve and now at Potijze, can be called upon for support by Gen. Hull.
6. The first objectives of the attack will be Fortuin (if occupied by the enemy), St. Julien and the wood in C10 and 11. After these points have been gained, General Hull will advance astride of the St.Julien-Poelcappelle road and drive back the enemy as far north as possible. All units holding the front line of trenches will follow up the attack and help to consolidate the ground gained.
7. The C.R.A. Canadian Division will arrange for artillery support of the counter attack and get into touch with the C.R.A.'s of the 27th and 28th Divisions regarding all possible artillery support from these Divisions.
8. The counter-attack will be launched at 3.30 a.m.
9. Divisional hqrs. will remain at the Chateau de Trois Tours near Brielen.

C.F. ROMER
Colonel,

8 p.m.   General Staff.

To: Eleventh Infantry Brigade, Canadian Division.
        Eighty-third Infantry Brigade
        Eighty-fourth Infantry Brigade
        Eighty-fifth Infantry Brigade
G.L.   Twenty-fifth

1. Eleventh Infantry Brigade has been placed under orders of G.O.C. 28th Division. This brigade will move so as to reach Fortuin not later than 9 p.m. tonight marching via road running north in square H.12.c – north side of Ypres – St. Jean – Wieltje – Fortuin. One platoon divisional cyclists has been ordered to report to eleventh infantry brigade at five-thirty p.m. and will remain attached to the brigade. This platoon will provide a guide for the road to Fortuin. Canadian division report present line runs from original trenches in D.2.d.10.0 – D.8.b.9.9 .- D.8.a.0.7. – thence straight to Fortuin – thence due west. Brigadier commanding eleventh infantry brigade will be responsible for this line from original trenches on the right to the road running south east in square C.18.d, and will if possible occupy it tonight and hold it strongly as security of the whole trench line southwards depends on the enemy being kept well to the north of the line. If the line named cannot be occupied then a new line will be dug in best position north of the Fortuin road in touch with the original trench line on the right and tenth infantry brigade on the left. The line will be immediately reconnoitred and reorganised. Brigadier commanding eleventh brigade will assume command of all troops at present holding or supporting this line – these include second Canadian brigade one battalion first Canadian brigade three battalions Durham Light Infantry brigade two battalions eighty-fourth infantry brigade besides various companies entrenched on south side of the Fortuin road. As soon as the situation permits all detached units will be withdrawn and collected in the rear of the line these units will be returned to the brigades to which they belong if they belong to the twenty-seventh twenty-eighth or Canadian divisions with the exception of the second Canadian brigade which will remain under orders of the eleventh infantry brigade till such time as it can be dispensed with. Such Territorial units as can be spared will be sent to Potijze to report to twenty-seventh division and eleventh brigade will report to twenty-eighth division stating what units are sent back. Brigadier commanding eleventh infantry brigade will report situation every three hours through eighty-fifth infantry brigade headquarters commencing at 9 p.m. Position of eleventh infantry brigade headquarters will be given in first report. Guides will be provided at second Canadian brigade headquarters C.27.d.7.6.

                                        Loch, Lt. Col

From Twenty-eighth Division
Time 6.25 p.m.

2nd ARMY OPERATION ORDER NO.8

Headquarters, 2nd Army,
26th April, 1915.

1. The present line of V Corps runs from where the original line of trenches crossed square D.9.(about Gravenstafel) by the north of Fortuin, to the Farm in C.15.c (Turco Farm), thence the French line continues by the road in C.7.c (N.N.W. to Canal) and along the West bank of the Canal to the West of Lizerne.

2. The French troops, strongly reinforced, are attacking the Germans on their front, with their right on the Ypres-Langemark road.

3. That portion of the 2nd Army facing North will assume the offensive, in conjunction with the French, in order to drive the enemy back from the position he now occupies.

4. For this purpose the Lahore Division will move today from about Ouderdom via Vlamertinghe and Ypres to an area North of Wieltje – St. Jean where it will deploy (with its left flank on the Ypres – Langemark road). Thence it will move to the line occupied by the V Corps, and echeloned slightly to the rear of the French advance will attack the enemy on a front of 1,000 yards, driving him back on Langemark. North of our present line the Ypres – Langemark road is allotted to the French.

5. Such artillery as is necessary for close support will accompany the Infantry. The remainder will be disposed on the West bank of the Canal under the general control of the V Corps.

The arrangements for the advance will be made by the V Corps and the Lahore Division acting in direct communication, and will be timed so that the attack can commence at 2 p.m. As many bridges as possible over the Canal at Ypres will be allotted to the Lahore Division.

6. The V Corps will co-operate in the attack, directing its main efforts on the right of the Lahore Division, and will arrange for the co-ordination of the necessary artillery bombardment and support.

7. Cavalry Corps, less on Division and Artillery, will remain in Army Reserve in their present positions, ready to move at half an hour's notice after 2 p.m.

8. An Army Report Centre will open at 12 noon near the Station in the Rue d'Ypres Poperinghe.

G.F. Milne
Major-General,
General Staff, II Army

Issued at 2.15 a.m.

V Corps

2nd Army
G444

Reference paragraph 6, Operation Order No.8 of 26th instant, it is considered advisable that the artillery at present in position should be employed in the support of the counter attack, and the Army Commander desires that the Artillery Adviser on your Staff should co-ordinate the work of the various

335

Artillery Commands. He should arrange, in conjunction with G.O.C., Lahore Division, for the preliminary bombardment of the enemy's positions and the subsequent artillery support, paying special attention to the wood in C.10 (d) and C.11 (c) from which the advance can be enfiladed.

G.F. Milne
M.G.G.S.
2nd Army

26th April, 1915.

V CORPS OPERATION ORDER NO 12

V Corps H.Q.
26.4.15

1. The French troops strongly reinforced are attacking the Germans on their front with their right on the Ypres – Langemark road.

The Lahore Division to attack this afternoon on the right of the French.

2. The V Corps will co-operate in the attack.

3. The Lahore Division is assembling as follows:

Jullundur Brigade on the right and

Ferozepore Brigade on the left assemble about Wieltje and St. Jean and will be deployed ready to begin an advance by 1.20 p.m. from an east and west line from Farm in C.28.a (Wieltje Farm) to Ypres – Langemark road.

The Sirhind Brigade will be in reserve about Potijze.

4. At 1.20 p.m. an artillery bombardment will begin and continue till 2 p.m. During this time the two brigades of the Lahore Division will advance.

At 2 p.m. rapid fire will begin and continue till 2.5 p.m. when the assault will take place on the German line between the wood on C.10.d (Kitchener's Wood) and the Ypres – Langemark road.

5. The Canadian Division will co-operate by pushing forward on the right of the Lahore Division in accordance with special instructions which have been given to G.O.C. Canadian Division.

The 27th and 28th Divisions will engage the enemy in their front with fire.

6. The artillery of all divisions not required on Divisional fronts will co-operate under instructions which have been issued separately.

7. Reports to Chateau H.11.a (Goldfish Chateau) after 1 p.m.

H.S. Jeudwine
B.G., G.S.
V Corps

Issued at 10.30 a.m.

OPERATION ORDER NO.10
BY
LIEUT. GENERAL E.A.H. ALDERSON, C.B.
Commanding Canadian Division.

26th April, 1915.

1. French troops strongly reinforced are attacking with their right on the Ypres – Langemark road. The Lahore Division which will be deployed by 1.20 p.m.

from the farm in C.28.a (Wieltje Farm) to Ypres – Langemark road. Will attack with its right on the wood in C.10.d (Kitchener's Wood). The V Corps will co-operate in the attack.

2. An artillery bombardment will begin at 1.20 p.m. and be continued until 2 p.m. during which time the Lahore Division will advance. At 2 p.m. rapid fire will begin and continue until 2.05 p.m., after which the assault will take place.

3. A battalion of the 10th Brigade will advance in co-operation with the Lahore Division between wood in C.10.d (Kitchener's Wood) and the Wieltje – St. Julien road. The Northumbrian Brigade will attack St. Julien and advance astride the Wieltje – St. Julien road at the same time as the Lahore Division moved forward.

4. The troops holding the front line of the Canadian Division will assist the attack by fire.

5. Colonel Geddes will move the three battalions now in reserve at St. Jean to the G.H.Q. 2nd Line in C. 23.c and 29.a (that is covering Wieltje) as soon as the Northumbrian Brigade clears the ground.

6. The 3rd Canadian Infantry Brigade will move to position south of Wieltje and form the divisional reserve as soon as the Lahore Division commences its advance.

7. The artillery of the Canadian Division will support the attack of the battalion of the 10th Brigade and Northumbrian Brigade by the heaviest possible artillery fire on the German position between the wood in C.10.d (Kitchener's Wood) and St. Julien inclusive.

8. Report to Chateau des Trois Tours

C.F. Romer, Colonel, G.S.

Issued at 12.30 p.m.

Advanced Headquarters, 2nd Army
27th April, 1915

My dear Robertson,

In order to put the situation before the Commander-in-Chief, I propose to enter into a certain amount of detail.

You will remember that I told Colonel Montgomery the night before last, after seeing General Putz's orders, that he was only putting a small proportion of his troops (and those at different points) to the actual attack, I did not antic-ipate any great results. You know what happened – the French right instead of gaining ground lost it, and the left of the Lahore Division, the Manchesters, did very well and took some enemy trenches and held them for a considerable time.

The Northumberland Brigade to their right made a very fine attack on St. Julien and got into it but were unable to remain there.

Away to the right, between St. Julien and our old trenches about square D10, there was a good deal of fighting but with fairly satisfactory results – the Germans eventually retiring.

The enemy losses are very heavy. Artillery observing officers claim to have mown them down over and over again during the day. At times the fighting appears to have been heavy, and our casualties are by no means slight.

I enclose you on a separate paper the description of the line the troops are on at this moment. I saw General Putz last night about today's operations, and he told me he intended to resume the offensive with very great vigour. I saw his orders, in which he claims to have captured Het Sas, but on my asking him what he meant he said the houses of that place which are to the west of the canal. He told me also that the success at Lizerne had been practically nil – in fact, that the Germans were still in possession of the village or were last night.

From General Putz's orders for today, he is sending one brigade to cross the river east of Brielen to carry forward the troops on the east of the canal in the direction of Pilckem, and he assured me that this brigade was going to be pushed in with great vigour.

It was not till afterwards that I noticed that, to form his own reserve, he is withdrawing two battalions from the east of the canal and another two battalions from the front line in the same part to be used as reserve on that bank of the river, so the net result of his orders is to send over six fresh battalions to the fighting line and to withdraw four which have already been employed.

I have lately received General Joppé's orders. He is the General commanding the attack towards Pilckem on the east of the canal, and I was horrified to see that he, instead of using the whole of this brigade across the canal for this offensive, is leaving one regiment back at Brielen, and only putting the other regiment across the canal to attack – so the net result of these latter orders with regard to the strength of the troops on the east of the canal for the fresh offensive is the addition of one battalion.

I need hardly say that I at once represented the matter pretty strongly to General Putz, but I want the Chief to know this as I do not think that he must expect that the French are going to do anything very great – in fact, although I have ordered the Lahore Division to co-operate when the French attack at 1.15 p.m., I am pretty sure that our line tonight will not be in advance of where it is at the present moment.

I fear the Lahore Division have had very heavy casualties, and so they tell me have the Northumbrians, and I am doubtful if it is worth losing any more men to regain this French ground unless the French do something really big.

Now, if you look at the map, you will see that the line the French and ourselves are now on allows the Germans to approach so close with their guns that the area to the east of Ypres will be very difficult to hold, chiefly because the roads approaching it from the west are swept by shell fire, and were all yesterday, and are being today. Again they are now able to shell this place, Poperinghe, and have done it for the last three days; all day yesterday at intervals there were shells close to my Report Centre and splinters of one struck the house opposite in the middle of the day, and splinters of another actually struck the house itself about midnight – in other words they will soon render this place unhealthy.

If the French are not to make a big push, the only line we can hold permanently and have a fair chance of keeping supplied, would be the G.H.Q.

line passing just east of Wieltje and Potijze with a curved switch which is being prepared through Hooge, the centres of squares I 18.d and I.24.b. and d., to join on to our present line about a thousand yards north-east of Hill 60.

This, of course, means the surrendering of a great deal of trench line, but any intermediate line, short of that, will be extremely difficult to hold, owing to the loss of the ridge to the east of Zonnebeke, which any withdrawal must entail.

I think it right to put these views before the Chief, but at the same time to make it clear that, although I am preparing for the worst, I do not think we have arrived at the time when it is necessary to adopt these measures. In any case a withdrawal to that line in one fell swoop would be almost impossible on account of the enormous amount of guns and paraphernalia which will have to be with-drawn first, and therefore, if withdrawal becomes necessary, the first contraction would be, starting from the left, "our present line as far as the spot where the Haanebeke stream crosses the road at the junction of squares D.7. and D.13. thence along the subsidiary line which is already prepared, as far as the South-East corner of square J.2., from whence a switch has been prepared into our old line on the east side of J.14.b, i.e. just excluding the Polygone *(sic)* Wood". I intend tonight if nothing special happens to re-organize the new front and to withdraw superfluous troops West of Ypres.

I always have to contemplate the possibility of the Germans gaining ground west of Lizerne, and this, of course, would make the situation more impossible – in fact, it all comes down to this, that unless the French do something really vigorous the situation might become such as to make it impossible for us to hold any line east of Ypres.

It is very difficult to put a subject such as this in a letter without appearing pessimistic – I am not in the least, but as an Army Commander I have of course to provide for every eventuality and I think it right to let the Chief know what is running in my mind.

More British troops, of course, could restore the situation – but this I consider to be out of the question, as it would interfere with a big offensive else-where which is after all the crux of the situation and will do more to relieve the situation than anything else.

Since writing above, our Cavalry report that the French actually took the whole of Lizerne last night capturing 120 Germans, and are now attacking the bridgehead covering the bridge leading over the canal to Steenstraat.

General Putz has answered my protest and has ordered General Joppé to put the whole of the fresh brigade and not to leave one Regiment of it in reserve at Brielen. The attack is to commence at 1.15 p.m. and we are to assist with heavy artillery fire, and the Lahore Division is only to advance if they see the French troops getting on.

Our Cavalry is where it was last night, one division west of Lizerne, one dismounted in reserve holding G.H.Q. trenches east of Ypres, one dismounted in huts at Vlamertinge.

I am still at my Advanced Headquarters in Poperinghe. Whether I remain here tonight again I do not know, the main advantage of my being here is my close touch with general Putz and my being able to impress my views upon him.

Yours sincerely

H.L. Smith-Dorrien

Telephoned Message

(The record is in the writing of the C.G.S. Lieut. Gen. Sir W.R. Robertson)
2.15 p.m. 27th April.

Chief does not regard situation nearly so unfavourable as your letter represents. He thinks you have abundance of troops and especially notes the large reserves you have. He wishes you to act vigorously with the full means available in co-operating with and assisting the French attack having due regard to his previous instructions that the combined attack should be simultaneous. The French possession of Lizerne and general situation on Canal seems to remove anxiety as to your left flank. Letter follows by Staff Officer.

Advanced Second Army
V Corps
O.A. 976   27th (April)

Chief directs you to hand over forthwith to General Plumer the command of all troops engaged in the present operations about Ypres. You should lend General Plumer your Brigadier General General Staff and such other officers of the various branches of your staff as he may require. General Plumer should send all reports direct to G.H.Q. from which he will receive his orders. Acknowledge. Addressed Second Army repeated V Corps.

R. Hutchinson, Major G.S.

From G.H.Q.
4.35 p.m.

APPENDIX V

The Withdrawal to the Frezenberg Line

The following documents give the preparatory discussions and arrangements for the withdrawal of the British Army from the eastern tip of the Ypres salient in May 1915. The idea of withdrawal was not popular with Sir John French or his French commander, General Ferdinand Foch, indeed it was one of the factors that speeded up General Smith-Dorrien being removed from his command. The French clearly did not like the idea, as is shown by Foch's note to Sir John French. However, by shortening the line at a critical time it is likely that many lives were saved.

The final document refers to the Canadian Division, however by the time the withdrawal was to take place the Canadians were in reserve, their place in the front line taken by three brigades of the 4th Division, to whom the instructions were then applied.

Lieut.-General Sir H. Plumer, K.C.B.   O.A. 983.

1. With reference to the failure of the French attack to-day and to the Chief's instructions given you by Brig. General Maurice, the Chief wishes you to consolidate the line you now hold so as to render it more secure against attack.
2. You are also requested to prepare a line east of Ypres joining up with the line now held north and south of that place ready for occupation if and when it becomes advisable to withdraw from the present salient. Please report early as to the position of the line you select for this purpose. It should be such as to avoid withdrawal from Hill 60. The necessary instructions, if any, will be sent by G.H.Q. to Second Corps on receipt of your report.

G.H.Q.   F. Maurice, B.G., G.S.,
27/4/15   for Lieutenant-General,
                                          Chief of General Staff

General adjoint to the Commander-in-Chief.

Headquarters
28th April 1915

Groupe Provisoire du Nord

NOTE

FOR THE FIELD MARSHAL COMMANDER-IN-CHIEF
OF THE BRITISH FORCES

1. In continuation of the interview of this morning, 28th April 1915, General Foch has the honour to put in writing for the Field Marshal the arguments which he developed verbally.

2. The Field Marshal indicated to General Foch the necessity in which he might find himself to retire to the line: Fortuin, Frezenberg, the Ypres-Menin road between Hooge and Veldhoek, old front Hill 60, for the reasons that

(a) the British troops established east of this line are very tired, have suffered heavily and are difficult to supply;

(b) the fighting around Ypres is a secondary matter in comparison to the scheme further south. It should absorb neither troops or resources.

3. Without denying the value of these arguments General Foch has the honour to observe:

(a) the new position selected for the British Army is at the foot of the ridges, and will be more difficult to hold than the present one on the crest.

(b) the enemy, master of the abandoned crest, will be able to attack under favourable conditions; he will be able to bring his artillery nearer to Ypres from the east and thus shell from a new direction that junction of communication.

(c) As long as the enemy occupies the Langemarck region and further south he holds under his guns Ypres, Vlamertinghe, Poperinghe, the British line of supply. Thus, the supply of troops facing east will remain difficult. To sum up, the supply can only be assured by the recapture by the Allies of the Langemarck region and not by a simple retirement.

(d) If we retire voluntarily to the line Fortuin-Hill 60 it may be anticipated that we shall be driven further back on Ypres and the Canal. The withdrawal will be over ground where the positions are less and less strong.

(e) The withdrawal of the present line to the line Fortuin-Hill 60 will be a confession of impotence, it will simply invite a very strong German effort. Besides the important tactical considerations already enumerated, the moral ascendance will pass to the Germans. A new battle of Ypres will be provoked and that under conditions materially and morally worse than those under which the former was fought.

(f) Even if the battle further south, towards Neuve Chapelle-Arras ought to be considered as more fertile in strategic results and more important, the preparation for it by a retirement is not to be thought of: for this would be the beginning of a set-back whose extent might well become very large.

342

4. The conclusions to be drawn from the above in the eyes of General Foch are:

(a) The retirement should not be ordered for the moment; it should be forbidden. If the enemy infantry does not attack in the region under consideration it should not be provoked to one by a retreat. His artillery alone is in action; its effects can be reduced by defensive arrangements.

(b) It is absolutely necessary for the Allied Armies to maintain their present attitude: the attack towards Langemark; to make fresh efforts to recover the ground lost there, the possession of which alone permits the holding of Ypres and its environs.

5. The 28th April may not be important but the 29th, thanks to the arrival of a strong force of heavy artillery, will without doubt give results if the British Army co-operates fully with the French effort.

6. General Foch in consequence has the honour to request the Field Marshal not to consider any further the retirement from the line on account of the serious consequences which would ensue, but to be good enough to keep to his present intention, and to support the French offensive to retake the Langemarck region at all costs, beginning at noon on the 29th.

F. FOCH

G.H.Q.

1. I beg to report that in accordance with instructions contained in telegram 0.A.976, dated 27th inst., I assumed command of the troops in the Ypres area last night, 27th inst.

2. I have received G.H.Q. letter 983 (Secret) dated 27th inst. with reference to it:

3. I have already given orders to G.O.C. Divisions to consolidate and strengthen the line we now hold.

4. Major Hutchinson has on his map the rough line I propose to occupy when it becomes advisable to withdraw from the present salient.

5. I note that para.3 of this letter [not included above but which refers to the planning for a French attack and which was modified as the battle progressed] has been modified by telegram O.A. 964 dated 28th inst. I have given instructions that the subsidiary French attack is to be supported by the Artillery and Infantry fire of the troops under the command of the G.O.C. Lahore, Canadian and 28th Divisions.

6. All the units which have been engaged have suffered heavy losses and have had repeated and continuous calls upon them, and in my opinion the support

I have indicated is all they should be called upon to give until the French have made appreciable progress and gained some material ground.

Further local attacks which were necessary in the first instance to keep back the enemy and retain as much ground as possible, will now only cause further heavy losses without affecting any material improvement in the general situation.

7. With regard to the situation generally, and especially in the retirement indicated in para.2 of G.H.Q. letter 983 of the 27th inst., I consider that:

(1) The present line we are now holding cannot be held permanently.

(2) Unless the French regain practically the whole of their trenches, the situation will not be improved materially from our point of view, without the employment of a very large force.

(3) If the retirement is to be carried out the longer it is delayed the more difficult and costly it will be.

(4) The French should be given a certain time to regain their trenches, and then we should begin our retirement on the second line I have referred to.

(5) It will take probably four nights to complete the retirement.

(6) If and when the retirement is carried out, there must be a complete understanding with the French as to their point of junction with us, and a definite undertaking on their part to hold and retain the section of the ground East of the Canal they now occupy.

HERBERT PLUMER, Lieut-General,
28th April 1915.   Commanding Plumer's Force.

PREPARATORY ORDER FOR WITHDRAWAL
FROM TIP OF SALIENT

1. In case it should be considered necessary to shorten our present line east of Ypres, the following is a general outline of the withdrawal:

(a) The north and north-east fronts will be maintained as long as possible unchanged, the movement of artillery commencing from the south and south-east.

(b) A reserve will be kept about Potijze throughout.

(c) Arrangements will be made so that during the movement flank protection by artillery posted west of the canal will be available.

2. During the withdrawal the following formations will be moved west of Ypres in the order stated

(a) Lahore Division;

(b) Northumbrian Division;

(c) 2nd Cavalry Division.

3. The line to be finally occupied will be as follows:

From the present trench line in I.30.b (in front of Armagh Wood) due north to Hooge Chateau, I.18.b., thence north-west to G.H.Q. line about C.29.a.c. (East of Wieltje) along G.H.Q. line to farm in C.22.b., (Mouse Trap Farm)

344

and thence along present British and French line.

A tracing of this line, which has been reconstructed during the last few days, is attached.

4. The line will be held, in order from south to north, by the following divisions:
   (a) 27th Division;
   (b) 28th Division;
   (c) Canadian Division.

5. The allotment of the new line will be as follows:

27th Division: From left of II Corps in I.30.d. (in front of Armagh Wood) to the level crossing in I.6.c. (1,000 yards south-west of Frezenberg) (exclusive of railway line).

28th Division: From the level crossing in I.6.c. (inclusive of railway line) to farm in C.22.b. (exclusive).

Canadian Division: From farm in C.22.b. (inclusive) to French right at farm in C.15.c. (Turco Farm) (exclusive).

6. The allotment of roads for carrying out this move will be as follows:

27th Division: All roads to the south and exclusive of road running west from crossroads Westhoek (J.7.b.).

28th Division: The above road (inclusive) and all roads up to and including the Passchendaele-Ypres road, but that part of the road from Wieltje (C.22.b.) to Ypres will be common to both 28th and Canadian Divisions under the control of the 28th Division.

Canadian Division: St. Julien-Wieltje road, with part use of that portion from Wieltje to Ypres and all roads and bridges west of it, excepting road leading to No.4 Bridge (C.25.a.) (Bridge east of the northern end of Brielen). This last road only to be used by arrangement with the French.

7. It is proposed, if the tactical situation permits, to carry out the withdrawal in four nights. In view of the fact that the movement will probably commence to-night, all preparations and plans should be considered.

8. The final withdrawal from the present trench line to the one detailed above in paragraph 3 will take place in one night. Arrangements will be made by divisions to make use of the "Subsidiary Line", in order to ensure co-operation as regards timing. The advisability of leaving a strong outpost line on the present front line should be seriously considered.

9. Detailed orders will be issued day by day.

G. F. MILNE, Major-General,
C.G.S. Plumer's Force

29th April 1915
9.30 a.m.

27th Division
28th Division
Canadian Division

1. In order to shorten the line now held to the East of Ypres, 27th 28th and Canadian Divisions will withdraw on the night 3rd/4th May to a line which has been prepared connecting the Subsidiary Line about Westhoek through Frezenberg with the fortified farm in C.22.b.7.7 (Mouse Trap Farm).On the right, this line connects by means of the Subsidiary Line with the present right of the trench line of the 27th Division.

2. This line will be held as follows:
From the right to the track (exclusive) just west of Westhoek by the 27th Division.
From the above track (inclusive) to the fortified farm in C.22.b. (Mouse Trap Farm) (exclusive) by the 28th Division.
From the above farm (inclusive) to farm in C.15.c. (Turco Farm) (exclusive) by the first Canadian Division.
From this farm (inclusive) North by the French.

3. Roads and tracks will be available as under:
27th Division and attached troops
Cross roads J.1.d.7.2. (500 yards N.W. of Westhoek) – Camp I.10.c. (near White Chateau) – Menin Gate – Grand Place Rue de Stuers – Railway Station – Kruisstraat – Groenen Jager and roads and tracks south of this.
28th Division and attached troops.
Roads and tracks North of the above as far as and including Fortuin-Wieltje-La Brique-No.2 bridge, I.1.b. (S.W. of La Brique) – road junction I.1.c. 10.8. (due West to Boesinghe road) – road junction B.29.d.9.1. (400 yards S.E. of Brielen) – Vlamertinghe road; but the Canadian Division to have joint use of this road under the control of the 28th Division. (N.B. This is a new road not shown on maps)
Canadian Division
Road as above under the control of 28th Division and No.3 (East of Brielen) bridge and roads approaching it. Also road running parallel to canal on west bank as far north as and including road on west bank from No.4 bridge to Brielen.

4. Artillery will begin withdrawal at 8.30 p.m.

5. The withdrawal of the Infantry of 27th Division and 28th Division will take place in three successive parties, viz.:
First parties – Half the troops in the trench line.
Second parties – Half the remainder.
Third parties – The troops still remaining followed by rear parties as required.

346

(a) First parties

At 9 p.m. half the Infantry of 28th Division will begin to withdraw; it will reach the following line by 10 p.m.:

North-western corner of Polygon Wood thence by Subsidiary Line to where the latter trench meets the present trench line about D.20.b.8.8. (Zonnebeke-Keerselare road).

Half the Infantry of 27th Division manning trenches in South face of Polygon Wood will be withdrawn in conjunction with right of 28th Division so as to reach the North-western corner of Polygon Wood at 10 p.m. On this line there will be a halt till 10.30 p.m. during which time any connection which has been lost will be regained along the whole of this line and maintained during the remainder of the withdrawal.

At 10.30 p.m. the withdrawal will be continued by both 27th and 28th Divisions, the former withdrawing detachments in succession from the right, but leaving half the troops to hold the trenches.

No troops will be withdrawn from the Canadian Division line East of farm C.22.b. (Mouse Trap Farm) at this date.

(b) Second parties

At 10.30 p.m., the withdrawal of Second parties will begin. It will be carried out in the same sequence as first parties, troops reaching subsidiary line at 11.30 p.m. halting there till 12 midnight, and completing withdrawal by 1 a.m. After it is completed First parties of troops of Canadian Division holding the trench line East of farm C.22.b. (Mouse Trap Farm) will withdraw.

(c) Third parties

The withdrawal of Third parties will begin at 12 midnight in the same order as First parties, troops reaching subsidiary line at 1 a.m. halting there till 1.30 a.m. and completing withdrawal by 2.15 a.m. After it is completed the Second and Third parties of Canadian troops holding trench line East of Farm C.22.b. will withdraw.

6. The disposal of troops after they have reached the new trench line is in the hands of Divisional Commanders, but all movements must be completed by 3.30 a.m.

7. 28th Division will be responsible for the timing of this retirement, and will keep 27th and Canadian Divisions frequently informed of the progress of it, and will give these Divisions adequate warning of the commencement of withdrawal of the units on its extreme right and left respectively. 27th and Canadian Divisions will regulate their retirement by that of the 28th Division, and will keep in close touch with it.

If before or after the retirement has begun the action of the enemy makes it advisable to postpone or delay it, the Division which becomes aware of the reasons for such delay will immediately inform both other Divisions as well as Force Headquarters, and failing special instructions, will conform to the movements of 28th Division.

8. The following points require regulation by Divisional Commanders, and instructions to every officer, N.C.O., and man concerned:

(a) Reconnoitring new trench line and determining exact extent of front to be occupied by each unit.

(b) Reconnoitring and marking routes from old to new trench line.

(c) Maintenance of communication between divisional and brigade and between brigade and battalion H.Q. during retirement.

9. No move in an easterly direction of troops or vehicles will be permitted East of the Canal, either North or South of Ypres, after 6 p.m.

All transport and horses not indispensable to the operation will be moved west of Ypres on the preceding night.

10. Areas for accommodation will remain as allotted to Divisions at present, with recent additions West of Poperinghe.

11. Divisional Commanders will inform Force Headquarters by 6 p.m. and where their Report Centres will be during the operations, and of any subsequent changes they contemplate.

12. Reports to Advanced Reports Centre, H.11.a. (Goldfish Chateau)

G. F. MILNE, Major-General,
C.G.S., Plumer's Force.

1st May 1915.

APPENDIX VI

Report on the Rumours of Gas

The following report dated 15th April was received at General Headquarters from General Putz's liaison officer in the Second Army.

A reliable agent of the Détachement of the French Army in Belgium reports that an attack in the Ypres salient has been arranged for the night of the 15th/16th April. A prisoner of the *234th Regiment, XXVI Corps*, taken on the 14th April near Langemarck, reports that an attack had been prepared for noon 13th. Reserves have been brought up and passages have been prepared across old trenches existing in rear of the present German trenches to facilitate bringing forward artillery.

The Germans intend making use of tubes with asphyxiating gas, placed in batteries of 20 tubes for every 40 metres along the front of the XXVI Corps [then as far as was known, in the line on either side of Langemarck, wholly opposite the French]. The prisoner had in his possession a small sack filled with a kind of gauze or cotton waste (cotton waste in a gauze bag) which would be dipped in some solution to counteract the effects of gas.

The German morale is said to be much improved lately, owing to the men having been told that there is not much in front of them.

It is possible that the attack may be postponed, if the wind is not favourable, so as to ensure that the gases blow over our trenches.

APPENDIX VII

A Note on Casualty Figures for the Second Battle of Ypres

It is always difficult to assess the exact number of casualties for both sides in any given battle during the Great War. There are a number of reasons for this, not the least being the numbers involved. Other factors, such as the method of recording battle casualties, differed between the belligerents and that complicates any direct comparison. Perhaps the most obvious feature to cause problems is the criterion used for the recording of a casualty. If a German soldier was treated at an aid post and was then able return to duty he was not counted as a casualty. This was not the case in the British army where any soldier treated was recorded as a casualty. This would clearly make a comparison of the wounded of the two armies very difficult – and, perhaps, this kind of "score sheet" is an invidious approach in any case.

The figures in Tables 1 and 2 are quoted from the Official History and the approach to reporting the data adopted by the Germans can be seen to be different. The British figures quoted relate to the period 22nd April to 31st May, 1915 and although they include the defence of Hill 60 in the early part of May they do not include casualties resulting from its capture in mid-April. The German casualty figures were returned as ten day totals and are for the period 21st April to 31st May, 1915 and hence include some of the casualties sustained in the heavy fighting at Hill 60 prior to the gas attack of the 22nd April. Further, it appears that at least some of the figures quoted for the British casualties are in error. If *Soldiers Died in the Great War* is consulted it would suggest that the numbers of killed are substantially higher than those quoted by the Official History for the same period. For instance, the 50th Division is shown as having 596 other ranks killed during fighting whereas *Soldiers Died* indicate 983 to have been killed or died of wounds. Presumably this difference of 387 is recorded in the Official History as "wounded" which in turn implies that the data for the table is older than that in *Soldiers Died* published in 1921.

Table 1: British Casualties of the 2nd Battle of Ypres.

Unit	Officers			Other Ranks			Total
	Killed	Wounded	Missing	Killed	Wounded	Missing	
1st Cav. Div.	17	59	9	151	638	329	1,203
2nd Cav. Div.	4	7	–	36	180	17	244
3rd Cav. Div.	31	60	3	273	1,057	194	1,618
4th Division	87	224	36	1,566	5,476	3,470	10,859
5th Division	71	209	13	1,068	5,478	1,155	7,994
27th Division	55	166	13	1,122	4,980	927	7,263
28th Division	97	300	98	3,177	5,548	6,313	15,533
50th Division	40	121	25	596	2,963	1,459	5,204
Canadian Div.	65	104	39	1,672	1,822	1,767	5,469
Lahore Division British	28	105	–	180	1,096	345	1,754
Lahore Division Indian	6	57	1	177	1,684	209	2,134
Total	501	1,412	237	10,018[2]	30,922	16,185	59,275

This sort of discrepancy occurs for all the units involved that can be readily researched using the *Soldiers Died* CD-ROM, of course unavailable to original compilers of the Official History. A summary of the casualty figures for British units is given in Table 3. An attempt to compile a similar table for the Canadian units based on the casualty returns of 30th June, 1915 was unsuccessful since at that stage many of those men killed were still listed as missing and some of the men listed as missing were prisoners.

To add to the figures for the main combatants it has been estimated that the French suffered 10,000 casualties – there is not a more precise figure available which perhaps says much about the French method of recording casualties! The Belgians, operating on the extreme left of the battle, sustained a further 1,530 casualties. Therefore, the total allied casualties for the period of interest was in excess of 70,000 whilst the Germans suffered aproximately 35,000 casualties. The Second Battle of Ypres had certainly been "one of the most murderous battles of the war".[1]

Table 2: German casualties for the 2nd Battle of Ypres.

	Killed	Wounded	Missing	Killed	Wounded	Missing
XXIII Reserve Corps						
21-30 April	40	89	13	977	3,862	1,780
1-10 May	3	8	0	161	524	0
11-20 May	14	23	5	279	1,349	515
21-30 May	9	7	0	193	694	47
Total	66	127	18	1,610	6,429	2,342
XXVI Reserve Corps						
21-30 April	50	119	4	998	4,247	813
1-10 May	19	45	2	519	2,408	208
11-20 May	14	20	2	380	1,079	323
21-30 May	8	26	1	346	1,144	70
Total	91	210	9	2,243	8,878	1,414
XXVII Reserve Corps						
21-30 April	16	38	2	319	1,121	144
1-10 May	24	121	0	660	2,785	74
11-20 May	4	21	2	346	1,120	185
21-30 May	12	27	1	331	1,242	57
Total	56	207	5	1,656	6,268	460
XV Reserve Corps						
21-30 April	7	10	1	101	437	28
1-10 May	13	26	0	269	900	15
11-20 May	3	6	0	129	397	4
21-30 May	2	2	1	91	397	5
Total	25	44	2	590	2,131	52

It is interesting to note that the "missing" account for thirty per cent of British casualties whilst in the German Army "missing" account for no more than twelve per cent. This reflects the fact that the Germans had advanced over ground once held by the British.

Table 3: Breakdown of British Fatalities by Unit.

The data for Table 3 has been gleaned by searching *Soldiers Died in The Great War* (CD-ROM Edition) using the search parameters 17th April to 31st May 1915 for the battalions involved thereby encompasing the fighting for Hill 60 and Second Ypres. It includes only other ranks since searching for officers by battalion proves difficult where certain officers were only "attached". Details of the officers killed in the battle can be found in Appendix I. Note also that the number of casualties for the Patricia's are an estimate (considered conservative) based on the List of Casualties issued on 30th June,1915.

4th Division

10 Brigade

1st Royal Warwickshire	245
1st Royal Irish Fusiliers	180
7th Argyll and Sutherland Highlanders	128
2nd Seaforth Highlanders	208
2nd Royal Dublin Fusiliers	405
Total	1,166

11 Brigade

1st Somerset Light Infantry	76
1st Hampshire Regiment	200
5th London (London Rifle Brigade)	143
1st East Lancashire Regiment	128
1st Rifle Brigade	230
Total	777

12 Brigade

1st King's Own Royal Lancaster Regiment	131
2nd Lancashire Fusilers	69
5th South Lancashire Regiment	93
2nd Royal Irish Regiment	172
2nd Essex	162
2nd Monmouthshire Regiment	77
Total	704

5th Division

13 Brigade

2nd King's Own Scottish Borderers	165
1st Royal West Kent	160
9th London (Queen Victoria's Rifles)	62
2nd Duke of Wellington's (West Riding)	287
2nd King's Own Yorkshire Light Infantry	142
Total	816

14 Brigade

1st Devonshire	75
1st Duke of Cornwall's Light Infantry	68
5th Cheshire	15
1st East Surrey	128
2nd Manchester Regiment	73
Total	359

15 Brigade

1st Norfolk	70
1st Cheshire	105
6th King's (Liverpool) Regiment	42
1st Bedfordshire	199
1st Dorsets	198
Total	614

27th Division

80 Brigade

2nd King's Shropshire Light Infantry	190
4th Kings Royal Rifle Corps	233
Princess Patricia's Canadian Light Infantry	161(approx)
3rd King's Royal Rifle Corps	115
4th Rifle Brigade	189
Total	888

81 Brigade

1st Royal Scots	69
2nd Cameron Highlanders	204
9th Royal Scots	48
2nd Gloucesters	127
1st Argyll and Sutherland Highlanders	122
9th Argyll and Sutherland Highlanders	118
Total	688

82 Brigade

1st Royal Irish Regiment	63
2nd Royal Irish Fusiliers	61
1st Cambridgeshire	32
2nd Duke of Cornwall's Light Infantry	115
1st Leinster	133
Total	404

28th Division
83 Brigade
2nd King's Own Royal Lancaster Regiment	399
1st King's Own Yorkshire Light Infantry	227
5th King's Own Royal Lancaster Regiment	128
2nd East Yorkshire	177
1st Yorks and Lancaster	293
3rd Monmouthshire Regiment	240
Total	1,464

84 Brigade
2nd Northumberland Fusiliers	278
2nd Cheshire	182
12th London (The Rangers)	158
1st Suffolk	263
1st Welsh	196
1st Monmouthshire Regiment	185
Total	1,262

85 Brigade
2nd Buffs	306
2nd East Surrey	305
8th Middlesex	99
3rd Royal Fusiliers	365
3rd Middlesex	199
Total	1,274

50th Division
149 Brigade
4th Northumberland Fusiliers	71
5th Northumberland Fusiliers	82
6th Northumberland Fusiliers	88
7th Northumberland Fusiliers	85
Total	326

150 Brigade
4th East Yorkshire	103
4th Green Howards	82
5th Green Howards	44
5th Durham Light Infantry	91
Total	320

151 Brigade
6th Durham Light Infantry	64
7th Durham Light Infantry	111
8th Durham Light Infantry	127
9th Durham Light Infantry	35
Total	337

Lahore Division
Ferozepore Brigade
Connaught Rangers	81
4th London (Royal Fusiliers)	55
Total	136

Jullundur Brigade
1st Manchester Regiment	68
4th Suffolks	22
Total	90

Sirhind Brigade
1st Highland Light Infantry	99
4th King's (Liverpool) Regiment	124
Total	223

1st Cavalry Division
1 Cavalry Brigade
Queen's Bays	36
5th Dragoon Guards	32
11th Hussars	29
Total	97

2 Cavalry Brigade
4th Dragoon Guards	31
9th Lancers	51
18th Hussars	70
Total	152

9 Cavalry Brigade
15th Hussars	15
19th Hussars	26
Total	41

2nd Cavalry Division
3 Cavalry Brigade
4th Hussars	19
5th Lancers	14
16th Lancers	12
Total	45

4 Cavalry Brigade
6th Dragoon Guards	19
3rd Hussars	8
Oxford Hussars	16
Total	43

5 Cavalry Brigade

Royal Scots Greys	12
12th Lancers	11
20th Hussars	18
Total	41

3rd Cavalry Division

6 Cavalry Brigade

3rd Dragoon Guards	60
1st Royal Dragoons	27
North Somerset Yeomanry	25
Total	112

7 Cavalry Brigade

1st Life Guards	25
2nd Life Guards	14
Leicestershire Yeomanry	90
Total	129

9 Cavalry Brigade

Royal Horse Guards	10
10th Hussars	40
Essex Yeomanry	65
Total	115

Canadian Division (undifferentiated)	1,672
Total Other Ranks Killed	14,195*

* Note this figure does not include the Indian troops who were killed during the battle since the available figures for them are totals of killed, wounded and missing. It also does not include the casualties from the support units such as the Royal Engineers, Royal Artillery and so on.

Notes

1. Falls 1959 (page 112).
2. Compare this figure with the total in Table 3.

BIBLIOGRAPHY

Aitkin, Sir M., *Canada in Flanders,* Hodder & Stoughton, London, 1916

Anderson, Brig. R.C.B., *History of the Argyll and Sutherland Highlanders. 1st Battalion 1909–1939,* T. & A. Constable Ltd., Edinburgh.

Anglesey, The Marquess of, *1996 A History of the British Cavalry 1816 to 1919. Volume 8. The Western Front 1914–1918,* Leo Cooper, London, 1996.

Anon., *Bond of Sacrifice: A Biographical Record of All British officers Who Fell in the Great War,* Anglo-African Publishing Contractors. (2 Vols.), 1915.

Anon., *History of the Dorsetshire Regiment 1914-1919,* Henry King Ltd, Dorchester.

Anon., *Officers Died in The Great War 1914-1919,* H.M.S.O. London, 1919 (Also as CD-ROM compiled by Naval and Military Press, Dallington.)

Anon., *Soldiers Died in The Great War 1914-1919,* (Relevant Parts). H.M.S.O. London, 1921 (Also as CD-ROM compiled by Naval and Military Press, Dallington)

Anon., *The History of the London Rifle Brigade 1859-1919,* Constable and Co. Ltd., London, 1921.

Anon., *Work of the Royal Engineers in the European War. Military Mining,* The Institution of Royal Engineers, 1922.

Anon,. *Historical Records of the Queen's Own Cameron Highlanders Vol II,* William Blackwood & Sons Ltd., London, 1931.

Anon., *History of the East Lancashire Regiment in the Great War 1914-1918,* Littlebury Bros. Ltd., Liverpool, 1936.

Ashby, J., *Seek Glory, Now Keep Glory. The Story of the 1st Battalion, the Royal Warwickshire Regiment 1914-18,* Heliol and Company, Solihull, 2000.

Ashurst, G., *My Bit. A Lancashire Fusilier at War 1914-1918,* (Ed. Richard Holmes). Crowood Press, Ramsbury, 1987.

Atkinson, C.T., *The Devonshire Regiment 1914-1918,* Eland Brothers, Exeter, 1926.

— *Regimental History The Royal Hampshire Regiment. Vol 2 1914-1918,* Robert Maclehose & Co. Ltd, The University Press, Glasgow,1952.

358

Bairnsfather, B., *Bullets and Billets,* (Edited by Mark Marsay), Great Northern Publishing, Scarborough, 2000.

Baker, A., *Battle Honours of the British and Commonwealth Armies,* Ian Allan Ltd., London, 1986.

Barrie, A., *War Underground. The Tunnellers of the Great War,* Tom Donovan, London, 1961.

Barrow, Lieut. Col. T.J. French, Major V.A. & Seabrook, J., *The Story of the Bedfordshire and Hertfordshire Regiment, Volume II. 1914–1958.*

Batchelor, P.F. & Matson, C., *VCs of the First World War. The Western Front 1915,* Sutton Publishing, Stroud, Gloucestershire, 1997.

Becke, Major A.F., *Order of Battle of Divisions. Part I – The Regular British Divisions,* Ray Westlake Military Books, Newport, 1989.

Bond, Lieut. Col. R.C., *History of the King's Own Yorkshire Light Infantry in the Great War,* Percy Lund, Humphries and Co., London.

Brett, Captain G.A., *A History of the 2nd Battalion the Monmouthshire Regiment,* Hughes & Son, The Griffin Press, Pontypool, 1933.

Brice, B., *The Battle Book of Ypres,* Spa Books, London, 1987.

Bruce, Brig. Gen. C.D., *History of the Duke of Wellington's Regiment. (1st and 2nd Battalions) 1881–1923.* The Medici Society Ltd., London.

Burgoyne, G.A., *The Burgoyne Diaries,* Thomas Harmsworth, London, 1985.

Burrows, J.W., *The Essex Regiment. 2nd Battalion (56th) (Pompadours),* John H. Burrows and Sons Ltd., Southend-on-Sea.

Byron, Lieut. Col. R. (Ed.), *The King's Royal Rifle Corps Chronicle. 1915,* Warren & Son Ltd., Winchester, 1916.

Cave, N., *Hill 60. Ypres.* Battleground Europe Series, Leo Cooper, Barnsley, 1998.

Christie, N., *For King and Empire. The Canadians at Ypres 22nd–26th April 1915,* Bunker to Bunker Books, Winnipeg, Canada, 1996.

Christie, N.M. (Ed.), *The Letters of Agar Adamson, Lieutenant Colonel, Princess Patricia's Canadian Light Infantry,* CEF Books, Nepean, Ontario, Canada, 1997.

— *Gas Attack. The Canadians at Ypres, 1915,* CEF Books, Nepean, Ontario, Canada, 1997.

Churton, Lieut. Col. W.A.V., *The War Record of the 1/5th (Earl of Chester's) Battalion The Cheshire Regiment,* Phillipson and Golder, Chester, 1920.

Clark, A., *The Donkeys,* Hutchison, London, 1961.

Clutterbuck Col. L.A., *The Bond of Sacrifice,* Naval and Military Press, Dallington, 1992.

Creagh, Sir O'M. & Humphries E.M., *The Distinguished Service Order 1886–1923,* J.B. Hayward and Son, London, 1979.

— *The Victoria Cross 1886–1923,* J.B. Hayward and Son, London, 1979.

Crookenden, A., *The History of the Cheshire Regiment in the Great War.*

Crutwell, C.R.M.F., *A History of the Great War 1914–1918 (2nd Edn),* Paladin, London, 1982.

Dancocks, D.G., *Gallant Canadians. The Story of the Tenth Canadian Infantry Battalion 1914–1919,* The Calgary Highlanders Funds Foundation, Alberta, Canada, 1990.

Davies, F. & Maddocks, G., *Bloody Red Tabs. General Officer Casualties of the Great War, 1914–1918,* Leo Cooper, London, 1995.

De Lisle, General Sir B., *Reminiscences of Sport and War,* Eyre and Spottiswoode, London, 1939.

De Ruvigny, The Marquis., *The Roll of Honour*, Naval and Military Press, Dallington, 2000.

Devereux, J. & Sacker, G., *Leaving All That Was Dear. Cheltenham and The Great War*, Promenade Publications, Cheltenham, 1997.

Dixon, J., *Out Since '14. A History of the 1/2nd Battalion The Monmouthshire Regiment 1914–1919*, Old Bakehouse Press, Abertillery, 2000.

Dixon, J. & Dixon, J., *With Rifle and Pick*, Cwm Press, Cardiff, 1991.

Doyle, P., *The Geology of the Western Front*, Geologist Association Guide No. 61, The Geologists Association, 1998.

Eastwood, S., *Lions of England. A Pictorial History of the King's Own Royal Regiment (Lancaster) 1680–1980*, Silver Link Publishing Limited, 1991.

Edmonds, Brig. Gen. J.E. & Wynne, Captain, G.C., *History of the Great War Based on Official Documents. Military Operations France and Belgium 1915, Vol. I*, Macmillan and Co. Ltd., London, 1927.

Ewing, Major J., *The Royal Scots 1914–1919*, Oliver and Boyd, London, 1925.

Falls, C., *The History of the First Seven Battalions The Royal Irish Rifles in the Great War*, Gale and Polden, Aldershot, 1925.

—— *The Great War 1914–1918*, Longmans, London, 1959.

Farndale, Gen. Sir M., *History of the Royal Regiment of Artillery. Western Front 1914–1918*, Henry Ling Ltd., The Dorset Press, Dorchester, 1986.

French, Field Marshal, J.D.P., *Complete Despatches 1914–1916*. Naval and Military Press. Dallington.

—— *1914*, Constable, London, 1919.

Gilbert, M., *First World War*, Weidenfield and Nicolson, London, 1994.

Gillon, Captain S., *The KOSB in the Great War*, Thomas Nelson and Sons Ltd., London, 1930.

Goeghegan, Br.Gen. S., *The Campaigns and History of the Royal Irish Regiment. Vol 2 From 1900 to 1922*, William Blackwood and Sons Ltd., Edinburgh and London, 1927.

Grieve, W.G. & Newman, B., *Tunnellers, The Story of the Tunnelling Companies, Royal Engineers, during the World War*, Herbert Jenkins Ltd., London, 1936.

Hart's *Army List for 1915*, Naval and Military Press, Dallington.

Haythornthwaite, P.J., *The World War One Source Book*, BCA, London, 1992.

Hodgkinson, A., *The King's Own T.F. Being a Record of the 1/5th Battalion The King's Own (Royal Lancaster Regiment) in the European War, 1914–1918*, The Lewes Press, Lewes, 1921.

Holmes, R., *The Little Field Marshal: Sir John French*, Jonathan Cape, London, 1981.

Home, Brig. Gen. Sir A., *The Diary of a World War I Cavalry Officer*, Costello, Tunbridge Wells, 1985.

Hossack, A. R., *The First Gas Attack* in *Fifty Amazing Stories of the Great War*, Odhams Press Ltd., London, 1936, pp 80–84.

Hughes, L. & Dixon, J., *Surrender Be Damned. A History of the 1/1st Battalion the Monmouthshire Regiment in the Great War 1914–1918*, Cwm Press, Caerphilly, 1995.

James, Brig. E.A., *British Regiments, 1914–1918*, Samson Books, London, 1978.

Jarvis, S.D. & Jarvis, D.B., *The Cross of Sacrifice. Officers who Died in the*

Service of British, Indian and East African Regiments and Corps. 1914–1919, Roberts Medals Ltd., Reading, 1993.

Keeson, Major C.A.C., *The History and Records of the Queen Victoria's Rifles 1792–1922*, Constable and Co. Ltd., London, 1923.

Latter, Major General J.C., *The History of the Lancashire Fusiliers 1914–1918*, Gale and Polden Ltd., Aldershot, 1949.

Liddell Hart, B.H., *History of the First World War*, Papermac, London, 1997.

MacDonald, L., *1915 The Death of Innocence*, BCA, London, 1993.

— *The Roses of no man's land*, Papermac, London, 1984.

McGilchrist, A.M., *The Liverpool Scottish 1900–1919*, Henry Young and Sons Ltd., Liverpool, 1930.

McWilliams, J. & Steel, R.J., *Gas! The Battle for Ypres, 1915*, Vanwell Publishing Ltd., St Catherines, Ontario, Canada, 1985.

Magnus, P., *Kitchener. Portrait of an Imperialist*, Murray, London, 1958.

Marden, Maj. Gen. T.O., *The History of the Welch Regiment. Vol. 2*, Western Mail and Echo Ltd., Cardiff, 1932.

Marsay, M., *Baptism of Fire*, Great Northern Publishing, Scarborough, 1999.

Maurice, Maj. Gen. Sir F., *The History of the London Rifle Brigade*, Constable and Co., London, 1921.

Merewether and Smith, *The India Corps in France*, E.P. Dutton and Co., New York, 2002.

Mitchinson, K.W., *Gentlemen and Officers. The Impact and Experience of War on a Territorial Regiment. 1914–1919 (5th Battalion the London Regiment – The London Rifle Brigade)*, The Inperial War Museum, London.

Molony, Major C.V., *"INVICTA" With the First Battalion the Queen's Own Royal West Kent Regiment in the Great War*, Nisbet & Co. Ltd., London.

Moore, W., *Gas Attack. Chemical Warfare 1915 to the Present Day*, Leo Cooper, London, 1987.

Morton, D. & Granatstein, J.L., *Marching to Armageddon. Canadians and the Great War 1914–1919*, Lester and Orpen Dennys Ltd., Toronto, 1989.

Murphy, Lieut. Col. C.C.R., *The history of the Suffolk Regiment 1914–1927*, Hutchinson and Co. Ltd., London, 1989.

Newman, S.K., *With the Patricia's in Flanders 1914–1918*, Bellewaerde House Publishing, Saanichton, Canada, 2000.

Pearse, Col. H.W. & Sloman Brig. Gen. H.S., *History of the East Surrey Regiment. Vol. II (1914–1917)*. The Medici Society Ltd., London, 1923.

Petre, F.L., *The History of the Norfolk Regiment 1685–1918. Vol. II 4th August, 1914, to 31st December, 1918*, Jarrold & Sons, Ltd., The Empire Press, Norwich, 1923.

Reed, P., *Walking the salient*, Battleground Europe Series, Leo Cooper, Barnsley, 1999.

Riddell Brig. Gen. E. & Clayton, Col. M.C., *The Cambridgeshires 1914 to 1919*, Bowes and Bowes, Cambridge, 1934.

Sandilands, Brigadier H.R., *The Fifth in the Great War. A History of the 1st and 2nd Northumberland Fusiliers 1914–1918*, G.W. Grigg and Son, 'St. George's Press', Dover, 1938.

Scott, Canon F.G., *The Great War as I saw it*, Clarke & Stuart Co. Ltd., Vancouver, 2nd Ed., 1999.

Shephard, E., *A Sergeant-Major's War. From Hill 60 to the Somme*, (Edited by B. Rossor) Crowood Press, Ramsbury, 1988.

Simpson, Major Gen. C.R., *The History of the Lincolnshire Regiment 1914–1918,* The Medici Society Ltd., London, 1931.

Somerset, W.H.B., Tyler, H.G. & Whitehead, L.D. (Eds), *On the Western Front. 1/3rd Battalion Monmouthshire Regiment.* Sergeant Bros Ltd., Abergavenny.

Southey, Stanley., *British Roll of Honour,* Published for Private Circulation.

Strachan, H., *The First World War. Vol 1: To Arms,* Oxford University Press, 2001.

Strange, Lieut. Col. L.A., *The Second Battle of Ypres* in *Fifty Amazing Stories of the Great War,* Odhams Press Ltd., London, 1936 pp 426–434.

Terraine, J., *The Great War 1914–1918,* Hutchinson, London, 1965.

Verner, Col. W., *The Rifle Brigade Chronicle for 1918,* John Bale, Sons & Danielsson Ltd., London, 1919.

Walker, Major G.G., *The Honourable Artillery Company in the Great War 1914–1919,* Sydney, Service and Co. Ltd., London, 1930.

Westlake, R., *British Battalions on the Western Front January to June 1915,* Leo Cooper, Barnsley, 2001.

Whalley-Kelly, Capt. H., *"Ich Dien" The Prince of Wales's Volunteers (South Lancashire) 1914–1934,* Gale and Polden Ltd., Aldershot.

Whitton, F.E., *The History of the Prince of Wales Leinster Regiment (The Royal Canadians). Part II The Great War and the Disbandment of the Regiment,* Gale and Polden Ltd., Aldershot.

Williams, J., *Princess Patricia's Canadian Light Infantry,* Leo Cooper, London, 1972.

Wood, Major W.de B., *The History of the King's Shropshire Light Infantry in the Great War. 1914–1918,* The Medici Society Ltd., London, 1925.

Wylly, Colonel H.C., *Crown and Company. The Historical Records of the 2nd Battalion Royal Dublin Fusiliers. Vol II. 1911–1922,* Gale and Polden Ltd., Aldershot, 1923.

— *History of the Manchester Regiment (late the 63rd and 96th Foot),* Forster Groom & Co. Ltd., London, 1925.

Wyrall, E., *The History of the Somerset Light Infantry (Prince Albert's) 1914–1919.* Methuen and Co. Ltd., London.

— *The History of the Duke of Cornwall's Light Infantry,* Methuen and Co. Ltd., London.

— *The History of the King's Regiment (Liverpool) 1914–1919. Vol.I 1914–1915,* Edward Arnold & Co., London.

— *The Die-Hards in the Great War,* Harrison and Son Ltd., London, 1926.

— *The East Yorkshire Regiment in the Great War 1914-1918,* Harrison and Sons Ltd., London, 1928.

The following War Diaries have also been consulted:

171st Tunnelling Company RE
9th Royal Scots
2nd East Kents (The Buffs)
1st King's Own Royal Lancaster Regiment
2nd King's Own Royal Lancaster Regiment
5th King's Own Royal Lancaster Regiment
1st Royal Warwickshire Regiment
3rd Royal Fusiliers
4th Royal Fusiliers
2nd East Yorkshire Regiment
1st Royal Scots Fusiliers
2nd King's Own Scottish Borderers
2nd Gloucestershire Regiment
2nd Duke of Cornwall's Light Infantry
2nd Duke of Wellington's (West Riding) Regiment
1st Royal West Kent Regiment
2nd King's Own Yorkshire Light Infantry
3rd Middlesex Regiment
1st Wiltshire Regiment
1st York and Lancaster Regiment
1st Highland Light Infantry
2nd Seaforth Highlanders
1st Gordon Highlanders
1st Royal Irish Fusiliers
2nd Royal Irish Fusiliers
7th Argyll and Sutherland Highlanders
1st Monmouthshire Regiment
2nd Monmouthshire Regiment
3rd Monmouthshire Regiment
9th London (Queen Victoria's Rifles) Regiment

Index

Saint Eloi, 14, 17, 178
Saint Jean, 50, 92–3, 120, 127, 155, 158
Saint Julien, 45, 47–49, 51, 56, 61, 65, 70, 74, 77, 88, 90–1, 93, 95–8, 100–1, 103, 105–7, 109–11, 113, 118, 121, 127, 130, 135–6, 138, 140, 155, 160, 254–6, 258, 276
Salier, Lieut. E.H., 282
Salverson, 2/Lieut. E.M., 107
Sanctuary Wood, 172, 178, 199, 206, 218, 243, 246, 248–9, 267, 276
Scott, Canon F., 51, 59, 118
Scrimger, Capt. F.A.C., 118–9, 322
Seymour Rfn. S., 37
Shaw, Lieut. Col. G.H., 97
Shell Trap Farm, 46–7, 51, 55, 59, 61, 67–8, 109, 118, 161–2, 172, 181, 193, 198–9, 201, 203, 206, 213–4, 216, 218, 230, 234–5, 237, 240, 250, 245, 256–8, 260, 272–7, 284
Shepard, Sgt. Maj. E., 174–7, 180, 186, 207–8
Smith, Cpl. I., 134, 322
Smith, Brig. Gen. W.E.B., 279–80
Smith-Dorrien, Gen. Sir H., 64, 70, 80, 100, 122–3, 125, 128, 135–6, 143–4, 146–8, 150–6, 159, 171, 212–3, 295
Snow, Major Gen. T.D'O., 90, 92, 95–7, 99, 119, 156, 229, 248
South Zwaanhof Farm, 76, 133
Stanton, Capt. C.W., 114
Steenstraat, 50, 71, 76–7, 80, 127, 161–3, 166–7, 178
Steel, Capt. O.W.D., 204, 297
Stephenson, Col., 66, 75
Stevens, Cpl. B., 227
Stevenson, Sgt. C., 56
Stevenson, Pte. J., 129
Stone, Major A.B., 230
Strange, Lieut. A.L., 61
Summerhayes, Lieut. D.L., 36

Taylor, Capt., 27
Taylor, Cpl., 185
Territorial Force, 4, 5
Thornton, Lieut. R.J., 132
Thurgood, Pte. W.C., 91
Toke, Major R.T., 278
Tomlinson, Capt. F.W., 50, 62, 77
Trench, 38 15, 21, 27, 35–7, 211
Trench 39, 211
Trench 40, 14, 27, 211, 212
Trench 41, 211
Trench 46, 176
Tuff, Capt., 26
Tulloh, Lieut. Col. G.S., 244
Turco Farm, 67, 75–6, 138, 153, 162, 178–80, 196, 199, 201, 216, 234, 252, 254, 264, 267, 272, 285
Turnbull, Lieut. Col. J., 113–4, 117
Turner, Lieut. Col., 27
Turner, Brig. Gen R.E.W., VC 47–8, 50–1, 55, 64, 69, 71, 86–7, 89–94, 97, 99, 112
Tuson, Lieut. Col. H.D., 72, 74, 151–2
Tuxford, Lieut. Col. G., 95, 112–3, 115–7
Tyrrell, Lieut. W., 164, 168, 181

Vanheule Farm, 107–8, 137, 223, 236
Venning, Lieut., 282
Verlorenhoek, 172, 236, 238, 240, 243, 269
Vlamertinge, 64, 76, 99, 120, 164, 201, 250

Wade, Lieut. G.H.T., 261
Walker, 2/Lieut. E.B., 24
Walker, Brig. Gen. W.G. VC,142, 148, 169
Wallace, Lieut. Col. W.B., 92, 96–8, 230
Wallace's Detachment, 92, 96, 109, 111, 115, 121–2, 129
Warner, Pte. E., 176–7, 322
Watkins,, Capt. I.E.M., 214
Watts, Pte. W., 233
Webb, Lieut., 94
Weeks, Rfn. R.S., 256
Wellesley, Capt. E., 22

Wheatley, L/Cpl. J.H., 256
White, Dmr. D., 213–4
White, Pte. J., 271
Wieltje, 67, 72, 75, 93–4, 101, 112, 120, 123, 127, 134–6, 155, 218, 252, 254, 256–8, 267, 272, 285
Wieltje Farm, 75, 127, 285
Williams, Lieut. Col. E.G., 175–6
Williams, Capt. O., 231–2
Williamson, Capt. G.M., 91
Wilson, Lieut. G.L., 31, 35
Wilson, Major Gen. H.F.M., 236, 284–5
Witte Poort Farm, 277–9, 282
Woodgate, Capt. A.B., 274
Wooley, Lieut. G.H., 36–7, 321
Worsley-Gough, Lieut. Col. H.W., 220, 222
Wreford-Browne, Capt. C., 277, 279
Wyllie, Capt. H., 61
Wynyard, Capt. D., 31–2

Y Wood, 278–9, 284
Young, Lieut. N.C.N.R., 107, 119
Ypres, 2, 4, 6–8, 11, 16, 22, 27, 44–5, 50, 61, 64–5, 70–2, 74, 77, 82, 94, 101, 111, 121, 127, 129, 130, 146–8, 153, 162, 170–2, 178, 185, 187, 192, 197, 201–2, 211, 218–20, 235–6, 239, 242–3, 246, 250–2, 254, 261, 266, 277, 279–80, 285, 287, 291
Ypres-Roulers Railway, 218, 235, 242, 269, 276
Yser Canal, 6, 45, 47, 57, 61–2, 76–8, 101, 121–2, 127, 129, 153, 171, 178, 201, 218, 237, 276

Zillebeke, 26, 216, 218
Zonnebeke, 96, 98, 112, 143, 172, 193, 195, 19708, 219, 235–6, 264, 267, 269, 272–3
Zonnebeke Ridge, 121
Zwaanhofbeek, 131–2
Zwartleen, 30, 242